Cambridge Semitic Languages and Cultures

General Editor: Geoffrey Khan

This is the first Open Access book series in the field; it combines the high peer-review and editorial standards with the fair Open Access model offered by OBP. The series includes philological and linguistic studies of Semitic languages, editions of Semitic texts, and studies of Semitic cultures. Titles cover all periods, traditions and methodological approaches to the field. The editorial board comprises Geoffrey Khan, Aaron Hornkohl, Esther-Miriam Wagner, Anne Burberry, and Benjamin Kantor.

You can access the full series catalogue here: https://www.openbookpublishers.com/series/2632-6914

If you would like to join our community and interact with authors of the books, sign up to be contacted about events relating to the series and receive publication updates and news here: https://forms.gle/RWymsw3hdsUjZTXv5

THE INTERTWINED WORLD OF THE ORAL AND WRITTEN TRANSMISSION OF SACRED TRADITIONS IN THE MIDDLE EAST

The Intertwined World of the Oral and Written Transmission of Sacred Traditions in the Middle East

Edited by Alba Fedeli, Geoffrey Khan and Johan Lundberg

UNIVERSITY OF CAMBRIDGE
Faculty of Asian and Middle Eastern Studies

OpenBook Publishers

https://www.openbookpublishers.com

All external links were active at the time of publication unless otherwise stated and have been archived via the Internet Archive Wayback Machine at https://archive.org/web

Any digital material and resources associated with this volume will be available at https://doi.org/10.11647/OBP.0498#resources

Semitic Languages and Cultures 40

ISSN (print): 2632-6906
ISSN (digital): 2632-6914

ISBN Paperback: 978-1-80511-740-7
ISBN Hardback: 978-1-80511-741-4
ISBN Digital (PDF): 978-1-80511-742-1

DOI: 10.11647/OBP.0498

Cover images: Karaite Arabic transcription of the Hebrew Bible into Arabic letters: British Library Or 2540, fol. 12r, Exodus 4.15–4.19. Hebrew Bible: Aleppo Codex, fol. 122r, Isaiah 44.16–45.11 (Courtesy of the Ben-Zvi Institute, Jerusalem. Photographer: Ardon Bar Hama). Arabic Qurʾān: Gotha Research Library of the University of Erfurt, Ms. orient. A 432, fol. 1r, Public Domain Mark 1.0, Q.3:51–3:52. Syriac Gospel: Staatsbibliothek zu Berlin, Phillips 1388, fol 30v, Matt. 12.33–41.
Cover design: Jeevanjot Kaur Nagpal

The fonts used in this volume are Charis SIL, SBL Hebrew, SBL Greek, Scheherazade New, Estrangelo Edessa, Serto Jerusalem and Allan.

CONTENTS

Contributors.. vii

Preface..xiii

Introduction.. 1

Jonathan Loopstra

Passing Down a Corpus of Reminders for the
Peshiṭta and the Harklean Bibles 27

Johan Lundberg

Taxonomies of Dots: The Context and Methodology
of the Early Treatises about the Syriac Accent Dots.... 95

George Kiraz

Multimodality in Liturgical Expression:
The Case of Textuality and Orality in Syriac
Orthodox Liturgies...129

Elvira Maria Martin-Contreras

Was There Ever an Oral Hebrew Masorah? 151

Robert Crellin

Main Clause Verbs are Prosodically Weaker than
Nouns in the Tiberian Cantillation of Biblical
Hebrew Prose Books 173

Geoffrey Khan

The Convergence of the Transmission of Jewish and Muslim Sacred Scriptures Reflected by the Medieval Karaite Transcriptions of the Hebrew Bible 229

Nick Posegay

A Jewish Translation of Genesis in 10th-Century Egyptian Arabic 275

Alba Fedeli

Patterns of Selective Vowel-Dotting in Early Qurʾānic Manuscripts 307

Alba Fedeli, Carolin Kinne-Wall, Hythem Sidky

New Approaches to Analysing the Vocalisation of Early Qurʾānic Manuscripts 387

Alicia González Martínez

A Computational System to Analyse the Layer of Tajwīd Notation in Contemporary Qurʾānic Orthography 437

Index 465

CONTRIBUTORS

Jonathan Loopstra is Professor of History at Redeemer University in Hamilton, Canada. He holds an MSt degree in Syriac Studies from the University of Oxford, a MA from Trinity Evangelical Divinity School, and a PhD from the Catholic University of America (2009). He works primarily in the fields of Patristics and Middle Eastern Studies, with an interest in the history, language, and theology of various Christian communities of the Middle East. In particular, he has published a variety of works on the development of Syriac biblical and patristic 'masoretic' traditions.

Johan Lundberg is a Leverhulme Early Career Fellow at the University of Oxford. He was awarded his PhD by the University of Cambridge (2020). His research focuses on Middle Eastern manuscripts and languages, specifically Syriac manuscripts. He is currently working on a history of Syriac punctuation and a reconstruction of classical Syriac prosody. He has also published on the relationship between punctuation and versification of Syriac Bibles and East Syriac word stress.

George A. Kiraz is a Senior Research Associate at the Institute for Advanced Study, Princeton, and teaches Syriac at Princeton University. He was awarded his PhD by the University of Cambridge in 1996. Specialising in Syriac studies, his research spans the intersections of philology, digital humanities, and cultural history. He pioneered the application of data science to Syriac, building large-scale corpora, developing tools for natural language processing, and designing infrastructures that link philological rigour with digital methodologies. His latest publications include *The Syriac Orthodox in North America* (2019), *Syriac-English New Testament* (2020), *Water the Willow Tree: Memoirs of a Bethlehem Boyhood* (2022), and *Algorithmic Musings in Syriac: A verse Poem on Computation Attributed to George of the Arabs* (2024).

Elvira Martín-Contreras is Senior Scientist at the Institute of Languages and Cultures of the Mediterranean and the Near East (ILC-CSIC). She was awarded her PhD by the Universidad Complutense, Madrid (2000). Her research focuses on the textual transmission and reception of the Hebrew Bible as attested in rabbinic literature and the Masora—the marginal annotations found in medieval Hebrew biblical manuscripts. She is also interested in annotation practices in medieval Hebrew Bibles and Hebrew palaeography. She is the author of several monographs and numerous articles, including *Masora. La transmisión de la Tradición de la Biblia Hebrea* (Navarra 2010), and co-editor of *The Text of the Hebrew Bible: From the Rabbis to the Masoretes* (Vandenhoeck & Ruprecht 2014).

Robert S. D. Crellin is an Academic Visitor at the Centre for the Study of Ancient Documents, Faculty of Classics, University of Oxford. He was awarded his PhD by the University of Cambridge (2012). He specialises in historical linguistics, focusing on the prosody, syntax and semantics of ancient languages, the structure of ancient writing systems and computational approaches to linguistic analysis. His publications include *The Semantics of Word Division in Northwest Semitic Writing Systems* (Oxbow, 2022) as well as (co-edited with Terry Joyce) *Writing systems: Past, Present (... and Future?)* (John Benjamins, 2019), and (co-edited with Thomas Jügel) *Perfects in Indo-European Languages and Beyond* (John Benjamins, 2020).

Geoffrey Khan is Regius Professor of Hebrew at the University of Cambridge. He was awarded his PhD by the School of Oriental and African Studies, London (1984). His research publications focus on three main fields: Biblical Hebrew language (especially medieval traditions), Neo-Aramaic dialectology, and medieval Arabic documents. He is the general editor of *The Encyclopedia of Hebrew Language and Linguistics* and is the senior editor of *Journal of Semitic Studies*. His most recent books include *The Tiberian Pronunciation Tradition of Biblical Hebrew* (University of Cambridge and Open Book Publishers, 2020), *Language Contact in Sanandaj* (with Masoud Mohammadirad as co-author, de Gruyter, 2023), and *Arabic Documents from Medieval Nubia* (University of Cambridge and Open Book Publishers, 2024).

Nick Posegay is an Alexander von Humboldt Postdoctoral Fellow in the Institute for Arabic and Islamic Studies at Ruhr University Bochum. He was awarded his PhD by the University of Cambridge (2021). He previously served as a Leverhulme Early Career Fellow at the Faculty of Asian and Middle Eastern Studies, Cambridge. His research focuses on interfaith exchange in the material, linguistic, and intellectual history of the medieval and early modern Middle East.

Alba Fedeli is a Research Associate at the Cluster of Excellence 'Understanding Written Artefacts' (University of Hamburg), where she serves as Principal Investigator of the research project

'What is in A Scribe's Mind and Inkwell'. She studied in Italy with Sergio Noja and was an awarded her PhD by the University of Birmingham (2015) on the history of Qur'ānic manuscripts in the Mingana Collection. Her publications reflect her research interests in early Qur'ānic manuscripts and include an edition of the Mingana-Lewis Qur'ān palimpsest. From 2004 to 2012, she taught at the University of Milan, and between 2004 and 2008, she served as Director of the Ferni Noja Noseda Foundation. She has participated in various projects on Qur'ānic manuscripts, such as the digitisation of the Sanaa Palimpsest at *Dār al-Makhṭūṭāt* in 2007 and the survey of the newly discovered manuscripts of the Great Mosque of Sanaa in 2008.

Carolin Kinne-Wall works as IT-coordinator at the Asien-Afrika-Institut, Universität Hamburg. She studied Computer Science in Mannheim (Berufsakademie), Bonn (Bachelor in Computer Science), Cologne (Master of Science, Information Systems) and Singapore (A*STAR Fellowship). She worked in different interdisciplinary projects as IT and data manager and joined the InterSaME project in 2022. Her research interests lie in digital humanities projects and applied information technology

Hythem Sidky is the Executive Director of the International Qur'ānic Studies Association. His research combines expertise in the sciences with a specialisation in Qur'ānic manuscripts and reading traditions. He brings together traditional philology and mathematical analysis to study the dynamics and evolution of the Qur'ān in early Islam. He has worked on the stemmatics of

Qur'ānic manuscripts, reconstruction of oral traditions, and applications of stylometry to the Qur'ān.

Alicia González Martínez is a Research Associate at Hamburg University with a backgroud in computer science, linguistics and Arabic studies. She was awarded her PhD by Universidad Autónoma de Madrid (2013). Her research focuses on developing digital tools and multipurpose platforms to enhance humanities scholarship, as well as applying advanced Natural Language Processing techniques to analyse and interpret cultural and textual data.

PREFACE

The project *The Intertwined World of the Oral and Written Transmission of Sacred Traditions in the Middle East* (known by the abbreviation InterSaME), which was funded jointly by the Deutsche Forschungsgemeinschaft (grant number 428993887) and the Arts and Humanities Research Council (grant number AH/T01282X /1), aimed to bring together strands of research related to various aspects of the transmission of the sacred scriptures of Christianity, Judaism, and Islam. The aim was to reach a deeper understanding of the intertwined world of the three major religions of the Middle East at their formative periods of development during the early Islamic centuries.

The researchers of the project undertook focused investigations of manuscripts of the Muslim Qurʾān (Alba Fedeli, Alicia González Martínez and Carolin Kinne-Wall), the Christian Syriac Bible (Johan Lundberg) and the Jewish Hebrew Bible (Geoffrey Khan). The project culminated in an international conference in Hamburg in September 2022, which brought together the researchers of the project and a group of additional scholars specialising in the transmission of the scriptures of the three religions in the Middle Ages. During the conference the connections between these traditions of transmission were discussed in detail. This volume brings together papers written by the project team and by participants of the Hamburg conference. The papers focus on various dimensions of transmission and methodologies of analysis.

We are grateful to the Deutsche Forschungsgemeinschaft and the Arts and Humanities Research Council for funding the project. We would also like to express our thanks to Tamar Karni for copyediting the volume and to the team of Open Book Publishers for their efficient work in its production.

The Editors, September 2025

INTRODUCTION

In the medieval Middle East, the scriptures of Christianity, Judaism, and Islam were transmitted in written and oral form. The means of written transmission and the textualisation of the oral reading of these scriptures exhibit many parallels, which reflect cultural contact and convergence across the various religious communities. The various different aspects of transmission that are relevant for understanding the connections between the traditions are the following.

1.0. Diacritical Dots and Vocalisation Signs

Syriac diacritical dots first began to be used in Syriac Bible manuscripts in late antiquity from the fifth to the seventh centuries, before the Islamic period (Segal 1953; Kiraz 2012, 2015). The main purpose of these dots was to make explicit the grammatical parsing of the written text by marking distinctions between different potential oral realisations. They marked, for example, distinctions between words that had the same written form but different oral forms, reflecting different morphology. They also marked different types of prosody in the oral reading of sentences of the text. This included the marking of different degrees of pausal strength, reflecting different degrees of grammatical connection, and distinctions in grammatical function such as the differentiation of interrogative sentences from declarative ones. These various functions of the dots came to be assigned specific technical terms, which are found in grammatical texts and handbooks used in the school curriculum (see the papers of Lundberg

 https://doi.org/10.11647/OBP.0498.00

and Loopstra in this volume). Full Syriac vocalisation systems that marked the vowels of the oral reading of the text were a later development in the early Islamic period (Knudsen 2015; Loopstra 2015). The earliest vocalisation system, known as the East Syriac system, used dots, some of which appear to have evolved from dots that marked the distinct vocalism of different morphological forms. Later, a system based on miniature Greek letters developed in the western Syriac ecclesiastical traditions in the Levant and adjacent regions, which came to be known as the western system (Coakley 2011). This innovative system is first attested in non-biblical texts, such as grammatical and poetic works, and subsequently came to be used in Syriac Bibles. The East Syriac system was used by ecclesiastical traditions in Mesopotamia and further east. Both the eastern and the western system continue to be used in their respective denominational traditions through the centuries without one becoming an overall standard.

Diacritical marks that distinguished homographic Arabic letters appear in the earliest Qurʾān manuscripts datable to the seventh century CE and also in Arabic epigraphy and papyri from the beginning of the Islamic period (Grohmann 1932, 40–43; Jones 1998; Al-Ghul 2004; Al-Ghabbān and Hoyland 2008). This coincides chronologically, therefore, with the emergence of diacritical dots in Syriac. Vocalisation signs that represented the vowels of the oral reading of the Arabic Qurʾān are first attested in manuscripts towards the end of the seventh century CE. The early systems of vocalisation used dots, as did the early Syriac systems of diacritical and vocalisation signs. Unlike Syriac, the Arabic sign system did not systematically mark prosody, though it did, in some cases, use signs to mark assimilations or pauses at the boundary of words (Fedeli 2024a). This is likely to reflect the fact that pitch modulation in Qurʾānic reading traditions was typically not fixed by tradition but was improvised by individual readers (Nelson 2001).

The earliest manifestations of vocalisation by dots in Qurʾān manuscripts reflect a selective marking by scribes of words and parts of words that were considered to require disambiguation for the reader (Muehlhaeusler 2016). These included words that were transmitted with different oral readings and also morphological inflections, many of which were homographs, and boundaries between words (see Fedeli in this volume). As with Syriac, therefore, the Arabic system began primarily as a system of distinguishing forms that were considered liable to be confounded. Even in the early period, however, there were some redundancies in this respect and the main function of the Arabic dots was to mark vowels rather than act as a lexical or morphological diacritic, as was the case in the earliest Syriac dot systems. Thus the Arabic system exhibits correspondence to the stage of development of the Syriac system in which dots marked specific vowels. There was not, however, an exact match between the phonetic value of the Syriac vocalisation dot signs and that of the corresponding Arabic dot signs. The non-systematic selective distribution of dots in such early systems varied across different circles of scribes and regions. A feature of these early dot systems that differed from Syriac is their use of different ink colours to distinguish vowels of variant oral reading traditions of the Qurʾān (Dutton 1999 and 2000; Cellard 2015; George 2015a and 2015b;

Fedeli 2020 and 2024a). The dot systems in Arabic Qurʾāns were subsequently replaced by stroke symbols that have continued to be used down to modern times (Fedeli, Kinne-Wall, and Sidky in this volume). Several of these symbols were stylised miniature forms of Arabic letters (Abbott 1939). This, therefore, is typologically parallel to the later development of miniature Greek letters to represent vowels in the western Syriac tradition. This shift to stroke symbols also coincided with a greater systematicity in marking of vowels, which may have been associated with attempts at standardisation of reading traditions at this period led by Ibn Mujāhid (859–936 CE) (Nasser 2020). The new system first appeared in non-Qurʾānic manuscripts in the ninth century (see the manuscripts discussed in Witkam 2015) and in Qurʾānic manuscripts in the tenth–eleventh centuries. This also parallels the development of the western Syriac system, which is first attested in non-biblical manuscripts, reflecting the greater conservativeness of the written form of sacred scripture. The process involved the transfer of non-sacred vocalisation practices to sacred texts. In the Qurʾānic tradition, a parallel to this is the transfer of cursive script, which is first attested in Arabic documents and non-sacred texts, to Qurʾānic manuscripts (Déroche 1992; Khan 2014; Witkam 2015, 380–81). Despite attempts at standardisation in the tenth century, a certain diversity in Qurʾānic reading traditions (*qirāʾāt*) continue down to modern times and this is reflected in variations in vocalisation in both manuscripts and printed editions. González Martínez (in this volume) describes an innovative computational tool that will facilitate the identification and analysis of variant vocalisation systems in Qurʾānic manuscripts and printed editions.

Diacritical and vocalisation signs are first attested in manuscripts of the Hebrew Bible dated to the late ninth or early tenth centuries. It is generally believed that the earliest sign systems that were developed were those of the so-called accent signs, which marked the prosody of the oral reading of the biblical text (Dotan 1981). Accent signs form a component of each of the three main Hebrew sign systems, namely the Babylonian, which was developed in Iraq (Shoshany 2013), the Palestinian (Revell 1977), and the Tiberian (Yeivin 1980), both of which developed in Palestine. These accents marked distinctions in the musical contour of the cantillation of the text and also the prosodic segmentation of the text. The latter function of segmentation reflected the grammatical parsing of the text. Crellin in his paper in this volume, for example, argues that the prosodic segmentation marked by the accents in the Hebrew Bible reflect distinctions in the grammaticalisation of different categories of words. The Hebrew accent systems, therefore, had a function that corresponds broadly to that of the Syriac prosody-marking signs, which constituted the earliest phase of the Syriac sign systems. There is no clear formal correspondence, however, in the form of most of the Hebrew accent signs with those of the Syriac prosody-marking signs. Moreover, Hebrew accent systems mark only prosodic segmentation and its associated pitch changes, whereas Syriac systems also mark pitch changes associated with communicative functions, such as commands and questions.

The earliest vocalisation systems that were developed predominantly used dots. These included the early layers of the Babylonian vocalisation system (Yeivin 1985) and the Palestinian vocalisation system (Revell 1970). Although it is possible that the idea of using dots to mark distinctions in vowels was borrowed from the Syriac or Arabic traditions, it is important to note that the phonetic value expressed by the signs in these early Hebrew vocalisation systems do not, for the most part, correspond to the phonetic value of the corresponding signs in the eastern Syriac or Arabic sign systems. The Babylonian vocalisation system subsequently developed systems consisting of a combination of dots, strokes and miniature Hebrew letters, which typologically parallels the later, stroke-based Arabic vocalisation system and the western Syriac vocalisation system.

The Tiberian vocalisation system, which is composed of signs consisting of strokes and dots, is also a later development. The Tiberian sign system, which was the one most systematically marked in the manuscripts, came to be regarded as the standard vocalisation for the Hebrew Bible and eventually replaced all other systems. Tiberian vocalisation was typically marked consistently on every word of the text, which can be regarded as a reflection of this prestigious status. The emergence of the Tiberian standard system of vocalisation and the growing prestige of the Tiberian reading tradition that it reflects may have been catalysed by the movement to standardise the Arabic Qurʾān led by Ibn Mujāhid during this same period in the ninth and tenth centuries. The introduction of the systematised, stroke-based Arabic vocalisation was, as remarked, possibly also associated with this standardisation movement. The innovation of the Tiberian system and the Arabic stroke-based system could, therefore, be reflections of a shared culture of standardisation. Unlike the innovative Arabic stroke system and the innovative western Syriac system, the Tiberian sign system does not appear to have been first used in non-sacred texts, but was introduced directly in biblical manuscripts. It is possible, however, that the idea of an innovative and systematic vocalisation was developed as a match for the innovative Arabic stroke system. So, in this respect, there was an external model. The introduction of the innovative Tiberian system directly into biblical manuscripts is likely to have been facilitated by the fact that the Tiberian oral reading tradition of the Hebrew Bible that it represented was regarded as the most prestigious reading tradition (Khan 2020). It should be noted, moreover, that the Tiberian vocalisation became the default type of vocalisation of non-biblical texts which did not have a tradition of vocalisation at the time of the standardisation of the Tiberian system. This included, for example, texts in Jewish languages written in Hebrew script, such as Judaeo-Arabic (see Posegay, this volume).

It is significant that sign systems appear at roughly the same period in manuscripts of the Syriac Bible and Arabic Qurʾān, but only about two centuries later do they appear in manuscripts of the Hebrew Bible. This can be correlated with the fact that in the Jewish tradition, it was only in the late ninth or early tenth century that the codex was adopted as the material medium for the transmission of the written text of the Hebrew Bible (Stern 2017). Prior to this, the Hebrew Bible was written in scrolls, the book format that was inherited from antiquity. The introduction of sign systems in the Hebrew Bible coincided with the introduction of the codex as a means of written transmission, whereas Syriac Bibles and Qur'ān manuscripts were being written in codices at the time of the introduction of the sign systems two centuries earlier (George 2010; Fedeli 2020). The adoption of the codex for Hebrew Bibles through convergence with the surrounding cultures of Christianity and Islam licensed the innovative addition of written accent and vocalisation signs to the written form of the sacred Hebrew text.

We see that there were various connecting strands between various dimensions of the emergence of the sign systems that were added to the written scripture of the three religions. It has been remarked that the three religious traditions did not, for the most part, share the use of signs with the same external form and value. Nonetheless, it should be noted that the external form of the various systems of signs of the three communities reflect, to a large extent, a shared theory of the physical articulation of vowels that was espoused by contemporary grammarians of Syriac, Hebrew and Arabic (Posegay 2021). Likewise, the diacritical signs that were written on Arabic consonants to distinguish homographs reflect the theory of articulation of consonants that was adopted by the medieval Arabic grammarians (Revell 1975). It is possible that the external forms of the signs were consciously kept distinct across the three religions since they were conceived as emblems of distinct communal identities. This would be analogous to the fact that the different alphabets were emblems of identity and they were transferred to the writing of different languages by members of a particular religious group: Arabic script for languages written by Muslim, e.g., Persian; Hebrew script for languages written by Jews, e.g., Judaeo-Arabic; and Syriac script for languages written by Christians, e.g., Christian Arabic known as Garshuni. The more abstract underpinning theory of vowels, on the other hand, did not serve as a marker of distinct identity and was shared across the communities.

2.0. Codicology

As has already been remarked, the three religious traditions shared the codex as a common physical form for the writing of sign systems in sacred texts. This was adopted in Judaism in the ninth–tenth centuries, later than in the other traditions. The ancient format of the scroll continued to be used in Judaism in addition to the codex, but vocalisation and accent signs were only written in codices.

The page layout of the codices differed across the traditions. The so-called 'model' Hebrew Bible codices, which were the most carefully executed and served as public authoritative bases for copying, were arranged in three columns on the page. This may have been a continuity of the column format of biblical scrolls. A similar column format is found also in Syriac Bible manuscripts, and so this also may have been a conditioning factor. Arabic Qur'ān codices, by contrast, were written in single columns. It is possible that this distinct page layout of Qur'āns was consciously conceived as a visual emblem of distinct communal identity.

Although model Hebrew Bible codices were written in columns, different page layouts were used in codices that did not have this public status but were rather private copies. Such medieval manuscripts of the Hebrew Bible, which have been termed 'popular' or 'common' Bibles (Arrant 2021; Outhwaite 2020), were frequently written in a single running text on the page without columns. This may have been motivated partly by the fact that many of them were smaller in size than the model manuscripts. In contrast, many of the popular Bibles had a page size that was large enough to have been comfortably arranged in columns, but nevertheless are written as a single block of text on the page. This could have been the result of convergence with the codicological format of Muslim Qurʾāns.

An even greater degree of external appearance convergence between Hebrew Bibles with Muslim Qurʾāns is exhibited by a corpus of Bibles written by Karaite Jews in the Middle Ages (Khan, this volume). The Bible manuscripts in the corpus in question are written with a single block of text on each page in Arabic transcription. The transcription represents the Hebrew oral reading tradition. Many such Karaite manuscripts also share other features of Qurʾān manuscripts, such as the use of inks of different colours for signs, which, as remarked above, is a feature of Qurʾān manuscripts. Moreover, the Karaite transcriptions also share with Qurʾāns decorative elements and sigla used to mark boundaries of verses and sections of text. Some of the Karaite manuscripts even used the Arabic word for God الله to represent the Hebrew name of God. These Karaite transcriptions fell into the category of private Bibles, since the Karaites also used and produced model codices at the same period. Two factors, therefore, facilitated the convergence of Hebrew Bible manuscripts with the external form of Muslim Qurʾāns. The first was their private status. Public, model Bibles were more conservative than private Bibles. This conservativism was, however, relative, since the codex format of the model Bibles was itself a result of some degree of convergence with external models. Moreover, some model codices exhibit decorative elements that are characteristic of contemporary Qurʾān manuscripts, such as elaborate carpet pages (Narkiss 1990; Bauer 2000; Gacek 2009; Stern 2017). The second factor was the ideological split of Karaite Judaism from the mainstream Rabbanite Judaism. This split facilitated a greater convergence with the external Muslim model and, indeed, this convergence was likely conceived of as an emblem of the distinct identity of the Karaites.

As remarked, the Karaites also used model Tiberian Bible codices written in Hebrew script. By the end of the tenth century, the Karaites had become the main custodians of model codices, as reflected by colophons (Khan 1992). It is worth mentioning here that the prestige of the Tiberian vocalisation system reached a climax at the period when the Karaites came to champion the Tiberian tradition. We have seen that a factor that gave rise to the standard Tiberian vocalisation system may have been the emergence of the innovative stroke-based Arabic vocalisation. This reflects a convergence with the Muslim tradition, which may have been driven by the Karaites, who were more open to convergence with the Muslim cultural environment than the Rabbanite Jews.

Also within the Muslim Qurʾānic tradition a distinction can be made between public model manuscripts and private manuscripts (Khan 1990; Fedeli 2019, 2024b; Kaplony and Marx 2018, 40–41; Connolly and Posegay 2021). Private Qurʾān manuscripts typically exhibit more assimilation to scribal practices of non-Qurʾānic manuscripts of the period, such as writing support, e.g., papyrus in the early period rather than parchment, or plene orthography. This is convergence to an external model, albeit within the Muslim Arabic tradition, which is typologically analogous to the convergence of popular Hebrew Bible manuscripts to external models.

Finally, verses of the Hebrew Bible and the Arabic Qurʾān that are cited within other texts often deviate from the form they have in scriptural codices, e.g., Hebrew Bible quotations in the Mishnah (Henshke 2013), in incantation bowls (Waller 2022; Molin 2019) and in medieval documents (Weiss 2008); and Qurʾān quotations in medieval documents (Kaplony and Marx 2018).

3.0. Masorah and Masoretic Treatises

In the three religious traditions, various ancillary works developed to ensure the preservation and correct transmission of scripture. The earliest of these are textual notes relating to the written form of the scripture, especially orthography, that in the Jewish Hebrew tradition are known as the Masoretic notes, or the Masorah. In Tiberian Hebrew model codices, the Masoretic notes are written in the margins of manuscripts. The same practice of writing Masoretic notes is found in the margins of Syriac Bible manuscripts. A corpus of Masoretic notes was associated with the Babylonian tradition of the Hebrew Bible, but this was transmitted as an independent work and not written in the margin of manuscripts (Ofer 2001).

A parallel to this is found in the Muslim Qurʾānic tradition, in which textual notes relating to the written text are not recorded in the margin of manuscripts but in separate works (e.g., al-Dānī, *Kitāb al-Muqniʿ fī Maʿrifat Marsūm Maṣāḥif ʾAhl al-Amṣār*). A feature of the marginal Masoretic notes in many Tiberian Bible manuscripts is that they sometimes describe details of orthography that are not found in the manuscript they are written in (Breuer 1977). This suggest that the notes are likely to have been transferred from originally independent lists, and so they were in origin closer to the Babylonian and Muslim model.

It is noteworthy that popular Tiberian Bible manuscripts frequently lack Masoretic notes (Arrant 2021), so this can be regarded as a convergence with the format of Arabic Qurʾāns. As we have seen, convergence of Hebrew Bibles with Qurʾāns was greater in popular Hebrew Bibles than model Bibles.

Martín-Contreras (this volume) examines the background of the Hebrew biblical Masorah and concludes that, although some embryonic forms of Masoretic textual notes can be found in pre-Islamic Jewish sources, such as Midrashic literature, the Masoretic notes that appear in Bible manuscripts and independent Masoretic works in the Middle Ages were not a direct continuation of these. This suggests that the emergence of such Masoretic notes in the Jewish tradition of the Hebrew Bible was catalysed by contact with the Muslim and Christian traditions of scripture.

In addition to independent works containing lists of Masoretic notes relating to the written biblical text, several treatises emerged in the Hebrew tradition that related to the oral reading tradition, including the vocalisation signs and accents. These typically incorporate grammatical theory and terminology (Eldar 1994; Khan 2020, vol. 2). Analogous treatises in the Syriac biblical tradition are the school texts described by Loopstra and Lundberg in this volume. The parallels in the Islamic tradition are the so-called *tajwīd* manuals (Nasser 2013; Nelson 2001). So, in here also there is a convergence across the communities.

4.0. Orality

The sacred scriptures of the three religious communities were transmitted in both a written and an oral form. A shared feature of the three traditions in the medieval Middle East was the textualisation of the oral reading traditions in the form of sign systems written onto the text. The degree of textualisation of the oral reading increased over the centuries of the early Islamic period. This increased textualisation of oral traditions, which was shared by the three traditions, can be correlated with the increasing literarisation of the culture in the Middle East from around the ninth century onwards. This involved the increased production of written texts and increased literacy. It also resulted in the increasing authority of written texts (Schoeler 2006). Kiraz's paper in this volume discusses a similar process of increasing textualisation over time of oral traditions in Syriac liturgical practice.

In the transmission of the Hebrew Bible in the Middle Ages there was a certain degree of discrepancy between the written form of the text and the oral reading reflected by the vocalisation signs. This reflected the conservative fixity of the Hebrew text at the period of this textualisation process, whereby the textualisation was restricted to the creation of added vocalisation and accent signs. The traditions of the Christian Syriac Bible and the Muslim Qurʾān exhibit a slightly lesser degree of fixity of the written text, so that some degree of variation in the written text appeared in manuscripts reflecting variations in oral reading traditions (Fedeli 2005; Déroche 2019). This can be regarded as reflecting a greater degree of textualisation of the oral reading traditions than in the transmission of the Hebrew Bible. It should be noted, however, that popular Hebrew Bible manuscripts often reflect a greater textualisation of the oral tradition than model Hebrew Bible manuscripts, in that they exhibit a lesser number of discrepancies between the written text and the oral reading tradition. This can be interpreted as a greater degree of convergence with the model of the other traditions.

There was, in general, more diversity in the authoritative form of the transmission of the Christian Syriac Bible and the Muslim Qurʾān than in the Hebrew Bible. In the Muslim tradition, the main manifestation of this was the acceptance of a diversity of authoritative oral reading traditions (*qirāʾāt*), although the number of these authoritative oral traditions became constrained after the activities of Ibn Mujāhid (ninth–tenth centuries) (Nasser 2020). A factor that may have contributed to the greater conservatism of the transmission of the Jewish scripture was the greater historical depth of Judaism than the other religions. The greater tolerance of diversity in the Christian and Muslim traditions than in Judaism may have arisen since the Eastern Christian and Muslim communities were expanding in the Middle Ages across an increasing large geographical extent whereas there was no equivalent expansion in the Jewish community. Moreover there was in Christianity and Islam increasing religious diversification, often associated with political fragmentation, whereas this did not take place to the same extent in Judaism. As we have seen, there were diverse traditions of sign notation of the Hebrew Bible. There are also allusions to small differences in readings in the Jewish Masoretic sources between eastern (Babylonian) and western (Tiberian) Masoretes, or between individual Masoretes in Tiberias. By the later Middle Ages, however, the Tiberian tradition of one particular, Aharon ben Asher, had become the sole authoritative tradition.

Another distinctive feature of the Jewish tradition of the Hebrew Bible was that the Tiberian vowel and accent notation signs became fossilised. Although they were originally textualisations of the living oral tradition of the Tiberian reading, by the later Middle Ages the Tiberian oral tradition ceased to be transmitted and the Tiberian signs were read with other reading traditions (Khan 2017). This differed from the Christian and Muslim sacred traditions, in which the written text, in principle, was adapted to variations in the oral reading. This reflects a lesser tolerance of diversity in the external form of the sacred text in Judaism than in Christianity and Islam. In this connection, the Samaritan tradition of the transmission of the Hebrew Pentateuch should be mentioned. The Samaritans seceded from Judaism in the first millennium BCE and transmitted the Pentateuch through the Middle Ages down to modern times in a textual form that deviated from the tradition of the fixed form of the Jewish Hebrew Bible at these periods. Furthermore, the written form of the Samaritan Pentateuch was adapted to the oral tradition and there were no discrepancies, as there were between the written and oral Jewish Hebrew Bible (Florentin and Tal 2025). The Samaritan tradition, therefore, reflects in this respect a greater convergence to the Muslim and Christian model of transmission of Scripture.

5.0. Concluding Remarks

We see, therefore, that there were many connections in various dimensions of the transmission of scripture across the various monotheistic religions in the medieval Middle East. These were expected, since the three communities co-existed in close contact and there was a rapprochement in other dimensions of culture of the communities at this period (Vorderstrasse and Treptow 2015).

There were, however, also a variety of differences. These differences can be attributed to various factors. These include the differences in conservativeness of individual traditions and differences in the tolerance of diversity. These factors, in turn, can be explained as arising from differences in the historical depth, geographical extent and intra-communal religious splits of the various communities. We have seen also that the degree of conservativeness depended to some extent on whether a manuscript of scripture was a public model manuscript or a private manuscript. In general, the public model manuscripts were more conservative, whereas private manuscripts exhibited more convergence with other sacred traditions in the region.

Another factor appears to have been the desire of the religious communities to maintain their distinct identity. Distinctions, especially in external features such as the form of vocalisation signs and codicological format, were exploited as emblems of communal identity.

References

Abbott, Nabia. 1939. *The Rise of the North Arabic Script and Its Ḳurʾānic Development, with a Full Description of the Ḳurʾān Manuscripts in the Oriental Institute*. Chicago: University of Chicago Press.

Al-Ghabbān, ʿAlī Ibrāhīm, and Robert Hoyland. 2008. 'The Inscription of Zuhayr, the Oldest Islamic Inscription (24 AH/AD 644–645), the Rise of the Arabic Script and the Nature of the Early Islamic State'. *Arabian Archaeology and Epigraphy* 19: 210–37.

Al-Ghul, Omar. 2004. 'An Early Arabic Inscription from Petra Carrying Diacritic Marks'. *Syria* 81: 105–18.

Arrant, Estara. 2021. 'A Codicological and Linguistic Typology of Common Torah Codices from the Cairo Genizah'. Ph.D. Thesis, University of Cambridge.

Bauer, Eva. 2000. 'Early Bible and Quran Illuminations: Preliminary Remarks'. In *Judaism and Islam: Boundaries, Communication, and Interaction*, edited by Benjamin H. Hary, John L. Hayes, and Fred Astren. Brill.

Breuer, Mordechai. 1977. *The Aleppo Codex and the Accepted Version of the Bible.* Jerusalem: Mossad ha-Rav Kook. [Hebrew].

Cellard, Eléonore. 2015. 'La vocalisation des manuscrits coraniques dans les premiers siècles de l'Islam'. In *Les origines du Coran, le Coran des origines*, edited by François Déroche, Christian J. Robin, and Michel Zink. Paris: Académie des Inscriptions et Belles-Lettres.

Coakley, James F. 2011. 'When Were the Five Greek Vowel-Signs Introduced into Syriac Writing?' *Journal of Semitic Studies* 56 (2): 307–25.

Connolly, Magdalen M., and Nick Posegay. 2021. 'A Survey of Personal-Use Qur'an Manuscripts Based on Fragments from the Cairo Genizah'. *Journal of Qur'anic Studies* 23: 1–40.

Déroche, François. 1992. *The Abbasid Tradition: Qur'ans of the 8th to the 10th Centuries A.D.* London: Nour Foundation.

———. 2019. *Le Coran, une histoire plurielle: essai sur la formation du texte coranique.* Paris: Editions du Seuil.

Dotan, Aron. 1981. 'The Relative Chronology of Hebrew Vocalization and Accentuation'. *Proceedings of the American Academy for Jewish Research* 48: 87–99.

Dutton, Yasin. 1999. 'Red Dots, Green Dots, Yellow Dots and Blue: Some Reflections on the Vocalisation of Early

Qur'anic Manuscripts—Part I'. *Journal of Qur'anic Studies* 1 (1): 115–40.

———. 2000. 'Red Dots, Green Dots, Yellow Dots and Blue: Some Reflections on the Vocalisation of Early Qur'anic Manuscripts—Part II'. *Journal of Qur'anic Studies* 2 (1): 1–24.

Eldar, Ilan. 1994. *The Study of the Art of Correct Reading as Reflected in the Medieval Treatise Hidāyat Al-Qāriʾ*. Jerusalem: Academy of the Hebrew Language. [Hebrew].

Fedeli, Alba. 2005. 'Early Evidences of Variant Readings in Qurʾānic Manuscripts'. In *Die dunklen Anfänge. Neue Forschungen zur Entstehung und frühen Geschichte des Islam*, edited by Klaus-Heinz Ohlig and Gerd-R. Puin. Berlin: Verlag Hans Schiler.

———. 2019. 'Isolated Qurʾānic Fragments: The Case of the Three Papyri from the Mingana Collection'. In *The Making of Religious Texts in Islam: The Fragment and the Whole*, edited by Asma Hilali and Stephen R. Burge. Dover, UK: Gerlach Press.

———. 2020. 'The Qurʾānic Text from Manuscript to Digital Form: Metalinguistic Markup of Scribes and Editors'. In *From Scrolls to Scrolling. Sacred Texts, Materiality, and Dynamic Media Cultures*, edited by Bradford A. Anderson. Berlin: De Gruyter.

———. 2024a. 'Early Qurʾānic Manuscripts: Re-Mediating Their Manuscript Page in the Most Recent Digital Form as Part of the InterSaME Project'. In *The Qurʾan and Its Handwritten Transmission*, edited by François Déroche. Leiden: Brill.

———. 2024b. 'Personal Qur'ans in Early Islam: A Case of Palimpsesting and Training'. In *Palimpsests and Related Phenomena across Languages and Cultures*, edited by Jost Gippert. Berlin: De Gruyter.

Florentin, Moshe, and Abraham Tal. 2025. *The Samaritan Pentateuch: An English Translation with a Parallel Annotated Hebrew Text*. Cambridge Semitic Languages and Cultures 30. Cambridge: University of Cambridge and Open Book Publishers.

Gacek, Adam. 2009. *Arabic Manuscripts. A Vademecum for Readers*. Leiden: Brill.

George, Alain. 2010. *The Rise of Islamic Calligraphy*. London: Saqi.

———. 2015a. 'Coloured Dots and the Question of Regional Origins in Early Qur'ans (Part I)'. *Journal of Qur'anic Studies* 17: 1–44.

———. 2015b. 'Coloured Dots and the Question of Regional Origins in Early Qur'ans (Part II)'. *Journal of Qur'anic Studies* 17: 75–102.

Grohmann, Adolf. 1932. 'Aperçu de Papyrologie Arabe'. In *Études de Papyrologie,* vol. 1. Cairo: L'Institut français d'archéologie orientale.

Henshke, Yehudit. 2013. 'Biblical Citations in the Mishnah: A Characterization of the Biblical Text Witnesses in Medieval Byzantium'. *Jewish Studies, An Internet Journal* 12: 1–47.

Jones, Alan. 1998. 'The Dotting of a Script and The Dating of an Era: The Strange Neglect of PERF 558'. *Islamic Culture* 72: 95–103.

Kaplony, Andreas, and Michael Marx. 2018. *Qurʾān Quotations Preserved on Papyrus Documents, 7th-10th Centuries*. Leiden: Brill.

Khan, Geoffrey. 1990. 'Standardisation and Variation in the Orthography of Hebrew Bible and Arabic Qurʾān Manuscripts'. *Manuscripts of the Middle East* 5: 53–58.

———. 1992. 'The Medieval Karaite Transcriptions of Hebrew in Arabic Script'. *Israel Oriental Studies* 12: 157–76.

———. 2014. 'The Development of Early Arabic Documentary Script'. In *Manuscrits hébreux et arabes: mélanges en l'honneur de Colette Sirat*, edited by Nicholas de Lange and Judith Olszowy-Schlanger. Turnhout: Brepols.

———. 2017. 'Learning to Read Biblical Hebrew in the Middle Ages: The Transition from Oral Standard to Written Standard'. In *Jewish Education from Antiquity to the Middle Ages: Studies in Honour of Philip S. Alexander*, edited by George J. Brooke and Renate Smithuis. Leiden: Brill.

———. 2020. *The Tiberian Pronunciation Tradition of Biblical Hebrew: Including a Critical Edition and English Translation of the Sections on Consonants and Vowels in the Masoretic Treatise Hidāyat al-Qāriʾ 'Guide for the Reader'*, vol. 2. Cambridge Semitic Languages and Cultures 1. Cambridge: University of Cambridge and Open Book Publishers. doi.org/10.11647/OBP.0163

Kiraz, George Anton. 2012. *Tūrrāṣ Mamllā : A Grammar of the Syriac Language*. Piscataway, NJ: Gorgias Press.

———. 2015. *The Syriac Dot: A Short History*. Piscataway, NJ: Gorgias Press.

Knudsen, Ebbe E. 2015. *Classical Syriac Phonology*. Piscataway, NJ: Gorgias Press.

Loopstra, Jonathan. 2015. *An East Syrian Manuscript of the Syriac "Masora" Dated to 899 CE : Introduction, List of Sample Texts, and Indices to Marginal Notes in British Library, Additional MS 12138*. Piscataway, NJ: Gorgias Press.

Molin, Dorota. 2019. 'The Biblical Quotations in the Aramaic Incantation Bowls and Their Contribution to the Study of the Babylonian Reading Tradition'. In *Studies in Semitic Vocalization and Reading Traditions,* edited by Geoffrey Khan. Cambridge Semitic Languages and Cultures. Cambridge: University of Cambridge and Open Book Publishers.

Muehlhaeusler, Mark. 2016. 'Additional Reading Marks in Kufic Manuscripts'. *Journal of Islamic Studies* 27: 1–16.

Narkiss, Bezalel. 1990. *Illuminations from Hebrew Bibles of Leningrad*. Jerusalem: The Bialik Institute.

Nasser, Shady Hekmat. 2013. *The Transmission of the Variant Readings of the Qurʾān: The Problem of Tawātur and the Emergence of Shawādhdh*. Leiden: Brill.

———. 2020. *The Second Canonization of the Qurʾān (324/936): Ibn Mujāhid and the Founding of the Seven Readings*. Leiden: Brill.

Nelson, Kristina. 2001. *The Art of Reciting the Qurʾan*. Cairo: American University in Cairo Press.

Ofer, Yosef. 2001. *Babylonian Masora of the Pentateuch, Its Principles and Methods*. Jerusalem: Academy of the Hebrew Language. [Hebrew].

Outhwaite, Ben. 2020. 'The Tiberian Tradition in Common Bibles from the Cairo Genizah'. In *Semitic Vocalization and Reading Traditions*, edited by Geoffrey Khan and Aaron Hornkohl. Cambridge Semitic Languages and Cultures 3. Cambridge: University of Cambridge and Open Book Publishers.

Posegay, Nick. 2021. *Points of Contact: The Shared Intellectual History of Vocalisation in Syriac, Arabic, and Hebrew*. Cambridge Semitic Languages and Cultures 10. Cambridge: University of Cambridge and Open Book Publishers.

Revell, E. John. 1970. 'Studies in the Palestinian Vocalization of Hebrew'. In *Essays on the Ancient Semitic World*, edited by John. W. Wevers. and Donald. B. Redford. Toronto: Toronto University Press.

———. 1975. 'The Diacritical Dots and the Development of the Arabic Alphabet'. *Journal of Semitic Studies* 20: 178–90.

———. 1977. *Biblical Texts with Palestinian Pointing and Their Accents*. Masoretic Studies, no. 4. Atlanta, GA: Scholars Press for the Society of Biblical Literature.

Schoeler, Gregor. 2006. *The Oral and the Written in Early Islam*. Edited by James Edward Montgomery. Translated by Uwe Vagelpohl. Routledge Studies in Middle Eastern Literatures 13. London: Routledge.

Segal, Judah Benzion. 1953. *The Diacritical Point and the Accents in Syriac*. Oxford: Oxford University Press.

Shoshany, Ronit. 2013. 'Biblical Accents: Babylonian'. In *Encyclopedia of Hebrew Language and Linguistics*, edited by Geoffrey Khan, Shmuel Bolozky, Steven E. Fassberg, et al., vol. 1. Leiden: Brill.

Stern, David. 2017. *The Jewish Bible: A Material History*. 1st ed. Samuel and Althea Stroum Lectures in Jewish Studies. Seattle: University of Washington Press.

Vorderstrasse, Tasha, and Tanya Treptow (eds). 2015. *A Cosmopolitan City: Muslims, Christians and Jews in Old Cairo*. Chicago: The Oriental Institute of the University of Chicago.

Waller, Daniel James. 2022. *The Bible in the Bowls: A Catalogue of Biblical Quotations in Published Jewish Babylonian Aramaic Magic Bowls*. With Dorota Molin. Cambridge Semitic Languages and Cultures 16. Cambridge: University of Cambridge and Open Book Publishers.

Weiss, Gershon. 2008. מובאות מן המקרא במסמכי הגניזה הקהירית. Beit Mikra 23: 341–62. [Hebrew].

Witkam, Jan Just. 2015. 'The Neglect Neglected. To Point or Not to Point, That Is the Question'. *Journal of Islamic Manuscripts* 6: 376–408.

Yeivin, Israel. 1980. *Introduction to the Tiberian Masorah*. Translated by E. John Revell. Masoretic Studies 5. Atlanta, GA: Scholars Press.

———. 1985. *The Hebrew Language Tradition as Reflected in the Babylonian Vocalization*. Jerusalem: The Academy of the Hebrew Language. [Hebrew].

PASSING DOWN A CORPUS OF REMINDERS FOR THE PESHIṬTA AND THE HARKLEAN BIBLES[1]

Jonathan A. Loopstra

1.0. Introduction

As in Hebrew and Arabic, the Syriac Scriptures were initially transmitted without reading dots, prosodic marks, or vowels, apart from what was already expressed by *matres lectionis*. These additions to the consonantal biblical text were developed only gradually, over hundreds of years, in order to set down in writing what were otherwise primarily oral traditions of reading and reciting the Scriptures (Coakley 2011, 307–25; Kiraz 2015, 68–123). In the case of Syriac, a fully-developed system appeared only after the contentious theological and ecclesiastical divisions of the fifth and sixth centuries. The resultant combinations of

[1] The author would like to thank the organisers of the working group for their kind invitation to participate in the Intersame conference in Hamburg. Thanks also to George Kiraz and Mark Dickens for their valuable feedback. The background work in collating these *šmāhe* manuscripts was made possible thanks to a fellowship at the Institute for Advanced Studies at Princeton in 2021, for which the author is very grateful.

 https://doi.org/10.11647/OBP.0498.01

added dots and vowels thus came to reflect distinct East Syriac (Church of the East) or West Syriac (Syrian Orthodox) traditions of reading and reciting the Syriac Bible. On occasion, these marks guide the reader in ways of understanding the text that differ from more contemporary readings of the Scriptures.

2.0. The Challenge of the Syriac Punctuation and Accent Dots

By the late seventh century CE, a relatively mature system of dots had been developed to mark punctuation and accents in biblical manuscripts, although the full spectrum of these dotted marks was not at first applied to the whole Syriac Bible. It is in some of these early biblical manuscripts that we also find evidence of added marginal notes—or reminders—written by later readers to elucidate these dots (Loopstra 2019, 159–176). For instance, a reader has added a number of such reminders to the margins of BL Add. 14448, dated to 699/701 CE, a relatively early manuscript of the New Testament (Juckel 2023, lxvii–lxvii). Five times this reader has added the abbreviation *m-š* (ܡܫ) as a reminder that one should read the dots in the corresponding passages as a 'question', the *mšalānā* (ܡܫܐܠܢܐ).[2] Likewise, we find that a later hand has inserted identical abbreviated reminders in the margins of the valuable eighth-century New Testament manuscript BL Add. 7157 (767/68 CE) (Juckel 2023, lxxvi–lxxvii). In Figure 1 below, this reader has noted that the phrase 'tell me' (ܐܡܪ ܠܝ ܐܢܬ.) in Acts

[2] Among these are reminders for James 3.12 (fol. 155v), James 4.1 (fol. 155v), James 4.12 (fol. 156r), and Rom. 3.1 (fol. 166r).

22.27 (line 2) should be read as a 'command' (ܦܘܩܕܢܐ = ܦܘܩ).[3] By the same token, the reader also notes that the following phrase 'are you a Roman citizen?' (ܪܗܘܡܝܐ ܐܢܬ܀)—with the single supralinear dot above 'Roman citizen' followed by two oblique dots after 'you' (ܐܢܬ܀)—should be read as a 'question' (ܡܫܐܠܢܐ = ܡܫ).[4] Both of these marginal notes, along with several others in BL Add. 7157, are attempts to clarify and interpret the various dots that had been added to the Syriac text of these relatively early Peshiṭta New Testament manuscripts.

---

[3] English translations of the New Testament are taken from the new Antioch Bible translation (Kiraz ed. 2020). Note that the same dotting can be found in the East Syriac *šmāhe* codex, BL Add. 12138, fol. 273v, though without these added reminders.

[4] We will frequently encounter a certain level of ambiguity regarding this marker of the question (cf. Job 2.19, Luke 1.29, John 7.42, and Ezek. 20.31 below). The *mšalānā* is often represented, as here in Acts 22.27, as a single supralineal dot. But the *mšalānā* can also be signified in combination with the double-dotted mark, possibly the *taḥtāyā* (Segal 1953, 86–87; Loopstra 2015, §8.4.7). That is, on occasion, copyists in *šmāhe* manuscripts refer to clauses that have a double-dotted supralineal mark (technically, the *zawgā ʿelāyā*) followed by dots on and below the line (the *taḥtāyā*) by the designation *mšalānā*. See, for instance, Job 7.19 in Appendix III, and Ezek. 20.31 below.

Figure 1: Marginal reminders for Acts 22.27 in BL Add. 7157, fol. 123r (767/68 CE) (© British Library)

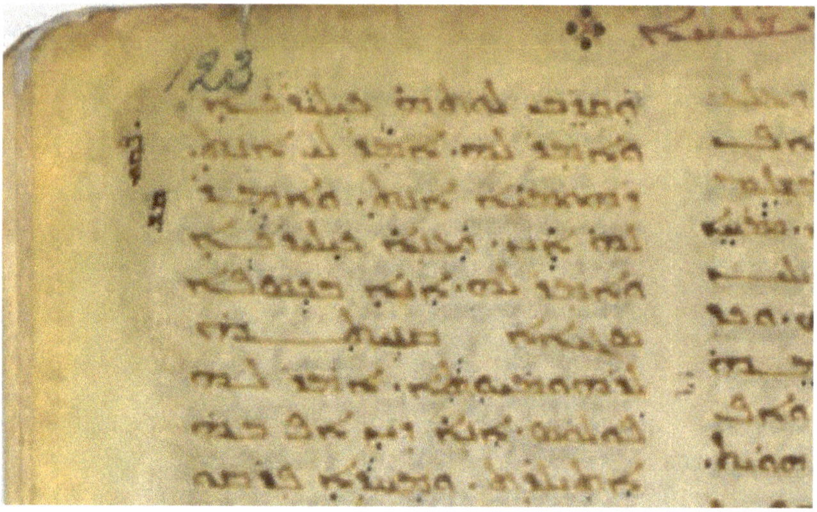

Only much later do we find anecdotal evidence that vividly illustrates the confusion that could result from this system of dotted punctuation and accents. In one rather humorous episode in his *Book of Rays,* the thirteenth-century West Syrian Bar ʿEbroyo tells of two teachers in Melitene who fell into a debate over the proper way to dot Mary's speech in Luke 1.29: 'and she pondered what this greeting might mean'. The images in Figure 2, below, from a Diyarbakir manuscript containing the *Book of Rays,* help us visualise how copyists would have placed these larger dots in the Syriac text.[5]

[5] In order to better visualise how scribes placed these dots in manuscripts, we have used Diyarbakir, Meryem Ana Kilisesi MS 167 for translations from the *Book of Rays* (DIYR 00167, fol. 187v). Curiously, Phillips does not include a scriptural citation for this passage in his English translation. It may be for this reason that he appears to have missed

> For I knew at one time of two old men (ܣܒ̈ܐ) in Melitene. Regarding the expression 'and she pondered what this greeting might mean' (ܘܡܬܚܫܒܐ ܗܘܬ ܕܡܢܘ ܫܠܡܐ ܗܢܐ), one, Michael, took ܡܢ̣ܘ ܫܠܡܐ ܗܢܐ, with a *mnaḥḥtā* (ܡܢܚܬܐ), as he had received from his teacher and our teacher George. But the other, Basil, read ܡܢ̇ܘ ܫܠܡܐ ܗܢܐ, with a *mšalānā* (ܡܫܐܠܢܐ), as he had received from his teacher Constantine. And thus, each scribe points (ܢܩܘܙ) in accord with what is good to him.

Figure 2: The dotting of Luke 1.29 in the *Book of Rays* (© HMML, DIYR 00167, fol. 187v)

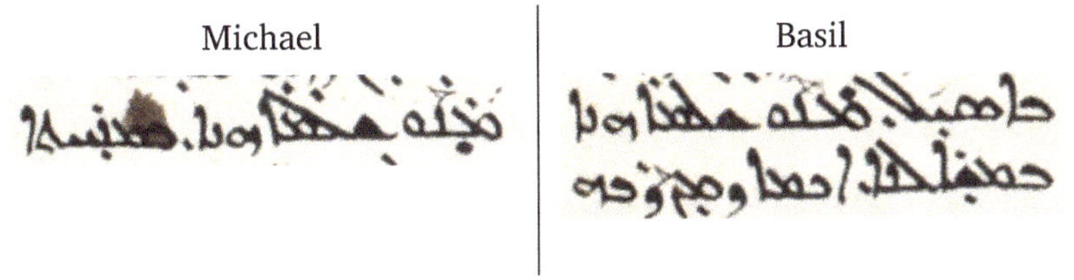

As Bar ʿEbroyo's anecdote makes clear, the first teacher, Michael, understood that there should be a large dot *under* the 'what is/does' (ܡܢ̣ܘ). This dot, the *mnaḥḥtā,* is often used to introduce a subordinate clause; hence, 'she wondered what this greeting might mean'. On the other hand, the second teacher, Basil, had been taught that the proper place for the accent dot was *above* the 'what is/does' (ܡܢ̇ܘ): 'she wondered, What does this greeting mean?' This large raised dot could suggest the presence of a *mšalānā*, marking a question. Moreover, Bar ʿEbroyo records that both teachers had 'received' (ܩܒܠ) their preferred method of dotting from their own teachers, hence the debate was also over

---

that the phrase 'and she pondered' (ܘܡܬܚܫܒܐ ܗܘܬ) is part of a biblical citation. (Phillips 1869, 39, ܟܛ).

which received tradition was correct. While anecdotal, it is possible that this could well have been a genuine debate over dotting. Perhaps we should not then be tempted to echo the rather disheartened observation of Judah Segal that these dots had become, by Bar ʿEbroyo's day, only "calligraphic debris, preserved out of respect for their antiquity" (1953, 1).

Indeed, earlier in his *Book of Rays*, Bar ʿEbroyo presents an argument for the value of these dots, suggesting "that the placing of the points of punctuation (ܢܘܩܙܐ ܕܢܝ̈ܫܐ، ܦܣܘܩܬ̈ܐ) is needed (ܐܠܝ،)" from a passage in John 7.42 (Phillips 1869, 34–35):[6]

> For the one who reads 'Has not the Messiah shone forth (ܕܢܚ) from the seed of David and from Bethlehem?'—if he were not to see the *taksa* with 'has not' (ܠܐ ܗܘܐ܆) and the *šwayā* with 'David' (ܕܘܝܕ܃), and the *mšalānā* with 'Messiah' (ܡܫܝܚܐ܂)—he would suppose that the Messiah was not born from the seed of David and of Bethlehem.

In other words, although he certainly recognised there were problems with the ability of scribes to competently place dots—as his predecessor Jacob of Edessa (d. 704) also recognised (Phillips 1869, 1–12)—Bar ʿEbroyo also suggested that these dots served an essential purpose. Without these ancient dotted marks, one could just as easily read what should be questions as statements, or what should be statements as questions. So, without the dots in the example from John 7.42 above, one could just as

[6] This translation is taken from Diyarbakir, Meryem Ana Kilisesi MS 167 (DIYR 00167, fol. 186r). We are presented here with a paraphrase of the Peshitta text in John 7.42, which reads in full, "Has not the scripture said that the Messiah comes (ܐܬܐ) from David's seed and from Bethlehem, the village of David?" (Phillips 1869, 34–35, ܗܡ).

readily read this passage as a statement: The Messiah 'has not [come] from the seed of David' (ܠܐ ܗܘܐ ܡܢ ܙܪܥܗ ܕܕܘܝܕ).

It was precisely because of this inherent ambiguity in the consonantal biblical text that these accent or punctuation dots were originally added as guides and correctives against possible misunderstanding. By the time Bar ʿEbroyo was writing, these dots had been in use for at least six hundred years. Therefore, it is little wonder that the two teachers from Melitene, Michael and Basil, took such an interest in debating which customary way of dotting Luke 1.29 was correct.

As interesting as the above anecdotes given by Bar ʿEbroyo are, these dotted passages are but two of the tens of thousands of excerpts that were included in a type of 'curriculum' of 'difficult' (ܥܣܩܐ) biblical exemplars by the late tenth century. First assembled nearly three centuries before Bar ʿEbroyo was writing, the collections of excerpts in this distinctive genre of Syriac reading handbook were designed to provide a solution to questions about how one should vocalise (or dot) the Scriptures. In answer to the types of problems that would have been raised by the two teachers in Bar ʿEbroyo's story above, the compilers of these massive codices collected difficult 'terms' *šmāhe* (ܫܡܗܐ) from the Syriac Bible and hundreds of other works, providing these excerpts with full vocalisation, dotting, and some annotations. Scholars today refer to these readers, somewhat misleadingly, as the Syriac 'Masorah'.

In Figure 3 below, we see that the passage debated by the two teachers of Melitene, Luke 1.29, appears with full dotting and vocalisation in both East Syriac and West Syriac manuscripts of these handbooks. We can also observe that both traditions include only the portion of the verse that was under debate, translated in the new Antioch Bible series as 'what this greeting might mean' (ܡܢܘ ܫܠܡܐ ܗܢܐ). The other parts of this verse have been omitted.

Figure 3: East Syriac and West Syriac *šmāhe* codices dot Luke 1.29

East Syriac *Šmāhe* Codex (899 CE)	West Syriac *Šmāhe* Codex (1004 CE)
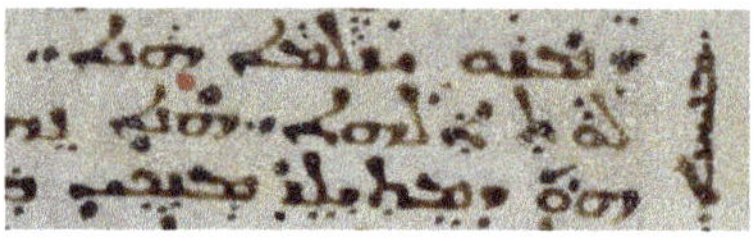	
© British Library (BL Add. 12138, fol. 247v)	© Patriarchate of Damascus (Dam. Syr. 7/16, fol. 140r)

We discover that the East Syriac *šmāhe* manuscript (899 CE), on the left, includes a large dot above 'what is' (ܡܢܘ), in keeping with the perspective of Basil, who argued for the presence of a *mšalānā* dot. An added note in the right margin of this manuscript suggests the presence of an additional dot, the *mnīḥānā* (in red ink), under the last word of the phrase, 'this' (ܗܢܐ).[7] On the other hand, most of the dozen manuscripts that have been preserved of the West Syriac *šmāhe* book also include a large dot above the *mīm*. Curiously, however, the copyist of one of these codices, Dam. Syr. 7/16 (1004 CE), on the right, records the presence of an additional dot below 'what is' (ܡܢܘ). This second dot does not appear in any other *šmāhe* manuscript. If these dots are 'accent' dots, Dam. Syr. 7/16 captures exactly the heart of the debate recorded

[7] The *mnīḥānā* ('providing rest') is a single dot that is often put under the last word of a clause ending a sentence with a *pāsuqā* (Loopstra 2015, §8.4.5).

by Bar ʿEbroyo;[8] should one read here a large dot above—the *mšalānā* (ܡܢܗ̇)—or a dot below—the *mnaḥḥtā* (ܡܢ̣ܗ)?

These *šmāhe* handbooks also speak to Bar ʿEbroyo's second example mentioned above, at least in part. In Figure 4 below, the copyist of Vat. sir. 152 (979/80 CE) has included a portion of the quote from John 7.42, including the double–dotted pausal mark, the *šwayā*, after 'David' (ܕܘܝܕ:), 'Has not the Scripture said that from the seed of David:'. However, looking at the surrounding verses in this manuscript, we find that scribes have inserted at least six rubricated reminders (ܡܫ) in these excerpts from John 7. These abbreviations are inserted after each excerpt and suggest that one should read the preceding phrase as a question, the *mšalānā* (ܡܫܐܠܢܐ). In the context of this chapter, these repeated insertions are not surprising; in John 7 the 'Jews' put forward a series of questions about Jesus in rapid sequence. We can also recall that these reminders (ܡܫ) are identical to a marginal note in BL Add. 7157 above (Fig. 1), with a notable exception. The difference here, in these *šmāhe* handbooks, is that the copyists themselves—or readers close to the tradition—added the vast majority of these reminders.

---

[8] However, we should also be careful as West Syriac 'accent' dots could also be confused with smaller 'tagging' dots concerned with phonology. The East Syriac manuscript in Figure 3 avoids this problem by exaggerating the size of these accent/punctuation dots.

Figure 4: John Chapter 7 in Vat. sir. 152, fol. 154v (© Vatican Library): sample text translation (with reminder ܙܘ)

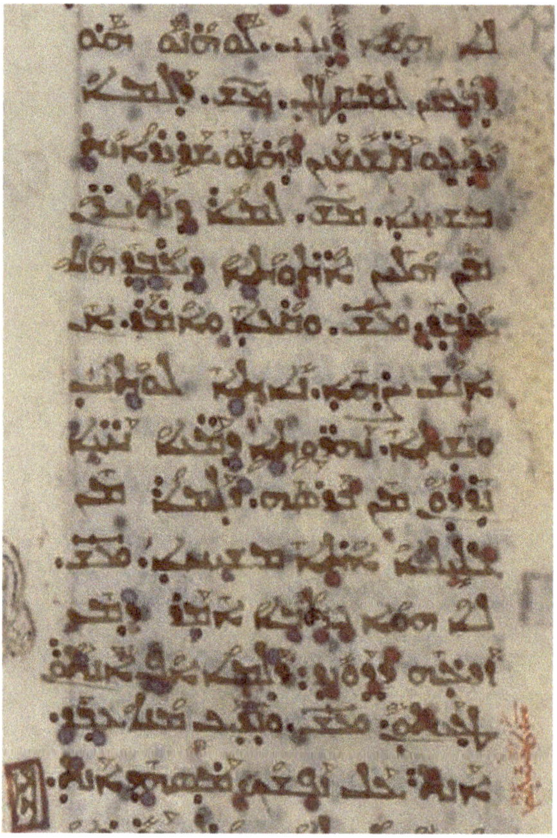

7.25 'Is not this the man they are seeking to kill?' ܙܘ
7.26 'Have our elders found out that he is really the Messiah?' ܙܘ
7.31 'Will he do more signs than those this man is doing?' ܙܘ
7.41 'The Messiah does not come from Galilee, does he?' ܙܘ
7.42 'Has not the scripture said that the Messiah comes from David's seed:'
7.47 'Has he deceived you too?' ܙܘ
7.51 'And finding out what he has done?'
8.13 'You testify about yourself. ܙܘ [mg.] Your testimony is not true'.

3.0. The Syriac 'Booklet of *Šmāhe*' (the Syriac 'Masorah')

Over twenty of these *šmāhe* handbooks, also known as the Syriac 'Masorah', have been preserved, all composed following the arrival of Islam. Our only example of an East Syriac *šmāhe* codex, dated to 899 CE, is titled 'gleanings of terms and readings' (ܠܘܩܛ̈ܐ

ܕܫܡ̈ܗܐ ܘܩܪ̈ܝܢܬܐ) (BL Add. 12138, fol. 1r). In West Syriac communities, from which most manuscripts come, these handbooks came to be known as 'a booklet of terms and readings' (ܟܘܪܣܐ ܕܫܡ̈ܗܐ ܘܩܪ̈ܝܢܬܐ) (Par. BnF syr. 64, fol. 1v.). Moreover, among these West Syriac codices, we find different categories of handbooks, each category made up of distinct extracts of 'difficult terms' (ܫܡ̈ܗܐ ܩܫܝ̈ܐ). However, whether East Syriac or West Syriac, all the *šmāhe* manuscripts in this Syriac genre functioned as a type of platform where users could expect to find sample texts from the Bible or the writings of the Greek Fathers fully vocalised and provided with a variety of dots (Loopstra, 2020, 123–26). At the time, apart from these handbooks, manuscripts were rarely provided with such a detailed level of additional helps; hence, the very real value of these handbooks. It was in these 'booklets' of fully vocalised and dotted sample texts that traditions of recitation (perhaps mostly oral) were set down in writing for tens of thousands of 'difficult' biblical excerpts.

The majority of the *šmāhe* handbooks that have come down to us were composed during the tenth and eleventh centuries, a period known as the Syriac Renaissance. Among these codices, the largest category consists of a fairly regular core of excerpted phrases from the Bible. For this reason, we refer to this category as model–text codices, to be distinguished from other *šmāhe* manuscripts that include different selections of biblical excerpts.

Nevertheless, while each model–text codex includes a regular core collection of biblical excerpts (or other sample texts), the manuscripts are also distinct from one another. To understand how this worked, we might think of this core as consisting of tens of thousands of set 'pockets' of phrases from the Bible. When compiling their handbooks, each copyist would have looked to these 'pockets' and chosen slightly different words or features to include in their *šmāhe* book. In other words, although these model–text codices include excerpts taken from roughly the same portions of Scripture, each copyist chose to include or exclude slightly different material from each portion. Taken together, these tens of thousands of sample texts from the Syriac Peshiṭta and Harklean Scriptures make up something approximating an established 'curriculum' of readings. It is with some irony, therefore, that this curriculum of vocalised and dotted sample texts—meant primarily as highly abbreviated reminders of what the educated reader should have known—now constitutes some of our earliest written repositories of what were otherwise oral traditions of reading the Syriac Bible (Brovender 1976, xiii).

Furthermore, from the notes left in these model–text *šmāhe* manuscripts, we can conclude that users would have approached these handbooks with some knowledge of which excerpts they could expect to find. Readers were able to locate and compare readings between manuscripts at a glance, thanks to the fairly stable collections of sample texts from the Syriac Bible. That users did compare readings is clear; some later readers refer in the margins to patterns of vocalisation or orthography they found in "all the booklets of vocalised terms" (Song 2.9 in Dam. Syr. MS 12/22, fol. 138r).

4.0. A Second Core: A 'Curriculum' of Reminders

Within this curriculum of thousands of excerpted sample texts, there is another core that has been even less explored—a curriculum of written reminders. We have already encountered examples of the abbreviated reminder for a 'question' (ܫܐ) among the sample texts from John in the model-text manuscript Vat. sir. 152 above (Fig. 4). However, the range of these *aides-mémoires* in *šmāhe* manuscripts is much broader, including supplementary short definitions, alternative biblical versions, and variant readings, in addition to reminders of accents and punctuation. All these reminders were added to assist the reader in bringing to mind what they were expected to recall about the corresponding biblical excerpt.

Occasionally, these notes suggest ways of reading the biblical text that are identical to explanations put forward by biblical commentators. For example, some of the definitions that were adjoined to sample texts in these tenth through eleventh-century model-text codices are identical to the definitions that would be recorded three-hundred years later by Bar ʿEbroyo (13th century). So, in 1 Tim. 5.6, several copyists have inserted the definition 'that is, sexual perversion' (ܗ̄ ܙܢܝܘܬܐ) after the word 'luxury' (ܣܛܪܐܢܝܐ / στρηνία) in the Peshiṭta translation. This is the same definition Bar ʿEbroyo provides in his commentary on the Pauline Epistles, as we see from Table 1 below.

Table 1: Defining 'Luxury' (ܣܦܛܪܐܝܐ) in 1 Tim. 5.6 in *šmāhe* manuscripts and Bar ʿEbroyo

Barb. orient. MS 118, fol. 117r	Bar ʿEbroyo (Loehr 1889, 38)
'whereas she who pursues only luxury that is, sexual perversion (ܣܦܛܪܐܝܐ ܗ̄ ܙܢܝܘܬܐ), is already dead while she is living'.	'"the widow who works for luxury (ܣܦܛܪܝܐ)," with an elided *ālaph*; that is, sexual perversion (ܗ̄ ܙܢܝܘܬܐ)'.

Moreover, the makeup of this body of reminders is similar, in some ways, to what we know about how these *šmāhe* manuscripts were compiled and used. That is, just as not every copyist included the same features from each 'pocket' of biblical text, so not every copyist included exactly the same reminders. For instance, only four *šmāhe* manuscripts include the above definition for 1 Tim. 5.6.

Among the over two hundred passages that include reminders of punctuation and accent dots, we can distinguish a group of scriptural texts that include a reminder in more than one manuscript. For a few passages, such as Job 38.28, every copyist has included the reminder. Yet, at the other extreme, for the sample text from 2 Kings 5.25 only one copyist, the compiler of the Mosul St. Thomas Church *šmāhe* manuscript, has included the reminder: 'Where have you been, Gehazi? *mšalānā* (ܡܫ̈ܠ)' (ܐܝܟܐ ܓܝܚܙܝ܆ ܡܫ̈ܠ•) (Mosul MS 16, fol. 63r). Most often, these reminders were included in between two to four manuscripts. Consequently, at a very practical level, these reminders reflect the combination of diversity and consistency so typical of this type of West Syriac model-text *šmāhe* manuscripts.

How these reminders were placed in these *šmāhe* manuscripts also reflects what we know of the copyists' style and the overall character of their work. For instance, both Vat. sir. 152 and Barb. orient. MS 118 include most of the same reminders, much as they also share similar biblical excerpts and vocalisation. Yet, they can also differ; in thirty–one passages, one of these copyists includes a reminder that the other will omit. The copyist of BL Add. 7183 adds reminders only in the margins, a characteristic we can similarly observe in other parts of his work. Again, two other manuscripts, Dam. syr. 7/16 and Dam. syr. 12/22, regularly omit the vast majority of these reminders. It seems these latter copyists were content to record the punctuation and accent dots on the sample texts, while omitting most of these additional written cues. In short, taken together, these abbreviated reminders reflect a distinct 'curriculum' within these West Syriac *šmāhe* codices. At the same time, the reminders also reveal the somewhat idiosyncratic ways the compilers chose to add or omit elements of this core to fit their own distinct needs.

4.1. Set Reminders of Accents and Punctuation

By far, those abbreviated reminders that are most insightful for our understanding of how the Syriac Scriptures would have been read are notes related to accentuation and punctuation. These prompts constitute a core of just over two hundred passages from the Peshiṭta and Harklean Scriptures. The two appendices at the end of this chapter provide a first glimpse at this large and significant collection of *aides-mémoires*. Appendix I lists 1) each biblical reference, followed by 2) the type of reminder, 3) the translation as found in the Antioch Bible, and 4) the place in each verse where the reminder has been inserted. Appendix II then clarifies which of the eight different *šmāhe* codices includes each reminder. Importantly, this second appendix also reveals whether each reminder has been written internally (int.), in-line with the text, or in the margin (mg.). In general, those notes written internally—after the associated sample text—can often be assumed to be the original work of the copyists.[9]

Altogether, the copyists of these *šmāhe* manuscripts remind the readers of seven different ways they should read the biblical text.[10] In order of frequency these include the *mšalānā* (ܡܫܐܠܢܐ), the question; the *taḥtāyā* (ܬܚܬܝܐ), the end of a major clause; the *paqūdā* (ܦܩܘܕܐ), a command or rising intonation; the *ʿelāyā* (ܥܠܝܐ), a pause; the *šuḥlāp̱ šwayā* (ܫܘܚܠܦ ܫܘܝܐ), a strong pause; the *rāhṭā d-pāseq* (ܪܗܛܐ ܕܦܣܩ), joining a word to the preceding

---

[9] By using the term 'in general', I acknowledge that there can be differences between how copyists place these reminders. For instance, internal notes in Dam. syr. 7/16 (see Figure 6 below), Dam. syr. 12/22, and Barb. orient. 118 appear most often in the same hand and script as the copyist. While in other manuscripts, such as Vat. sir. 152 (see Figure 4 above), the original copyist has often left space for the reminders, which sometimes appear to be in a slightly different hand. Moreover, in Mosul, St. Thomas Church MS 16, a much later reader has gone through and added internal reminders throughout Job and other books. But these additions are easily discerned as later additions, and they have not been added to our Appendices below. For a more detailed survey, see my forthcoming introduction to these *šmāhe* manuscripts.

[10] Overall, the copyists and readers of these manuscripts appear to have the corresponding dotted marks in mind when these reminders are named. Yet, it is sometimes possible that these reminders refer to how the passage should be read (not merely the dots). For example, *mšalānā* can refer to the dotted marks, though it also translates as 'question'.

word; and the *rāhṭā d-lā pāseq* (ܪܗܛܐ ܕܠܐ ܦܣܩ), joining a word to the following word or phrase (Loopstra 2015, §8.4.7, §8.4.19, §8.4.16, §8.4.13, §8.4.1, §8.4.17). In other words, although a primary focus of these West Syriac model–text codices was to help the reader place 'Greek vowels', reading dots, and *rūkkāḵā* and *qūššāyā* marks (Diettrich 1899, xi), the added reminders suggest that attention was likewise given to punctuation and accentuation.

4.1.1. A Disconnect with the Well–known Tracts Attributed to Jacob of Edessa and Thomas the Deacon

One of the unexpected features of this core of reminders is that they are often associated with a different set of biblical exemplars than those used to illustrate the placement of dots in some of the well-known tracts found towards the back of these same *šmāhe* codices (Phillips 1869, 1–33, 66–68).[11] These tracts, attributed to Jacob of Edessa (d. 704) and Thomas the Deacon (7th cent.), became a standard feature of the model-text codices from at least the tenth century onwards. However, there appears to be very little overlap between the exemplars in these tracts and these

[11] At least three tracts concerning these dotted marks became standard in most model-text manuscripts, apart from the anonymous tract present only in BL Add. 12178. Phillip's publication, dated to 1869, was based on only a few *šmāhe* manuscripts and omits portions of these tracts. See my forthcoming edition and translation of these tracts based on all available *šmāhe* manuscripts.

sample texts with added reminders in the first part of these codices. These two collections have in common five biblical passages, as Table 2 shows, but only one of these shared passages includes the same dotted mark. Both the tract attributed to Jacob of Edessa and the *šmāhe* reminders use the same excerpt from 2 Kgs 2.18 to illustrate the placement of the *mšalānā*. The other four passages that are common to both collections either include different parts of the same verse or use the same verse to illustrate different dotted marks.

Table 2: Shared Biblical Exemplars between the Corpus of Reminders and Tracts

	Reminders	**West Syriac Tracts**
Gen. 4.9	*mšalānā*: 'Am I my brother's guardian? (ܡܫܠ)'	Jacob of Edessa, *mšalānā* (repeated twice): 'Where is Abel your brother?'
2 Kgs 2.18	*mšalānā*: 'Did I not say that you should not go? (ܡܫܠ)'	Jacob of Edessa, *tāḵsā* and *mšalānā*: 'Did I not say to you that you should not go?
Jer. 4.30	*mšalānā*: 'when you deck yourself with golden ornament, (ܡܫܠ) when you paint your eyes with kohl? It is in vain that you deck yourself',	Jacob of Edessa, *mḇakkyānā* which is *msaqqʿānā*: 'when you clothe yourself in scarlet, when you deck yourself with golden ornament, when you paint your eyes with kohl?'
Lam. 2:20	*mšalānā*: 'the women shall eat their fruits, the infants be dashed (ܡܫܠ)'	Thomas the Deacon, *zawʿā* and *sāmkā*: 'the women shall eat their fruits, the infants be dashed'
Luke 17.9	*mšalānā*: 'Does that servant receive his thanks because he did what was commanded him? (ܡܫܠ)'	Thomas the Deacon, *taḥtāyā* and *šḥimā*: *taḥtāyā*: 'Does that servant receive his thanks because what he did was commanded him?' *šḥimā* : 'I think not'

Our only copy of the East Syriac *šmāhe* manuscript, BL Add. 12138 (899 CE), also includes a tract on punctuation and accent dots on folios 303v–308r (Loopstra 2014, 606–615; Loopstra 2015, 396–407). Judah Segal relied heavily upon this tract in his own work (1953, 78–118). Yet, as with our comparison with West Syriac tracts, we likewise find no significant correlation between the corpus of exemplars in this East Syriac tract and the body of reminders in the West Syriac *šmāhe* manuscripts. As Appendix III shows, of the eleven passages that are shared between the East Syriac tract and the West Syriac *šmāhe* manuscripts, only six include exactly the same dotted marks. But even then, each Syriac tradition uses slightly different terminology for some of these same marks, as one might expect.[12] So, in the exemplar from Job 2.19, the West Syriac tradition reminds the reader to read a question, the *mšalānā*, while the copyist of the East Syriac tract reminds his readers of the *zawgā ʻelāyā* and *taḥtāyā* dotted marks. In this case, both traditions may be saying the same thing, though with different terminology. As with the example above from John 7.42, cited by Bar ʻEbroyo, phrases marked as questions often include double-dotted supralineal dots followed by a dot below and on the line at the end of the clause (Segal 1953, 87; Kiraz 2015, 112–113).

[12] Interestingly, when we step away from the tracts and compare the wider body of sample texts in both the East and West Syriac *šmāhe* manuscripts, only in Amos 6.13 has the same reminder been added to the margins by both traditions (BL Add. MS 12138, fol. 190v, 31 = Vat. sir. 152, fol. 77v).

4.1.2. Distinctions Between East and West Syriac Dotting Practices

On occasion, these reminders can also highlight differences between East Syriac and West Syriac ways of punctuating the biblical text. This divergence can also be seen in Appendix III, where these two traditions use slightly different terminology for the same dotted marks. These distinctions are especially apparent when West Syriac copyists remind their readers of the double-dotted *taḥtāyā* (·.) for passages where East Syriac scribes prefer the triple-dotted *taḥtāyā da-tālāt* (·.̣). Although both East and West Syriac scribes use the *taḥtāyā* to mark the end of a clause, in certain passages the East Syriac tradition continued to use the *taḥtāyā da-tālāt* (·.̣) instead. This is a longstanding difference between the two traditions. We find the *taḥtāyā da-tālāt* in East Syriac biblical manuscripts such as BL Add. 14448 and BL Add. 7157, as early as the seventh and eighth centuries (cf. Fig. 1). Although this triple-dotted mark does appear in some West Syriac manuscripts,[13] it is more regularly incorporated by East Syriac scribes. Most often the *taḥtāyā da-tālāt* is used in passages of direct address that include admonitions or warnings (Loopstra 2017, 109–137). Thus, in the following examples from 1 Tim. 6.20 and Acts 9.34, the copyist of the East Syriac *šmāhe* manuscript has placed the triple-dotted *taḥtāyā da-tālāt* after 'Oh, Timothy' and 'Aeneas', whereas West Syriac copyists add reminders

---

[13] A number of West Syriac examples that include the *taḥtāyā da-tālāt* appear among the 'Demonstrations' from Scripture in the earliest commentary manuscript to Gregory's Orations, BL Add. 17147 (cf. fol. 82r-v, 87v, 91v).

that one is to read the double–dotted *taḥtāyā* (Tables 3 and 4).[14] Moreover, as the following images in Figure 5 show, the difference between the *taḥtāyā* and the *taḥtāyā da-tālāt* are clearly visible, even in those *šmāhe* manuscripts that do not include added reminders (as in the example from Dam. Syr. 12/22 in Figure 5).

Table 3: 1 Tim. 6.20 in both East and West Syriac *Šmāhe* Manuscripts

East Syriac: *taḥtāyā da-tālāt*	West Syriac: *taḥtāyā*
BL Add. 12138, fol. 297v:	Vat. sir. 152, fol. 130r:
ܐܘ ܛܝܡܬܐܐ ⁝	ܐܘ ܛܝܡܬܐܐ ⁖ ܬܚܬܝܐ
‘Oh Timothy ⁝’	‘Oh Timothy ⁖’ *taḥtāyā*

Table 4: East and West Syriac *šmāhe* Manuscripts Punctuate Acts 9.34

East Syriac: *taḥtāyā da-tālāt*	West Syriac: *taḥtāyā*
BL Add. 12138, fol. 269r:	Vat. sir. 152, fol. 120v:
ܐܝܢܐ ⁝	ܐܝܢܐ ⁖ ܬܚܬܝܐ
‘[Simeon said to him] Aeneas ⁝’	‘[Simeon said to him] Aeneas ⁖’ *taḥtāyā*

Figure 5: 1 Tim. 6.20: ‘Oh Timothy!’ *taḥtāyā da-tālāt* (left) and *taḥtāyā* (right)

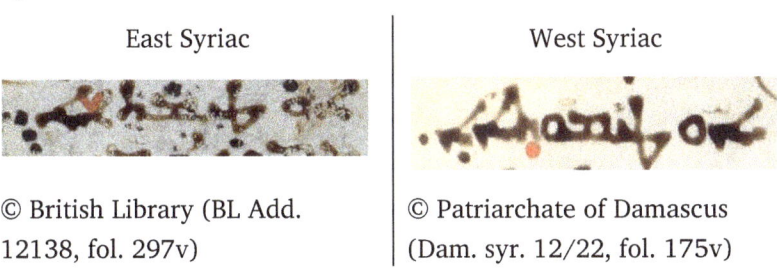

East Syriac	West Syriac
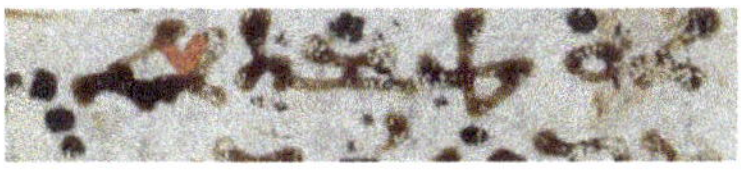	
© British Library (BL Add. 12138, fol. 297v)	© Patriarchate of Damascus (Dam. syr. 12/22, fol. 175v)

[14] Some other examples from among these reminders include 1 Kings 3.17 (‘I beg of you, my Lord ⁖’), Ezek. 36.13 (‘You have devoured men and are bereaved of her people ⁖’), and Acts 20.26 (‘On account of this, I testify to you today ⁖’).

4.1.3. Distinguishing a Question or a Statement

The vast majority of these reminders were added to bring to mind a 'question', *mšalānā* (ܡܫܐܠܢܐ). In Syriac, the dotted marks used to indicate the presence of a question were developed centuries after the translation of the Peshiṭta Bible (Coakley 2012, 193–213). Without these helps, many passages in the Syriac scriptures could be read either as a question or a statement. While context can help the reader to make this distinction, this is not always true. It is perhaps for this reason that so many of the passages singled out for reminders in these Syriac *šmāhe* codices include the prompt *mšalānā* (ܡܫܐܠܢܐ = ܡܫ) as a way to clarify otherwise ambiguous passages. Then again, in other passages the copyist appears to have placed the reminder at a particular position in the verse to separate the question (ܡܫܐܠܢܐ) clause from the subsequent statement. Accordingly, in Rom. 7.13, the question, 'Does that mean that something good became death for me?' is divided from the following statement 'God forbid!' by the reminder *m-š* (ܡܫ).[15] In a similar way, in Ps. 58.1, two reminders of the *mšalānā* have been used to distinguish two different questions.[16]

As Appendix II shows, there are only a handful of passages where nearly every copyist has added a reminder to their codices, and these are most often used to mark a 'question' (*mšalānā*). For instance, in Job 38.28 every manuscript includes a reminder that

---

[15] See also, Isa. 42.14, Mic. 5.2, Mal. 1.2, Luke 12.6, John 6.70, and Rom. 11.11.

[16] Other examples include 2 Kgs 4.28, Ps. 58.1, and Matt. 13.55.

one is to read the passage as a 'question' (*mšalānā*): 'Does the rain have a father?' (Loopstra 2016, 217). Yet, it would have been equally possible to read the passage as a statement: 'There is a father for the rain'. Although we do not know for certain, it is possible that such passages would have posed challenges for readers, hence the high number of added reminders.

Figure 6: Job 38.28: 'Does the rain have a father? *mšalānā*' (© Patriarchate of Damascus, Dam. Syr. 7/16, fol. 38r)

Far fewer copyists include a reminder in Psalm 22.2, though the glossator of BL Add. 7183, among others, is quite explicit: 'this is a question' (ܗܢܐ ܡܫܐܠܢܐ). Consequently, instead of rendering the passage as it is interpreted in the Antioch Bible and in many modern translations, this *šmāhe* manuscript encourages the reader to interpret the verse as a question: 'but [God] do you not remain with me?'

Antioch Bible	Syriac *Šmāhe* Manuscripts
'My God, I cry out to you [during the day], but you do not answer me; and during the night, but you do not remain with me' (Taylor 2020, 73).	'My God, I cry out to you [during the day], but do you not answer me; and during the night, and do you not remain with me?'

Figure 7: Ps. 22.2: 'This is a *mšalānā*' (© British Library, BL Add. 7183, fol. 40v)

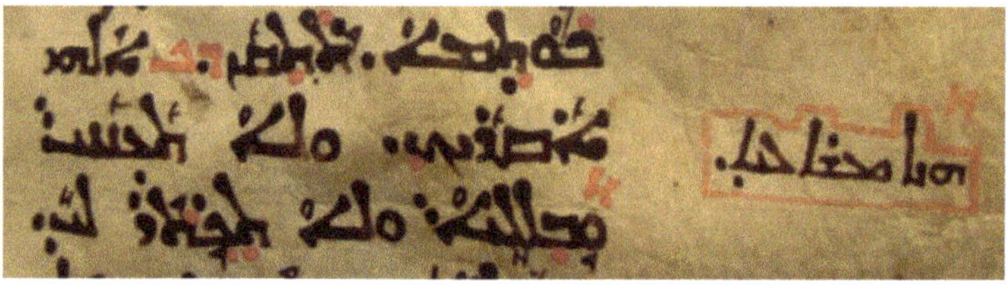

Although very rare, at times these notes remind the reader how *not* to read the passage. So, in Ezekiel 44.9 the glossator of BL Add. 7183 has added a note in the margin: 'it is not a question (*mšalānā*)'. As is his style, this glossator has connected his note to the text by a rubricated siglum approximating the Greek Π.

Ezek. 44.9: ܕܥܪܝܠ ܠܒܗ: ܘܥܪܝܠ. [ܠܐ ܐܝܬܘܗܝ ܡܫܐܠܢܐ] ܠܡܩܕܫܝ.

Antioch Bible: '[No]… uncircumcised of heart, uncircumcised [of flesh, shall enter] my sanctuary' (Greenberg and Walter 2015, 269).

Figure 8: Ezek. 44.9: 'This is not a *mšalānā*' (© British Library, BL Add. 7183, fol. 71r)

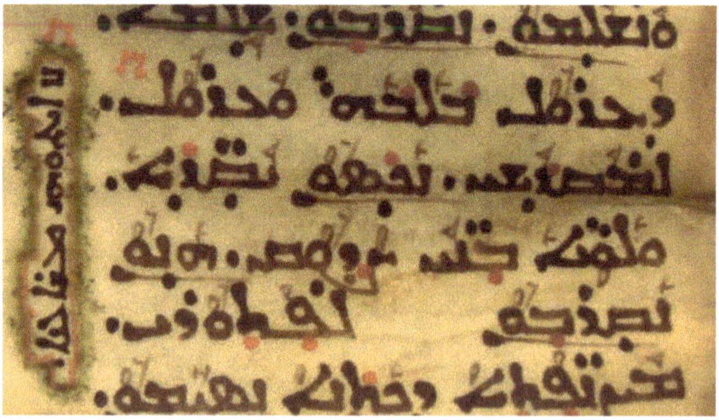

One rather remarkable feature of this corpus is that the reminders in these *šmāhe* manuscripts are almost always in agreement. Out of over two hundred biblical passages, only once, in

Ezekiel 20.31, do copyists disagree among themselves regarding the type of reminder that should be placed in the associated scriptural passage. Vat. sir. 152 and Barb. orient. MS 118 include a *mšalānā*, while the copyist of Par. BnF syr. 64 prefers the *taḥtāyā*. Given what we have already seen in passages discussed above, such as John 7.42 and Job 2.19, this confusion is understandable. Clauses that function as questions often end with the double-dotted *taḥtāyā* or two separate dots (Weiss 1933, 58–59; Loopstra 2015, §8.4.7). In a sense, both interpretations could be correct.

> Ezek. 20.31, *mšalānā* or *taḥtāyā*
>
> Vat. sir. 152/Barb. orient. MS 118: '—yet wanting to inquire of me, O house of Israel?—(ܡܫ)'
>
> Par. BnF syr. 64: '—yet wanting to inquire of me, O house of Israel?—(ܬܚܬ)'

4.2. Readings Differ from some English Translations

Given such ambiguities, it is not unexpected that these reminders occasionally suggest ways of reading the text of Scripture that differ from what we find in modern translations. Although this is true for passages that include disjunctive or pausal marks, such as the *taḥtāyā* (ܬܚܬܝܐ) or *šuḥlāp̱ šwayā* (ܫܘܚܠܦ ܫܘܝܐ),[17] such differences can be seen most visibly in passages for which we have reminders of a question, the *mšalānā* (ܡܫܐܠܢܐ).

One of the most prominent examples of this divergence occurs in 1 Kings 1.21. Here, every model–text *šmāhe* codex written between the tenth through twelfth centuries suggests that this

[17] See also Job 38.31, Ps. 143.10, Isa. 66.23, Zech. 5.3, Zech. 9.3, 2 Cor. 4.6, 2 Cor. 4.17, Matt. 3.17.

passage is to be read as a question.[18] This includes other manuscripts such as Deir al-Surian MS 14, a *šmāhe* manuscript we have not taken into account when compiling these appendices. The result is a different way of interpreting Bathsheba's speech to the dying, elderly King David. On the one hand, most modern English translations generally read this passage as a statement, as does the Antioch Bible. The latter attempts to make sense of the Syriac text by adding the clarifying phrase 'treated as': 'when my lord king shall sleep peacefully with his fathers, I and my son Solomon will be (treated as) sinners' (Greenberg and Walter 2018, 7). On the other hand, every model-text *šmāhe* manuscript includes a note suggesting that we are to read this verse as a question (*mšalānā*): 'Would my son Solomon and I be sinners? *mšalānā* (ܡܫܐܠܢܐ)'.[19] Assuming this interpretation, Bathsheba is not so much suggesting that she and Solomon *will be* sinners after David's death. Rather, she is raising a hypothetical question: '*would* we be sinners?'

---

[18] Only the youngest of these model-text manuscripts, Lund Medeltidshandskrift MS 58 (1204/5 CE), does not include a reminder here. This very late codex omits most of these reminders, although it includes extended commentary instead. Notably, Deir al-Surian MS 14 includes this reminder for 1 Kgs 1.21 as well. The excerpts in this a model *šmāhe* codex, located today in Egypt, can be quite different than what we find in other model codices.

[19] For another example present in almost every *šmāhe* manuscript, see Deut. 1.33, which is a statement in the Antioch Bible, but a question according to these reminders. 'Who goes before you on the way, to establish a place for you, in which you might camp' (McCarthy 2013, 9).

Figure 9: 1 Kgs 1.21: 'would we be sinners? *mšalānā*' (© Patriarchate of Damascus, Dam. Syr. 7/16, fol. 47v)

Because translators have rarely taken these *šmāhe* codices into consideration, this body of reminders of punctuation and accentuation has gone largely unnoticed. It is true that these model–text manuscripts are relatively late. However, it does not necessarily follow that they are entirely devoid of at least some helpful insights into how the Syriac Scriptures would have read among Syriac Christians over a millennium ago.

This much is evident when these reminders speak to ambiguities that have also been raised by the translators of the new Antioch Bible edition. On occasion, these translators have recorded in their footnotes questions over whether the Syriac should be taken as a question or as a statement. In seven separate passages, the reminders added by the copyists of the Syriac *šmāhe* manuscripts speak directly to the ambiguities raised by these modern translators. In Appendix I, these footnoted readings have been recorded as 'AB-n-var'. For instance, two of these exemplars from the Antioch Bible translation of the Book of Ezekiel are included below (Greenberg and Walter 2015, 49, 107). Notably, in neither passage did the translators choose the interpretation recommended by the copyists of the West Syriac *šmāhe* manuscripts.

Ezek. 11.3. Antioch Bible: 'It was not in its midst that we built houses'. AB-n-var.: 'It was not in its midst that we built houses' or 'Was it not in its midst that we built houses?'	*šmāhe* text: 'Was it not in its midst that we built houses? *mšalānā* (ܡܫ)'
Ezek. 20.3. Antioch Bible: 'You come to inquire of me'. AB-n-var.: "You come to inquire of me' or 'Do you come to inquire of me?' (as in MT)'	*šmāhe* text: 'Do you come to inquire of me? *mšalānā* (ܡܫ)'

4.3. Agreement with Later Syriac Commentators

Lastly, some of the reminders of a question in these West Syriac model-text *šmāhe* manuscripts agree with interpretations that would be set down much later by Bar ʿEbroyo. At least five passages in Appendix I agree with reminders provided by Bar ʿEbroyo in his biblical commentary, the *Storehouse of Mysteries.*[20] In these verses, Bar ʿEbroyo chose, for whatever reason, to remind his readers that they should interpret these passages as questions and not as statements. In each of these cases, the same clarification had also been provided by the copyists of these *šmāhe* handbooks centuries earlier.

For instance, the modern translator of Numbers 20.10 for the Antioch Bible read this passage as a statement: 'From this

[20] These passages include Num. 20.10, Judg. 8.2, 1 Sam. 16.11, Job 14.19, and Rom. 3.27. In all of these, Bar ʿEbroyo specifies the need for reading as a 'question'.

rock we shall bring out water for you' (Cook 2015, 125). This reading is certainly possible in Syriac. However, Bar ʿEbroyo suggests a different approach, one closer to modern translations of this passage from the Hebrew. He contends that the story of Moses striking of the rock in the desert should instead be read as a question. It is to be understood "as a question," Bar ʿEbroyo notes, as in the Greek. This is because Moses struck the rock with "words of doubt and dispute," not with "praise and consecration" (Sprengling and Graham 1931, 206 [Syr.]).

> Should be read as a question (ܡܫܐܠܐܝܬ). The Greek (reads): "From this rock will we bring out water for you?" That is, so he should not himself boast in many revelations, God allowed him to act like a fool. Rather than that he should strike the stone with words of praise and consecration, as he was commanded, he struck it with words of doubt and dispute.

For this passage, the copyists of at least two *šmāhe* manuscripts agree with Bar ʿEbroyo, adding notes that the reader was to understand this passage as a question. Bar ʿEbroyo did not provide such specific insights in every passage for which we have these reminders in the *šmāhe* manuscripts. Nonetheless, even this small degree of correspondence lends legitimacy to these *aides-mémoires* in model-text codices as valid expressions of how West Syriac Christians would have read their Scriptures.

5.0. Concluding Appendices

Syriac *šmāhe* (or 'Masorah') manuscripts remain a relatively untapped repository of information about how the Syriac Bible was read between the tenth and thirteenth centuries. More specifically, the category of West Syriac *šmāhe* codices we have labelled as 'model–text' manuscripts include something very much like a set 'curriculum' of biblical and patristic sample texts. Yet, within this set curriculum is another core, a collection of abbreviated reminders specifying how one was to punctuate or accentuate just over two hundred biblical passages. The copyists of these West Syriac *šmāhe* codices appear to have drawn upon this core, adding or omitting reminders as needed.

The following appendices are an initial attempt to gather together these hundreds of reminders as they occur in eight of the most prominent model-text *šmāhe* manuscripts. In a few of these passages, the interpretation hinted at by these added reminders differs from our own familiar ways of reading the text, allowing us access to how earlier generations would have read and recited these verses. Moreover, at another level, these appendices allow us more insights into the nature of these large, rather complicated reading handbooks. The information in Appendix II, in particular, provides data that helps us to deepen our awareness of the possible relationships between these *šmāhe* codices. We can gain a better sense of how this distinct Syriac genre functioned—for copyists and readers alike.

Finally, this corpus of 211 reminders of punctuation and accentuation in the Peshiṭta and Harklean Bibles can allow us to make sense of similar abbreviated reminders in regular non–*šmāhe* biblical manuscripts. Unlike these *šmāhe* manuscripts, where it is the copyists who often add reminders, in regular biblical manuscripts these notes are generally added by much later readers. On occasion, we find that the reminders present in these *šmāhe* codices match exactly the marginal notes that have been added to the biblical manuscripts. As Figure 10 shows, a reader of Par. BnF syr. 11 has added a note indicating the presence of a 'question', *mšalānā* (ܡܫܐ), for Isaiah 10.15. As it happens, four different *šmāhe* manuscripts have also added this reminder, including BL Add. 7183 (left). One hopes that the following appendices, comprising this corpus of *šmāhe* reminders, can support future attempts to understand how these added marks would have functioned across a wider range of Syriac biblical and liturgical manuscripts.

Figure 10: Isaiah 10.15: 'Should the axe be praised more than the man who hews with it? [ܡܫ]' (Greenberg and Walter 2012, 51)

BL Add. 7183

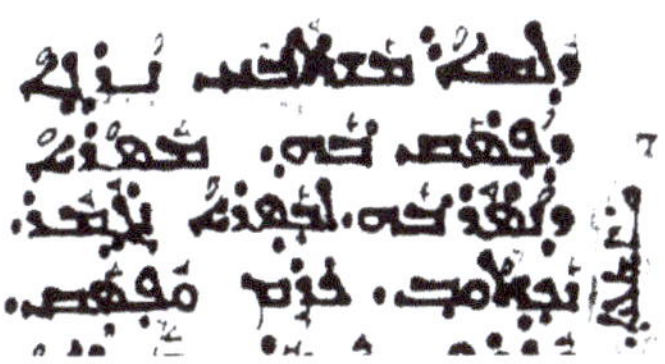

© British Library (BL Add. 7183, fol. 52v)

Par. BnF syr. 11

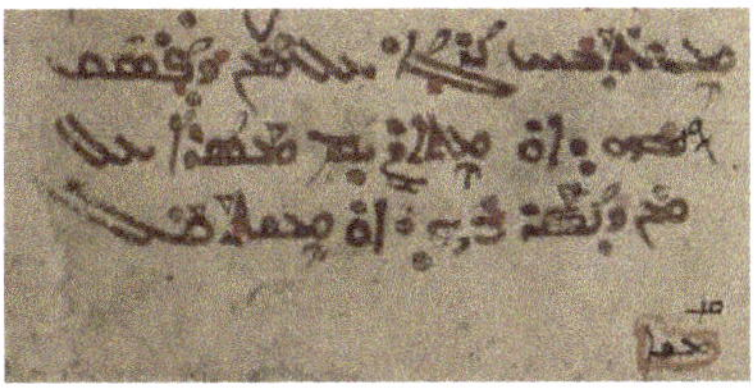

© Par BnF. (Par. BnF syr. 11, fol. 6r)

Appendix I: Core Reminders of Punctuation/ Accents in the West Syriac Model-Text *Šmāhe* Manuscripts

Reminders:

taḥtāyā (ܬܚܬܝܐ) marks the end of a clause
ʿelāyā (ܥܠܝܐ) marks a pause
rāhṭā d-pāseq (ܪܗܛܐ ܕܦܣܩ) joins to preceding word
rāhṭā d-lā pāseq (ܪܗܛܐ ܕܠܐ ܦܣܩ) joins to following word
mšalānā (ܡܫܐܠܢܐ) marks a question
šuḥlāp̱ šwayā (ܫܘܚܠܦ ܫܘܝܐ) marks a strong pause
paqūdā (ܦܩܘܕܐ) marks a command or rising intonation

Abbreviations and siglum:

- AB – Antioch Bible translation (whether or not the translation agrees with the reminders in *šmāhe* manuscripts)
- ‘AB-n-var.’ – indicates that the translators of the Antioch Bible indicated in the footnote a variable translation, whether as question or statement.
- int. – internal (written after the associated sample text)
- lac. – lacunae
- mg. – margin (written in the margin)
- var. – variant reading
- [] text omitted from sample text in *šmāhe* manuscripts
- () addition in sample text in *šmāhe* manuscripts
- {} additional remarks

Scriptural Passage / *Type of Reminder* / Translation in AB with Abbreviated Reminder

1. Gen. 4.9, *mšalānā* / AB: 'Am I my brother's guardian? (ܡܫ)'
2. Gen. 16.8, *mšalānā* / AB: '['from where are you coming'] and where are you going? (ܡܫ)'
3. Gen. 24.6, *paqūdā* / AB: 'Be careful [not to bring my son back there] (ܦܩܘܕ)'
4. Gen. 29.6, *mšalānā* / AB: 'Is he well? (ܡܫ)'
5. Gen. 30.2, *mšalānā* / AB: 'Can I replace God, who has withheld from you the fruits of the womb? (ܡܫ)'
6. Exod. 4.11, *mšalānā* / AB: 'Is it not I, the Lord? (ܡܫ)'
7. Num. 11.12, *mšalānā* / AB: 'Have I conceived all this people? (ܡܫ) Or have I given birth to them?'
8. Num. 20.10, *rāhṭā d-pāseq* and *mšalānā* / AB: 'Hear now, you complainers! (ܪܗܛܐ ܕܦܣܩ) From this rock we shall bring out water for you. (ܡܫ)' {Bar 'Ebroyo, *Storehouse of Mysteries*: question}[21]
9. Num. 21.29, *rāhṭā d-lā pāseq* / AB: 'Woe to you, Moab! The people of Chemosh (ܪܗܛܐ ܕܠܐ ܦܣܩ) have perished. He gives his sons as hostages and his daughters as captives'.
10. Num. 36.3, *mšalānā* / AB: 'And it shall be taken away from the lot of our inheritance. (ܡܫ)'
11. Deut. 1.33, *mšalānā* / AB: 'Who goes before you on the way, to establish a place for you, in which you might camp. (ܡܫ)'

[21] Sprengling and Graham (1931, 205).

12. Deut. 29.19, *ʿelāyā* / AB: ‘[Who] when he hears the words of this sworn agreement. (ܥܠܝܐ)’
13. Deut. 30.7, *paqūdā* / AB ‘[The Lord your God will place] all these curses on your enemies and on those that hate you, who persecute you. (ܦܩܘܕ)’
14. Deut. 30.11, *paqūdā* / AB ‘[For this commandment…] is not hidden from you, nor is it far away. (ܦܩܘܕ)’
15. Deut. 32.6, *mšalānā* / AB: ‘Has he not been your father who acquired you? (ܡܫ)’
16. Judg. 8.2, *mšalānā* / AB: ‘Is not the gleaning of Ephraim better than the vintage of Jezreel? (ܡܫ)’ {Bar ‘Ebroyo, *Storehouse of Mysteries*: a question}[22]
17. Judg. 8.11, *ʿelāyā* / AB: ‘Gideon went up, towards those who were in the camp. (ܥܠܝܐ)’
18. Judg. 9.28, *mšalānā* / AB: ‘Who is Abimelech? (ܡܫ)’
19. Judg. 9.32, *paqūdā* / AB: ‘and lie in wait in the field. (ܦܩܘܕ)’
20. Judg. 9.38, *mšalānā* / AB: ‘Was this not the people whom you despised? (ܡܫ)’
21. Judg. 11.24, *mšalānā* / AB: ‘It was not something that your god Chemosh made you take possession of, that you possess. (ܡܫ)’ {AB-n-var ‘or “Was it not”’}[23]
22. Judg. 11.25, *mšalānā* / AB: ‘Now are you any better than Balak son of Zippor king of Moab? (ܡܫ)’
23. Judg. 12.5, *mšalānā* / AB: ‘Are you an Ephraimite? (ܡܫ)’

---

[22] Sprengling and Graham (1931, 285).

[23] Walter and Greenberg (2015, 85, n3).

24. Job 6.5, *mšalānā* / AB: 'Does the wild ass bray over the grass, or the ox bellow over the fodder? (ܡܫ)'
25. Job 7.19, *mšalānā* / AB: 'nor let me be till I have swallowed my spit? (ܡܫ)'
26. Job 8.3, *mšalānā* / AB: 'Does God distort justice? (ܡܫ)'
27. Job 8.11, *mšalānā* / AB: 'Can a marsh spread out in an arid land? (ܡܫ)'
28. Job 10.13, *mšalānā* / AB: 'Still, you have hidden these things in Your heart. (ܡܫ)'
29. Job 11.9, *mšalānā* / AB: 'Its measure is longer than the earth and broader than the sea. (ܡܫ)'
30. Job 13.25, *mšalānā* / AB: 'You crush a dry leaf that falls. (ܡܫ)'
31. Job 14.18, *mšalānā* / AB: 'In truth, does a strong mountain fall down? (ܡܫ)'
32. Job 14.19, *mšalānā* / AB: 'Does a stone erode water? (ܡܫ)' {Bar 'Ebroyo, *Storehouse of Mysteries*: a question}[24]
33. Job 23.6, *mšalānā* / AB: 'And if not, he sets fear against me. (ܡܫ)'
34. Job 30.20, *mšalānā* / AB: 'I would cry out to You, but You will not answer me. (ܡܫ)'
35. Job 38.12, *mšalānā* / AB: 'In your days, have you commanded the dawn? (ܡܫ)'
36. Job 38.18, *mšalānā* / AB: 'You have observed the entire extent of the earth! (ܡܫ)'

[24] Bernstein (1858, 195).

37. Job 38.28, *mšalānā* / AB: ‘Does the rain have a father? (ܡܫ)’
38. Job 38.31 *taḥtāyā* / AB: ‘Are you holding fast the Pleiades? (ܬܚܬ)’
39. Job 39.3, *mšalānā* / AB: ‘[W]hen they crouch down and give birth? (ܡܫ)’
40. Job 39.9, *mšalānā* / AB: ‘Perhaps the wild ox can be persuaded to work for you? (ܡܫ)’
41. Job 39.26, *mšalānā* / AB: ‘By your wisdom does the hawk come into being, so he stretches his wings to the south? (ܡܫ)’
42. 1 Sam. 9.11, *mšalānā* / AB: ‘[Saul said to them:] Is the seer here? (ܡܫ)’
43. 1 Sam. 10.24, *mšalānā* / AB: ‘You have seen that God delights in him. (ܡܫ)’
44. 1 Sam. 11.13, *mšalānā* / AB: ‘[F]or today the Lord has saved Israel. (ܡܫ)’
45. 1 Sam. 16.5, *mšalānā* / AB: ‘Do you come in peace?’ (ܡܫ)’
46. 1 Sam. 16.11, *mšalānā* / AB: ‘Are the children complete? (ܡܫ)’ {Bar ‘Ebroyo, *Storehouse of Mysteries*: a question}[25]
47. 1 Sam. 17.43, *mšalānā* / AB: ‘Am I a dog, that you come against me with a stick? (ܡܫ)’
48. 1 Sam. 30.8, *mšalānā* / AB: ‘Shall I pursue this troop? Shall I overtake it? (ܡܫ)’
49. 2 Sam. 2.26, *mšalānā* / AB: ‘Do you not know that in the end it will be bitter? (ܡܫ)’

---

[25] Sprengling and Graham (1931, 313).

50. 2 Sam. 7.7, *mšalānā* / AB: ‘Did I say a word to one of the tribes of Israel, that I had commanded to feed my people Israel? (ܡܫܐ)’
51. 2 Sam. 11.20, *mšalānā* / AB: ‘Did you now know that they would shoot from the wall? (ܡܫܐ)’
52. 2 Sam. 11.21, *mšalānā* / AB: ‘Was it not a woman who threw at him a piece of an upper millstone, from the wall, and he died? (ܡܫܐ)’
53. 2 Sam. 13.4, *taḥtāyā* and *mšalānā* / AB: ‘[He said to Hamnon] the king’s son: (ܬܚܬ) Why are you so, from day to day? Will you not tell me? (ܡܫܐ)’[26]
54. 2 Sam. 17.6, *mšalānā* / AB: ‘Shall we do what he has said? (ܡܫܐ)’
55. Ps. 10.15, *mšalānā* / AB: ‘[Break the arm of the sinner] and the wicked; may his sin seek him and may he not be found. (ܡܫܐ)’
56. Ps. 22.2, *mšalānā* / AB: ‘My God, I cry out to you during the day, but you do not answer me; and during the night, but you do not remain with me. (ܡܫܐ)’
57. Ps. 58.1, *mšalānā* and *mšalānā* / AB: ‘Do you truly speak righteousness? (ܡܫܐ) Are you judging with integrity, human beings? (ܡܫܐ)’
58. Ps. 59.11, *mšalānā* / AB: ‘Do not kill them, so that they not cause my people to forget. (ܡܫܐ)’

---

[26] The copyist of 10m1 records a *mšalānā* after ‘the king’s son’ instead of a *taḥtāyā*, perhaps because he then omits the following question ‘Will you not tell me?’

59. Ps. 78.19, *mšalānā* / AB: ‘Is God able to spread tables for us in the wilderness? (ܡܫܠ)’
60. Ps. 78.20, *mšalānā* / AB: ‘is he able also to give us bread? (ܡܫܠ)’
61. Ps. 143.10 {MT 144}, *taḥtāyā* / AB: ‘he delivered David his servant from the evil sword. (ܬܚܬ)’
62. Ps. 143.15 {MT 144}, *mšalānā* / AB: ‘Blessed are the people who thus it is to him; (ܡܫܠ)’
63. 1 Kgs 1.21, *mšalānā* / AB: ‘I and my son Solomon will be (treated as) sinners. (ܡܫܠ)’
64. 1 Kgs 1.27, *mšalānā* / AB: ‘From before you, my lord the king, it was this word ,(ܡܫܠ) [though you did not tell your servants?]’
65. 1 Kgs 2.13, *mšalānā* / AB: ‘Do you come in peace? (ܡܫܠ)’ {AB-n-var: ‘It is your coming’}[27]
66. 1 Kgs 2.42, *mšalānā* / AB: ‘you will know for sure that you will certainly die? (ܡܫܠ)’
67. 1 Kgs 3.17, *taḥtāyā* / AB: ‘I beg of you, my lord: (ܬܚܬ)’
68. 1 Kgs 21.7, *mšalānā* / AB: ‘[Jezebel said to him:] May you prosper! You are the king of Israel! (ܡܫܠ)’
69. 1 Kgs 21.19, *mšalānā* / AB: ‘See! You have taken possession. (ܡܫܠ)’
70. 2 Kgs 2.18, *mšalānā* / AB: ‘Did I not say that you should not go? (ܡܫܠ)’
71. 2 Kgs 4.28, *mšalānā* / AB: ‘Did I ask my lord for a son? (ܡܫܠ) Did I not say to you, ‘Do not ask on my behalf? (ܡܫܠ)’

---

[27] Greenberg and Walter (2018, 17, n3).

72. 2 Kgs 5.7, *mšalānā* / AB: ‘Am I a god, who kills or gives life, that he has sent me this, that I should cure the man of leprosy? (ܡܫ)’
73. 2 Kgs 5.25, *mšalānā* / AB: ‘Where have you been, Gehazi? (ܡܫ)’
74. 2 Kgs 6.32, *mšalānā* / AB: ‘You have seen that this son of a murderer has sent to behead me. (ܡܫ)’
75. 2 Kgs 19.12, *mšalānā* / AB: ‘Did the gods of the nations save what my fathers destroyed, (ܡܫ) Gozan, Haran, Rezeph, and the children of Eden who are in Delasar?’
76. 2 Kgs 19.26, *mšalānā* / AB: ‘That their inhabitants, their power became little, (ܡܫ) they were broken, put to shame’.
77. Isa. 7.13, *mšalānā* / AB: ‘but will you also weary my God? (ܡܫ)’
78. Isa. 10.15, *mšalānā* / AB: ‘Should the axe be praised more than the man who hews with it? (ܡܫ)’
79. Isa. 22.2, *mšalānā* / AB: ‘You have filled the city with tumult, (ܡܫ)’
80. Isa. 29.16, *mšalānā* / AB: ‘Does the work say to its maker: You did not make me? (ܡܫ)’
81. Isa. 42.14, *mšalānā* / AB: ‘I have been silent; I will be silent forever; (ܡܫ) I have endured like a woman in labor. I will astonish, I will confound, at once’.
82. Isa. 44.28, *taḥtāyā* / AB: ‘Who said to Cyrus: My shepherd; (ܬܚܬ) for he will fulfill all my desire’,

83. Isa. 49.6, *mšalānā* / AB: '[It is a small thing, that you would be my servant,] that you would establish the tribe of Jacob, return the scion of Israel; (ܡܫ)'
84. Isa. 49.24, *mšalānā* / AB: 'Shall the prey of the mighty be carried off (ܡܫ)?'
85. Isa. 50.2, *mšalānā* / AB: 'My hand reaped the harvest: did it fall short? (ܡܫ)' {AB-n-var: 'or "it fell short"'}[28]
86. Isa. 57.6, *mšalānā* / AB: 'shall I be comforted by these? (ܡܫ)'
87. Isa. 58.5, *mšalānā* / AB: 'This is the fast that I have chosen: that a man should humble himself, should bend his neck like a hook, humbling himself with sackcloth and ash: (ܡܫ)'
88. Isa. 66.9, *mšalānā* / AB: 'is it I who causes birth, I who withholds? says your God. (ܡܫ)'
89. Isa. 66.22, *taḥtāyā* / AB: 'As the new heavens and new earth that I am making, that stand before me, says the Lord, (ܬܚܬ)'
90. Isa. 66.23, *taḥtāyā* / AB: '[And it will be, month by month,] and Sabbath by Sabbath, (ܬܚܬ)'
91. Joel 1.13, *paqūdā* / AB: 'The priests have put on sackcloth, (ܦܩܘܕܐ)'
92. Amos 3.4, *mšalānā* / AB: 'Does the lion roar in the forest when he has no prey? (ܡܫ)'
93. Amos 6.13, *mšalānā* /AB: 'Was it not with our strength that we took a city? (ܡܫ)'

[28] Greenberg and Walter (2012, 247, n3).

94. Amos 7.12, *taḥtāyā* / AB: ‘Amaziah said to Amos the seer: (ܬܚܬ)’
95. Jon. 4.2, *mšalānā* / AB: ‘was not this what I said, when I was in my own country? (ܡܫܠ)’
96. Mic. 3.1, *mšalānā* / AB: ‘was it not fitting for you to understand justice? (ܡܫܠ)’
97. Mic. 5.2, *mšalānā* / AB: ‘But you, Bethlehem Ephrathah – though you are the least among the thousands of Judah – (ܡܫܠ) a ruler will come forth from you’,
98. Mic. 5.5, *taḥtāyā* / AB: ‘the Assyrian, when he has come to our land, trodden down our palaces – (ܬܚܬ)’
99. Hag. 1.4, *mšalānā* / AB: ‘Is this a time for you to live in your (well)-roofed houses, while this house has been laid waste? (ܡܫܠ)’
100. Hag. 2.3, *mšalānā* / AB: ‘Did it count for nothing in your eyes? (ܡܫܠ)’
101. Hag. 2.13, *mšalānā* / AB: ‘If one who is unclean touches any of these things, is it not defiled? (ܡܫܠ)’
102. Zech. 1.5, *mšalānā* / AB: ‘Do they live forever? (ܡܫܠ)’
103. Zech. 1.6, *taḥtāyā* / AB: ‘which I commanded my servants the prophets: (ܬܚܬ)’
104. Zech. 3.7, *taḥtāyā* / AB: ‘If you will walk in my way and keep my commandments, (ܬܚܬ)’
105. Zech. 5.3, *taḥtāyā* / AB: ‘for everyone who steals from it (ܬܚܬ), like it, free from blame’;
106. Zech. 5.4, *taḥtāyā* / AB: ‘it will dwell within his house, (ܬܚܬ)’

107. Zech. 7.6, *mšalānā* / AB: 'is it not for yourself that you eat and drink? (ܡܫ)'

108. Zech. 9.3 *taḥtāyā* / AB: 'Tyre built a citadel for itself, (ܬܚܬ)'

109. Mal. 1.2, *mšalānā* / AB: 'Was Esau not Jacob's brother? (ܡܫ) Says the Lord'

110. Mal. 2.10, *mšalānā* / AB: 'Is there not one father for all of us? (ܡܫ)'

111. Mal. 3.2, *mšalānā* / AB: 'He will return, to refine (ܡܫ)'

112. Jer. 2.22, *taḥtāyā* / AB: 'Even if you cleanse yourself with nitre, and use more soap, (ܬܚܬ) your sins have made their mark [on you before me]'

113. Jer. 2.31, *mšalānā* / AB: 'Was I a wilderness to Israel? (ܡܫ)'

114. Jer. 2.32, *mšalānā* / AB: 'Does a maiden forget her modesty? or a bride her elegant dress? (ܡܫ)'

115. Jer. 4.8, *taḥtāyā* / AB: 'Put on sackcloth for this, lament and wail, (ܬܚܬ)'

116. Jer. 4.30, *mšalānā* / AB: 'when you deck yourself with golden ornament, (ܡܫ) when you paint your eyes with kohl? It is in vain that you deck yourself',

117. Jer. 13.12, *mšalānā* / AB: 'Every bottle will be filled with wine. (ܡܫ)'[29]

118. Jer. 22.15, *mšalānā* / AB: 'Do you rule because you rejoice in cedars? (ܡܫ)'

---

[29] Var. in 10m1: .ܕܟܠܗܘܢ ܙ̈ܩܐ ܡܬܡܠܝܢ ܚܡܪܐ. ܡܫ

119. Jer. 22.23, *mšalānā* / AB: 'Dweller in Lebanon (ܡܫܠ)... how you will groan' {AB-n-var: 'or 'why will you'}[30]
120. Jer. 22.26, *taḥtāyā* / AB: 'I will cast you out, you and your mother who gave birth to you, (ܬܚܬ)'
121. Jer. 25.29, *mšalānā* / AB: 'and are you completely innocent? (ܡܫܠ)'
122. Jer. 26.8, *taḥtāyā* / AB: 'When Jeremiah had finished saying everything that the Lord had commanded him to speak to all the people, (ܬܚܬ)'[31]
123. Jer. 44.19, *taḥtāyā* / AB: ' 'When we burnt incense to the queen of heaven, and poured libations to her, (ܬܚܬ)'
124. Jer. 48.27, *mšalānā* / AB: 'Was Israel not a laughing-stock to you? (ܡܫܠ)'
125. Jer. 49.3, *paqūdā* / AB: 'Put on sackcloth, (ܦܩܘܕ)'
126. Jer. 49.12, *mšalānā* / AB: 'you thought that you would be found innocent, (ܡܫܠ) will not be found innocent'.
127. Lam. 2.20, *mšalānā* / 'should women eat their offspring, the infants of their care? (ܡܫܠ)'
128. Ezek. 8.6, *mšalānā* / AB: 'O mortal man, (ܡܫܠ) do you see what they are doing?'
129. Ezek. 11.3, *mšalānā* / AB: 'It was not in its midst that we built houses. (ܡܫܠ)' {AB-n-var: 'Was it not in its midst that we built houses?'}[32]

---

[30] Greenberg and Walter (2012, 135, n4).

[31] *šmāhe* manuscripts om. 'all'.

[32] Greenberg and Walter (2015, 49, no. 1).

130. Ezek. 18.13, *mšalānā* / AB: 'Practice usury, take interest, shall he indeed live? (ܡܫ)'
131. Ezek. 18.27, *taḥtāyā* / AB: '[And if the wicked man should turn away from his iniquity,] act justly and rightly, (ܬܚܬ) [his soul will live.]'
132. Ezek. 20.3, *mšalānā* / AB: 'You come to inquire of me. (ܡܫ)' {AB-n-var: 'Do you come to inquire of me?'}[33]
133. Ezek. 20.31, *mšalānā* or *taḥtāyā* / AB: '— yet wanting to inquire of me, O house of Israel — (ܡܫ or ܬܚܬ)'[34]
134. Ezek. 28.2, *taḥtāyā* / AB: '[I am a god,] I sit in the seat of a god on the deep sea (ܬܚܬ)'
135. Ezek. 33.13, *taḥtāyā* / AB: 'he put his trust in his righteousness and then acted wickedly (ܬܚܬ)'
136. Ezek. 36.13, *taḥtāyā* / AB: 'You have devoured men and are bereaved of her people. (ܬܚܬ)'
137. Dan. 5.20, *taḥtāyā* / AB: 'his strong spirit made him arrogant, (ܬܚܬ)'
138. Bel 17, *mšalānā* / AB: 'Do the seals stand, Daniel? (ܡܫ)'
139. Sus. 53, *mšalānā* / 'And you said, Is our God righteous? (ܡܫ)'[35]
140. Wis. 11.19, *taḥtāyā* / 'These were not only their destroyer, (ܬܚܬ)'[36]
141. Wis. 15.17, *taḥtāyā* / 'he who lays aside life (ܬܚܬ)'

[33] Greenberg and Walter (2015, 107, no. 1).

[34] Var. between *šmāhe* manuscripts. See Appendix II.

[35] Text differs from AB Syriac: 10m1: ܘܐܡܪܬ ܐܢܬ܃ ܕܐܠܗܢ ܙܕܝܩ ܗܘ܂ ܡܫ.

[36] Wisdom and Sirach are not yet translated in AB.

142. Eccl. 6.6, *mšalānā* / AB: 'is not every one going to the same place? (ܡܫܐ)'
143. Sir. 26.12 *taḥtāyā* / 'drinks from any water, so she will sit in front of every tent peg and open her quiver to the arrow (ܬܚܬ)'
144. Sir. 27.17, *paqūdā* / 'Prove your friend, be confident with him (ܦܩܘܕ)'
145. Sir. 28.24, *taḥtāyā* / 'Bind your silver and gold, (ܬܚܬ)'
146. Acts 5.28, *mšalānā* /AB: 'Did we not strictly command you not to teach in this name? (ܡܫܐ)'[37]
147. Acts 9.34, *taḥtāyā* / AB: '[Simeon said to him,] Aeneas, (ܬܚܬ) [Jesus, the Messiah, heals you]'.
148. Acts 12.15, *mšalānā* /AB: '[They said to her,] You are really disturbed. (ܡܫܐ)'
149. Acts 16.37, *mšalānā* /AB: 'And now they are releasing us quietly? (ܡܫܐ)'
150. Acts 20.26, *taḥtāyā* / AB: 'On account of this I testify to you today. (ܬܚܬ)'
151. Acts 22.25, *mšalānā* / AB: 'Is it permissible for you to flog a Roman citizen who is not condemned? (ܡܫܐ)'
152. Jas. 3.11, *mšalānā* / AB: 'Is it really possible for both sweet water and bitter water to come from a single spring? (ܡܫܐ)'
153. Rom. 2.26, *mšalānā* / AB: 'then would not this person be reckoned as if they were circumcised? (ܡܫܐ)'

---

[37] The following English translations are taken from the Antioch Bible New Testament (Kiraz, ed. 2020).

154. Rom. 3.27, *mšalānā* / AB: ‘Where does that leave our boasting? [It is made worthless.] By a Law that involves works? (ܡܫ)’ {Bar ‘Ebroyo, *Storehouse of Mysteries*: a question}[38]

155. Rom. 7.13, *mšalānā* / AB: ‘Does that mean that something good became death for me? (ܡܫ) Not at all’.

156. Rom. 7.17, *šuḥlāp̱ šwayā* / AB: ‘But then it isn’t really me who is doing this thing. (ܫܘܚܠܦ ܫܘܝܐ)’

157. Rom. 11.11, *mšalānā* / AB: ‘But I ask, they did not trip and fall right over, did they? (ܡܫ) Not at all’.

158. 1 Cor. 1.13, *mšalānā* / AB: ‘Surely the Messiah isn’t divided! (ܡܫ)’

159. 1 Cor. 5.2, *mšalānā* / AB: ‘And you are proud of yourselves! (ܡܫ)’

160. 1 Cor. 6.2, *mšalānā* / AB: ‘surely you are competent to judge in insignificant matters, aren’t you? (ܡܫ)’

161. 1 Cor. 7.16, *mšalānā* / AB: ‘[For how do] you, being a wife, know whether you will bring to life your husband (ܡܫ)’

162. 1 Cor. 9.1, *mšalānā* / AB: ‘Aren’t I a free man? (ܡܫ)’

163. 1 Cor. 9.5, *mšalānā* / AB: ‘Do I not have the right to go around with a sister-wife (ܡܫ)?’

164. 1 Cor. 9.24, *mšalānā* / AB: ‘Don’t you realize that when people race on the track, although all of them are running, (ܡܫ) [only one of them is victorious]?’

---

[38] Loehr (1889, 3).

165. 2 Cor. 4.6, *taḥtāyā* / AB: because God, who said, ‘may the light shine from the darkness’, (ܬܚܬ) has shone in our hearts to enlighten us with the knowledge of God’s glory’
166. 2 Cor. 4.17, *šuḥlāp̱ šwayā* / AB: ‘[since the difficulties that we experience now…] are preparing for us a great glory that will be forever and ever. (ܫܘܚܠܦ ܫܘܝܐ)’
167. 2 Cor. 10.7, *mšalānā* / AB: ‘Do you look merely at the outside of people? (ܡܫ)’
168. Gal. 4.16, *mšalānā* / AB: ‘Have I become your enemy by preaching the truth to you? (ܡܫ)’
169. 1 Tim. 6.20, *taḥtāyā* / AB: ‘Oh Timothy, (ܬܚܬ)’
170. Matt. 3.14, *mšalānā* / AB: ‘I need to be baptized by you, and you have come to me? (ܡܫ)’
171. Matt. 3.17, *taḥtāyā* / AB: ‘And behold, a voice from heaven said, (ܬܚܬ) This is my [beloved] Son’,
172. Matt. 7.10, *mšalānā* / AB: ‘And if he asks him for a fish, will he hand him a snake? (ܡܫ)’
173. Matt. 13.55, *mšalānā* / AB: ‘Is this not the carpenter’s son? (ܡܫ) …and his brothers James, Joses, [Simon, and Judas]? (ܡܫ)’
174. Matt. 16.3, *mšalānā* / AB: ‘Sky is [dark] and red… You do not know how to interpret the signs of this time. (ܡܫ)’
175. Matt. 18.12, *mšalānā* / AB: ‘[A]nd look for the one that wandered away? (ܡܫ)’
176. Matt. 18.33, *mšalānā* / AB: ‘Should you not have had mercy on your fellow servant too, just as I had mercy on you? (ܡܫ)’

177. Matt. 20.13, *mšalānā* / AB: ‘Did you not contract with me for a denarius? (ܗܘ)’
178. Matt. 21.16, *mšalānā* / AB: ‘From the mouths of children and infants you have ordained praise? (ܗܘ)’
179. Matt. 24.2, *mšalānā* / AB: ‘Look, do you see all these? (ܗܘ)’
180. Matt. 26.50, *mšalānā* / AB: ‘Is that why you have come, my friend? (ܗܘ)’
181. Matt. 26.62, *mšalānā* / AB: ‘Do you have no answer to give? (ܗܘ)’
182. Mark 6.37, *mšalānā* / AB: ‘Shall we go and spend 200 denarii on bread and give it to them to eat? (ܗܘ)’
183. Mark 14.19, *mšalānā* / AB: ‘Is it I? (ܗܘ)’
184. Mark 14.37, *mšalānā* / AB: ‘Simon, are you sleeping? (ܗܘ)’
185. Luke 4.22, *mšalānā* / AB: ‘Is this not Joseph’s son? (ܗܘ)’
186. Luke 11.11, *mšalānā* / AB: ‘And if he asks him for a fish, will hand him a snake instead of a fish? (ܗܘ)’
187. Luke 11.40, *mšalānā* / AB: ‘Did not he who made what is outside also make what is inside? (ܗܘ)’
188. Luke 12.6, *mšalānā* / AB: ‘Are not five sparrows sold for two pennies? (ܗܘ) And not one of them is forgotten before God’.
189. Luke 17.9, *mšalānā* / AB: ‘Does that servant receive his thanks because he did what was commanded him? (ܗܘ)’
190. John 6.70, *mšalānā* / AB: ‘Have I not chosen you twelve? (ܗܘ) And one of you is Satan’.
191. John 7.25, *mšalānā* / AB: ‘Is this not the man they are seeking to kill? (ܗܘ)’

192. John 7.26, *mšalānā* / AB: ‘Have our elders found out that he is really the Messiah? (ܡܫ)’
193. John 7.31, *mšalānā* / AB: ‘When the Messiah comes, will he do more signs than this man is doing? (ܡܫ)’
194. John 7.41, *mšalānā* / AB: ‘The Messiah does not come from Galilee, does he? (ܡܫ)’
195. John 7.47, *mšalānā* / AB: ‘Has he deceived you too? (ܡܫ)’
196. John 7.51, *mšalānā* / AB: ‘and finding out what they have done? (ܡܫ)’
197. John 8.13, *mšalānā* / AB: ‘You testify about yourself. (ܡܫ) Your testimony is not true’.
198. John 9.19, *mšalānā* / AB: ‘Is this your son, (ܡܫ)?’
199. John 11.40, *mšalānā* / AB: ‘Did I not tell you that if you believe, you will see the glory of God? (ܡܫ)’
200. John 12.19, *mšalānā* / AB: ‘See, [we are not accomplishing anything,] because the whole world is following him. (ܡܫ)’[39]
201. John 14.9, *mšalānā* / AB: ‘I have been with you this whole time… and you do not know me, Philip? (ܡܫ)’
202. John 18.35, *mšalānā* / AB: ‘Am I a Jew? (ܡܫ)’
203. John 19.10, *mšalānā* / AB: ‘Do you not realize that I have the power to set you free and I have the power to crucify you? (ܡܫ)’

For Harklean Reminders, see Appendix II.

[39] Var. in 10m1: ܚܙܝ ܐܢܬܘܢ܆ ܕܥܠܡܐ ܟܠܗ ܗܘܐ ܐܙܠ ܒܬܪܗ܂.

Appendix II: Core Reminders of Punctuation/ Accents Across Eight West Syriac Model-Text *Šmāhe* Manuscripts

	10m1 BL Add. 12178	10m3 Vat. sir. 152	11m1 Dam. Syr. 7/16	11m2 BL Add. 7183	11m4 Mosul MS 16	11m5 Par. BnF sir. 64	11m6 Barb. orient. 118	11m7[40] Dam. Syr. 12/22
Gen. 4.9		mg.		mg.			lac.	
Gen. 16.8		mg.					lac.	
Gen. 24.6	int.	int.					lac.	
Gen. 29.6		mg.					lac.	
Gen. 30.2		mg.					lac.	
Exod. 4.11		mg.		mg.			lac.	
Num. 11.12		mg.		mg.			lac.	
Num. 20.10 (ܪܗܠܐ ܕܦܩܘ)				mg				
Num. 20.10 (ܡܢ)		mg.		mg.			lac.	
Num. 21.29				mg				
Num. 36.3		mg.					lac.	
Deut. 1.33	int.	mg.		mg.	int.	int.	lac.	

[40] A sigla was not previously assigned to Dam. syr. 12/22 by the editors of the Leiden Peshitta Project. Therefore, we have assigned the nomenclature '11m7' to this valuable *šmāhe* manuscript.

	10m1 BL Add. 12178	10m3 Vat. sir. 152	11m1 Dam. Syr. 7/16	11m2 BL Add. 7183	11m4 Mosul MS 16	11m5 Par. BnF sir. 64	11m6 Barb. orient. 118	11m7[40] Dam. Syr. 12/22
Deut. 29.19				mg.				
Deut. 30.7	int.	int.				int.		
Deut. 30.11				mg.				
Deut. 32.6				mg.				
Judg. 8.2		mg.		mg.			int.	
Judg. 8.11				mg.				
Judg. 9.28		mg.		mg.			int.	int.
Judg. 9.32	int.	int.			int.	int.	int.	mg.
Judg. 9.38		mg.		mg.			int.	
Judg. 11.24		mg.		mg.			int.	
Judg. 11.25		mg.		mg.			int.	
Judg. 12.5		mg.		mg.			int.	
Job 6.5		mg.		mg.			int.	
Job 7.19		mg.		mg.			int.	
Job 8.3		mg.		mg.			int.	
Job 8.11		mg.		mg.			int.	
Job 10.13		mg.		mg.			int.	
Job 11.9		mg.		mg.			int.	
Job 13.25		mg.		mg.				

	10m1 BL Add. 12178	10m3 Vat. sir. 152	11m1 Dam. Syr. 7/16	11m2 BL Add. 7183	11m4 Mosul MS 16	11m5 Par. BnF sir. 64	11m6 Barb. orient. 118	11m7[40] Dam. Syr. 12/22
Job 14.18		mg.		mg.			int.	
Job 14.19		mg.		mg.			mg.	
Job 23.6		mg.					int.	
Job 30.20		mg.		mg.				
Job 38.12		mg.		mg.			int.	
Job 38.18	int.	mg.		mg.	int.	int.	int.	mg.
Job 38.28	int.	mg.	int.	mg.	int.	int.	int.	mg.
Job 38.31	int.	int.		mg.		int.	int.	mg.
Job 39.2–3		mg.		mg.			int.	
Job 39.9		mg.		mg.			int.	
Job 39.26		mg.		mg.			int.	
1 Sam. 9.11		mg.		mg.			int.	
1 Sam. 10.24		mg.		mg.				
1 Sam. 11.13		mg.		mg.			int.	
1 Sam. 16.5				mg.			int.	
1 Sam. 16.11		mg.		mg.			int.	
1 Sam. 17.43		mg.		mg.			int.	
1 Sam. 30.8				mg.			int.	
2 Sam. 2.26		mg.		mg.			int.	

	10m1 BL Add. 12178	10m3 Vat. sir. 152	11m1 Dam. Syr. 7/16	11m2 BL Add. 7183	11m4 Mosul MS 16	11m5 Par. BnF sir. 64	11m6 Barb. orient. 118	11m7[40] Dam. Syr. 12/22
2 Sam. 7.7		mg.		mg.				
2 Sam. 11.20	int.	mg.		mg.		int.	int.	
2 Sam. 11.21		mg.		mg.				
2 Sam. 13.4 (ܬܡܪ)		int. (ܬܡܪ)					int. (ܬܡܪ)	
2 Sam. 13.4 (ܐܢܐ)	int. (ܐܢܐ)			mg. (ܐܢܐ)		int. (ܐܢܐ)	int. (ܐܢܐ)	
2 Sam. 17.6		mg.		mg.			int.	
Ps. 10.15		mg.					int.	
Ps. 22.2		int.		mg.			int.	
Ps. 58.1 (ܐܢܐ$_1$)		mg.		mg.			int.	
Ps. 58.1 (ܐܢܐ$_2$)		mg.					int.	
Ps. 59.11		mg.		mg.			int.	
Ps. 78.19		mg.		mg.				
Ps. 78.20		int.		mg.	int.		int.	
Ps. 143.10 {MT 144}	int.							
Ps. 143.15 {MT 144}		int.			int.		int.	

	10m1 BL Add. 12178	10m3 Vat. sir. 152	11m1 Dam. Syr. 7/16	11m2 BL Add. 7183	11m4 Mosul MS 16	11m5 Par. BnF sir. 64	11m6 Barb. orient. 118	11m7[40] Dam. Syr. 12/22
1 Kgs 1.21	int.	mg.	int.	mg.	int.	int.	int.	mg.
1 Kgs 1.27		mg.		mg.	int.		int.	
1 Kgs 2.13		mg.		mg.	int.		int.	
1 Kgs 2.42					int.			
1 Kgs 3.17		mg.			int.			
1 Kgs 21.7		mg.		mg.	int.		int.	
1 Kgs 21.19		int.		mg.	int.		int.	
2 Kgs 2.18		int.			int.		int.	
2 Kgs 4.28 (ܠܐ$_1$)		mg.		mg.			int.	
2 Kgs 4.28 (ܠܐ$_2$)		int.			int.		int.	
2 Kgs 5.7		mg.		mg.			int.	
2 Kgs 5.25					int.			
2 Kgs 6.32		mg.		mg.	int.			
2 Kgs 19.12		int.		mg.	int.		int.	
2 Kgs 19.26		mg.		mg.			int.	
Isa. 7.13		int.		mg.			int.	
Isa. 10.15		mg.		mg.	int.		int.	
Isa. 22.2		mg.			int.		int.	

	10m1 BL Add. 12178	10m3 Vat. sir. 152	11m1 Dam. Syr. 7/16	11m2 BL Add. 7183	11m4 Mosul MS 16	11m5 Par. BnF sir. 64	11m6 Barb. orient. 118	11m7[40] Dam. Syr. 12/22
Isa. 29.16		int.			int.		int.	
Isa. 42.14		mg.		mg.	int.		int.	
Isa. 44.28		int.					int.	
Isa. 49.6		mg.		mg.	int.		int.	
Isa. 49.24		int.		mg.	int.		int.	
Isa. 50.2	int.	mg.		mg.	int.		int.	
Isa. 57.6		mg.		mg.	int.	int.	int.	
Isa. 58.5		int.		mg.	int.		int.	
Isa. 66.9		int.		mg.	int.		int.	
Isa. 66.22		int.			int.		int.	
Isa. 66.23		int.					int.	
Joel 1.13	int.	mg.	int.			int.	int.	
Amos 3.4		int.		mg.	int.		int.	
Amos 6.13		mg.		mg.	int.		int.	
Amos 7.12		int.			int.		int.	
Jonah 4.2		int.		mg.	int.		int.	
Mic. 3.1		mg.		mg.	int.		int.	
Mic. 5.2		mg.		mg.	int.		int.	
Mic. 5.5		mg.					int.	

	10m1 BL Add. 12178	10m3 Vat. sir. 152	11m1 Dam. Syr. 7/16	11m2 BL Add. 7183	11m4 Mosul MS 16	11m5 Par. BnF sir. 64	11m6 Barb. orient. 118	11m7[40] Dam. Syr. 12/22
Hag. 1.4		int.		mg.	int.		int.	
Hag. 2.3		mg.		mg.	int.		int.	
Hag. 2.13		mg.		mg.	int.		int.	
Zech. 1.5		int.			int.		int.	
Zech. 1.6		int.			int.		int.	
Zech. 3.7		int.			int.		int.	
Zech. 5.3		int.			int.		int.	
Zech. 5.4		int.			int.		int.	
Zech. 7.6		mg.		mg.			int.	
Zech. 9.3		int.					int.	
Mal. 1.2				mg.			int.	
Mal. 2.10		mg.					int.	
Mal. 3.2							int.	
Jer. 2.22		int.			int.		int.	
Jer. 2.31		mg.		mg.	int.[41]		int.	
Jer. 2.32		mg.		mg.	int.		int.	
Jer. 4.8			int.			int.		

[41] Jer. 2.31 and 2.32 are reversed in Mosul, St. Thomas Church MS 16.

	10m1 BL Add. 12178	10m3 Vat. sir. 152	11m1 Dam. Syr. 7/16	11m2 BL Add. 7183	11m4 Mosul MS 16	11m5 Par. BnF sir. 64	11m6 Barb. orient. 118	11m7[40] Dam. Syr. 12/22
Jer. 4.30					int.		int.	
Jer. 13.12		int.		mg.	int.		int.	
Jer. 22.15		int.		mg.	int.		int.	
Jer. 22.23		int.			int.		int.	
Jer. 22.26		mg.			int.			
Jer. 25.29		mg.		mg.	int.		int.	
Jer. 26.8		mg.			int.		int.	
Jer. 44.19		mg.					int.	
Jer. 48.27		int.					int.	
Jer. 49.3						int.		int.
Jer. 49.12		mg.		mg.			int.	
Lam. 2.20		int.					int.	
Ezek. 8.6		mg.		mg.			int.	
Ezek. 11.3		mg.					int.	
Ezek. 18.13		int.		mg.			int.	
Ezek. 18.27		int.					int.	
Ezek. 20.3		int.		mg.			int.	
Ezek. 20.31		int. (ܡܪܝܐ)		mg. (ܡܪܝܐ)		int. (ܐܢܬ)	int. (ܡܪܝܐ)	
Ezek. 28.2		int.					int.	

	10m1 BL Add. 12178	10m3 Vat. sir. 152	11m1 Dam. Syr. 7/16	11m2 BL Add. 7183	11m4 Mosul MS 16	11m5 Par. BnF sir. 64	11m6 Barb. orient. 118	11m7[40] Dam. Syr. 12/22
Ezek. 33.13		int.					int.	
Ezek. 36.13		mg.					int.	
Dan. 5.20	int.	int.	int.		int.	int.		
Bel 17				mg.				
Sus. 53		int.		mg.			int.	
Wis. 11.19		int.						
Wis. 15.17		int.						
Eccl. 6.6		int.		mg.				
Sir. 26.12		int.						
Sir. 27.17					int.			
Sir. 28.24		mg.						
Acts 5.28		int.					int.	
Acts 9.34		int.						
Acts 12.15		int.		mg.			int.	
Acts 16.37		int.		mg.			int.	
Acts 20.26		mg.						
Acts 22.25		int.		mg.		mg.	int.	
Jas. 3.11		mg.					int.	
Rom. 2.26		int.		mg.			int.	
Rom. 3.27		int.		mg.			int.	

	10m1 BL Add. 12178	10m3 Vat. sir. 152	11m1 Dam. Syr. 7/16	11m2 BL Add. 7183	11m4 Mosul MS 16	11m5 Par. BnF sir. 64	11m6 Barb. orient. 118	11m7[40] Dam. Syr. 12/22
Rom. 7.13		int.		mg.			int.	
Rom. 7.17	int.	mg.	int.		int.		int.	
Rom. 11.11		int.		mg.			int.	
1 Cor. 1.13		int.		mg.			int.	
1 Cor. 5.2	int.	int.		mg.			int.	
1 Cor. 6.2		int.		mg.			int.	
1 Cor. 7.16				mg.			int.	
1 Cor. 9.1		mg.		mg.			int.	
1 Cor. 9.5		int.		mg.				
1 Cor. 9.24		int.		mg.			int.	
2 Cor. 4.6		int.					int.	
2 Cor. 4.17		mg.						
2 Cor. 10.7		mg.		mg.			int.	
Gal. 4.16		int.		mg.			int.	
1 Tim. 6.20		mg.					int.	
Matt. 3.14		mg.		mg.			int.	
Matt. 3.17							int.	
Matt. 7.10		int.		mg.			int.	

	10m1 BL Add. 12178	10m3 Vat. sir. 152	11m1 Dam. Syr. 7/16	11m2 BL Add. 7183	11m4 Mosul MS 16	11m5 Par. BnF sir. 64	11m6 Barb. orient. 118	11m7[40] Dam. Syr. 12/22
Matt. 13.55 (ܐܡܗ$_1$)		int.		mg.			int.	
Matt. 13.55 (ܐܡܗ$_2$)		int.		mg.			int.	
Matt. 16.3		int.		mg.			int.	
Matt. 18.12					int.			
Matt. 18.33		int.		mg.			int.	
Matt. 20.13		int.		mg.			int.	
Matt. 21.16		int.						
Matt. 24.2							int.	
Matt. 26.50		int.					int.	
Matt. 26.62		int.		mg.				
Mark 6.37							int.	
Mark 14.19		int.		mg.			int.	
Mark 14.37		int.		mg.			int.	
Luke 4.22		int.						
Luke 11.11		int.		mg.			int.	
Luke 11.40		int.					int.	
Luke 12.6		int.		mg.			int.	
Luke 17.9		int.					int.	

	10m1 BL Add. 12178	10m3 Vat. sir. 152	11m1 Dam. Syr. 7/16	11m2 BL Add. 7183	11m4 Mosul MS 16	11m5 Par. BnF sir. 64	11m6 Barb. orient. 118	11m7[40] Dam. Syr. 12/22
John 6.70		int.					int.	
John 7.25		int.		mg.			int.	
John 7.26		int.		mg.			int.	
John 7.31		int.		mg.			int.	
John 7.41		int.		mg.			int.	
John 7.47		int.		mg.			int.	
John 7.51		int.		mg.	int.		int.	
John 8.13		mg.					int.	
John 9.19				mg.			int.	
John 11.40		mg.		mg.			int.	
John 12.19		mg.		mg.			int.	
John 14.9		int.		mg.			int.	
John 18.35		int.		mg.			int.	
John 19.10		mg.		mg.			int.	

Harklean

	10m1 BL Add. 12178	10m3 Vat. sir. 152	11m1 Dam. Syr. 7/16	11m2 BL Add. 7183	11m4 Mosul MS 16	11m5 Par. BnF sir. 64	11m6 Barb. orient. 118	11m7 Dam. Syr. 12/22
1 Cor. 3.19		int.		mg.			int.	
1 Cor. 9.1							int.	
1 Cor. 10.18							int.	
Matt. 7.12				mg.			int.	
Matt. 17.24				mg.				
John 7.25				mg.			int.	
John 7.45				mg.			int.	
John 14.9				mg.			int.	

Appendix III: Scriptural Passages Common to West Syriac Reminders in *Šmāhe* Codices and the East Syriac Tract in BL Add. 12138

	West Syriac *Šmāhe* Reminders	East Syriac *Šmāhe* Tract
Num. 36.3 {2} But if they become wives in any of the tribes of Israel… {1} and it shall be taken away from the lot of our inheritance.	*mšalānā*: {1} ܘܡܢ ܦܣ̈ܝ ܬܐ ܕܝܪܬܘܬܢ ܬܬܒܨܪ ܪ: ܡܫܐܠܢܐ	*mzī ʾāne* and *zawgā*: {2} ܘܐܢ ܢܗܘܝ̈ܢ ܠܚܕ ܡܢ ܫܒܛ̈ܐ ܕܒܢ̈ܝ ܝܣܪܐܝܠ ܢܫ̈ܐ:
Job 7.19 {1 + 2} [N]or let me be till I have swallowed my spit?	*mšalānā*: {1} ܠܐ ܬܫܒܩܢܝ: ܥܕܡܐ ܕܐܒܠܥ ܪܘܩܝ: ܡܫܐܠܢܐ	*zawgā ʿelāyā* and *taḥtāyā*: {2} ܠܐ ܬܫܒܩܢܝ: ܥܕܡܐ ܕܐܒܠܥ ܪܘܩܝ:
1 Sam. 16.11 {1 + 2} Are the children complete?	*mšalānā*: {1} ܫܠܡܘ ܛܠܝ̈ܐ: ܡܫܐܠܢܐ	*paqūdā* and *taḥtāyā*: {2} ܫܠܡܘ ܛܠܝ̈ܐ:
2 Sam. 13.4 {1 + 2} the king's son: {1} Why are you so, from day to day? {1 + 2} Will you not tell me?	*taḥtāyā* and *mšalānā*: {1} ܒܪ ܡܠܟܐ: ܬܚܬܝܐ. ܗܢܘ ܕܗܟܢܐ ܐܙܠܐ ܐܢܬ ܡܢ ܨܦܪ ܠܨܦܪ. ܕܡܛܠ ܟܠ ܒܨܦܪ ܠܐ ܐܡܪ ܐܢܬ ܠܝ: ܡܫܐܠܢܐ.	*mnaḥḥtā* and *taḥtāyā*: {2} ܒܪ ܡܠܟܐ: ܠܐ ܐܡܪ ܐܢܬ ܠܝ:
1 Kgs 3.17 {1} I beg of you, {1 + 2} my lord:	*taḥtāyā*: {1} ܒܒܥܘ ܐܢܐ ܡܢܟ ܡܪܝ: ܬܚܬܝܐ.	*šḥīmā*, on one word: {2} ܡܪܝ:
Isa. 44.28 [Who] {1} said to Cyrus: My shepherd; for he will fulfill all my desire, {2} to tell Jerusalem that she will be rebuilt, and the temple restored.	*taḥtāyā*: {1} ܕܐܡܪ ܠܟܘܪܫ ܪܥܝ: ܬܚܬܝܐ. ܕܟܠܗ ܨܒܝܢܝ ܢܫܠܡ. ܬܚܬܝܐ.	*mzī ʾānā* and *sāmkā*, twice: {2} ܠܡܐܡܪ ܠܐܘܪܫܠܡ. ܕܬܬܒܢܐ ܘܗܝܟܠܐ. ܢܬܬܟܠܠ.

	West Syriac *Šmāhe* Reminders	East Syriac *Šmāhe* Tract
Jer. 25.29 {1 + 2} and are you completely innocent?	*mšalānā*: {1} ܘܐܢܬܘܢ ܡܙܟܐ ܬܙܟܘܢ ܡܫܐܠܢܐ.	*zawgā ʿelāyā* and *paqūdā* and *taḥtāyā*: {2} ܘܐܢܬܘܢ ܡܙܟܐ ܬܙܟܘܢ
Jer. 49.12 {1 + 2} you, who thought that you would be found innocent, will not be found innocent.	*mšalānā*: {1} ܘܐܢܬ ܣܒܪܬ ܕܬܙܟܐ. ܠܐ ܬܙܟܐ ܡܫܐܠܢܐ.	*zawgā ʿelāyā* and *paqūdā* and *taḥtāyā*: {2} ܘܐܢܬ ܣܒܪܬ ܕܬܙܟܐ. ܠܐ ܬܙܟܐ
Lam. 2.20 {1 + 2} should women eat their offspring, the infants of their care? {2} Should prophet and priest be killed in the tabernacle of the Lord?	*mšalānā*: {1} ܐܢ ܢܐܟܠܢ ܢܫ̈ܐ ܦܐܪܝܗܝܢ ܠܥܘ̈ܠܐ ܕܡܫܬܡܫܝܢ ܡܫܐܠܢܐ	*zawgā ʿelāyā* and *mzī ʾānā* and *zawgā ʿelāyā* and *taḥtāyā*: {2} ܐܢ ܢܐܟܠܢ ܢܫ̈ܐ ܦܐܪܝܗܝܢ ܠܥܘ̈ܠܐ ܕܡܫܬܡܫܝܢ ܐܢ ܢܬܩܛܠ ܒܡܩܕܫܗ ܕܡܪܝܐ ܟܗܢܐ ܘܢܒܝܐ
Acts 5.28 {1 + 2} Did we not strictly command you {1} not to teach in this name?	*mšalānā*: {1} ܠܐ ܗܘܐ ܒܪ ܡܦܩܕ ܦܩܕܢ ܗܘܝܢ ܠܟܘܢ ܕܠܐܚ ܠܐ ܬܐܠܦܘܢ ܒܫܡܐ ܗܢܐ ܡܫܐܠܢܐ	*mzī ʾāne* and *zawgā*: {2} ܠܐ ܗܘܐ ܡܦܩܕ ܦܩܕܢ ܗܘܝܢ ܠܟܘܢ
Luke 11.40 {2} Fools! {1} Did not he who made what is outside also make what is inside?	*mšalānā*: {1} ܠܐ ܗܘܐ ܡܢ ܕܥܒܕ ܕܠܒܪ ܘܠܓܘ ܗܘ ܥܒܕ ܡܫܐܠܢܐ	*rāhṭā d-pāseq*: {2} ܚܣܝܪܝ, ܪܥܝܢܐ.

References

Bernstein, Georgius H. (trans.). 1858. *Gregorii Bar-Hebraei scholia in librum Iobi*. Vratislaviae: Typis Universitatis.

Brovender, Chaim. 1976. 'The Syriac SHEMAHE MSS: A Typological and Comparative Study'. PhD dissertation, Hebrew University of Jerusalem. [Hebrew].

Coakley, J. F. 2011. 'When Were the Five Greek Vowel Signs Introduced into Writing?'. *Journal of Semitic Studies* 56: 307–25.

———. 2012. 'An Early Syriac Question Mark'. *Aramaic Studies* 10: 193–212.

Cook, Edward (trans.). 2015. *Numbers. The Syriac Peshitta Bible with English Translation*. Piscataway, NJ: Gorgias Press.

Diettrich, Gustav. 1899. *Die Massorah der ostlichen und westlichen Syrer in ihren Angaben zum Propheten Jesaia nach fünf Handschiften des British Museum*. London: Williams and Norgate.

Greenberg, Gillian and Donald M. Walter (trans). 2012. *Isaiah. The Syriac Peshitta Bible with English Translation*. Piscataway, NJ: Gorgias Press.

———. 2013. *Jeremiah. The Syriac Peshitta Bible with English Translation*. Piscataway, NJ: Gorgias Press.

———. 2015. *Ezekiel. The Syriac Peshitta Bible with English Translation*. Piscataway, NJ: Gorgias Press.

———. 2015. *Judges. The Syriac Peshitta Bible with English Translation*. Piscataway, NJ: Gorgias Press.

———. 2018. *Kings. The Syriac Peshitta Bible with English Translation*. Piscataway, NJ: Gorgias Press.

Juckel, Andreas, and Inetje Parlevliet-Flesseman. 2023. *The New Testament in Syriac Peshiṭta Version. Vol. III The Pauline Epistles*. Piscataway, NJ: Gorgias Press.

Kiraz, George. 2015. *The Syriac Dot*. Piscataway, NJ: Gorgias Press.

———. (ed.). 2020. *Syriac-English New Testament*. Piscataway, NJ; Gorgias Press.

Loehr, Maximilianus (trans.). 1889. *Gregorii Abulfaragii Bar Ebhraya in Epistulas Paulinas Adnotationes*. Gottingen: In Aedibus Dieterichianis.

Loopstra, Jonathan. 2014. *An East Syrian Manuscript of the Syriac 'Masora' Dated to 899 CE. A Facsimile Reproduction*. Piscataway, NJ: Gorgias Press.

———. 2015. *An East Syrian Manuscript of the Syriac 'Masora' Dated to 899 CE—Introduction, Lists of Samples, and Indices to Marginal Notes*. Piscataway, NJ: Gorgias Press.

———. 2016. *Job. The Syriac Peshitta Bible with English Translation*. Piscataway, NJ: Gorgias Press.

———. 2017. 'Reading the Bible with the *Tahtāyā da-tlāta*'. In *From Ancient Manuscripts to Modern Dictionaries*, edited by Tarsee Li and Keith Dyer, 109–137. Piscataway, NJ: Gorgias Press.

———. 2019. 'The Syriac Reading Dot in Transmission—Consistency and Confusion'. In *Studies in Biblical Philology and Lexicography*, edited by Daniel King, 159–176. Piscataway, NJ: Gorgias Press.

———. 2020. *The Patristic 'Masora'—A Study of Patristic Collections in Syriac Handbooks from the Near East.* CSCO 689; Scriptores Syri, Tomus 265. Leuven: Peeters.

McCarthy, Carmel (trans.). 2013. *Deuteronomy. The Syriac Peshitta Bible with English Translation.* Piscataway, NJ: Gorgias Press.

Morrison, Craig E., Claudio Balzaretti, and Mirko Pozzobon (trans). 2019. *Genesis. The Syriac Peshitta Bible with English Translation.* Piscataway, NJ: Gorgias Press.

Phillips, George (trans. and ed.). 1869. *A Letter by Mār Jacob, Bishop of Edessa, on Syriac Orthography; Also a Tract by the Same Author, and a Discourse by Gregory bar Hebraeus on Syriac Accents.* London: Williams and Norgate.

Segal, Judah. 1953. *The Diacritical Point and the Accents in Syriac.* London Oriental Series 2. Oxford: Oxford University Press.

Sprengling, Martin, and William Creighton Graham (trans and eds). 1931. *Barhebraeus' Scholia on the Old Testament. Part I: Genesis-II Samuel.* Chicago: University of Chicago Press.

Taylor, Richard (trans.). 2020. *Psalms. The Syriac Peshitta Bible with English Translation.* Piscataway, NJ: Gorgias Press.

Weiss, Theodor. 1933. *Zur ostsyrischen Laut- und Akzentlehre.* Bonner Orientalistische Studien. Stuttgart: Verlag W. Kohlhammer.

TAXONOMIES OF DOTS: THE CONTEXT AND METHODOLOGY OF THE EARLY TREATISES ABOUT THE SYRIAC ACCENT DOTS

Johan Lundberg

1.0. Placing Points

In the fifth century, Syriac scribes developed a system of punctuation. This system of dots was used to divide the text, and to mark pauses, pitch contours, and stress (cf. Lundberg 2022, 2025). The core of this system was used in both biblical and non-biblical manuscripts. From a visual perspective there are nine or ten dots in the early system (cf. Martin 1875; Segal 1953, 67; Weiss 1953; Merx and King 2023, 148).[1] There are differences between earlier and later manuscripts and there are even differences within the eastern and western traditions. David Bar Pawlos recounts an episode in which two monks of Beṯ Rāmīšoʿ—both well-known

[1] The western and eastern used different names for these signs. I use the western names and spelling for dots in western treatises, and vice versa for the eastern names. In a few instances the result is similar but different names for visually identical dots, e.g. ܦܩܘܕܐ pronounced *pāqūḏā* in the western tradition and *pāqoḏā* in the eastern.

 https://doi.org/10.11647/OBP.0498.02

for their ability to recite the Scriptures—were asked to retreat into a cell and add dots to an un-pointed manuscript (Posegay 2021, 155–56). We do not have these manuscripts, and we do not know where they differed, but a similar tradition has probably been preserved in British Library Add. 12138. This is the only preserved eastern Masoretic manuscript and one of its unusual features is that Babai, the scribe, recorded more than one reading tradition. He includes the traditions of the *maqryānē*[2] and the tradition of Rāmīšoʿ. The traditions of the *maqryānē* were recorded with black ink, whereas red dots was used to mark places where Rāmīšoʿ read the text differently. Babai also used other signs, especially lines, and marginal notations to clarify readings, and to indicate which readings he considered correct.[3]

BL Add. 12138 is a compilation of quotes from the Syriac Bible—from Genesis 1.1 to the end of the New Testament. A survey of the red dots in the quotes from Genesis (BL Add. 12138, 1v–24r) suggests that there is a very large degree of agreement between Rāmīšoʿ and the *maqryānē*. Moreover, when a red dot is added, it is there to mark a stressed word, or to slightly modify a

---

[2] Becker compares these 'readers' with the Grammarians in Greek schools (2006, 71). Loopstra notes that their main role was teaching students how to read the Syriac Bible (2015, viii).

[3] See Loopstra for a facsimile of the manuscript (2014). Loopstra contains a description of the manuscript, indices of Biblical passages, editions and translations of some treatises, and more (2015). See Loopstra for Babai's description of his methodology and how he used black and red dots (2025, xxxiv, 409; cf. BL Add. 12136, 309v–310r).

dot used by the *maqryānē*. These differences are neither immaterial nor major, and they suggest that the two traditions were very similar.

After the main body of text there is a treatise about accent dots. It is one of four early treatises preserved in Masoretic manuscripts, e.g., BL Add. 12138, BL Add. 12178, and Vat. sir. 152. This chapter is about these early treatises: their origin, context, and scope. Who wrote these treatises? Did they originate in a specific school? How were they used, and what can they tell us about the system of pointing in Biblical manuscripts?

The treatises included in western Masoretic manuscripts are not always the same, and the boundaries between treatises are not always clear. In BL Add. 12178, Jacob's *On Persons and Tenses* is divided into chapters but, unlike the letter that precedes it, which is also written by Jacob, the ending is not clearly marked.

Moreover, the content is often similar. The introduction to the longer anonymous treatise contains references to Aristotle and Epiphanius. References to the former are also found in a treatise attributed to Thomas the Deacon (Vat. sir. 152, 192v). BL Add. 12138 is the only eastern Masoretic manuscript, but it is not the only manuscript that preserves an eastern treatise on punctuation. Two similar treatises are preserved in Petermann 9 (22r–27v, 228v–230r), a manuscript in the Staatsbibliothek zu Berlin.

2.0. The Context and Authors

The discussion in this chapter centres on four treatises: three western and one eastern. They are preserved in ninth and tenth century manuscripts, but they are almost certainly older. Segal suggests that the accents had become a recondite subject by the eleventh century, and that discussions were restricted to classrooms and dissertations (1953, 143). However, the schools were probably always the main place where these dots were discussed and where theories were formulated. The question is, can we be more precise? Where did these ideas develop, and can they be connected with specific schools?

2.1. The Early Western Treatises

The earliest western treatises are likely to be a product of the sixth and seventh century, describing a system of dots that is very similar to the one we find in the late sixth century Rabbula gospels (Biblioteca Medicea Laurenziana, Plut. 1.56). Most western Masoretic Bibles contain two treatises, one written by Jacob of Edessa and another written by Thomas the Deacon. In BL Add. 12178 there is also a third treatise.

These three are the main witnesses of the early western grammatical tradition. One is perhaps anonymous, one was written by a named but possibly unknown author, and the last was written by Jacob of Edessa. In terms of content and basic terminology, these treatises share a lot of material. For example, all three treatises often quote the same examples from the Syriac Bible; and Thomas' treatise and the longer anonymous treatise mention Aristotle as a source of inspiration for early grammarians.

There are also differences. The anonymous treatise is only focused on individual dots, while the other treatises mention compound dots, i.e., two or more dots combined in the same pausal unit. The anonymous treatise divides the dots into seven groups according to their position, while the other treatises list dots but do not divide them into specific groups. While Jacob's treatise has a clear structure, it does not follow this organising principle. The similarities between these treatises suggest that they were the product of the same tradition, school, or intellectual milieu.

Then there are references to Greek. The introduction to the anonymous treatise mentions Epiphanius and Aristotle; the latter is mentioned by Thomas as well. In Thomas' treatise the Syriac accent *gārūrā* is called ܦܪܐܘܟܣܘܛܘܢܘܣ (παροξύτονος) 'stressed penultimate syllable' (Vat. sir. 152, 191v; BL Add. 12178, 141r; cf. Phillips 1869, 22–23). When Jacob and the anonymous author writes about the accent *mḥawwyānā* 'demonstrative,' they quote John 1.29, mentioning that this accent dot is accompanied by an act of pointing with a finger (Phillips 1869, 30). This reference is certainly connected with the Greek grammatical discussion of demonstratives. We could continue, but these references show, with sufficient clarity, that these treatises originated in a milieu where Greek was an integral part of grammatical discussions.

If we try to establish whether these treatises were connected to a specific school, we should look for a place that combined Syriac and Greek education. The bilingual monastery of Qenneshre was the training ground for most of the Miaphysite Bishop-Scholars of the seventh and eighth centuries, including Jacob of Edessa (Tannous 2018, 171). Bar ʿEbroyo mentions that Jacob's education included Greek and the accurate reading of Scripture (Wilmshurst 2016, 100; cf. Salvesen 2008, 1). The system of dots is found already in sixth century manuscripts, so it is not difficult to imagine that Jacob's generation of students learned to read with dots. Quite the contrary, it is actually unlikely that they learned to read the Syriac Bible without dots. Jacob is often thought of as a great innovator, but most of what we find in *On Persons and Tenses*—certainly most of the examples—are found in an earlier treatise, attributed to Thomas the Deacon.

When Phillips edited the treatises in BL Add. 12178 he suggested that Thomas the Deacon was Thomas of Ḥarqel. This suggestion was followed by both Merx and Segal (Phillips 1868, 91–92; Segal 1953, 63–64; Merx and King 2023, 183;). The identification is mainly based on comments made by Bar ʿEbroyo, who writes that Thomas of Ḥarqel equates the two accent dots *mqallsānā* and *yāheḇ ṭūḇā*. Bar ʿEbroyo makes a distinction between these two, but he also writes that the same sign is used for both (Phillips 1869, 52, 92). Thomas' treatise contains the following quote:

> ܝܗܒ ܛܘܒܐ ܐܘܟܝܬ ܡܩܠܣܢܐ.
>
> *yāheḇ ṭūḇā*, that is *mqallsānā* (BL Add. 12178, 240r; Vat. sir. 152, 191v).

Bar ʿEbroyo also writes that Thomas of Ḥarqel viewed *mḥayyḏānā* and *zāqūrā* as one and the same accent dot (Phillips 1869, 55–

56, 92). This comment is found in Thomas' treatise (BL Add. 12178, 240r; Vat. sir. 152, 191v). The anonymous treatise also contains the same observations (BL Add. 12178, 233v, 234r), but it seems more likely that Bar ʿEbroyo is thinking of Thomas' treatise than the anonymous one. If Thomas the Deacon was Thomas of Ḥarqel, it would tie the western treatises closely to Qenneshre, because this is where Thomas was educated (Wilmshurst 2016, 92).

Thomas' treatise could be the earliest one written about accent dots, perhaps in the late sixth century. The title is:

ܬܘܒ ܫܡܗܐ ܕܢܘܩܙܐ ܕܥܒܝܕܝܢ ܠܬܐܘܡܐ ܡܫܡܫܢܐ.

> Again the names of the dots that were made by Thomas the Deacon (BL Add. 12178, 240r; Vat. sir. 152, 191v).

Because virtually all these dots are attested in early manuscripts, it is unlikely that Thomas invented the signs. If this is a sixth century author—the bishop of Ḥarqel or not—it is more likely that this title refers to the names and classification of dots.

The anonymous treatise may be from the same period as Thomas' text and the shared nomenclature suggest that it is part of the same tradition (cf. Phillips 1869, 66–7; Merx and King 2023, 183). If Thomas invented these names, it is possible that this treatise was the product of the late sixth century or the early seventh century. Phillips suggests that it preceded Jacob's treatise because it avoids the subject of compound dots (1869, 67). While both Jacob and Thomas mention compound dots, neither provides what could be considered an exhaustive treatment of the subject. In short, the shared names are sufficient to show that the anonymous treatise is part of the same grammatical tradition as Thomas' treatise, but the more systematic structure probably points to a later date. In fact, this treatise is mentioned in Elias of Ṭirhan's eleventh-century grammar (Petermann 9, 224r).[4]

> ܐܫܟܚܬ ܒܝ ܣܝܥܐ ܕܪܫܝܡ ܠܥܠܘܗܝ، ܕܝܥܩܘܒ ܐܘܪܗܝܐ ܕܡܟܬܒ ܥܠ ܦܘܚܡܐ ܕܡܫܘܕܥ ܥܠ ܦܣܘ̈ܩܝܬܐ ܩܪܐ ܠܗܘܢ ܕܝܢ ܢܝܫܐ ܣܟܪ ܠܗܘܢ ܕܝܢ ܬܚܝܬ ܫܒܥܐ ܙܢ̈ܝܐ.
>
> I found, in a section which was inscribed with 'by Jacob of Edessa', that he wrote about the *puḥḥāmā* which marks sentences. He calls them *nīšā*, confining them to seven categories.

The last observation is intriguing. We know that he is not referring to Jacob's *On Persons and Tenses,* because that treatise does not divide accent dots into seven categories; the longer anonymous treatise is the only extant one that does this. The chapter in Elias' grammar also follows the same structure as this early western treatise. Segal, aware of this reference, suggests that Elias mistakenly ascribed the anonymous treatise to Jacob (1953, 145). Why did Elias make this mistake? There are several possibilities. Perhaps he had a manuscript where this treatise was ascribed to Jacob. Perhaps he had a manuscript like BL Add. 12138; the title of the longer anonymous treatise, in the British Library manuscript, is:

> ܬܘܒ ܡܛܠܠܬܗܘܢ ܕܠܗܘܢ ܕܢܘ̈ܩܙܐ ܗܠܝܢ ܕܐܡܝܢܐ ܡܬܬܢܝܢܐ ܕܡܠܘܬܐ ܕܥܠ ܚܕ ܚܕ ܡܢܗܘܢ܀ ܗܢܘܢ ܕܐܝܟ ܐܢ̈ܫܝܢ ܫܘܦ̈ܠܐ ܐܬܬܘܣܦܘ.

[4] Baethgen (1880); cf. Segal (1953, 145).

> Again, about the same dots: how the place of each one of them is known, which careful men devised (BL Add. 12178, 232r).

Is something missing? Phillips thought so, suggesting that this was a letter, and that its beginning was lost (1869, 66). Another alternative, and an equally plausible one, is that this title refers to the preceding treatise. If so, and if Elias had access to a similar manuscript, he may have assumed that the absence of a named author suggests that this treatise was written by Jacob.

Back to the big picture. One of the western treatises was written by Jacob of Edessa, and can be connected to the school at Qenneshre. The authorship of the other two is uncertain. Thomas of Ḥarqel may be the author of the oldest one, providing another connection to Qenneshre. The author of the third is unknown but the system is close to what we find in Thomas' treatise. It almost certainly comes from the same kind of Greek-Syriac milieu as the other two, and perhaps Jacob was the author. There are, in other words, several possible connections to Qenneshre. This does not mean that the western classification was invented a Qenneshre, although that is certainly possible.

2.2. The Early Eastern Treatise

The eastern Masoretic manuscript, BL Add. 12138, contains one of the most important treatises for understanding the eastern grammatical tradition about accent dots. The treatise is anonymous, and it has a different character than the western treatises. Most of the treatise consists of headings and quotes. The quotes in each heading have the same combination of dots, while headings are used to identify patterns and to distinguish between different clauses with the same pattern.

Where did this treatise originate? The note that mentions red and black ink, specifically mentions the books of Rabban Rāmīšoʿ and the *maqryānē* (cf. Loopstra 215, 409). The treatise, however, contains mostly black dots. It is therefore possible, perhaps even likely, that this is a compilation of material from Nisibis. It is difficult to know whether Babai copied a single treatise or combined material from several treatises; there may even be a trace of Rāmīšoʿ in heading 97 (BL Add. 12137, 307r; Loopstra 2015, 402, 406). Perhaps it is best to conclude that this was a state-of-the-art East Syriac compilation consisting of material available in 899 at the monastery of Mār Gabriel in the city of Ḥarrān (cf. Loopstra 2015, vii–viii).

2.3. Qenneshre and Nisibis

Segal suggests that accent dots eventually become a "recondite subject for written dissertations or for discussion in the schools" (1953, 143). Yet, the schools were always the main place where these theories were discussed. While students were taught how to read the text, and scribes were taught how to point a manuscript, the classification and systematization that we find in these treatises was probably the domain of the masters of the schools. Perhaps it would be better to say that it was always a recondite subject.

3.0. Methodologies and Taxonomies

Phillips found that Jacob's treatise was 'perfectly useless' as a teaching manual for students (1869, vi). This is a harsh judgement. Perhaps he was right, or perhaps he misunderstood its purpose. Regardless, it is essential that we consider the structure and methodology of these treatises. Without this, it is easy to misunderstand what the ancient writers tried to achieve. Here I want to focus on three areas: how accent dots are grouped, the types of names and distinctions that the authors make, and how they use biblical quotations.

3.1. The Grouping of Accent Dots

These ancient treatises have different ways of grouping the various accent dots. Some are more overt: the anonymous treatise has the most systematic and the most clearly defined groups. The other authors are less overt, but the groups are there, nonetheless.

3.1.1. Seven Groups and Four Organising Principles

Seven groups of accents—this is the main organising principle in the anonymous treatise. The author divides 23 accents into seven groups according to the position and shape of the accent dots. These groups are:

(1) dots above the last letter of a word
(2) dots below the last letter of a word
(3) vertical pairs of dots
(4) horizontal pairs of dots
(5) dots above the first letter of a word

(6) dots below the first letter of a word

(7) dots that do not fit into any of the other categories

Some of these classifications may seem arbitrary at first glance. For example, why are *tāḵsā* (ܡܠܟܐ̇) and *rāhṭā ḏlā pāseq* (ܡܠܟܐ̈) not placed in the first group with dots above the last letter.[5] There is a simple reason for this. *Rāhṭā ḏpāseq* (ܡܠܟܐ..) and *rāhṭā ḏlā pāseq* (ܡܠܟܐ̈) have the same shape and related functions: both are used after vocative phrases, the former when there is a pause and the latter when there is no pause. The same is true for *tāḵsā* (ܡܠܟܐ̇) and *šwayā* (ܡܠܟܐ:). The close connection between the latter two is highlighted in the eastern tradition where *šwayā* is called *zāwgā* and *tāḵsā* is called *zāwgā ʿelāyā*. Segal and Merx, however, do not connect the latter two. Segal discusses *tāḵsā* among dots above the last letter and *šwayā* among dots on the line of writing, while Merx classifies *šwayā* as a logical accent and *tāḵsā* 'rebuke' as a rhetorical accent (Segal 1953, 127, 135; Merx and King 2023, 159–161). The grouping in the longer anonymous treatise suggests that, this author saw a connection. Groups (3) and (4) consist of accent dots with the same shape, and these dots alternate between two positions: above the last letter of a word, and on the line of writing after the last letter. There is a similar interchange in group (1), where *ʿelāyā* is a combination of a dot above the last letter of a word and a dot on the line of writing (ܡܠܟܐ.̇), while the other two dots are only placed above the last letter of the word (ܡܠܟܐ̈). The same is true for the accents in

[5] Segal includes all dots where one or all of the dots is placed above the word in the same group (1953, 127–128). This includes all of the dots in group (1), (4), and (5), as well as one of the dots in group (3).

group (2), where *taḥtāyā* and *mḇakkyānā* combine a dot below the last letter with a dot on the line of writing (ܡܠܟܐ̣.), while *sāmkā* is a dot below the last letter (ܡܠܟܐ̣). In short, position and shape are the main organising principles of the anonymous treatise, but not the only ones.

A third principle is function. *Rāhṭā ḏpāseq* (ܡܠܟܐ̈.) and *rāhṭā ḏlā pāseq* (ܡܠܟܐ̈) illustrate this, since both are used to mark vocative phrases. *Taḥtāyā* and *sāmkā* are also used in the same grammatical constructions, e.g., at the end of temporal clauses and after conditional protases (Lundberg 2022, 378–380). The examples in group (5) are also functionally related. Three out of six examples are imperatives and the dot above the first letter of these imperatives is almost certainly connected to their imperative mood or, perhaps more accurately, the rising pitch contour associated with these verbal forms (cf. Lundberg 2025).

The fourth organising principle is pitch contour. This is another reason why *sāmkā* and *taḥtāyā* are placed in the same group, even though they probably mark different types of pauses. This is also the reason why *rāhṭā ḏpāseq* (ܡܠܟܐ̈.) and *rāhṭā dlā pāseq* (ܡܠܟܐ̈) are grouped together. In the eastern tradition *rāhṭā ḏpāseq* consists of three dots: a horizontal pair above the last letter, like *rāhṭā dlā pāseq*, and a dot on the line of writing after the last word (ܡܠܟܐ̈.). This suggests that both dots mark a rising pitch contour. Whether the same is true for *šwayā* and *tāḵsā* is less certain. Regardless, pitch contour appears to be another organising principle in the anonymous treatise. The names, and descriptions of the accent dots, needs to be understood within this framework.

3.1.2. Pausal and Non-pausal Dots

Jacob's treatise *On Persons and Tenses* does not have the same groups as the anonymous treatise. It uses the same names and quotes many of the same examples, but it does not have the same principles governing the grouping of dots. Jacob does not mention that the accent dots can be grouped according to position. Equally important, he does not list them in an order that suggests that position is one of his organising principles.

Pause is the most important principle in this treatise. The first five dots in his list of examples are: *ʿelāyā, taḥtāyā, šwayā, šuḥlāp̄ šwayā*, and *pāsūqā*. The next six are *rāhṭā d̲p̄āseq, mb̲akkyānā, šuḥlāp̄ ʿelāyā, šuḥlāp̄ taḥtāyā, pāqūd̲ā*, and *šḥīmā* (BL Add. 12178, 229v). The list of dots, which precedes the list with examples is similarly structured: *ʿelāyā, taḥtāyā, šwayā, šuḥlāp̄ šwayā, rāhṭā d̲p̄āseq, pāsūqā, mb̲akkyānā, šuḥlāp̄ ʿelāyā, šuḥlāp̄ taḥtāyā, pāqūd̲ā, šḥīmā* (BL Add. 12178, 229r–229v). With the exception of *pāqūd̲ā*, all these accent dots are pausal dots. This suggests that Jacob wanted to highlight the distinction between pausal accent dots and non-pausal accent dots.

There is also a logic to the order of the first 11 accent dots. If we consider these dots through the lens of the anonymous treatise, we might wonder why *ʿelāyā* is not followed by *šuḥlāp̄ ʿelāyā*, or why *taḥtāyā* is not followed by *šuḥlāp̄ taḥtāyā*. Similarly, why is *pāsūqā* the fifth accent dot and *šḥīmā* the eleventh, even though they are identical. The order of these dots show that position is not a key principle. Instead, Jacob divided the pausal dots into two categories: primary pausal dots and variant dots. *ʿelāyā, taḥtāyā, šwayā*, and *pāsūqā* are the primary pausal dots, while the other dots are variants. For example, *taḥtāyā* is primary while *šuḥlāp̄ taḥyāyā* and *mb̲akkyānā* are variants. The perceptive reader might wonder: if this is the case, why is *šuḥlāp̄ šwayā* mentioned among the first five accent dots? I think the answer lies in the specific quotes used to illustrate these accent dots. *Šwayā* is illustrated with a quote from Gen. 6.5 while *šuḥlāp̄ šwayā* is illustrated with a quote from Gen. 6.4. The proximity of these quotes probably influenced the order of the examples. This is probably why *pāqūd̲ā* is mentioned among the pausal dot, since both *pāqūd̲ā* and *šḥīmā* are illustrated with quotes from Joel 2.16. You may have noticed that *rāhṭā d̲p̄āseq* follows *pāsūqā* in in the list of examples, but precedes it in the list of dots. Does this make the order unreliable? Maybe, but only slightly. Crucially, *rāhṭā d̲p̄āseq* does not fit neatly into either category: it is not a variant of a primary accent dot, and there is no **šuḥlāp̄ rāhṭā d̲p̄āseq*. Perhaps Jacob, or a later scribe, first thought of it as primary—placing it before *pāsūqā*—but then changed his mind. This could be an example of an editorial mistake, or the absence of editing. Regardless, this list points to the fact that pause is one of the primary organising principles in this treatise.

The list of examples is then followed by a discussion of identical dots. In this section Jacob compares *rāhṭā d̲p̄āseq* and *rāhṭā d̲lā pāseq*. This is hardly surprising given the almost identical names of these dots, but it is still noteworthy that this is the only instance where he compares a pausal dot with a non-pausal dot.

3.1.3. A List with Some Order

The treatise ascribed to Thomas the Deacon is primarily a list of examples. It does not have the same structure as either of the other two treatises, but it shares some similarities with both. The list of examples begins with *ʿelāyā*, *taḥtāyā*, *sāmkā* and *šwayā*. If we removed *sāmkā* from this list, it would be identical to the order in Jacob's treatise. At the same time, the mention of *sāmkā* after *taḥtāyā* is a nod to the grouping of these two in the anonymous treatise. Another parallel between Thomas and Jacob is the use of quotes from the same context, like the quotes from Gen. 6.4–5 and Joel 2.16. The grouping of quotes is even clearer in Thomas' treatise:

> ܪܗܛܐ ܕܦܣܩ. ܠܐ ܠܟܘܢ ܥܒܪ̈ܝ ܐܘܪܚܐ.. ܙܘܥܐ ܐܬܒܩܘ ܘܚܙܘ.
> ܡܢܚܚܬܐ. ܐܢ ܐܝܬ ܟܐܒܐ ܐܝܟ ܟܐܒܝ ܕܥܒܕ ܠܝ ܡܪܝܐ.
>
> *rāhṭā ḏpāseq*. Is it nothing to you, all you who pass by? (Lam. 1.12) *zawʿā*. 'Look and see' (Lam. 1.12) *mnaḥḥṯā*. 'If there is a sorrow like my sorrow, which the Lord did to me' (Lam. 1.12) (Vat. sir. 152, 192r; cf. BL Add. 12178, 240v).

These three quotes come from the same verse, and they are quoted in order. From a pedagogical perspective it is easy to understand why these quotes are combined. If the student memorised this verse, he would have memorised three accent dots, and he would know how to recite them together.

The combination of accent dots is another characteristic of Thomas' treatise. Jacob writes that most dots can be combined with other dots: e.g., *pāqūḏā* and *sāmkā*, *taḥtāyā* and *sāmkā*, or *zawʿā* and *sāmkā* (BL Add. 12178, 229r; cf. Phillips 1869, 17–18). The anonymous author mentions that he is not going to write about the combination of accent dots. This is another indication that the combination of two or more dots was discussed among the western grammarians. The combination of quotes from Lam. 1.12 also suggests that this was one of the principles influencing the order in Thomas' treatise. This is even clearer in the next example, which lists the compound dot *mšalānā and zawʿā and rāhṭā ḏp̄āseq* (Vat. sir. 152, 192r; BL Add. 12178, 240v).

The combination of accent dots was not central to the western grammatical tradition. These writers are certainly aware that different accent dots were combined in the Syriac Bible, but the masters of this discipline belonged to the eastern grammatical tradition.

3.1.4. A Catalogue of Combinations

On Persons and Tenses gives a few examples of compound dots, but Jacob never attempts to list all the different combinations. The challenge of making such a list is highlighted by the early eastern treatise (BL Add. 12138, 303v–308r). It contains several hundred quotes divided into 134 headings. While some of these headings contain the same combination of accent dots, it is safe to say that this is a monumental task.

What can the structure of this treatise tell us about the organising principles of the eastern grammarians? The first and perhaps the most important observation, must be the importance of compound dots. The eastern grammarians would never have written this treatise if they were convinced that these accent dots were used in isolation.

The eastern treatise also has a clear structure that mirrors something we see in Jacob's treatise. After the list of pausal dots, Jacob gives four examples of *tāḵsā*: one with *tāḵsā* alone, and three examples where it is combined with other accent dots: *tāḵsā* (Lam. 2.20), *tāḵsā* and *šwayā* (Jer. 5.9), *tāḵsā* and *mšalānā* (2 Kgs 2.18), *tāḵsā* and *taḥtāyā* (Luke 12.28). The eastern treatise does something very similar, but on a much larger scale. In fact, the treatise begins with the following headings:

1. ***taḥtāyā*** *šḥīmā*
2. ***znā ḥrēnā*** 'another kind'
3. ***taḥtāyā*** *ḏreṯme*
4. *pāqoḏā* and ***taḥtāyā***
5. ***znā ḥrēnā*** 'another kind'

The first heading is followed by four examples illustrating the use of *taḥtāyā* without any other accent dots. The same is true for the examples in the second heading which has the title 'another kind'. The first 41 headings in this treatise contain compound dots where *taḥtāyā* is combined with other accent dots. This is the overarching structure of the eastern treatises:

Headings	Dots
1–41	Combinations with *taḥtāyā*
42–51	Combinations with *zāwgā*
52–64	Combinations with *ʿelāyā*
65	Combinations with *mḏammrānā*
66–72	Combinations with *mšalānā*
73–79	Combinations with *meṯkaššpānā*
80–92	Combinations with *rāhṭā*
93–134	Combinations with *pāsoqā*

This division of headings reveals several things about the methodology and classification of the eastern treatise. Almost half of the headings are devoted to combinations with the three pausal dots *taḥtāyā, zāwgā* and *ʿelāyā*, and almost a third of the treatise is devoted to combinations with *pāsoqā*. This shows that the pausal dots were very important to the eastern grammarians. It is interesting that, in spite of all the quotes and headings in this treatise, there is no heading that lists compound dots with more than one of the pausal dots *taḥtāyā, zāwgā, ʿelāyā*, and *pāsoqā*. The exception is perhaps a few of the headings in the section about *ʿelāyā*, which lists examples *after ʿelāyā* (ܒܬܪ ܥܠܝܐ), but even these quotes contain only one pausal dot. This structure suggests that the eastern grammarians thought of compound dots as a string of non-pausal accent dots followed by a single pausal dot.

The eastern grammarians also listed similar constructions under the same heading. Three examples from headings 4, 5, and 16 can illustrate this:

ܡܢܐ ܥܒܕ: ܐܢܬ ܗܪܟܐ ܐܠܝܐ.

What are you doing here, Elijah? (1 Kgs 19.9; BL Add. 12138, 303v)

ܫܠܡܘ ܛܠܝܐ.

Are the sons complete? (1 Sam. 16.11; BL Add. 12138, 303v)

ܐܢܬ ܠܟ ܕܪܥܐ ܐܝܟ ܕܐܠܗܐ.

Do you have an arm like God? (Job 40.9; BL Add. 12138, 304r)

Heading 4, where we find the first quote, has three variable questions beginning with the interrogative word ܡܢܐ 'what'. The second quote comes from heading 5, which contains two polar questions and a statement. Lastly, heading 16 has five polar questions of the same kind as Job 40.9. Why are these quotes placed under different headings? One could argue that the examples in headings 4 and 5 illustrate variable questions and polar questions with the same pattern. The repetition of the heading *pāqoḏā and taḥtāyā* in 16 might seem odd, but these questions, although polar, are highly biased. The division of these questions into three different headings shows that the type of construction was an important organising principle for the early eastern grammarians, even if this treatise does not mention or define these grammatical categories.

The eastern treatise has three levels of division. The first level divides constructions into larger groups, focusing on eight accent dots: *taḥtāyā, zāwgā, ʿelāyā, mḏammrānā, mšalānā, meṯkašspānā, rāhṭā* and *pāsoqā.* The second level divides the larger groupings into smaller groups where each quote has the same dotting pattern, e.g., *pāqoḏā and taḥtāyā.* Some headings, especially those with the title 'another kind', differentiate between clauses with the same dotting pattern. Structurally, the eastern approach is radically different from the approach of the western grammarians and they take the discussion of compound dots to another level.

3.2. How to Make Distinctions

3.2.1. Names as Categories

We have seen that the eastern grammarians use different headings to distinguish between different types of constructions with the same dotting pattern. The early western tradition used additional names to make similar distinctions. For example, the first group in the longer anonymous treatise consists of three accent dots: *ʿelāyā*, *ʿeṣyānā*, and *zawʿā*. *ʿelāyā* is distinguished from the other two because it consists of two dots: one on the line of writing and one above the last letter. There is nothing visual to distinguish between *ʿeṣyānā* and *zawʿā*. The difference between these dots is explained as follows:

> ܒ܀ ܟܕ ܕܝܢ ܗܘ ܢܘܩܙܐ ܢܫܬܟܚ ܕܣܝܡ ܐܝܟܐ ܕܐܡܝܪܐ: ܣܛܪ ܡܢ ܗܘ ܕܦܣܩ ܠܦܬܓܡܐ: ܟܕ ܠܝܬ ܣܩܘܒܠܗ ܕܗܢܐ ܚܕ ܡܢ ܡ̈ܐܡܪܐ ܗܢܘܢ ܕܒܬܪܗ܁ ܠܗܢܐ ܚܢܢ ܩܪܝܢܢ ܥܨܝܢܐ. ܐܝܟ ܗܝ ܕܐܡܝܪܐ܇ ܒܗܘ ܝܘܡܐ ܬܕܥܘܢ ܕܐܢܐ ܒܐܒܝ܆ ܘܐܢܬܘܢ ܒܝ ܐܢܬܘܢ܀ ܓ܀ ܐܡܬܝ، ܬܘܒ ܕܗܘ ܦܣܩܐ: ܐܝܟ ܕܐܝܬܘܗܝ، ܢܩܘܦ: ܘܡܫܩܘܒܠܗ ܕܗܢܐ ܢܫܬܟܚ ܚܕ ܡܢ ܡ̈ܐܡܪܐ ܕܒܬܪܗ܁ ܠܗܢܐ ܙܘܥܐ ܩܪܝܢ. ܐܝܟ ܗܝ ܕܐܡܝܪܐ. ܕܠܐ ܐܬܝܬ ܕܐܫܪܐ ܢܡܘܣܐ ܐܠܐ ܕܐܡܠܐ.
>
> 2. When a dot is found, which is placed where it is said; without the one that pauses the *peṯḡāmā* [pausal unit]; when it is not contrary to one of the words that follow it; this one, we call *ʿeṣyānā*, just as it is said: 'On that day you will know that I am in my Father, **and** you are in me' (John 14.20). 3. Again, when this dot remains as it is, and it is found contrary to one of the words that follow it, this is called *zawʿā*, as it is said: 'I did not come to abolish the law **but** to fulfil' (Matt. 5.17) (BL Add. 12178, 232v–233r).

The difference between these two, according to this treatise, is the relationship between the phrases. The key term is ܣܘܩܒܠܐ 'contrary'. In John 14.20 there is no contrast between the two clauses, but there is one in Matthew 5.17, marked by the contrastive conjunction *ʾellā* 'but'.

Jacob also distinguishes between *ʿeṣyānā* and *zawʿā*, but his definition is based on the presence or absence of *sāmkā*:

> ܥܨܝܢܐ ܕܝܢ ܘܙܘܥܐ ܡܬܦܪܫܝܢ ܟܕ. ܕܥܨܝܢܐ ܠܚܘܕܝܗ ܗܘ ܒܦܬܓܡܐ.
> ܘܙܘܥܐ ܕܝܢ ܥܡ ܣܡܟܐ ܡܬܬܣܝܡ܀
>
> Now *ʿeṣyānā* and *zawʿā* are distinguished because *ʿeṣyānā* is alone in the *peṯgāmā*, but *zawʿā* is placed with *sāmkā* (BL Add. 12178, 231r).

Like the western treatises, the eastern treatise has two accent dots that are placed above the last letter of a word: *reṯmā* and *mziʿānā* (cf. Weiss, 1933, 48, 50; Loopstra 2015, lxvi, lxxxi). Here it is not necessary to try to distinguish between these dots, but it is important to note that the authors of the early eastern treatise do not provide a definition of either dot.

This brings us to the large number of names in the western treatises. The anonymous treatise mentions 23 accent dots and Jacob adds more dots to this list. The dots mentioned in the eastern treatise are fewer, but this does not mean that western manuscripts had more accent dots. On the contrary, eastern manuscripts often have more dots than western ones. The difference is that the western tradition used names to make distinctions. One example is the distinction between *ʿeṣyānā* and *zawʿā*. Another example is the distinctions between some of the accent dots placed above the first letter of a word. The three dots *qārūyā*, *pāqūḏā*, and *mp̄īsānā* are placed above imperatives, but in different types of constructions.

> ❖ܝܕ❖❖ ܕܬܠܝܬܝܐ ܕܝܢ ܐܝܟ ܗܝ ܕܐܬܐܡܪܬ ܠܦܪܘܩܢ ܡܠܬܐ ܐܠܗܐ
> ܒܐܘܢ̈ܓܠܝܘܢ ܕܝܠܗ܇ ܕܬܘ ܟܠܟܘܢ ܠܠܐܝ̈ܐ ܘܫܩܝܠܝ ܡܘܒ̈ܠܐ ܘܐܢܐ
> ܐܢܝܚܟܘܢ ❖ܗܘ❖ ܕܐܪ̈ܒܥܐ ܐܝܟ ܗܝ ܐܬܐ ܕܐܬܐܡܪܬ ܡܢ ܝܘܢܬܢ ܠܘܬ
> ܛܠܝܐ܇ ܕܙܠ ܠܘܩܛ ܓܐܪ̈ܐ ܕܐܢܐ ܫܕܐ. ❖ܗܘ❖ ܕܚܡܫܐ ܕܝܢ ܕܐܝܟ ܗܢܐ
> ܐܝܬܘܗܝ܆ ܐܡܬܝ ܕܡܢ ܗܘ ܕܙܥܘܪ ܠܘܬ ܗܘ ܕܪܒ ܡܬܩܪܒܐ ܡܠܬܐ܇ ܐܝܟ
> ܗ̈ܢܝܢ ܕܗܘ ܒܪܐ ܐܣܘܛܐ ܠܘܬ ܐܒܘܗܝ ܡܬܚܫܒ ܗܘܐ ܕܢܐܡܪ. ܕܥܒܕܝܢ
> ܐܝܟ ܚܕ ܡܢ ܐ ܐܓܝ̈ܪܝܟ. ܘܗܝ، ܕܡܢ ܐ̈ܢܫܐ ܒܒܥܘܬܐ ܠܘܬ ܐܠܗܐ ܡܬܩܪܒܐ
> ܕܐܥܒܪ ܚܛ̈ܗܝܢ. ܠܚܝ ܥܘ̈ܠܢ. ܠܐ ܬܬܕܟܪ ܠܢ ܣܟ̈ܠܘܬܢ. ܗܢܐ
> ܡܦܝܣܢܐ ܡܬܩܪܐ. ܡܕܝܢ ܗܘ ܟܕ ܗܘ ܦܩܘܕܐ ܘܡܦܝܣܢܐ. ܟܕ ܡܢ ܗܘ ܕܪܒ
> ܠܘܬ ܗܘ ܕܙܥܘܪ ܡܬܐܡܪ ܦܩܘܕܐ ܗܘ. ܡܛܠ ܕܦܩܘܕܐܝܬ ܡܬܐܡܪ. ܐܢܕܝܢ
> ܐܝܟ ܕܗܦܟܐ ܡܦܝܣܢܐ❖

> 14. Now the third [*qārūyā*] is as was said by our saviour, the word of God, in his gospels: '**Come** all of you who are weary and carry burdens and I will give you rest' (Matt. 11.28) The fourth [*pāqūḏā*] is like the sign that was spoken by Jonathan to the boy: '**Go** and **take** the arrow that I shoot' (1 Sam. 20.36). 'Now the fifth [*mp̄īsānā* 'petition'] is like this, when a word from one who is small approaches one who is great, as those which the prodigal son planned to say to his father '**Receive** me as one of your hired workers' (Luke 15.19), and that which is brought from men to God to pass over sins: '**Blot out** our iniquities, **do not remember** our foolish wrongdoing'. This is called *mp̄īsānā*. Consequently, when is it *pāqūḏā* and *mp̄īsānā*? When from he who is great to he who is small, it is called *pāqūḏā* because it is spoken commandingly; now if it is as the opposite, it is *mp̄īsānā* (BL Add. 12178, 233v–234r).

The name *pāqoḏā* is used in the eastern tradition for each of these dots even though the imperatives have slightly different functions in each sentence. *Pāqoḏā* is also used for dots above interjections or demonstratives, where the western tradition uses the name *mḥawwyānā* 'demonstrative'. The point is not so much that the western grammarians made distinctions that the eastern tradition did not—although, they did—but that these treatises used names differently and that they made different types of distinctions.

3.2.2. Patterns, Headings, and Different Constructions

The structure and nomenclature of these treatises gives them certain possibilities. Heading 25 in the eastern treatise has the title *pāqoḏā and taḥtāyā* and contains a set of questions:

ܐܢܬ ܗܘ ܝܘܐܒ:

Are you Joab? (2 Sam. 20.17; BL Add. 12138, 304v)

ܢܡܚܐ ܠܗܘܢ ܒܣܦܣܪܐ:

Shall we strike them with the sword? (Luke 22.49; BL Add. 12138, 304v)

The questions in this heading are confirmation-seeking questions. This means that headings 5, 16, and 25 contain examples of polar questions with the pattern *pāqoḏā and taḥtāyā*. The questions in 5 are neutral questions, the questions in 16 are strongly biased or rhetorical questions, and the questions in 25 are confirmation-seeking questions. The use of different headings shows that the eastern grammarians were aware of these types of distinctions.

One of the advantages of the eastern nomenclature is that it allows the grammarians to place different questions in the same categories. These two are among the biased questions in heading 16, and both have a dot above the first word:

ܚ̇ܙܐ ܐܢܬ ܒܪܢܫܐ:

Do you see, son of man? (Ezek. 8.12; BL Add. 12138, 304r)

ܗ̇ܐ ܬܦܘܩ ܥܓܠܬܐ ܒܙܒܢܗ:

Do you bring out the chariot in its season? (Job 38.32; BL Add. 12138, 304r)

As the heading suggests, this dot was called *pāqoḏā*. In the second question the dot is placed above the interjection ܗ̇ܐ. This example is not quoted by the western grammarians, but Jacob's *On Persons and Tenses* contains quotes from John 1.29 and 1.30, which suggest that *mḥawwyānā* was the western name used for dots above the interjection ܗ̇ܐ and the demonstrative ܗ̇ܢܐ:

ܡܚܘܝܢܐ ܕܐܝܟ ܐܝܟ ܗܘ ܕܒܨܒܥܐ ܡܚܘܐ ܐܝܟ ܗܝ ܕܐܡܝܪܐ: ܕܗܐ ܐܡܪܗ ܕܐܠܗܐ ܗܘ ܕܫܩܠ ܚܛܝܬܗ ܕܥܠܡܐ. ܘܬܘܒ ܗ̇ܢܘ ܗܘ ܕܐܡܪܬ ܕܒܬܪܝ ܐܬܐ.܀

mḥawwyānā is just as when one shows with the finger, as it is said: 'Behold the lamb of God, who takes away the sins of the world'; and again 'This is the one about whom I said: "He comes after me"' (BL Add. 12178, 231r).

Would the western grammarians use *mḥawwyānā* for the dot in Job 38.32? *Pāqūḏā* is used when someone speaks commandingly, so it is unlikely that they would have used that term. Perhaps they could use *mšalānā* for the first dot, since this is a question, although *On Persons and Tenses* also contains a reference that suggests that the name *mšalānā* could be used for the dot at the end of polar questions. When Elias of Ṭirhan, working with the longer anonymous treatise, mentions the eastern names of dots, he says that they call the pattern in John 1.29 *pāqoḏā* and *pāsoqā* (Petermann 9, 224v; Baethgen 1880, 53, لد). While some of these terms can be reconciled more easily than others, it is clear that there was no universal terminology.

3.3. The Use of Biblical Quotations

The use of quotations is one of the areas where the western and eastern treatises differ most. The western treatises typically provide one quotation for each dot, although Jacob provides a few more examples when he lists compound dots, and in the discussion of similar accent dots. Nevertheless, this approach is fundamentally different from the approach of the eastern treatise.

A comparison between the quotes in the western treatises show that they often quote the same passages. For example, the same quotes are used to illustrate *ʿelāyā*, *ʿeṣyānā*, *taḥtāyā*, *šwayā*, *mḥawwyānā*, *qārūyā*, *pāqūḏā*, and *mḇaṭṭlānā*. They also use the same phrase to illustrate *mṣallyānā*. It is somewhat surprising that no quote is used to exemplify *pāsūqā*, but that is another feature these treatises share. The longer anonymous treatise and the treatise of Thomas the Deacon also use the same quote for *šrāyā*, *mšalānā*, *mp̄īsānā*, *metdammrānā*, and *mnaḥḥṯā*—and both treatises have what looks like a reference to the beatitudes, illustrating *yāheḇ ṭūḇā*. Jacob and Thomas also share quotes. They use the same passages to illustrate *tāḵsā*, *rāhṭā ḏp̄āseq*, *mp̄īsānā*, *metdammrānā*, and *mnaḥḥṯā*. Jacob sometimes uses several quotes, and in the case of *tāḵsā*, he also shares a quote with the anonymous author.

Accent Dot	Anonymous Treatise	Thomas the Deacon	Jacob's Treatise
ʿelāyā	Matt. 1.1	Matt. 1.1	Matt. 1.1
ʿeṣyānā	John 14.20	John 14.20	John 14.20
zawʿā	Matt. 5.17	Lam. 1.12	Ezek. 28.13
taḥtāyā	Acts 1.1	Acts 1.1	Acts 1.1
sāmkā	Ps. 104.15	John 1.1	Prov. 2.21–22, John 1.1
mṣallyānā or metkaššpānā	'I seek you'	'I seek you'	'I seek you'
šwayā	Gen. 6.5	Gen. 6.5	Gen. 6.5
tāksā	Ps. 94.9	Lam. 2.20	Ps. 94.9, Lam. 2.20, etc.
šrāyā	Rom. 11.36	Rom. 11.36	Gen. 6.4
rāhṭā dlā pāseq	Lam. 5.1	Lam. 2.20	Ps. 9.14 and Bar. 2.16[6]
rāhṭā dpāseq	Ps. 88.15	Lam. 1.12	Lam. 1.12, Ps. 9.14
mhawwyānā	John 1.29	John 1.29	John 1.29
mšalānā	John 11.34	John 11.34	Gen. 4.9
qārūyā	Matt. 11.28	Matt. 11.28	Matt. 11:28 etc.
pāqūdā	1 Sam. 20.36	1 Sam. 20:36	1 Sam. 2036 etc.
mpīsānā	Luke 15.19	Luke 15.19; Liturgical phrases	Liturgical phrases
yāheb ṭūbā	Reference to beatitudes	Reference to Beatitudes	Ps. 1.1

[6] Jacob illustrates this *rāhṭā* with a quote that appears to be built on two quotes, perhaps Bar. 2.16 and Ps. 9.14.

metdammrānā	2 Sam. 1.25	Ob. 6, Lam. 2.1, 2 Sam. 1.25	Ob. 6, Ps. 73.19
mnaḥḥṭā	Gospel reference (Matt. 4.21)	Lam. 1:12, Gospel reference (Matt. 4.21)	Lam. 1.12
mbaṭṭlānā	John 1.1	John 1.1, etc.	John 1.1, etc.
pāsūqā	no quote	no quote	no quote

In short, the same examples were recycled, much like the use of examples in many modern reference grammars. While the shared material is both relevant and interesting, it also limits the scope of these treatises. The small number of examples makes it difficult to determine where specific dots were used and how often. The pausal dots are very good examples of this. *Pāsūqā*—the dot which resembles a full stop—is more common than any of the other pausal dots, but these treatises give no examples of where this dot is used. They only mention that it is placed at the end of a *peṯgāmā*, a term which refers to a pausal unit.

In the anonymous treatise, *taḥtāyā* and *mṣallyānā* are identical, and in Jacob's treatise *taḥtāyā*, *mḇakkyānā*, and *šuḥlāp̄ taḥtāyā* are identical. In each quote, these dots are placed after a vocative phrase. This means that we have several examples of double dots that look like *taḥtāyā*—one dot on the line of writing and one dot beneath the last letter. A survey of Syriac manuscripts, including the Masoretic codices, would yield further examples of this dot at the end of vocative phrases. Yet, this is not the only environment where these dots are used and, as other examples show, *rāhṭā ḏpāseq*, *rāhṭā ḏlā pāseq*, and *ʿelāyā* can also be used after a vocative phrase. If we rely on these quotations to provide a comprehensive picture of the use of these dots, our understanding will be hampered and limited by the small and non-representative sample. The dot called *ʿelāyā* is exemplified by a quote from Matthew 1.1 and Jacob adds James 1.2 as a variant: *šuḥlāp̄ ʿelāyā*. The contexts are different: the former is followed by a noun phrase which provides additional information about Jesus, and the quote from James 1.2 follows a vocative phrase. Still, these are only two examples. It is difficult to determine where these dots should be used based on this sample. I suspect that there is a reason behind this choice. Even if Jacob add a few more examples than the anonymous treatise, it is unlikely that he tried to be comprehensive. These examples are not meant to cover all the possible constructions where different dots were used. As I mentioned in the introduction, and as I have argued elsewhere, the accent dots were either used to mark boundary tones at the end of a phrase, or a rising pitch contour associated with a specific word (Lundberg 2022, 2025). This could explain why the western grammarians only mentioned one or, occasionally, two examples. If the student memorised Matthew 1.1 and Acts 1.1, or had heard the beginning of these books recited, these examples would be sufficient to show him which boundary tones *ʿelāyā* and *taḥtāyā* marked.

3.4. A Long List of Examples

The eastern treatise has a rather different approach to biblical quotations. Some of these quotes may have been well known, and it is possible that students had memorised some of them, but the large number of quotes makes this less probable. Some quotes come from the same passage, but this is not the norm, suggesting that these quotations were chosen because they were good examples of a particular dotting pattern or grammatical construction, not because they were next to another example. Heading 16 illustrates strongly biased polar questions with the pattern *pāqoḏā* and *taḥtāyā*. Three of the quotes are drawn from the end of Job (38.32, 39.20, 40.9); presumably, this is because these chapters contain a large number of biased polar questions, making it an excellent place to find quotations.

The different use of accent dots is also underscored by the fact that the eastern treatise draws on a different set of quotations. Only a small number of passages in the western treatises are also quoted in the eastern treatise, even though the latter contains a very large number of quotations. Perhaps this is not surprising, given that there are often hundreds or thousands of examples that the grammarians could quote.

There is a convergence between the western and eastern tradition at one point. This happens when the grammarians quote examples of western *metdammrānā* and eastern *mḏammrānā*. These dots look different: in the western treatises it is a dot below the first letter, and in the eastern tradition it is a pair of dots placed above the first letter. Heading 65 is the only one in the eastern treatise that mentions *mḏammrānā*. This is rather unusual, but it underscores the fact that this accent dot and the constructions where it is used are very rare. This means that both traditions had relatively few examples to draw from.

4.0. The Origin and Purpose of these Treatises

The descriptive capabilities of these treatises are limited. Phillips called Jacob's *On Persons and Tenses* 'perfectly useless' (1869, vi). He could have said this about any of the early western treatises, or the eastern treatise. If we read the western treatises to understand when and where to place specific accent dots, we may come away with more questions than answers. For example, when should you use a *taḥtāyā*? It is used in Acts 1.1 after the vocative phrase 'Theophilus' (ܬܐܘܦܝܠܐ.), but that is not the only place where it is used. This accent dot is regularly used after vocative phrases so this is perhaps a good example, but this is not sufficient to teach us when to use *taḥtāyā*. Jacob also lists examples where *rāhṭā ḏpāseq*, *mḇakkyānā*, *šuḥlāp̄ 'elāyā*, and *šuḥlāp̄ taḥtāyā* are placed after vocatives. This shows that all of these dots could follow vocatives, but it also limits the scope of the description. This leads to several conclusions: first, the western treatises were not meant to teach students a theory about accent dots. Second, if the accent dots mark a phrase boundary, the reader does not need a lot of examples; one or two might suffice, especially if the examples are taught by someone who knows how to recite them, like a *maqryānā*. Third, the western treatises are more descriptive than prescriptive. Crucially, it is about classification, and they are not trying to teach anyone how to point a manuscript.

The eastern treatise is in many ways much more comprehensive than its western counterparts. It contains a plethora of examples illustrating different combinations of dots as well as different constructions with the same patterns. Like the western treatises, it is descriptive. The feature that makes this treatise difficult to understand is the absence of terminology and explanations. Like the examples in the western treatises, this collection of examples could have been used to teach students to recite the Syriac Bible. The large number of examples and combinations of dots would have allowed students to learn how to recite different clauses, and to associate certain patterns with specific grammatical constructions.

I think it is important to keep in mind that these treatises were probably not produced for self-study. In fact, while these examples could have been used by students to learn how to recite the Syriac Bible, these treatises were not necessarily handbooks for students to read. If we assume that the reader has memorised and studied portions of the Syriac Bible and that he has learned how to recite these texts, then these treatises are neither perfectly useless nor a tiresome mess, they are simply a compendium of examples that can be used to teach students.

References

Baethgen, Friedrich (ed.). 1880. *Syrische Grammatik des Mar Elias von Tirhan*. Leipzig: Hinrichs.

Becker, Adam H. 2006. *Fear of God and the Beginning of Wisdom: The School of Nisibis and Christian Scholastic Culture in Late Antique Mesopotamia*. Philadelphia: University of Pennsylvania Press.

Loopstra, Jonathan (ed.). 2014. *An East Syrian Manuscript of the Syriac "Masora" Dated to 899 CE: A Facsimile Reproduction of British Library, Add. MS 12138*. Piscataway, NJ: Gorgias Press.

———. (ed.). 2015. *An East Syrian Manuscript of the Syriac "Masora" Dated to 899 CE: Introduction, List of Sample Texts, and Indices to Marginal Notes in British Library, Additional MS 12138*. Piscataway, NJ: Gorgias Press.

Lundberg, Johan M. V. (2022). 'Dots, Versification and Grammar'. *Dead Sea Discoveries: A Journal of Current Research on the Scrolls and Related Literature* 29 (3): 366–387.

———. 2025. 'Dots and Word Stress in Classical East Syriac'. In *Interconnected Traditions: Semitic Languages, Literatures, Cultures: A Festschrift for Geoffrey Khan*, edited by Aaron D. Hornkohl et al., 821–842. Cambridge: Open Book Publishers.

Martin, J. P. P. 1875. *Histoire de la ponctuation ou de la Massore chez les Syriens*. Paris: Impr. Nationale.

Merx, Adalbert, and Daniel King. 2023. *A History of the Study of Grammar among the Syrians: An English Translation of Historia Artis Grammaticae Apud Syros*. Piscataway, NJ: Gorgias Press.

Phillips, George (ed.). 1869. *A Letter by Mār Jacob, Bishop of Edessa, on Syriac Orthography: Also a Tract by the Same Author, and a Discourse by Gregory Bar Hebrœus on Syriac Accents*. London: Williams and Norgate.

Posegay, Nick. 2021. 'Men of Letters in the Syriac Scribal Tradition: Dawid Bar Pawlos, Rabban Rāmišoʿ, and the Family of Beṯ Rabban'. *Hugoye* 24 (1): 127–186.

Salvesen, Alison. 2008. 'Jacob of Edessa's Life and Work: A Biographical Sketch'. In *Jacob of Edessa and the Syriac Culture of His Day*, edited by Bas Ter Haar Romeny, 1–10. Leiden: Brill.

Segal, Judah B. 1953. *The Diacritical Point and the Accents in Syriac*. London: Oxford University Press.

Tannous, Jack Boulos Victor. 2018. *The Making of the Medieval Middle East: Religion, Society, and Simple Believers*. Princeton: Princeton University Press.

Weiss, Theodor. 1933. *Zur ostsyrischen Laut- und Akzentlehre: auf Grund der ostsyrischen Massorah-Handschrift des British Museum; mit Facsimiles von 50 Seiten der Londoner Handschrift*. Stuttgart: W. Kohlhammer.

Wilmshurst, David (ed.). 2016. *Bar Hebraeus. The Ecclesiastical Chronicle: An English Translation*. Piscataway, NJ: Gorgias Press.

MULTIMODALITY IN LITURGICAL EXPRESSION: THE CASE OF TEXTUALITY AND ORALITY IN SYRIAC ORTHODOX LITURGIES[1]

George A. Kiraz

Liturgical texts can be thought of as palimpsests. While the term was originally coined to describe ancient manuscripts or leaves that have been written on, erased, and then written over again with new texts, its scope has been broadened in literary and cultural studies to refer to texts—even objects—that reflect layers of history or multiple iterations over time (Kalaga et al. 2011; Colwell 2022). Notwithstanding Anton Baumstark's seminal work on comparative liturgy (1958), one can think of liturgical texts as layers that interact with versions that have preceded them, often revealing a complex and interwoven relationship between different time periods that go back to Late Antiquity.

Indeed, the earliest forms of Syriac liturgical expression hail from the fourth and fifth centuries, primarily in the form of

---

[1] I am grateful to Roger Akhrass (aka Mor Severus) for reading a penultimate version and making many valuable suggestions. Baby Varghese answered questions regarding Malankara publications. Many thanks are also due to two anonymous reviewers.

 https://doi.org/10.11647/OBP.0498.03

poetry (Brock 2011). Ephrem of Nisibis (d. 373) is the most famous of poets who produced texts for liturgical use, followed by other known and anonymous authors. Some of their poetry made it to the modern period.[2] As such, metrical and stanzaic texts become a cornerstone of Syriac worship, contrasted with prose texts. How all this poetry was incorporated in a liturgical schema is less understood (Varghese 2020; 2021).

It is only from the sixth and seventh centuries that we begin to receive liturgical texts in the genre of ܛܟܣ̈ܐ *tekse* or 'orders'. That is, texts with prose and poetic elements, marked by some sort of heading or rubric that give a hint of structured services. We know this from later manuscripts that are attributed to writers of this period, most notably Jacob of Edessa (d. 708) in the West Syriac rite.

Jacob's function was that of a reformer, restructuring existing texts, probably adapting them to the needs of his time. Jacob was active a century or so after intense Christological conflicts that widened the gap between the East and West Syriac rites. His activities also coincide with the Islamic *Futūḥ* or conquests. How much these socioreligious and sociopolitical changes affected the reform of liturgical texts is hard to know. Another reform was the introduction of a genre unique to the West Syriac rite known as *sedre* or 'ordered [lists of] petitions'. The Syriac Orthodox Patriarch John (d. 648) put together a good number of *sedre* so much

[2] One hymn that quite known to the faithful of the Syriac Orthodox tradition is Ephrem's ܗܘ ܡܠܟܐ ܒܡܪܘܡ that became ܗܘ ܡܠܟܐ ܗܘ ܒܡܪܘܡ for metrical purposes. See Brock's translation (Brock and Kiraz 2006, 112–121). The metrical aspects are discussed by George Kiraz (2024, 178).

that he was named 'John of *Sedre*'. Whether Jacob and John committed oral elements to writing is difficult to ascertain as transmission history is not so kind to liturgical manuscripts: they tend to get replaced often by newer ones. One of the very few manuscripts that survived—British Library Add. 17,129 from the seventh or eighth century (Wright 1870, I:383)—gives the ܛܟܣܐ ܕܒܘܪܟ ܡܝ̈ܐ ܕܥܐܕܐ ܕܕܢܚܐ 'the Order of the Blessing of Water of Epiphany'. The title continues, ܐܝܟ ܕܢܩܦ ܡܬܦܫܩ ܡܢ ܝܘܢܝܐ ܠܣܘܪܝܝܐ 'as it was *recently* translated from Greek into Syriac', another indication of the reform activities of this early period.

A few more liturgical manuscripts exist from the ninth and tenth centuries. For example, a later monk at Deir al-Suryān in Egypt named Malachus was the user of British Library Add. 14,494 (Wright 1870, I:217–218), consisting of many *tekse* 'orders': ܛܟܣܐ ܕܒܘܪܟ ܡܝ̈ܐ ܕܕܢܚܐ 'the Order of the Blessing of Water of Epiphany', ܛܟܣܐ ܕܫܝܓܬܐ ܒܚܡܫܒܫܒܐ ܕܐܪ̈ܙܐ 'the Order of the Washing [of the feet] on the Thursday of Mysteries', ܛܟܣܐ ܕܣܓܕܬܐ ܕܨܠܝܒܐ ܒܥܪܘܒܬܐ ܕܚܫܐ 'the Order of the Adoration of the Cross on the Friday of Passion', in addition to a collection of *sedre*. While a modern user can recognise elements and texts here and there, the liturgical schemata of this period remain understudied. It is only with manuscripts from the Early Modern period that we begin to see recognizable content and structure. In theory, a modern clergy can pick up a late manuscript and *use* it.

This does not necessarily imply that the modern user can perform the liturgical rites in the exact manner as those who wrote them. This is so because liturgical expression is multimodal. There is the written and the oral. There is the audible and the inaudible. And there is the kinaesthetic—physical movement (e.g., extending the hands, making the sign of the cross) and physical engagement with objects (e.g., lifting a spoon, waving a cloth). It is this complex, multimodal interplay that is the focus of this paper.

Section 1 gives an overview of the textual repository of the Syriac Orthodox tradition, with references to modern editions that have become standard.[3] Section 2 describes the liturgical space (in order to give us a visual of *where* the texts are physically placed) and the timing of the canonical hours. Section 3 delves into the interplay between textuality and orality, audibility and inaudibility. Finally, section 4 gives a few concluding remarks.

Throughout, I make use of the term 'Received Tradition' referring to texts that have been passed down to us through generations of scribes and are accepted and practiced in the present day. This is arguably the last palimpsest layer—thus far—in a long transmission. I make no effort to connect the Received Tradition with earlier layers, a task that must await further developments in Syriac liturgical studies.

1.0. Textuality Repository

Barsoum, in his *Kitāb al-Luʾluʾ al-Manthūr* (Barsoum 1956, ch. 15), gives an account of Syriac Orthodox liturgical texts.[4] The most frequent among them in terms of usage is the Liturgy of the Hours. Textually, weekday texts are found in the book of *Šḥimo*

[3] Books with titles in the Latin script give the Latin-script title; otherwise, the Syriac title is given.

[4] All subsequent references to Barsoum are from this 1956 work.

(Barsoum, ch. 15, §2), called so since weekdays are known as ܝܘ̈ܡܐ ܫܚܝ̈ܡܐ *yawme šḥime* 'simple days'. The standard edition was prepared by Barsoum himself.[5] The text follows the days of the week in sequence. Texts for Sundays and feast days are split by genre (poetry vs prose): poetic material is found in the *Phenqitho* (Barsoum, §§5–7), while prose material (opening Prayer, *Ḥusoyo*, *ʿEṭro*, and concluding Prayer) in the book of *Ḥusoyo*. Each comes in four primary volumes that cover the entire year cycle:

1. Winter volume starts off with the Sunday of the Sanctification of the Church (ܩܘܕܫ ܥܕܬܐ) (the first Sunday of the liturgical calendar) up to the Sunday before the beginning of Lent[6]
2. Lent volume covers the Lent period (ܨܘܡܐ ܪܒܐ)
3. Passion volume covers Passion Week (ܚܫܐ)
4. Summer volume covers the Resurrection period (ܩܝܡܬܐ)

A fifth volume covers Feasts of the Lord (ܥܐܕ̈ܐ ܡܪ̈ܢܝܐ: Christmas, Circumcision, Epiphany, Entrance to the Temple, Palm Sunday, Resurrection, Ascension, Pentecost, Transfiguration, Feast of the Cross, and Feasts of the Virgin Mary) and Saint Days (ܩܕ̈ܝܫܐ) throughout the year. Some manuscripts bind Lent and Passion together. The order of texts within each volume follows the liturgical calendar. Until the end of the twentieth century, most

[5] Afram Barsoum, *kthobo da-ṣlawotho d-šabtho šḥimto* (Jerusalem, 1934). The church in India follows Matthew Konat's edition, *kthobo da-ṣlutho šḥimto* (1915). See also Kiraz 2022.

[6] In the Maphrianate of Takrit tradition, the first Sunday of the liturgical calendar is the Sunday of the Renewal of the Church (ܚܘܕܬ ܥܕܬܐ) which is the second Sunday in the Antiochene tradition.

parishes still relied on manuscripts for the *Phenqitho* and *Ḥusoyo* volumes. As photocopy technology became popular in the 1980s and 1990s, diaspora parishes began to photocopy manuscripts and use highlights to colour rubrics and headings. It is only with the first and second decades of the twenty-first century that the texts of the *Phenqitho*[7] and *Ḥusoyo*[8] were edited and parishes gradually began to move to using these editions.

---

[7] In Malankara, Abraham Konat edited a set in Pampakuda titled ܦܢܩܝܬܐ ܕܚܘܕܪܐ ܫܠܝܚܝܐ: I Winter (1962); II Lent and Passion (1963); III Resurrection (1963). It is only during the twenty-first century that *Pheniqtho* sets where published by Syriacs from the Middle East as follows:

1. Tur Abdin, Turkey, by the scribe Gabriel Aktaş: I Winter (ܦܢܩܝܬܐ ܣܬܘܬܐ) 2001; II Lent and Passion (ܦܢܩܝܬܐ ܕܨܘܡܐ ܩܕܝܫܐ ܘܕܐܘܚܕܢ) 2002; III Resurrection (ܦܢܩܝܬܐ ܕܩܝܡܬܐ) 2000; IV Saints (ܦܢܩܝܬܐ ܕܕܘܟܪܢܐ ܕܩܕܝܫܐ) 2005.
2. Paderbon, Germany, by Abdulmesih Nergiz and Yuhanon Savci: I Winter (ܟܬܒܐ ܕܦܢܩܝܬܐ ܕܩܘܕܫ ܥܕܬܐ) 2016; II Lent and Passion (ܟܬܒܐ ܕܦܢܩܝܬܐ ܕܨܘܡܐ ܩܕܝܫܐ ܘܕܐܘܚܕܢ ܥܡ ܫܒܘܥܐ ܕܚܫܐ ܦܪܘܩܝܐ) 2015; III Resurrection (ܟܬܒܐ ܕܦܢܩܝܬܐ ܕܩܝܡܬܐ ܦܪܘܩܝܬܐ) 2014; IV Saints (ܦܢܩܝܬܐ ܕܕܘܟܪܢܐ ܕܩܕܝܫܐ ܘܕܥܐܕܐ ܡܪܢܝܐ) 2015.
3. Gütersloh, Germany, by Issa Bulut and Aziz Georg: I Winter (ܦܢܩܝܬܐ ܕܩܘܕܫ ܥܕܬܐ) 2019; II Lent and Passion (ܦܢܩܝܬܐ ܕܨܘܡܐ ܩܕܝܫܐ ܘܕܐܘܚܕܢ ܥܡ ܫܒܬܐ ܕܚܫܐ ܦܪܘܩܝܐ); III Resurrection (ܦܢܩܝܬܐ ܕܩܝܡܬܐ ܦܪܘܩܝܬܐ).

[8] A set was published in Paderbon by Yuhanon Savci: I Winter (ܟܬܒܐ ܕܚܘܣܝܐ ܕܩܘܕܫ ܥܕܬܐ) 2010; II Lent (ܟܬܒܐ ܕܚܘܣܝܐ ܕܨܘܡܐ ܩܕܝܫܐ ܘܕܐܘܚܕܢ) 2011; III Resurrection (ܟܬܒܐ ܕܚܘܣܝܐ ܕܩܝܡܬܐ) 2009. A bilingual set in Classical Syriac and Turoyo was published in Paderbon, Germany, by Abdulmesih Nergiz and Yuhanon Savci titled: I Winter (ܟܬܒܐ ܕܚܘܣܝܐ ܕܩܘܕܫ ܥܕܬܐ ܥܡ ܦܘܫܩܐ); II Lent and Passion (ܟܬܒܐ ܕܚܘܣܝܐ ܡܦܫܩܝܐ ܕܡܢ ܒܟܢܐ ܕܨܘܡܐ ܪܒܐ... ܥܡ ܫܒܬܐ ܕܚܫܐ ܦܪܘܩܝܐ) 2015; III Resurrection (ܟܬܒܐ ܕܚܘܣܝܐ ܕܩܝܡܬܐ ܥܡ ܦܘܫܩܐ) 2014.

The next liturgical service in terms of frequency is the Eucharistic liturgy, practiced weekly on Sundays, on feast days, and—in monastic settings—on every Wednesday and Friday throughout the year. (The Eucharistic liturgy is not practiced on Good Friday unless Annunciation falls on that day.) The Eucharistic liturgy stands on its own in terms of content and schema. The service gives voice to three actors: the celebrant (addressing God in prayers, and only addressing the people when giving a blessing), the deacon (inviting the celebrant to bless or addressing the people by giving them instructions), and the people (addressing God in prayers or responding to the celebrant). The text is given in the book of Anaphora (Barsoum, §4), but only from the perspective of the celebrant. Parts pertaining to the deacon, or the people are denoted in the Anaphora with brief rubrics (usually one or two words). While Anaphora manuscripts are known from the ninth or tenth century, it is rare to find the deacon portions before the Early Modern period. Barsoum does not even discuss them, although he edited them in a small diaconal service book.[9] Multiple modern editions of the Anaphora[10] and

---

[9] Afram Barsoum, ܟܬܒܐ ܕܫܘܡܫܐ ܕܩܘܪܒܐ ܠܟܘܠܗ̇ ܫܢܬܐ ܕܒܝܬ ܬܫܡܫܬܐ ܠܐܘܪܚܐ ܫܘܡܫܐ (Dayro d-Kurkmo, 1912).

[10] The primary editions are: *Anaphora* (Syriac, Arabic, and partial Turkish) edited by Yulius Çiçek (Holland, 1985); *Anaphoras* edited by Athanasius Y. Samuel and translated into English by Murad S. Barsom (NJ, 1991 [Syriac typesetting by George A. Kiraz]); *Lahmo Dhayé* (with Arabic translation) edited by Roger Akhrass and published by Thewofilos G. Saliba (Beirut, 2002); *The Anaphora* (Syriac, English, and Arabic) edited by Philoxenos M. Nayiş and Matta al-Koury and published under the auspices of Ignatius Z Iwaz (Damascus, 2012, 5th ed.).

the diaconal service book exist.[11] On major feast days, the Eucharistic liturgy is augmented with a special service that pertains to the feast in question. These texts are given in the book of Mʿadʿdono (Barsoum, §11) whose standard edition was edited by Jacob III.[12]

Next in frequency are liturgical services performed on behalf of lay people such as baptism, matrimony, anointing of the sick, repentance, and funerals (Barsoum, §§9, 12).[13] And there is a set of liturgies that can only be celebrated by the Episcopal rank

---

[11] Numerous editions exist, the most important being: Yuhanna Dolabani's ܛܟܣܐ ܕܬܫܡܫܬܐ ܕܩܘܪܒܐ (Jerusalem, 1929); Ni'matallah Dinno, ܟܬܒܐ ܕܛܟܣ̈ܬܐ ܐܘܟܝܬ ܡܫܬܘܬܐ ܡܢ ܙܘܥܪܐ ܡܩ̈ܝܡܬܐ ܘܡܫܡܫܢܐ ܕܩܘܪܒܐ ܘܠܡܫܡ̈ܫܢܘܬܐ (Mosul, 1936); Yulius Çiçek's ܛܟܣܐ ܕܩܘܪܒܐ ܐܠܗܝܐ (1988 with many subsequent editions). Matthew (or Abraham, his son, the authorship is uncertain) Konat edited the Malankara edition (Pampakuda, n/d, reprint 1989).

[12] Matthew (or Abraham) Konat published a Syriac-Malayalam edition titled ܟܬܒܐ ܕܡܥܕܥܕܢܐ (Pampakuda, n/d); Jacob III published a Syriac-Arabic (Garshuni) edition titled ܛܟܣܐ ܕܡܥܕܥܕܢܐ (Beirut, 1978). A bilingual Syriac-English edition was edited by Athanasius Y. Samuel and translated by Murad S. Barsom (NJ, 1991).

[13] The first editions upon which later editions are based are:

1. Baptism: Syriac-Arabic (Garshuni) edited by Afram Barsoum titled ܛܟܣܐ ܕܥܡܕܐ ܩܕܝܫܐ (Beirut, 1950); Syriac-English *The Sacrament of Holy Baptism* (Syriac-English) edited by Athanasius Y. Samuel and translated by Murad S. Barsom (Beirut, 1974).
2. Matrimony: Syriac-Arabic (Garshuni) edited by Afram Barsoum titled ܛܟܣܐ ܕܒܘܪܟ ܟܠ̈ܝܠܐ ܘܡܟ̈ܠܠܐ (Lebanon, 1948); *The Order of Slemnisation of the Sacrament of Matrimony* edited by Athanasius Y. Samuel and translated by Murad S. Barsom (Beirut, 1974).

(Barsoum, §10) on special occasions such as ordinations and sanctifications of churches, of the chrism, etc.[14]

Obviously, all liturgical services include scripture readings. These are given in Lectionaries (Barsoum, §3) for the year cycle or in the texts of specific liturgies (e.g., baptism). Within each Sunday or feast day, the readings are given for *Ramšo*, *Saphro*, and the Eucharistic liturgy. There are four readings: Old Testament, Acts (which includes the Major Catholic Epistles), the Pauline Epistles, and the Gospels, each in its own volume.[15] (The Minor Catholic Epistles and Revelation are not part of the Syriac Peshitta canon and are absent liturgically.) While the scripture readings do not vary much from one manuscript to another, the selections of lections do vary. Revised editions of lection readings are being prepared by Archbishop Severus Roger Akrass under the auspices of a Synodal liturgical committee.

---

3. Funeral: Syriac-Arabic (Garshuni) edited by Jacob III titled ܛܟܣܐ ܕܩܘܦܠܐ ܕܥܢܝ̈ܕܐ (Beirut, 1972); Syriac-English edited by edited by Athanasius Y. Samuel and translated by Murad S. Barsom (Lebanon, 1974).
4. Anointing of the sick known as Qandilo: *Kandilo* edited by Yulius Çiçek (Holland, 1983).

[14] The only edition that currently exists is ܟܬܒܐ ܕܩܘܕ̈ܫܐ, for sanctifications, edited by Yuyakin Unval and Nahir Akçay (Damascus 2009) and ܟܬܒܐ ܕܣܝ̈ܡܝܕܘܬܐ, for ordinations, edited by Yuyakin Unval (Damascus 2009).

[15] See Dolabani's *Mukaddes Ayrıllarıın Fihristi* (Mardin, 1954) for a list of lection readings. The Gospel was scribed and reproduced by Yulius Çiçek, ܐܘܢܓܠܝܘܢ ܩܕܝܫܐ (Holland, 1987). The Pauline Epistles were edited by George A. Kiraz titled, ܦܘܠܘܣ ܫܠܝܚܐ ܕܐܓܪ̈ܬܐ (Holland, 1991).

In addition to the above, the book of Beth Gazo (Barsoum, §8) consists of collections of hymnals as a reference. Older manuscripts of the Beth Gazo may also contain the book of Anaphora and/or the *Šḥimo* and whatever other services the scribe feels a priest needs as a *handbook*. A modern brief Beth Gazo has become a reference for how to chant hymns. If a lexicon defines words in language, the brief Beth Gazo defines the melodies of hymns (cf. with the *Irmologion* in the Byzantine rite).

Table 1: Summary of entire textual repository

Purpose	**Item**	**Book**	**Barsoum, Ch. 15, §:**
Liturgy of the			
Hours:	1	*Šḥimo*	2
a. Weekdays	2	*Phenqitho* (for poetry).	
b. Sundays and		Volumes:	5
Feasts		a. Winter	7
		b. Lent	7
		c. Passion Week	5
		d. Summer	6
	3	e. Feasts and Saints	8
		Ḥusoyo (for prose).	
		(Volumes as *Phenqitho*)	
Eucharist	4	*Anaphora* (for the celebrant)	4
	5	Diaconal Service Book	N/A
Major Feasts	6	*Mʿadʿdono*	11
Lay Services	7	Baptism	9
	8	Matrimony	9
	9	Funerals	12
	10	Anointing of the sick (*Qandilo*)	9
Episcopal Services	11	Ordinations	10
	12	Consecrations	10
Lectionaries	12	Old Testament	3
	14	Acts and Minor Epistles	
	15	Pauline Epistles	
	16	Gospels	
References and	17	Beth Gazo (short)	13
Aids	18	Oral aids booklets	N/A

Items 15 and 18 are absent in Barsoum. Frequent prayers that are not written in the above books are sometimes collected in *aid* manuscripts. This includes certain hymns, prayers, or psalms. These were edited only recently with much fluctuation in content.

2.0. Setting the Stage

Before embarking on the interplay between textuality and orality, it is important to understand the *where*, *when* (and *how*) of liturgical worship.

2.1. Where: The Liturgical Space

A traditional Syriac church consists of three primary sections: the nave, the choirs (*gude*), and the altar. Jacob of Serug (451–521), in his *Mimro* on the destruction of *Amida*, gives us a visual of *where* the various voices are coming from (Akhrass and Syryany 2017, II:344–351). Amida under attack speaks,

149 ܒܛܠ ܗܘ ܕܒܚܐ ܕܚܝܐ ܕܗܘܐ ܚܠܦ ܥܢܝ̈ܕܐ܆
ܘܝܩܕ ܡܕܒܚܝ ܘܣܦܝܩܐ ܐܢܐ ܡܢ ܚܘܣܝܐ.
150 ܘܪܘܡ ܗܘܠܠܐ ܡܢ ܠܡܥܡܕܝܬܐ ܘܡܢ ܡܫܡܫܐ܆
ܘܦܣܩ ܡܢ ܦܘܡܝ ܗܠܠ ܕܡܘܫܐ ܘܕܘܝܕ܀
151 ܐܒܪܘ ܡܝ̈ܬܐ ܒܠܥܕ ܩ̈ܒܪܐ ܕܟܘܡܪ̈ܐ܆
ܘܫܒܪ[ܘ] ܦܘܡܗܘܢ ܡܢ ܠܡܥܡܕܝܬܐ ܕܒܗ ܐܬܝܠܕܘ
152 ܒܠܗ ܫܒܐ ܘܡܚܠܗ ܫܪܪܐ ܕܒܢ̈ܝܬܐ܆
ܘܒܛܠ ܥܠܐ ܕܡܫܡܫܢܐ ܕܙܟܐ ܗܘܐ ܒܝ܀

149 The sacrifice [i.e., Holy Eucharist] that is offered on behalf of the departed ceased. My altar burnt; I am emptied from petitions

150 My **naves** became deserted from (liturgical) service and from deacons;
And the voice of praise and the chanting of hallelujah are cut off from my mouth.

151 The swords flashed [like lightning] between the crowded **choirs [*gude*]**
And shut their mouths from glorification with the blood they shed.

152 The captors entered and spoiled the rows of the congregations;
And the voice of the ones singing praise that sounded like thunder within me ceased.

Jacob alludes to the three parts of the church: my **naves** became deserted (150a), the swords flashed between the crowded **choirs** [*gude*] (151a), and my **altar** burnt (149b). There are actors: the deacons (*šamoše*, 150a), the choirs (*gude*, 151a), the congregation (*knušotho*, 152a), and the ones singing praise (*mšabḥone*, 152b). And there are voices: the voice (*qolo*) of praise and the chanting of hallelujah (*hulolo*, 150b), the choirs' mouth (*fumo*) with which they utter glorification (*tešbuḥto*, 151), and the voice (*qolo*) of the ones signing praise (*mšabḥone*, 152b). Additionally, Jacob gives us an image of how the congregation (*knušotho*) may have organised itself in the pew-less space: in *sedre* 'rows' or 'lines' (152a). The closest likeness today that could depict this image from Late Antiquity are Muslims solemnly standing in mosques in rows and lines (keeping in mind that Jacob wrote his Mimro just over 50 years before the *Futūḥ*).[16] This division of the liturgical space into three main parts persists to the present day.

[16] First observed by George Kiraz in a Facebook post dated 21 December 2023.

Two lecterns are placed in the *gudo* section, usually elevated by a step or two. The lectern as an object became to be known as *gudo* as well. The one on the northern side is called ܓܘܕܐ ܕܢܒܝܐ '*gudo* of the prophets' and the other on the southern end called ܓܘܕܐ ܕܫܠܝܚܐ '*gudo* of the apostles', representing continuity between the Old and New Testaments. The lecterns hold all books pertaining to the Liturgy of the Hours (nos 1–3), as well as references and aids (nos 17–18). A third lectern, also set in the southern side, holds the book of *Ḥusoyo* (no. 3). (Some churches have only one *gudo* for the *Phenqitho* on the Northern side and the left *gudo* holds the book of *Ḥusoyo*.)

The sanctuary, elevated by another step or two, has an altar in the middle. The altar usually has a bookstand that holds the book of Anaphora (no. 4) to be used by the celebrant for the Eucharist liturgy. A movable *bema* 'throne' is set in the middle, western edge of the sanctuary and has a bookstand that holds the Gospel lectionary. (In Late Antiquity, the *bema* was set in the middle of the nave.) There are no lectors or bookstands for other lectionaries; these are held by hand by the reader.

2.2. When: Canonical Hours

The Liturgy of the Hours is celebrated daily, the canonical hours being: 1) ܪܡܫܐ (hereafter, *Ramšo*) 'evening'; 2) ܣܘܬܪܐ (*Sutoro*) 'covering, protection', corresponding to Latin *compline*; 3) ܠܠܝܐ (*Lilyo*) 'night', corresponding to Latin *nocturnes*; 4) ܨܦܪܐ (*Ṣaphro*) 'morning', which is the apposition of *Ramšo* and corresponds to Latin *lauds*; 5) ܬܠܬ ܫ̈ܥܝܢ or the Third Hour, corresponding to Latin *terce*;

6) ܫܬ ܫܥܝ̈ܢ or the Sixth Hour, corresponding to Latin *sext*; and 7) ܬܫܥ ܫܥܝ̈ܢ or the Ninth Hour corresponds to Latin *none*.

The ecclesiastical day—following the Jewish tradition—begins at sunset with *Ramšo* being the first Hour. Our modern calendrical day, however, begins at midnight. As such, each liturgical day spans two calendrical days; compare this with the Jewish Sabath that begins at sunset on calendrical Friday and ends at sunset on calendrical Saturday.

Take for example the feast of Ascension which occurs on a Thursday. The day begins on calendrical Wednesday afternoon with the *Ramšo* hour. To complicate matters further, the seven canonical hours have been reduced in the Received Tradition to two synaxes (ܣܘܢܗܕ̈ܘܣ): an evening synaxis and a morning synaxis. The evening synaxis takes place on calendrical Wednesday and starts off with the Ninth Hour of liturgical Wednesday (being the last Hour of the liturgical day). Usually, the prayers of the Ninth Hour last less than five minutes after which the liturgical day flips to Thursday (but still on calendrical Wednesday evening). The evening synaxis then resumes with the *Ramšo* and *Sutoro* of liturgical Thursday.

The morning synaxis is more straightforward. It is held during the morning of calendrical and liturgical Thursday. It consists of *Lilyo*, *Ṣaphro*, Third Hour, and Sixth Hour, all of liturgical Thursday. The following evening synaxis, held on calendrical Thursday afternoon, begins with the Ninth Hour of liturgical Thursday. After a few minutes, the liturgical day flips to liturgical Friday with the *Ramšo* and *Sutoro*.

Recall that the Liturgy of the Hours make use of the book of *Šḥimo* (no. 1) for simple weekdays and the *Phenqitho* (no. 2) for feast days. This entails not only flipping between liturgical days, but also switching between different books.

3.0. Textuality and Orality; Audibility and Inaudibility

During the Liturgy of the Hours, the chanters gather around the *gudo*. Sometimes, as Jacob portrays, their voices do sound like thunder. But occasionally, those gathered *around* the lectern line up—in *sedre* 'lines' to use Jacob's words—and enter either a state of what seems to be complete silence or a state of murmur. The faithful usually stand at this moment and follow suit. Everyone would be making the sign of the cross a few times, sometimes bowing their heads, sometimes prostrating all the way down. The Syriac liturgy has no space for complete silence; what seems to be silence is in fact a recitation of a *qawmo*, lit. 'rising' or *statio*. It is *recited* inaudibly. Roger Akhrass points out that this is to the chanter an opportunity to rest as the liturgy has no room for complete silence.[17]

Recall that a synaxis consists of multiple canonical hours. Each canonical hour begins with a *qawmo* and ends with another. As such, one can think of the *qawmo* as a delimiter of canonical hours. The *qawmo* is completely absent in the *Šḥimo* (no. 1) and the *Phenqitho* (no. 2). There is not even a rubric that denotes its

---

[17] Roger Akhrass (personal communication, 1 January 2024).

existence. As such, it can be categorised as inaudible and oral (i.e., non-textual).

The text of the *qawmo* was recently committed to writing in non-liturgical guidebooks, the most common is a book on prayer by Barsoum.[18] The text consists of the Trisagion and the Lord's prayer. The *qawmo* is recited twice between two canonical hours: the first to conclude one canonical hour and the second to commence the next hour.

Certain canonical hours terminate with other fixed elements just before the concluding *qawmo*. These also belong to the realm of orality as there is no mention of them in the *Šḥimo* nor in the *Phenqitho*. But unlike the *qawmo*, they are audible. Some canonical hours convert the Trisagion of the concluding *qawmo* from inaudibility to audibility. Other canonical hours contain psalms and other biblical elements (e.g., the Beatitudes, Matt. 5.3–12). These are usually denoted in the *Šḥimo* and the *Phenqitho* with a brief rubric of a few words. Seasoned deacons know them by heart. Less experienced deacons use aid booklets (no. 18). These fluctuate between orality and textuality.

The Eucharistic liturgy as well as all other liturgies that include a consecration or sanctification element contain recitative audible prayers which, over time, became inaudible. These are textual and marked with the heading ܓܘܢܬܐ *ghonto* lit. '[prayer with a] lowered [voice or head?]' to denote their inaudibility, or sometimes with the heading ܦܫܝܛܬܐ '[prayer with] stretched

[18] Barsoum, *Kitāb al-Tuḥfah al-Rūḥiyyah fī al-Ṣalāh al-Farḍiyyah* (Aleppo, 1956, 5th ed.).

[hands]'. Notice that the headings indicate kinaesthetic movements.

During the Eucharistic liturgy, deacons recite elements—usually instructions to the faithful—while the priest is performing a *ghonto*. The deacon elements are absent from the Anaphora, but denoted with a rubric. Traditionally, they have always been within orality, although modern editions are pushing them towards textuality, writing them explicitly. During consecrations and sanctifications, the deacon recites the 'Kyrie eleison' audibly. It is almost completely oral, usually without an indication of it even in the form of a rubric.

It is clear from the above that there is a certain degree of elasticity between the textual and the oral, and between the audible and inaudible. In recent years, as the ability of deacons to remember elements by heart decreased, helping manuals are increasingly published, committing the oral to writing. As modern events (such as retreats and conventions) became part of the liturgical life of the nonclergy, even the *qawmo* is moving to audibility. Finally, computer monitors became a common fixture in churches,[19] the *qawmo* is being committed to the born-digital.

4.0. Conclusion

This paper has explored the dynamic and intricate relationship between orality and textuality within the Syriac Orthodox liturgical tradition. Through a close examination of the Received Tradition, it becomes evident that Syriac liturgy is characterised by

[19] George Kiraz proposed the use of monitors for Church worship during the Syriac Orthodox Convention held in Oregon, 1999.

a unique multimodal expression that is not solely dependent on written texts but rather integrates oral, auditory, and kinaesthetic dimensions to create a comprehensive worship experience. This complexity, underscored by both the audible and inaudible elements, reflects a sophisticated interplay that embodies centuries of historical, social, and theological developments.

The study of Syriac liturgy is an understudied field, and this paper's examination highlights the need for further exploration into the transmission history and development of liturgical practices in this tradition. Unlike other more extensively studied liturgical traditions, Syriac liturgy offers a distinctive example of how ritual practice adapts over time, responding to the needs of the community while retaining core elements. Recent works, such as Baby Varghese's *The Early History of the Syriac Liturgy: Growth, Adaptation and Inculturation* (2021), have begun to address this gap, contributing to a growing, though still limited, scholarly interest in Syriac liturgical history. Yet the depth of the tradition and its intricate evolution suggest that much remains to be uncovered, particularly regarding the sociopolitical and theological factors that influenced changes in liturgical practice and form.

One of the central contributions of this paper is the identification of Syriac liturgical texts as 'palimpsests', layered with historical traces from different periods. Each layer reflects adaptations and reforms by figures such as Jacob of Edessa and Patriarch John of Sedre, whose work likely shaped the structure and content of Syriac liturgy in response to the sociocultural contexts of their time. This palimpsest nature emphasises that Syriac liturgical texts are more than static documents; they are dynamic, evolving expressions of faith that have continuously interacted with oral traditions and community practices.

Furthermore, the paper underscores the elasticity between textuality and orality in Syriac liturgy. Traditionally oral elements, such as the *qawmo,* which once lacked textual representation, have gradually been committed to writing and even incorporated into digital formats for modern liturgical use. This movement from orality to textuality exemplifies the adaptability of Syriac liturgy, where community practices, memory, and written texts intersect. This shift raises questions about how the Syriac Orthodox tradition will continue to navigate this balance as more traditionally oral practices are committed to writing, potentially altering the experiential aspect of worship.

Finally, the study reaffirms the critical role of further research in understanding the multimodal aspects of Syriac worship. Future studies should aim to map out the relationship between local practices and the Received Tradition, exploring how variations across regions have contributed to the rich tapestry of Syriac liturgy. This focus on multimodal expression—encompassing the textual, oral, audible, inaudible, and kinaesthetic—adds a new dimension to our understanding of Syriac worship practices and underscores the need for interdisciplinary approaches to study liturgy, incorporating insights from anthropology, theology, and historical linguistics.

In sum, this paper contributes to a deeper understanding of Syriac Orthodox liturgy as a living tradition, embodying both a heritage of textual transmission and an oral, communal experience that continues to evolve. By highlighting the multilayered and adaptive nature of Syriac liturgy, this study offers a foundation for future research that will further illuminate the history and significance of one of Christianity's most ancient and enduring worship traditions.

This paper has briefly described the interplay between textuality and orality in the liturgical worship of the Syriac Orthodox tradition based on the Received Tradition. It has also touched upon the audible and inaudible. This complex multimodal expression is further complicated by local traditions, not to mention the palimpsest layers of yesteryear. Understanding the transmission history of multimodal expression in more detail is going to require further developments in the understudied field of Syriac liturgy.

References

Akhrass, Roger; and Syryany, Imad. 2017. *160 Unpublished Homilies of Jacob of Serugh.* Damascus.

Barsoum, Afram. 1956. *Kitāb al-Luʾluʾ al-Manthūr fī Tārīkh al-ʿUlūm wal-ʾĀdāb al-Suryāniyya.* Aleppo.

Baumstark, Anton. 1958. *Comparative Liturgy.* Translated by Frank L. Cross. Pine Beach: The Newman Press.

Brock, Sebastian P. 2011. 'Liturgy'. In *Gorgias Encyclopedic Dictionary of the Syriac Heritage*, edited by Sebastian P. Brock, Aaron Butts, George Kiraz, and Lucas Van Rompay, 334–336. Piscataway, NJ: Gorgias Press.

Brock, Sebastian, and Kiraz, George. 2024. *Ephrem the Syrian: Select Poems*. Provo, UT: Brigham Young University Press.

Colwell, Chip. 2022. 'A Palimpsest Theory of Objects'. *Current Anthropology* 63 (2): 129–157.

Kalaga, Wojciech, Bożena Shallcross, and Ryszard Nycz (eds). 2011. *The Effect of Palimpsest: Culture, Literature, History*. Literary and Cultural Theory 36. Lausanne: Peter Lang.

Kiraz, George A. 2022. 'Schema of the Syriac Šḥimo'. *Hugoye: Journal of Syriac Studies* 25 (2): 455–483.

———. 2024. *New Syriac Primer*. Piscataway, NJ: Gorgias Press.

Varghese, Baby. 2020. 'Saint Ephrem and the Early Syriac Liturgical Traditions'. *Parole de l'Orient* 46: 254–83.

———. 2021. *The Early History of the Syriac Liturgy: Growth, Adaptation and Inculturation*. Wiesbaden: Harrassowitz Verlag.

Wright, William. 1870. *Catalogue of the Syriac Manuscripts in the British Museum*. London: The British Museum.

WAS THERE EVER AN ORAL HEBREW MASORAH?[1]

Elvira Martín-Contreras

In his famous article 'Masorah', Aron Dotan (2007, 609) distinguished between oral Masorah and written Masorah:

> Therefore one must differentiate quite clearly between the oral Masorah which is endless and cannot be defined even though there are allusions to it and evidence thereof, and between the written Masorah whose notations were written in the margins of the codices and which is called simply 'the Masorah'.[2]

According to Dotan, the annotations on the text of the Bible, and the instructions on how to properly pronounce and copy it, were transmitted orally from generation to generation before being put

[1] This article was completed under the auspices of a research project entitled 'Lengua y Literatura del Judaísmo Rabínico y Medieval (JuRaMe)', funded by the Plan Nacional de I + D + i (PID2019–105305GB–I00).

[2] Later in his article, Dotan divides written Masorah into two categories: (1) the Masoretic notes in the margins of the text and the longer lists which accompany the text or are appended to it—the Masorah in the narrow sense; (2) the graphemes which, by their nature, are of two types: (a) vocalisation signs; (b) accentuation signs (see Dotan 2007, 614). In this chapter, the term 'written Masorah' refers specifically to Masorah in the narrow sense.

 https://doi.org/10.11647/OBP.0498.04

into writing. The existence of this oral Masorah is, in his opinion, a key point in the debate on the relationship between the Hebrew written Masorah and the Syriac Masorah—between which there are several contact points. Dotan argued that the Hebrew Masorah is "as old as the public reading of the text of the Bible and which was finally written down", and thus "undoubtedly precedes the 'Syriac Masorah'" (2007, 621).[3] Therefore, the written Hebrew Masorah is the original and the one that has influenced the Syriac. This assertion has been one of the obstacles to carrying out comparative analyses of the two systems.

Moreover, the belief in the ancient origin of the written Hebrew Masorah has prevented scholars in Masoretic studies from exploring possible contacts with other nearby textual traditions that developed similar annotation systems. This paper reviews the concept and existence of the oral Hebrew Masorah as the starting point for an interdisciplinary debate.

1.0. The Idea of a Hebrew Oral Masorah

The concept of an oral Masorah that preceded our written testimony can be traced back to the 16th century. Jacob ben Ḥayyim was the first to suggest, in the introduction to the first printed edition of the Hebrew Bible accompanied by the entire apparatus of the Masorah (the Second Rabbinical Bible), that all the Masoretic statements were laws delivered to Moses at Sinai (Ginsburg 1968, 57).

---

[3] The opposite has been defended from the field of Syriac studies, see Juckel (2007, 107–21).

Elías Levita further developed this idea in his book *Masoret ha-masoret*, when explaining what *masoret* (מסרת) means and what its etymology is (Ginsburg 1867, 102–3):

> Thus it is said in the Mishna, Moses received the Law from Sinai (ומסרה), and delivered it to Joshua, etc. [Mishna, Aboth, i.1]; and this is the meaning of the word מסר in question. Since it was transmitted to sages, from mouth to mouth, till the time of Ezra and his associates, and by them again to the sages of Tiberias, who wrote down, and called it Massorah.

Levita drew a parallel between the oral Torah and the Masorah, both being laws handed down to Moses at Sinai. He developed the idea of the oral transmission of the written Masorah in a similar way to how the oral Torah was transmitted. Just as the latter was finally put into writing by the rabbis (the men of the great assembly), the Masorah was put in writing by the men of Tiberias.

Levita also put forth the theory of the existence of independent treatises as an intermediate step between the oral and written Masorah added in the codices (Ginsburg 1867, 138). C. D. Ginsburg, the revitalizer of the study of the Masorah in the nineteenth century, reiterated these assumptions in his *Introduction to the Massoretico-critical edition of the Hebrew Bible* (1897).

In the second half of the twentieth century, Dotan echoed these ideas and developed them. He conceptualized the oral Masorah as the issue, apart from the method of writing the Bible (i.e., the order of the books, the *sedarim* and *parašiyyot*, the *petuḥot* and *setumot*) and the orthographic irregularities in the writing, that are part of the oral transmission, namely, "the notes concerning the text of the Bible and the instructions for its proper pronunciation and its exact copying" before they were written down. He assumed that such commentaries could have been written when the codex format was adopted by the Jews. From that moment on, we can speak of written Masorah or simply 'Masorah' to refer to the annotations found in the margins of the codices (Dotan 2007, 609).

This theory has been accepted and reproduced by many other scholars without further research (for example, Yeivin 1980, 122–23; Ofer 2019, 125).

2.0. A Critical Review

However, the question remains: is there any evidence for the existence of an oral Masorah? What are the arguments in favour of the existence of an oral precursor to the written Masorah?

As occurs in the field of textual criticism regarding the history of the transmission of the Hebrew biblical text, rabbinic literature plays a key role in explaining what happened in the period before the Masorah was written down in the codices we know today. Dotan, like Ben Ḥayyim, Levita and Ginsburg before him, took the following as evidence for the existence of an oral Masorah: the rabbinical accounts referring to the process of copying and transmitting the biblical text; the role and the activity of the *sopherim* ("those scholars who specialized in the written Torah and in its exact transmission"); the oral transmission of the *miqra sopherim*; the *ʿiṭṭure sopherim*; the *Qere we-la' Ketiv* and *Ketiv we-la Qere* phenomena; references to the tradition of division into verses, as well as of internal verse division by accentuation, alongside differing traditions concerning both division of the text into verses and division within verses; and, finally, how to reach decisions about such divisions (Dotan 2007, 609-12).[4] The same rabbinic texts are used by other scholars in the field of Masoretic studies (e.g., Ofer 2019a, 1269–1270) and those in the field of textual criticism for similar purposes (e.g., Tov 2003; Lange 2009, esp. 75–6).[5]

2.1. Study of Rabbinic and Masoretic Sources

The apparent continuity or relationship between rabbinic literature and the written Masorah has been the focus of my research for many years. The presence of references to text-preserving observations stated in a language similar to the Masorah that I identified in the midrash *Bereshit Rabbah* (Martín-Contreras 1999, 2002, 2003), was the starting point of my project, 'The Role of Rabbinic Literature in the Textual Transmission of the Hebrew Bible'. Here, a text-preserving observation refers to one component of the midrashic unit—an exclusively meta-linguistic description of details in the biblical text, often followed by an exegetical interpretation of the detail. For example, *Ruth Rabbah* 7:2 on the word הבי in Ruth 3.15 says: 'it is written *habi'* [הביא כתב].

[4] Kid. 30a; Ned. 37b–38a; Meg. 4:4; Meg. 3a; y. Meg. 4:1, 74d; Kid. 30a; Ned. 37a; y. Bezah 2:4 (61c); Yoma 52a for 1 Kgs 6:19; Bava Mezia 58a; Bava Mezia 73b; Hag. 6b; Yoma 52b.

[5] For the problematic use of rabbinic literature as a straightforward historical source see Alexander (2010, 7–24), Martín-Contreras and Miralles Maciá (2014, esp. 21–7).

It teaches that he addressed her in the masculine, that none should notice her'.[6]

The aim of the project was to clarify and understand the role of the rabbis and their literary production in the process of transmitting the Hebrew Bible text (Martín-Contreras 2014). To achieve this, I analysed all midrashim that can be 'clearly'[7] dated before the appearance of the written Masorah (usually established as the seventh century). These include: Bereshit Rabbah, Lamentations Rabbah (Martín-Contreras 2002a), Mekhilta de R. Yishmael (Martín-Contreras 2003a), Sifra, Sifre Numbers (Martín-Contreras 2003b), Sifre to Deuteronomy, Leviticus Rabbah, Pesiqta de Rab Kahana, Ruth Rabbah (Martín-Contreras 2011).

After studying the data (Martín-Contreras 2014, esp. 89–90), I reached the following conclusions:

- The identified text-preserving observations, although numerous (over 150), are not significant in proportion to the vast number of Masoretic annotations included even in a single biblical book of a codex.
- The phenomena and textual information contained in these text-preserving observations are varied, but compared to the variety found in the textual information collected in the Masoretic annotations, they are quite limited and uniform. Aside from the references to orthographic irregularities—the inverted *nun*, extraordinary points, large and small letters, suspended letters, and

[6] For a detailed explanation see Martín-Contreras (2009).

[7] On dating problems see Stemberger (2008, esp. 82–83).

other unusual letters—and those mentioned in the oral tradition that are attributed to the *sopherim*, most text-preserving observations concern *plene* and defective spelling of a word on which the interpretation is based. There are likewise many that deal with numerical information, which I have referred to as 'counting'.

- Technical terms found in rabbinic literature which refer to textual phenomena are few or non-existent. The term *ketiv* is used to name a variety of phenomena, such as the *plene* and defective spelling, odd spelling, the difference between written and read, etc. Exceptionally, some other terms such as *lašon neqeva/zakhar* (Mek Shirata 1), *male/ḥaser*, found in the Masorah, are also used. However, the possibility that they are late insertions or later glosses must be taken into account (Stemberger 2014).

I have also analysed the extra-textual details of the biblical text discussed in the rabbinic literature, comparing them with those found in the Masoretic codices. Emanuel Tov argued that these details prove the unalterable transmission of not only the biblical text but also paratextual elements, particularly those presented in the Leningrad codex (2003). However, my comparative analysis of the phenomena that he mentions—the open and closed sections, the scribal annotations, the versification, as well as the reading of Scripture—in both sources, reveals significant divergences not only between what is found in rabbinic literature and what is written in the main Masoretic codices, but also among the various Masoretic codices themselves. Therefore, the apparent continuity and similarity between the two sources are not supported by my study (Martín-Contreras 2024).

An example that I have examined, which illustrates the results well, is the phenomenon of dotted words or *puncta extraordinaria* (words bearing dots over one or more letters), interpreted by some scholars as evidence of critical textual activity by the *sopherim* (Ginsburg 1897, esp. 320–21.334; Harris 1898–1899, esp. 34; Lieberman 1950, 43–6; Weil 1964, 30–1; Kelley, Mynatt, Crawford 1998, 32; Yeivin 1980, 44–6).

This phenomenon has been widely discussed in rabbinic literature. Lists with the ten cases found in the Torah (Gen. 16.5, 18.9, 19.33, 33.4, 37.12; Num. 3.39, 9.10, 21.30, 29.15; Deut. 29.28) appear in Sifre Numbers 69, Avoth di Rabbi Nathan a 34.5, Avoth di Rabbi Nathan b 37.6, Midrash Rabbah Numbers 3.13, Midrash Mishle 26.6, Sopherim 6.3, and the Midrashic compilations *Oṣar ha-midrashim parasha rabenu haqodesh* 9 and 2 Batei Midrashot 53.1. With the exception of the list in Sopherim 6:3, each case is followed by an interpretative explanation of why the word or words in question have dots. Together with the lists, independent references to this phenomenon can also be found. The five verses of Genesis that include a punctuated word or letter are noted and commented on in Midrash Bereshit Rabbah[8] and in Midrash Bereshit.[9] The case of Gen. 33.4 is also

[8] Gen. 16.5 (*GenR* 45,5), 18.9 (*GenR* 48,15), 19.33 (*GenR* 51,8), 33.4 (*GenR* 78,9), 37.12 (*GenR* 84,13), see Martín-Contreras (2010, esp. 154–59).

[9] Gen. 16.5 (MGen 45,5); 18.9 (MGen 48,21); 19.33 (MGen 51,12); 33.4 (MGen 78,13); 37.12 (MGen 84,20).

commented on in Shir ha-Shirim Rabbah 4,7 and in Midrash Tanhuma *wa-yislah* 4. The case of Num. 9.10 is commented in Pes 9, 2. Finally, Ber. 4a contains the only case found in the Writings, Ps. 27.13.

The Masoretic lists (Frensdorff 1864 §96; Baer and Strack 1879, especially 45–6; Ginsburg 1975, especially III:§14, 38 and §39, 364–65) and the Masorah of the main Tiberian manuscripts indicate 15 cases. The Cairo Prophets codex (Cairo) has two Masorah Magna (MM) annotations attached to 2 Sam. 19.20 and Isa. 44.9 giving the fifteen cases and their location: הׄי נקדות ׄי בתוׄר דׄ' בנבׄי אׄ בכתׄו 'fifteen [words] dotted, ten in the Torah, four in the Prophets and one in the Writings': Gen. 16.5, 18.9, 19.33, 33.4, 37.12; Num. 3.39, 9.10, 21.30, 29.15; Deut. 29.28; 2 Sam. 19.20; Isa. 44.9; Ezek. 41.20, 46.22; Ps. 27.13 (fig. 1). However, due to its fragmentary state, only four of the fifteen cases—those of the Prophets—are present. In the Masorah Parva (MP) annotations to 2 Sam. 19.20, Ezek. 41.20 and 46.22, the information given in the MM annotations is repeated without the *simanim*, and the MP annotation to Isa. 44.9 states: דׄ נקוד בנבׄ 'four [words] dotted in the Prophets'. All the letters of the words involved in the four cases are dotted.

Figure 1: Cairo codex, Isa. 44.9 MM (photographs held by the Masorah team at the CSIC)

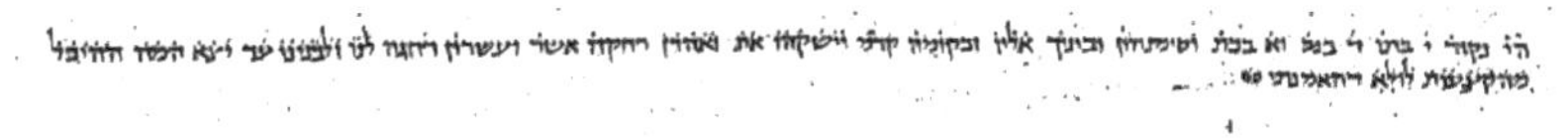

In the Aleppo codex, there are no MM annotations. Due to its fragmentary situation, only six of the fifteen cases are present, and five of them have MP annotations. In the Prophets, it is said three times: דׄ נקדׄ בנביׄא 'four dotted in the Prophets' and at 2 Sam.

19.20 it is said: נקוד 'dotted'. In the only case from the Writings, it is said: נקוד מלמע̇ ולמטה 'dotted above and below'. In five cases all the letters of the word are dotted and in 2 Sam. 19.20 just two of the letters of the word are dotted.

There are no MM annotations in the Leningrad codex, but fourteen of the fifteen cases have MP annotations (Deut. 29.28 has no annotation). In six of the cases of the Pentateuch it is said: י̇ נקד בתור̇ 'ten dotted in the Torah', and in the other three cases it is said: נקוד 'dotted'. In the Prophets, in three cases it is said: ה̇י̇ נקוד 'fifteen dotted', and in Ezek. 41.20 it is said: נקוד 'dotted'. In the only case of the Writings, it is said: ל̇ נקוד מלעל ומלרע ב̇מ̇ו̇ 'dotted above and below with the exception of the *waw*'. In nine cases (Gen. 18.9, 33.4, 37.12; Num. 3.39; Deut. 29.28; 2 Sam. 19.20; Isa. 44.9; Ezek. 41.20, 46.22), all the letters of the words involved are dotted, in four cases (Gen. 16.5; Num. 9.10, 21.30, 29.15) just one letter of the word is dotted, and in two cases (Gen. 19.33; Ps. 27.13) three of the letters of the word are dotted.

When comparing the Masoretic and the rabbinic sources, divergences can be found not only between the two sources but also within each source. The Masorah lists fifteen cases of the phenomenon, but the four cases listed for the Prophets have no reference in the rabbinic literature. Additionally, Midrash Mishle deviates from other rabbinic lists by excluding Gen. 18.9 and including Num. 10.35 instead (table 1). In Midrash Mishle it is said concerning this verse 'dotted above and below' (נקוד בין למעלה בין למטה), and the interpretation is focused on this phenomenon (see Leiman 1974, Levine 1976). However, in the Masoretic codices, this verse has no dots over the word, but instead an inverted *nun*.[10] Moreover, the order of the verses in the list differs among the rabbinic testimonies.

Table 1: Rabbinic literature 1 (SNm 69; ARNa 34.5; ARNb 37.6; Midrash Rabbah Num. 3.13; Sopherim 6.3; *Oṣar ha-midrashim parasha rabbenu haqodesh* 9 and 2 Batei Midrashot 53.1, and independent references), and Rabbinic Literature 2 (list of the ten cases in Midrash Mishle 2.6)

	Rabbinic Literature 1	**Rabbinic Literature 2**	**Masorah**
Gen.	16.5	16.5	16.5
	18.9		18.9
	19.33	19.33	19.33
	33.4	33.4	33.4
	37.12	37.12	37.12
Num.	3.39	3.39	3.39
	9.10	9.10	9.10
		10.35	
	21.30	21.30	21.30
	29.15	29.15	29.15
Deut.	29.28	29.28	29.28
2 Sam.			19.20
Isa.			44.9
Ezek.			41.20
			46.22
Ps.	27.13		27.13
Total	**10**	**10**	**15**

Furthermore, there are numerous differences in the placements of the dots, including variations across different rabbinic testimonies (Martín-Contreras 2005, 332–33), and between the

[10] The inverted *nun* appears nine times in the biblical text, twice in the Pentateuch, Num. 10.35–36, and seven times in Ps. 107, in verses 23–28 and 40 according to some manuscripts, or in verses 21–26 according to others. See Martín-Contreras (2010, esp. 161–62).

extant manuscripts of each testimony, which can be seen in the critical editions' apparatus.[11] Variations can also be found between the main Masoretic codices, such as the placement of the dots over the words in Deut. 29.28, 2 Sam. 19.20, and Ps. 27.13 (table 2). The letters of the words לָנוּ וּלְבָנֵינוּ עַד (apart from the *dalet*) are dotted in Aleppo, whereas in Leningrad, only the words לָנוּ וּלְבָנֵינוּ are dotted. The three letters of the word in 2 Sam. 19.20 are dotted in Cairo and Leningrad, in Aleppo only two of the letters are dotted. Lastly, in Ps. 27.13 all letters are dotted in Aleppo, but only three are dotted in Leningrad. This is the only instance where dots appear both above and below the text in both codices, and this is explicitly stated in their respective MP annotations. Finally, there are differences in the placement of the dots between both sources. While the rabbinic testimonies are homogeneous in indicating that in Gen. 18:9 the dotted letters in אליו are *ʾalef*, *yod*, *waw*, in the Leningrad codex all the letters of the word are dotted. In the case of Deut. 29.28, the placement of the dot over the letter *ʿayin* in Aleppo is also found in two rabbinic sources, namely Avoth di Rabbi Nathan a 34.5 and Sopherim 6.3 (in this case the dot is not reported on the other words), but they disagree with the other rabbinic sources and the Leningrad codex.

---

[11] An example is the divergences in the placement of dots in Deut. 29.28 across different manuscripts of Sifre Numbers; for a detailed list see Kahana (2011, esp. 1168).

Table 2: Differences in the placement of the dots:

	Cairo	**Aleppo**	**Leningrad**
Deut. 29.28			
2 Sam. 19.20		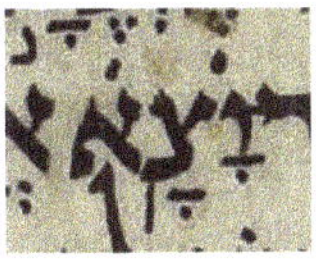	
Ps. 27.13			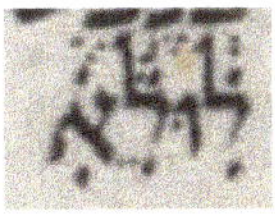

Moreover, while nearly all rabbinic testimonies include interpretive explanations of the dots found in each verse, only two of the Masoretic lists offer such explanations.[12] The Masorah of Cairo, Aleppo, and Leningrad also display several differences in their approach to indicating the phenomenon (table 3). Cairo provides a list identifying the fifteen cases and their distribution as ten in the Torah, four in the Prophets and one in the writings. It also refers only to the four cases of the Prophets. In the annotations of the MP of Leningrad there are also references to the number fifteen (without the identification and distribution of the cases), and to just the ten cases in the Torah. In Aleppo, only the four cases of the Prophets are mentioned. In both Aleppo and Leningrad, there is also information on individual cases, and in one

[12] For a comparative of the interpretations in different lists and the presence of such interpretations in the Masorah of the biblical manuscript BH MSS1 see Ázcarraga Servert (1999) and Martín-Contreras (2005).

instance (Deut. 29.28) there is no MP annotation in either codex, but the words are dotted in the text in both.

Table 3: Differences in the Masorah information

	Cairo	Aleppo	Leningrad
15 dotted	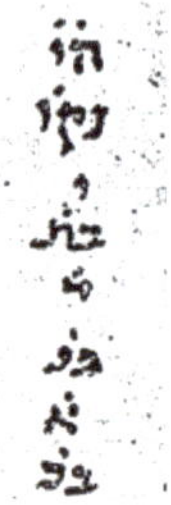		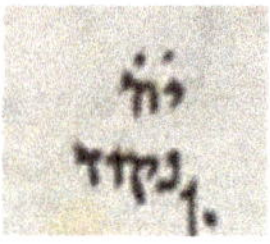
10 dotted in the Torah			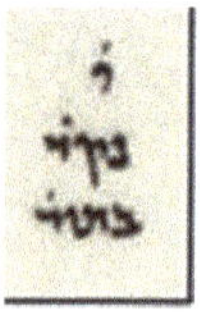
4 dotted in the Prophets	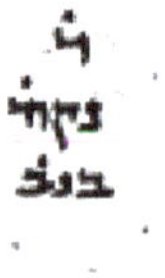	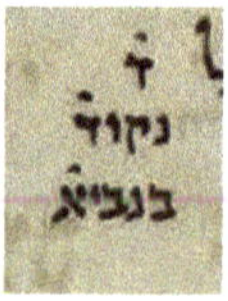	
Individual cases		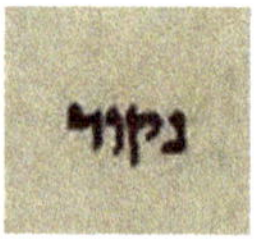 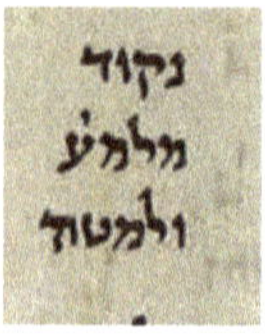	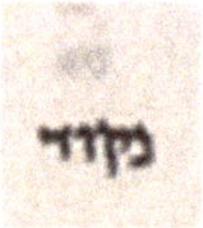 

The results of both studies call into question the existence of an originally oral Masorah that was eventually written down. Despite certain similarities, there is a relatively scant number of text-preserving observations in rabbinic literature. The few referred textual phenomena observed and the few technical terms used in the text-preserving observations have little or nothing to do with the richness and variety of phenomena and technical terminology collected in the annotations found in the margins of the earliest biblical codices. These annotations imply an enormous effort to gather information, systematise it (which does not necessarily entail standardisation) and create a whole system of annotation: technical terms, graphic markers, abbreviations, etc. Indeed, this implies a substantially different approach to the biblical text. While the text-preserving observations found in the rabbinic literature are the precursor or trigger of this interpretation, the annotations in the Masoretic codices must be considered to stand on their own. These annotations transmit widely different types of information about the biblical text: how it is written, and how it should be read, understood, and copied.

The differences between the text-preserving observations in rabbinic literature and the annotations in the Masoretic codices are so numerous and significant that it is not possible to maintain that one is the continuation of the other. It seems more reasonable to consider them as separate entities, with some shared traditions, and sometimes sharing textual traditions that each one treats, names and uses differently. The numerous differences in the same phenomena found in both sources further call into question the notion of an unalterable textual transmission, which is one of the pillars of the idea of an oral Masorah. The differences suggest that the traditions were not yet fixed or closed, and the plurality exhibited among the annotations in the Masoretic codices—with no two Masorahs being the same—underscores the state of flux in these traditions (Martín-Contreras 2023).

In conclusion, the evidence we have from the rabbinic literature does not support the existence of an oral Masorah, nor does it trace an unalterable textual line of transmission from the Second Temple period to the ninth century. It does not corroborate the idea of Masoretic activity having begun in the Talmudic period, as some scholars have claimed (Harris 1898–1899, esp. 130–31, 142; Mulder 1988, esp. 93–4; Yeivin 1980, esp. 132). On the contrary, the multiple differences detected between the supposed 'oral Masorah' as it appears in the rabbinic literature, and the written Masorah, suggest that other reasons beyond the change of medium from scroll to codex must have determined the development of the annotation system added in the margins of the codices. As this system was a new creation, with no ancient origin, it seems logical to look to other nearby textual traditions with similar processes, such as Arabic and Syriac, and the systems they developed, in order to explore possible connections or influences.

References

Alexander, Philip. 2010. 'Using Rabbinic Literature as a Source of the History of Late-Roman Palestina: Problems and Issues'. In *Rabbinic Texts and the History of Late-Roman Palestine*, edited by Martin Goodman and Philip Alexander, 7–24. Oxford, New York: Oxford University Press.

Azcárraga Servert, Mª Josefa. 1999. 'The Orthographic Irregularities in the Manuscript M1 of the Library of the Universidad Complutense de Madrid'. *Sefarad* 59 (2): 239–50.

Baer, Seligman, and Hermann L. Strack. 1879. *Diqduqe ha-teamim. With Prefatory Note and Appendix*. Leipzig: Verlag von L. Fernau.

Dotan, Aron. 2007 (1971). 'Masorah'. In *Encyclopaedia Judaica*, 2nd ed., edited by Michael Berenbaum and Fred Skolnik. XXIII: 603–56.

Frensdorff, Solomon. 1864. *Ochlah W'ochlah*. Hannover: Hahn.

Ginsburg, Christian D. 1867. *The Massoreth ha-massoreth of Elias Levita: being an Exposition of the Massoretic Notes on the Hebrew Bible: or the Ancient Critical Apparatus of the Old Testament: in Hebrew, with an English Translation and Critical and Explanatory Notes*. London: Longmans, Green, Reader & Dyer. https://archive.org/details/themassorethhama00ashuuoft/page/n169/mode/2up.

———. 1966. *Introduction to the Massoretico-Critical Edition of the Hebrew Bible*. New York: Ktav Publishing House. Originally published Christian D. Ginsburg. 1897. *Introduction to the Massoretico-Critical Edition of the Hebrew Bible*. London: Trinitarian Bible Society.

———. 1968. *Jacob ben Chajim ibn Adonija's Introduction to the Rabbinic Bible*, 2nd ed. New York: Ktav Publishing House. https://archive.org/details/introductiontor00ginsgoog/

page/n95/mode/2up. Originally published in Christian D. Ginsburg. 1865. *Jacob ben Chajim ibn Adonija's Introduction to the Rabbinic Bible*. London: Mitchell and Son.

———. 1975. *The Massorah Compiled from Manuscripts Alphabetically and Lexically Arranged. With an Analytical Table of Contents and Lists of Identified Sources and Parallels by A. Dotan.* 4 vols. New York: Ktav Publishing House.

Harris, Isidore. 1898–1899. 'The Rise and Development of the Massorah'. *JQR* 1: 128–42.

Juckel, Andreas. 2007. 'The "Syriac Masora" and the New Testament Peshitta'. In *The Peshitta: Its Use in Literature and Liturgy: Papers Read at the Third Peshitta Symposium*, edited by Bas Ter Haar Romeny, 107–21. Leiden, Boston: Brill.

Kahana, Menachem. 2011. ספרי במדבר: מהדורה מבוארת [Sifre of Numbers: An Annotated Edition]. Jerusalem: Magnes.

Kelley, Page H., Daniel S. Mynatt, and Timothy G. Crawford. 1998. *The Masorah of Biblia Hebraica Stuttgartensia: Introduction and Annotated Glossary*. Grand Rapids: Eerdmans Publishing.

Lange, Armin. 2009. '"They Confirmed the Reading" (y. Ta'an. 4.68a): The Textual Standardisation of Jewish Scriptures in the Second Temple Period'. In *From Qumran to Aleppo. A Discussion with Emanuel Tov about the Textual History of Jewish Scriptures in Honor of His 65th Birthday*, edited by Armin Lange, Matthias Weigold, and József Zsengellér, 29–80. FRLANT, 230. Göttingen: Vandenhoeck & Ruprecht.

Leiman, Sid Z. 1974. 'The Inverted Nuns at Num. 10:35–36 and the Book of Eldad and Medad'. *Journal of Biblical Literature* 93: 348–54.

Levine, Baruch A. 1976. 'More on the Inverted Nuns of Num. 10: 35–36'. *Journal of Biblical Literature* 95: 122–24.

Lieberman, Saul. 1950. *Hellenism in Jewish Palestine. Studies in the Literary Transmission, Beliefs and Manners of Palestine in the I Century B.C.E.—IV Century C. E.* Texts and Studies of the Jewish Theological Seminary of America, 18. New York: Jewish Theological Seminary of America.

Martín-Contreras, Elvira. 1999. 'Terminología masorética en la exégesis de Génesis Rabbâ (secciones Beresith y Noah)'. *Sefarad* 59 (2): 343–52.

———. 2002. *La interpretación de la Creación. Técnicas exegéticas en Génesis Rabbah.* Navarra: Verbo Divino.

———. 2002a. 'Noticias masoréticas en el midrás Lamentaciones Rabbah'. *Sefarad* 62 (1): 125–41.

———. 2003. 'Comments on Textual Details: Relationships between Masorah and Midrash'. *Journal of Jewish Studies* 54 (1): 62–70.

———. 2003a. 'Rethinking Hermeneutical Techniques: Suggestions from their Practice'. *Henoch* 25: 79–92.

———. 2003b. 'Noticias masoréticas en los midrašîm halákicos más antiguos y su comparación con los midrašîm exegéticos'. *Sefarad* 63 (1): 119–39.

———. 2005. 'The Continuity of the Tradition. Masorah with Midrashic Commentaries'. *Journal of Semitic Studies* 50 (2): 329–39.

———. 2009. 'Masoretic and Rabbinic Lights on the Word הבי, Ruth 3.15: יהב or בוא?'. *Vetus Testamentum* 59: 257–265.

———. 2011. 'Text Preserving Observations in the midrash Ruth Rabbah'. *Journal of Jewish Studies* 62 (2): 311–23.

———. 2014. 'Rabbinic Ways of Preservation and Transmission of the Biblical Text in the Light of Masoretic Sources'. In *The Text of the Hebrew Bible. From the Rabbis to Masoretes,* edited by Elvira Martín-Contreras and Lorena Miralles Maciá, 79–90. Journal of Ancient Judaism, Supplements 13. Göttingen: Vandenhoeck & Ruprecht.

———. 2023. 'Remarks on the Plurality of the Masora'. In *Mélanges en hommage à Philippe Cassuto,* edited by Élodie Attia and Manuel Sartori, 81–95. Aix-en-Provence: Press Universitaires de Provence.

———. 2024. 'El mito de la transmisión inalterable del texto bíblico hebreo. Revisión crítica desde la literatura rabínica y la masora'. *El Olivo: documentación y estudios para el diálogo entre judíos y cristianos* 48: 191–208.

Martín-Contreras, Elvira, and Lorena Miralles Maciá. 2014. 'Interdisciplinary Perspectives for the Study of the Text of the Hebrew Bible: Open Questions'. In *The Text of the Hebrew Bible. From the Rabbis to Masoretes,* edited by Elvira Martín-Contreras and Lorena Miralles Maciá, 17–34. *Journal of Ancient Judaism, Supplements* 13. Göttingen: Vandenhoeck & Ruprecht.

Martín-Contreras, Elvira, and Guadalupe Seijas de los Ríos. 2010. *Masora. La transmisión de la tradición de la Biblia hebrea.*

Prólogo de Emilia Fernández Tejero. Instrumentos para el estudio de la Biblia 20. Navarra: Editiorial Verbo Divino.

Mulder, Martin J. 1988. 'The Transmission of the Biblical Text'. In *Miqra: Text, Translation, Reading and Interpretation of the Hebrew Bible*, edited by Martin J. Mulder, 87–135. Philadelphia: Van Gorcum Assen, Maastricht Fortress Press.

Ofer, Yosef. 2019. *The Masorah on Scripture and its Methods*. Berlin, Boston: De Gruyter.

———. 2019a. 'Masorah, Masoretes'. In *Encyclopaedia of the Bible and Its Reception*, edited by Brennan Breed et al., XVII: 1269–1270. Berlin: De Gruyter.

Stemberger, Gunter. 2008. 'Dating Rabbinic Traditions'. In *The New Testament and Rabbinic Literature*, edited by Reimund Bieringer, Florentino García Martínez, Didier Pollefeyt, and Peter Tomson, 79–96. JSJSup 136. Leiden: Brill.

———. 2014. 'Preliminary Notes on Grammar and Orthography in Halakhic Midrashim: Late additions?'. In *The Text of the Hebrew Bible. From the Rabbis to Masoretes*, edited by Elvira Martín-Contreras and Lorena Miralles Maciá, 91–200. Journal of Ancient Judaism, Supplements 13. Göttingen: Vandenhoeck & Ruprecht.

Tov, Emanuel. 2003. 'The Text of the Hebrew/Aramaic and Greek Bible Used in the Ancient Synagogues'. In *The Ancient Synagogue from Its Origins until 200 C.E.: Papers Presented at an International Conference at Lund University October 14–17, 2001,* edited by B. Olsson and M. Zetterholm, 237–59. Coniectanea Biblica. New Testament Series 39. Stockholm: Almqvist & Wiksell International.

Weil, Gerard. E. 1964. *Initiation à la Massorah*. Leiden: Brill.

Yeivin, Israel. 1980. *Introduction to the Tiberian Masorah*. Translated and edited by Ernest J. Revell. Masoretic Studies 5. Missoula, MT: Scholars Press.

MAIN CLAUSE VERBS ARE PROSODICALLY WEAKER THAN NOUNS IN THE TIBERIAN CANTILLATION OF BIBLICAL HEBREW PROSE BOOKS

Robert S. D. Crellin

1.0. Foundations

1.1. Word Classes

Morphemes in the world's languages are typically separated into classes, including verbs, nouns, adjectives, adverbs, prepositions and (e.g., discourse) particles. These classes are known as 'word classes' (and 'parts of speech', 'grammatical categories', or 'lexical categories', see Payne 1997, 32–70). Depending on the language, these categories can overlap: thus in Homeric Greek, for instance, there is considerable overlap between the category of preposition and that of adverb (cf. Haug 2009). The present study is concerned with the relationship between a morpheme's prosodic status and its word class.

 https://doi.org/10.11647/OBP.0498.05

1.2. Functional vs Lexical Classes

Word classes may themselves be categorised into 'functional' (or 'grammatical') and 'content' (or 'lexical') classes (for the distinction see Sapir 1921; Fries 1952). Distinguishing function words from lexical (content) words is the fact that they relate entities in the discourse to one another, whether that be lexical words, clauses or sentences etc. By contrast, content words refer to entities outside the discourse (cf. Crellin 2022a, 11–12). For instance, the preposition 'on', as in 'The cat is on the sofa', relates 'the cat' to 'the sofa', which are named participants in the discourse. By contrast, 'cat' and 'sofa' give labels in the discourse to entities outside it.

Functional word classes are typically closed (Gelderen 2004). This is to say that new members cannot readily be added (Caink 2008, 491). By contrast, lexical word classes are open, meaning that new members may be readily generated by the community of language users.

1.3. Syntactic Structure: Phrase Structure Grammar

Words may be combined to form larger units. It has been a convention for several decades to analyse the surface structure of a sentence as a tree, where each node dominates a contiguous sequence of words. Figure 1 provides a phrase structure representation of Gen. 1:1, as analysed in the Macula treebank.

Figure 1: Phrase structure representation of Gen. 1.1 (Macula)

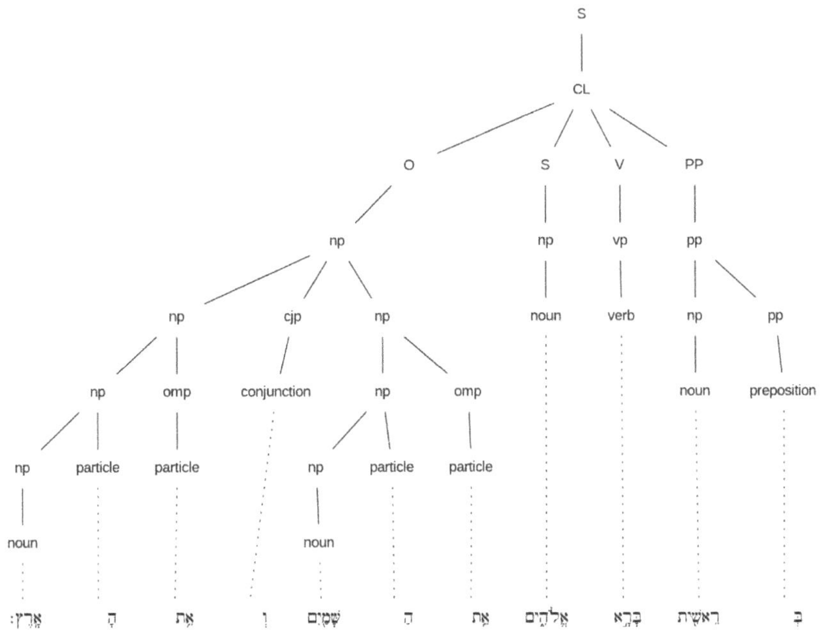

The central insight in phrase structure representations of syntax is that a constituent—viz. a string dominated by a single node in the tree—may be exchanged with another string with the same class as the first string. In Figure 1, the sentence is analysed into prepositional phrase (PP), verb (V), subject (S) and object (O) phrases. By far the longest of these is O: אֵת הַשָּׁמַיִם וְאֵת הָאָרֶץ. In principle this string could be exchanged for an alternative object constituent consisting of a single word or morpheme, e.g., a pronoun.

The tree is hierarchical: in בְּרֵאשִׁית the node for the phrase as a whole (PP) stands above the nodes for each of the constituents (P and NP) respectively.

1.4. Prosodic Structure

The utterance is structured in phrases in a way parallel to the syntax of a sentence. Various levels have been identified (for a helpful overview see Goldstein 2016, 44–46). For our purposes here, it is sufficient to identify three levels: (1) the utterance itself; (2) the prosodic phrase; (3) the prosodic word.

1.4.1. Utterance

This is the highest level of the prosodic hierarchy. Nespor and Vogel define it as follows (2007, 221):

> The last phonological constituent we will consider is the phonological utterance (*U*), the largest constituent in the prosodic hierarchy. A *U* consists of one or more intonational phrases, the category just below it in the hierarchy, and usually extends the length of the string dominated by the highest node of a syntactic tree, which we will refer to as X^n.

They are at pains to point out (2007, 221),

> This is not to say, however, that *U* is simply the phonological counterpart of X^n, a phonological constituent introduced only to avoid making direct reference to syntax in the formulation of phonological rules. In fact, X^n and *U* are not always the same, as will be demonstrated on the basis of several phonological rules that operate within the U domain, but not within the confines of X^n.

For the purpose of the analysis of the Tiberian cantillation tradition of Biblical Hebrew, I take the utterance to correspond to the *verse*, since this is the highest level of the phonological hierarchy. One consequence of this decision is that an utterance will potentially contain more than one sentence.

1.4.2. Prosodic Word

The prosodic word is identified cross-linguistically as the domain of the single main stress or word accent (cf. Truckenbrodt 1999, 220; Crellin 2022a, 12–16 for application in the context of Northwest Semitic, including Biblical Hebrew, and Greek; cf. Fortson 2008, 261 and Crellin 2022b for Latin; see also references in the cited works).

1.4.3. Prosodic Phrase

Prosodic phrases are identified *inter alia* by pauses of varying lengths existing between sequences of prosodic words as they are pronounced (Dresher 1994, 23–25). Prosodic phrases can be nested in a hierarchy. The longer the pause relative to the other pauses in the sentence, the greater the strength of the division, and the higher in the hierarchy the position of the two phrases adjacent to the pause.

1.4.4. Phonological Clisis

Not all morphemes are able to stand as prosodic words in their own right. This arises because the morpheme in question is too short in prosodic terms (where prosodic length may be construed either in terms of syllables or morae, depending on the language, and the prosodic word is minimally binary either in syllables or morae). Such morphemes are incorporated into the prosodic structure of the utterance by being incorporated into a neighbouring prosodic word (the host). Such morphemes are accentually dependent on their host.

There are at least three kinds of phonological clitics: 'free clitics', 'internal clitics', and 'affixal clitics' (for details see Anderson 2005, 46; Goldstein 2016, 48). These are represented in Figure 2, Figure 3 and Figure 4 respectively.

Figure 2: Free clitic

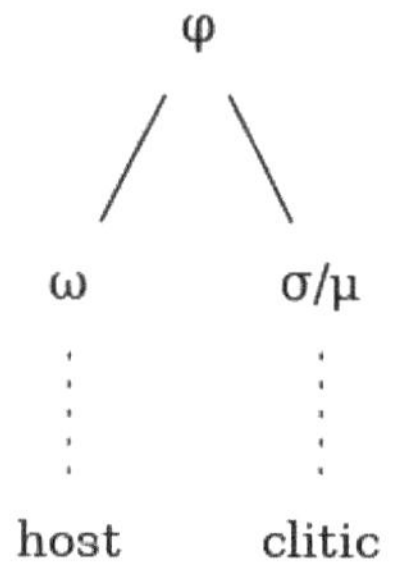

Figure 3: Internal clitic

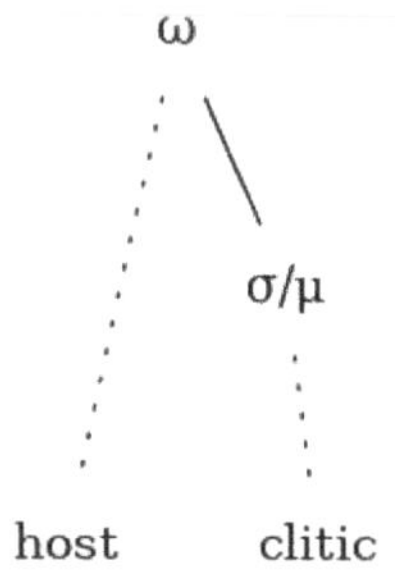

Figure 4: Affixal clitic

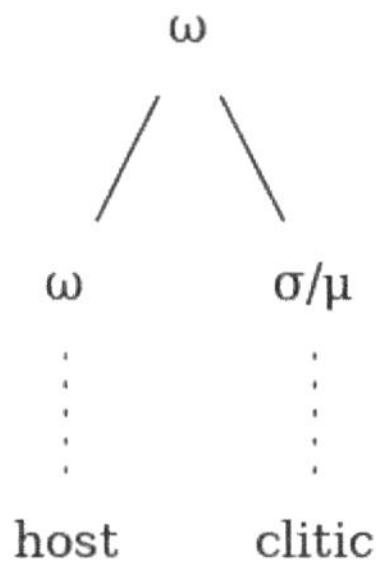

What these all have in common is that the clitic is not a prosodic word in its own right. The prepositions *b-*, *k-* and *l-* are always clitics in Biblical Hebrew, since, standing at not more than one mora in length, they always fall short of the two-mora threshold for prosodic wordhood.

1.5. Relationship Between Word Class and Prosodic Status

A relationship has been observed to exist between the functional status of a morpheme and its prosodic strength: function words are more likely to be prosodically 'weak' or 'deficient' than content words (see Gelderen 2004, Evertz 2018, 140, and references therein). This is to say, function words are more likely to be incorporated into the prosodic structure of neighbouring morphemes at the level of the prosodic word.

Content words are held to be incapable of prosodic deficiency, unless they are members of a special grammaticalised subclass, e.g., auxiliary verbs. Caink is explicit on this point (2008, 491):

> Items that are clitic vary across languages but are always grammatical (or functional) words and thus members of closed classes in that they cannot be coined (Emonds, 1985, Chap. 4); they may include auxiliary verbs, pronouns (as in many Indo-European languages), question particles (Slavic *-li* in (9) or Finnish *-ko* in Nevis, 1988, 9), negative particles (Slavic verbal negation ne -in (9)), and conjunctions (Latin *-que* 'and'). There are no clitic forms for open-class items such as the lexical noun *wood*, despite the homophony with the modal auxiliary *would* (cf. I'd really like that).

While clitics must be function words, according to this view, functional status is not enough to guarantee prosodic deficiency: some function words—such as 'too' and 'off' in English, and 'weil' and 'aus' in German—carry their own word accent despite their functional status (see Evertz 2018, 140, with references).

1.6. Prosody and Syntax Above the Prosodic Word

Just as prosody interacts with morphosyntax at the level of the word, so it does at the level of syntax. This relationship is not, however, isomorphic (Truckenbrodt 1999, 220). It is lexical rather than functional items that are viewed as critical for the alignment of prosodic structure with syntactic. Truckenbrodt identifies a 'lexical category condition' under which "[c]onstraints relating syntactic and prosodic categories apply to lexical syntactic elements and their projections, but not to functional elements and their projections, or to empty syntactic elements and their projections" (1999, 226).

Selkirk is categorical (1996, 191):

> *[T]he set of constraints governing the interface between morphosyntactic and prosodic structure makes no reference to functional categories at all.* Rather, it is only lexical categories and their phrasal projections which would figure in the statement of morphosyntactic constraints on prosodic structure; GCat would stand only for "LexCat" in any constraint of the Align (GCat PCat variety).

The phenomenon under which the phrasal projections of lexical categories align with prosodic phrase boundaries is known as 'edge alignment' (for further explanation and references see Truckenbrodt 2007, 437–438).

2.0. Accessing Syntactic and Phonological Structure in Biblical Hebrew: The TanakhML Treebank

In the preceding section we gave an overview of some foundational concepts in syntax and phonological structure. In the present section I consider the means of accessing syntax and phonological structure in Biblical Hebrew.

Very unusually for a document, or set of documents, with as deep a history as the Hebrew Bible, not only have we received the 'text', that is, the characters corresponding (in the case of Hebrew) to the consonant (and some vowel) phonemes of the spoken language, but also more than one system of 'accents'. The present study is concerned with the Tiberian system, as recorded and described by the medieval community of scholars known as the Masoretes.

These accents were designed to record the system of chanting the Hebrew Bible, recording both the position of the primary accent on prosodic words, and the musical contour of the chant (Yeivin 1980, §178; Aronoff 1985, 33; Dresher 1994, 5–6; Khan 2020, 51).

The accents' connection with the reading tradition or practice of chanting the Hebrew Bible is not disputed. Also not disputed is that the accents have a purpose beyond the marking of the contours of the reading tradition, and that this further purpose has to do with the sense of the text. This is suggested, not least, by the meaning of the Hebrew term טעמים 'senses' (Aronoff 1985, 35; Janis 1987, 4; Dresher 1994, 6). Where there is not agreement is on the linguistic domain of the units demarcated by the accents. It has been proposed that the accents demarcate 'semantic' (Yeivin 1980, §178), syntactic (Aronoff 1985) and prosodic (Dresher 1994) units. For the purposes of the present study, I follow Dresher in taking the accents as denoting prosodic structure.[1]

2.1. Structure Overview

The prosodic structure of Biblical Hebrew for this investigation is provided by the TanakhML treebank (https://www.tanakhml.org/). The structure of the tree is a direct representation of the prosodic structure of the Tiberian accents. As with any tree, a TanakhML tree comprises two fundamental types of node: terminal (= leaves) and non-terminal. Figure 5 gives the hierarchy of dominance in a TanakhML tree.

[1] Space does not permit me to go into the details of why this analysis is preferable. Relevant issues are discussed in Crellin (2022a).

Figure 5: Hierarchy of dominance in a TanakhML tree

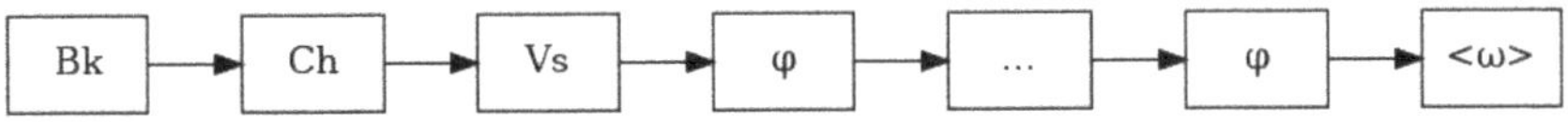

2.2. Terminal Nodes

Terminal nodes correspond to graphematic words (<ω> in Figure 5). Graphematic words are marked up for their accent. The accent may be of one of the following three types: (a) *Maqqef*; (b) Conjunctive; and (c) Disjunctive. Disjunctives are always phrase-final, whereas conjunctives and *maqqef* are never phrase-final.

In Figure 6, terminal nodes are labelled with their accents:

tifḥa, disjunctive (TIP)
munaḥ, conjunctive (MUN)
atnaḥ, disjunctive (ATN)
merka, conjunctive (MER)
tifḥa, disjunctive (TIP)
merka, conjunctive (MER)
silluq, disjunctive (SLQ)

Figure 6: Representation of Gen. 1.1 (TanakhML)

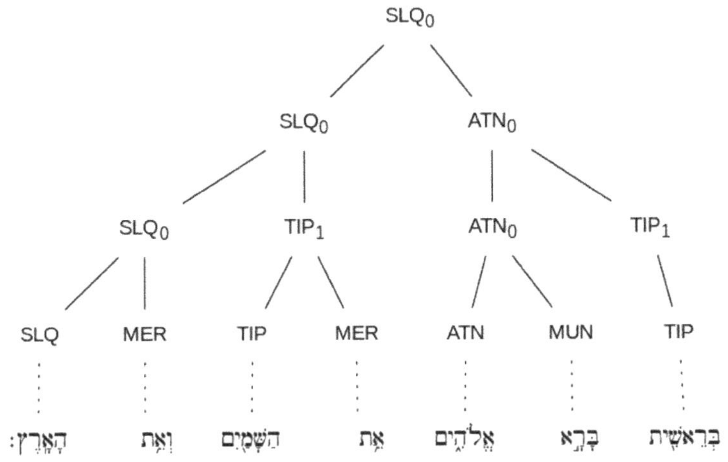

2.3. Non-terminal Nodes

Non-terminal nodes in TanakhML are phrase-level nodes (φ in Figure 5). Non-terminal nodes are labelled for the final disjunctive descendant. The subscript number indicates the position of the accent within the accent hierarchy, to which I now turn.

2.4. Prosodic Strength and the Hierarchy of Accents

Disjunctive accents in Tiberian Hebrew may be divided into four categories according to the strength of the prosodic division which follows (Dresher (1994, 4; Park 2020, 14) ranging from D0 (the strongest) to D3 (the weakest).[2] In purely numerical terms, therefore, the values range from 0 to 3, in reverse order of disjunctive strength.

In this study the conjunctive accents, which indicate that the following item belongs to the same prosodic phrase, are accorded a reverse strength score of 4. In turn, *maqqef*, which indicates that the following item belongs to the same prosodic word, is accorded a reverse strength score of 5.[3]

Since it is more intuitive for prosodic strength to increase in line with numerical value, for this study the prosodic strength of an accent is calculated by subtracting the reverse prosodic strength from 5. In these terms the weakest accent (*maqqef*) obtains a prosodic strength score of 0, while *silluq* and *atnaḥ* obtain

[2] For a recent overview of the accent hierarchy in Tiberian Hebrew, see Park (2020, 9–22).

[3] This is the practice of the TanakhML treebank, where words carrying conjunctive and *maqqef* in TanakhML are given reverse strength scores of 4 and 5 respectively.

a score of 5. In these terms the weakest disjunctive accent has strength 2.

2.5. Contextual Strength of the Disjunctive Accents

Whilst in principle the higher the position of a disjunctive accent is in the hierarchy, the stronger the prosodic pause associated with it, this is not always the case in practice. Specifically, when a series of disjunctives of the same hierarchical level appear in sequence—with or without intervening conjunctives—the strength of the break decreases successively. Park puts the matter as follows (2020, 18):

> [T]he first D_{i+1} level accent presents the greatest relative pause, and the following D_{i+1} level accents indicate progressively lesser pauses. This case presents a unique situation in that the last D_{i+1} level accent appears just before the next level domain (i.e., the D_i level) even though it itself carries the weakest pause.

In the present study, the strength of the *nth* disjunctive in a series of disjunctives of level *i*, without interruption by a disjunctive of a different level, is given by the following formula:

$$s' = s - 1 + 1 / n$$

where s' is the modified disjunct strength, s is disjunct strength and n is the number of consecutive disjunctive accents at level i.

The formula ensures that the contextual disjunctive strength will always be between the nominal disjunctive strength and the disjunctive strength of the next weakest accent class, but never weaker than the latter.

Figure 7: Representation of Gen. 3.1b in TanakhML

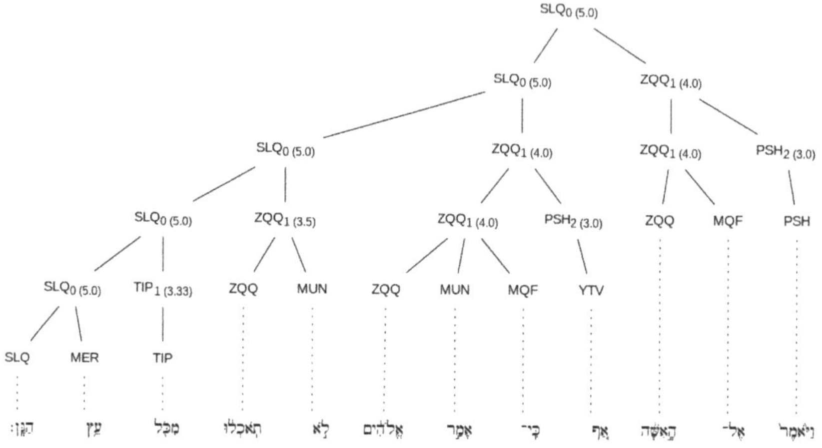

To illustrate how this works, an analysis of Gen. 3.1b is given in Figure 7.[4] The phrase לֹא תֹאכְלוּ terminates in a disjunctive, *little zaqeph*. This is at place D1 in the hierarchy, and is therefore initially accorded disjunct strength 5 − 1 = 4 on my scale. However, it follows immediately on from the phrase אַף כִּי־אָמַר אֱלֹהִים, which also carries *little zaqeph*. Since לֹא תֹאכְלוּ contains no additional disjunctives, we have a case of two disjunctive phrases at the same level in the hierarchy following on from one another. The second of these, לֹא תֹאכְלוּ, therefore carries a lower disjunctive strength than would be expected based on its nominal position in the hierarchy. Specifically its disjunctive strength becomes 4 − 1 + ½ = 3.5.

After this follows the single-word phrase מִכֹּל, carrying the disjunctive accent *tifḥa*. Like *little zaqeph*, *tifḥa* is at place D1 in

[4] The suffixes a, b, c, etc. after verse references distinguish main clauses in the verse.

the hierarchy. Here again then we have a sequence of D1 accents. Since מִכֹּל is the third in the sequence, its adjusted disjunctive strength becomes $4 - 1 + ⅓ \approx 3.33$.

3.0. Analysing Syntax in Biblical Hebrew

3.1. Introduction

If (as we will take to be the case henceforth) the Tiberian Biblical Hebrew accents provide an analysis of prosodic structure rather than syntactic structure, it is important to address briefly the question of how the syntax of Biblical Hebrew is accessed and analysed.

Syntax is a more abstract notion than prosody: prosody can be measured empirically in terms of length of pause, pitch contours etc. Syntax, by contrast, is an abstraction from the surface order of the text into a structure that exposes directly the relationship between the elements. This structure is not provided by (instances of) the language itself, but must be derived by the application of a syntactic theory. The resulting syntactic structure is therefore dependent on the syntactic theory one applies. The syntactic analyses used in the present study are those provided by the Macula treebank.

3.2. Structure of the Macula Treebank

3.2.1. Overview

A schematic representation of the dominance hierarchy in a Macula syntax tree is given in Figure 8.

Figure 8: Hierarchy of dominance in a Macula syntax tree

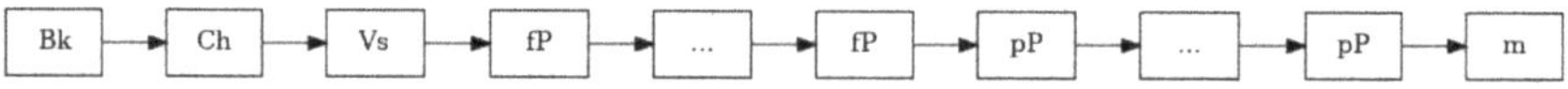

As in the case of the TanakhML treebank, terminal and non-terminal nodes correspond to different functions (see Tan and Wu 2022, 2).

3.2.2. Terminal Nodes

Terminal nodes (corresponding to *m* in Figure 8) are 'word-level' units in some sense: "A terminal node is the basic unit of syntactic analysis, usually corresponding to the type of speech analysis for each *word* as provided by the OSHB morphology" (Tan and Wu 2022, 5). While Tan and Wu (2022) use the term 'word', these units are not graphematic words, as in the TanakhML treebank, but rather 'morphosyntactic words'. Thus in Figure 1 the article הָ and the conjunction וְ occupy separate terminal nodes, despite not being graphematic words. This is, of course, reasonable, since, though these morphemes are never written as separate words in our texts, they do not have the same morphosyntactic function as their graphematic hosts (see further Crellin 2022a).

3.2.3. Non-terminal Nodes: Phrase-level Syntactic Categories

Non-terminal nodes in Macula are of two kinds: clause-level and phrase-level. These are indicated in Figure 8 by the labels *fP* ('f' for 'functional') and *pP* ('p' for 'phrase'), respectively. Tan and Wu (2022, 6) describe the phrase level as follows:

> The phrase level is the intermediate level between word level and clause level. Phrase level nodes are either non-

terminal nodes that are the immediate parent nodes of the part-of-speech terminal nodes or parent nodes of other phrase level non-terminal nodes that together form multi-word phrases. From the perspective of the clause, single words or combinations of words form phrases, which are the minimal constituents with a specific function at the clause level.

3.2.4. Non-terminal Nodes: Clause-level Syntactic Categories

The purpose of clause-level nodes is apparently to provide information on the grammatical function of its descendant nodes within the sentence. From Figure 1 it may be seen that each clause level node (S, O, V, etc.) has a single daughter phrase level node.[5]

An exception to this is where a clause-level node comprises a clause in its own right, in which case a clause-level node dominates a CL node containing its own clause. In Figure 9 the object (O) constituent of the first clause (CL) immediately dominates a CL node, which in turn immediately dominates another CL node, which in turn immediately dominates a subject (S) and a predicate (P) node.[6]

---

[5] Tan and Wu (2022, 6) describe the role of clause-level nodes as follows: "The clause level differs from the phrase level by using a dependency-like structure. The terminology used to describe the functions of clause level constituents is purposely conservative for ease of understanding and to preserve a clearer link between clause level terminology and phrase and word level terminology."

[6] As explained below, clause-level nodes with nominal categories (S, O and PP) containing subclauses (CL nodes) are excluded from this study.

Figure 9: Graphical representation of Macula syntax tree of Gen. 1.4a

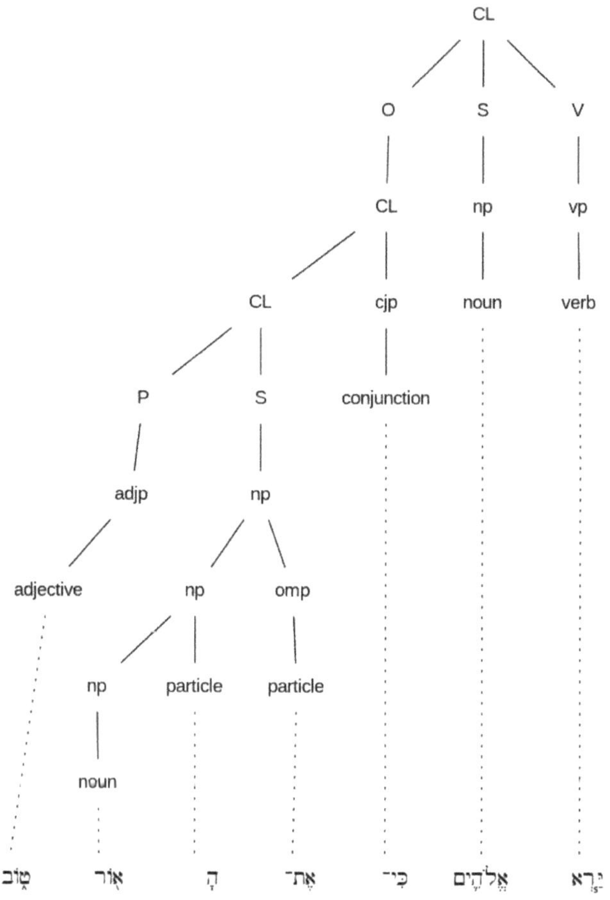

3.2.5. Predicative Sentences Involving היה

In sentences containing predications made with היה, the predicative constituent is labelled O in Macula, per Figure 10.

Figure 10: Gen. 4.2b (syntax)

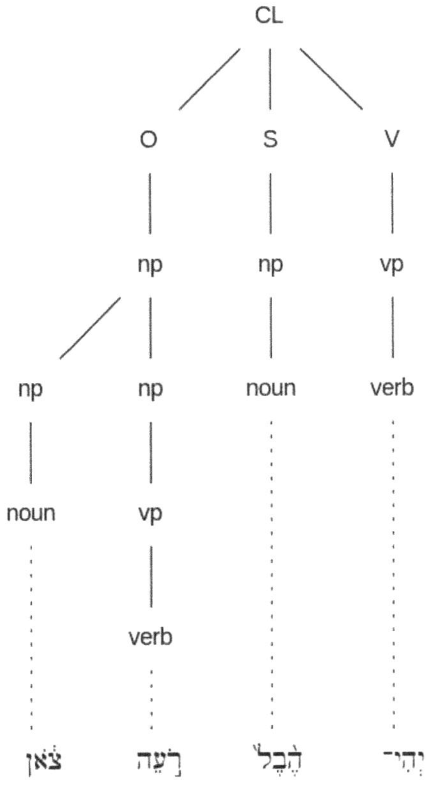

3.2.6. Sentences and Verses

The Macula treebank has an idiosyncratic feature when viewed from a purely syntactic perspective: the root node of a syntactic tree in Macula corresponds to a verse of the Biblical text rather than a sentence: "[T]he Greek trees are sentence-based and frequently cross verse boundaries, whereas the Hebrew trees are verse-based" (Tan and Wu 2022, 2).

Syntactically Gen. 1.1 (Figure 1) comprises a single sentence (= main clause) whereas Gen. 1.4 (Figure 9) comprises two sentences (= main clauses). The alignment of root nodes with the verse level is shown in the fact that both verses have a single S node as its root: the separate sentences of Gen. 1.4 are headed by separate CL nodes joined by means of conjunctions. In the purely syntactic sense, therefore, sentences correspond to top-level CL nodes.

4.0. Integrating Syntactic and Prosodic Treebanks

4.1. Indexing and Minimal Word-level Units

Crucial to integrating two treebanks that were not specifically designed with one another's structure in mind is referencing and indexing. This is to say, it is critical that, when a given word-unit is identified in one treebank, its counterpart in the other treebank can be unambiguously identified.

The Macula and TanakhML treebanks are aligned at the levels of the book, chapter and verse, and at the level of the graphematic word (<ω>) (see Figure 11). The two are not aligned at the levels of the phonological phrase (φ) and the syntactic phrase (P), since the purpose of the treebank is to investigate the relationship between these two.

Figure 11: Alignment of Macula and TanakhML treebanks

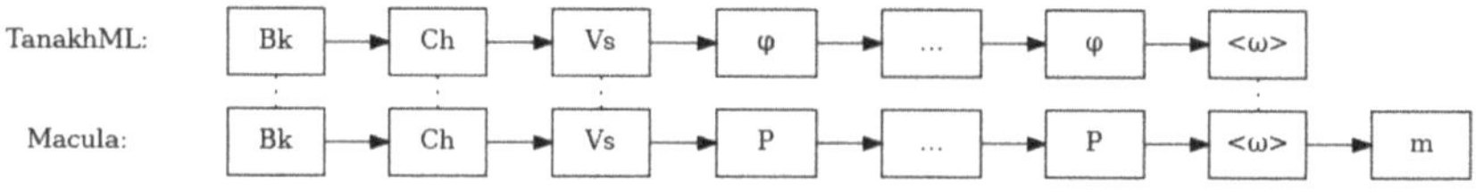

Alignment at the level of the verse is rendered straightforward by the fact that the root node of a Macula tree corresponds to its root node corresponding to the same root node in TanakhML, namely, the verse (see above).

4.2. Alignment at the Level of the Graphematic Word

As we have seen, the minimal unit (= terminal node) in a TanakhML tree is the graphematic word, while the minimal unit in a Macula tree is the morphosyntactic word. This is indicated in Figure 11 by the domination by the terminal syntactic phrase node (P) of the morphosyntactic word node (m).

The alignment at the level of the graphematic word is crucial for analysing the relationship between morphosyntax and prosody in Biblical Hebrew. This is because the graphematic word may be said to correspond to the minimal prosodic word (Crellin 2022a). This means that phonological phrase divisions cannot intervene between elements of the graphematic word, even if morphosyntactic divisions do. A prosodic division will, therefore, never occur within a graphematic word, and the minimal unit for the purpose of this study is therefore the graphematic word.

While the graphematic word is a category native to TanakhML, it is not to the Macula treebank. In order to align the treebanks at the level of the graphematic word, therefore, it was necessary to generate this category secondarily in the Macula object model.

4.3. Corpus

The corpus chosen for the present analysis was that of three (Classical) Biblical Hebrew books consisting largely of prose: Genesis, Exodus and 1 Kings. Poetic books were excluded on the grounds that it is not implausible that the relationship between syntax and prosody might be different in Biblical Hebrew poetry.[7]

4.4. Textual Differences

A significant issue in aligning the treebanks is that the underlying texts of Macula and TanakhML are not identical. For the most part the differences are minor: the vast majority of differences pertain to the order of the unicode encoding of the diacritics in unicode. There are, however, some more significant differences: for example, at Gen. 36.5, TanakhML is lacking the object marker אֶת before יְעֽוּשׁ.

For the purposes of the present study, if the consonantal texts of a verse are the same in both Macula and TanakhML, the verse's graphematic words are analysed; if the consonantal texts differ, or the analysis is lacking in one or both treebanks, the verse is excluded.[8]

At first sight, the use of the consonantal text as a yardstick of identity might be surprising for a (combination of) treebanks fundamentally concerned with phonology and, therefore, with the vocalised text. However, the use of the consonantal text as a

[7] My thanks to James Cuénod and Ryder Wishart (personal communication, March 2023) for highlighting the importance of considering genre at this point.

[8] In practice, the following verses are excluded on these grounds: Gen. 5.29, 8.18, 14.17, 18.18, 35.22, 36.5, 36.14 and 39.20; Exod. 4.10, 9.22, 10.13, 20.2, 20.3, 20.4, 20.5, 20.6, 20.7, 20.8, 20.9, 20.10, 20.13, 20.15, 21.8, 22.4, 28.1 and 38.12; 1 Kgs 1.27, 4.7, 6.2, 6.3, 6.10, 6.38, 8.11, 8.48, 9.18, 14.2, 16.19, 16.33, 17.15, 19.11, 20.5, 20.29 20.25, 21.29 and 22.49.

yardstick of similarity is justified since, although the purpose of combining the treebanks is to provide the possibility of querying on the syntax-phonology interface, it is not a requirement that the vocalised text with accents be the same in both treebanks, only that it be visible in one of them.

5.0. Prosodic Strength by Word Class in Biblical Hebrew: Quantitative Analysis of the Depth of Prosodic Division at the Level of the Graphematic Word

Figure 12: Gen. 1–50: Depth of prosodic division at the level of the graphematic word

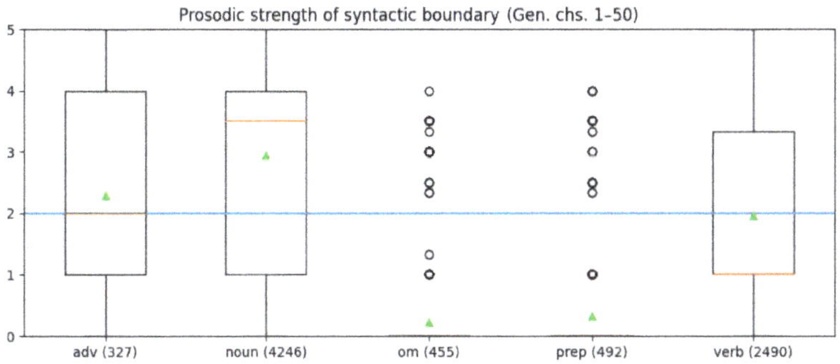

Figure 13: Exod. 1–40: Depth of prosodic division at the level of the graphematic word

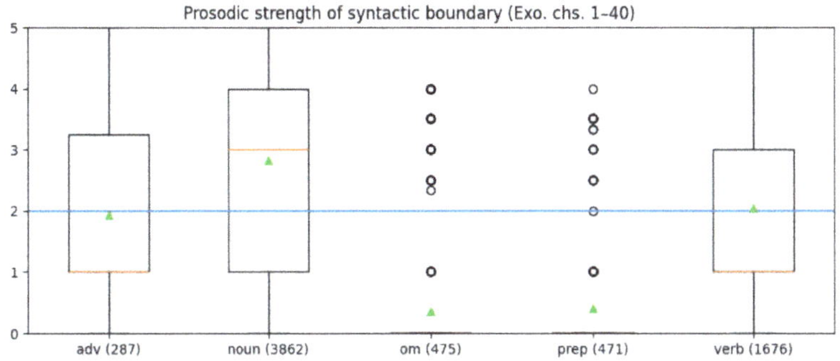

Figure 14: 1 Kgs 1–22: Depth of prosodic division at the level of the graphematic word

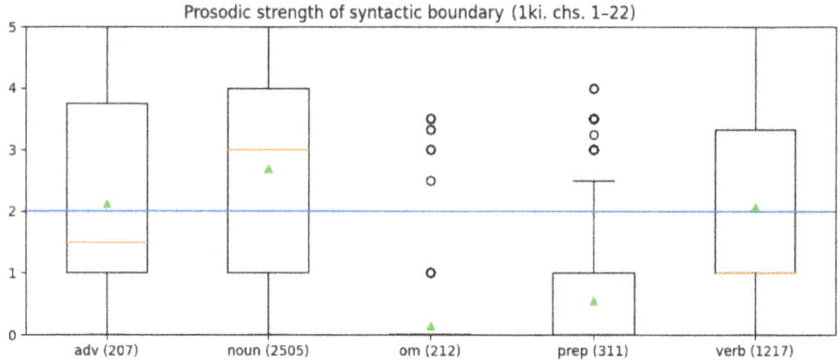

Figures 12–14 give the distribution of the strength of the prosodic boundary after instances of each word class (noun, verb, object marker [*om*], and preposition [*prep*]) in Genesis, Exodus and 1 Kings. Only sentences consisting exclusively of a main clause were included (i.e., subordinate clauses were excluded).

The figures show that the median accent on verbal forms is conjunctive (strength 1).[9] By contrast, the median accent on the noun is disjunctive (> 2). In terms of mean the verb also has a lower disjunctive strength than the noun: ≈ 2 vs ≈ 3. On both

[9] The results of this part of the investigation are here presented as 'box plots', plotted using *Matplotlib* (Hunter 2007). Box plots show the distribution of the data. Distributions are represented as boxes, where the lower edge of the box gives the first quartile (= median of the lower half of the dataset), the upper edge gives the third quartile. The box as a whole, therefore, provides a visualisation of the interquartile range. The lower and upper whiskers of the box plot identify the minimum and maximum respectively. The green triangle marks the mean, while the orange line marks the median. For further information on box plots, see https://en.wikipedia.org/wiki/Box_plot, last accessed 23 September 2022.

measures, therefore, the verb shows a lower propensity to bound prosodic phrases than nominal forms.

Prosodically weakest are the object marker (*om*) and the preposition, with a median boundary strength of 0 (*maqqef*), while the distribution of the adverb generally parallels that of the verb (see further below) although its disjunctive strength is perhaps marginally greater than the verb (see especially distributions in Genesis and 1 Kings).

From the average strength of the following prosodic division, a cline of prosodic status can be inferred:

noun > adverb > verb > object marker, preposition

The prosodic weakness of the object marker and the preposition is to be expected: both are closed word classes, and their members are highly grammaticalised. The prosodic weakness of adverbs is similarly expected, since (in the Macula scheme) important grammatical words such as the negative adverb are included in their number. By contrast, verbs are prosodically weaker than nouns. This is *a priori* unexpected, since the verb in Biblical Hebrew is an open lexical class, just like the noun, and would therefore be expected to behave prosodically like the noun. It is the goal of the rest of this chapter to ascertain a reason for this unexpected difference.

6.0. Prosody and Syntax in Tiberian Biblical Hebrew

6.1. Introduction

I turn first to the interface between prosody and syntax: in many syntactic models the verb forms a syntactic constituent, at some level of analysis, with the object (see e.g., 'Verb phrase', https://en.wikipedia.org/wiki/Verb_phrase, last accessed 28 March 2023). A related point is that many models expect the deepest prosodic divide in the sentence to be between the subject and the predicate (Dresher 1994, 25; Devine and Stephens 1994, 386;). Given the relationship that is generally found to exist between syntax and prosody, one might expect to find the strongest phonological divide to be between the subject and the predicate. The corollary of this is that the subject and the verb would be "unlikely to form a phonological phrase" (Devine and Stephens 1994, 386). It could be, therefore, that the relatively lower prosodic strength of the verb relative to the noun is due to the verb's tendency to form a prosodic phrase with a following object or non-subject phrase.[10]

---

[10] Constituent order in Biblical Hebrew has received considerable attention in recent years (see e.g., Holmstedt 2009; Hornkohl 2018; Khan and van der Merwe 2020). Indeed, there has been a growing appreciation of the importance of pragmatics and semantics, as well as syntax, in providing a context for understanding the surface word order of Biblical Hebrew sentences.

6.2. Quantitative Analysis of Prosodic Depth and Constituent Order

6.2.1. Constraints

The prosodic strength at the boundaries of major constituents in the same corpus was analysed, namely: Genesis, Exodus and 1 Kings. The constraints adopted were as follows: (a) sentences included consist only of the elements labelled, i.e., an SVO sentence starts with the subject constituent and ends with an O constituent; (b) constituents do not contain subclauses, i.e., an O constituent contains no subclause; (c) functional categories are calculated on the final element of the graphematic word. An important consequence of this is that VO sequences involving a verb and suffix pronoun, which will always manifest as O, were excluded.[11] This is helpful for the analysis, since, as enclitics, there is no prosodic boundary after V in such sentences, and these could skew the results to make the verbs look prosodically weaker than they in fact are; (d) non-verbal predicates (denoted P in Macula) are excluded.

To summarise: the sentences included in this study are main clauses containing no subordinate clauses. Consequently all verbs are main verbs. The reasons for restricting the corpus of verses in this way are: (a) since we are interested in the boundaries of verbal and non-verbal forms, it is important that we exclude the possibility of a boundary between a verb and non-verb

---

[11] This is because, from the perspective of the query engine such sentences will appear to have no verb, and so will not feature in the analysis, since only sentences including V constituents are included.

occurring at the right edge of a subordinate clause; and (b) the prosody of verbs in subordinate clauses is known to differ from that of main clause verbs in some languages (see below in this chapter for an example from Indo-European).[12]

6.2.2. Prosodic Boundary after First Syntactic Constituent

The distribution of prosodic strengths after the first functional phrase are given in the form of box plots in Figures 15–17.

Figure 15: Gen. 1–50 X|XX

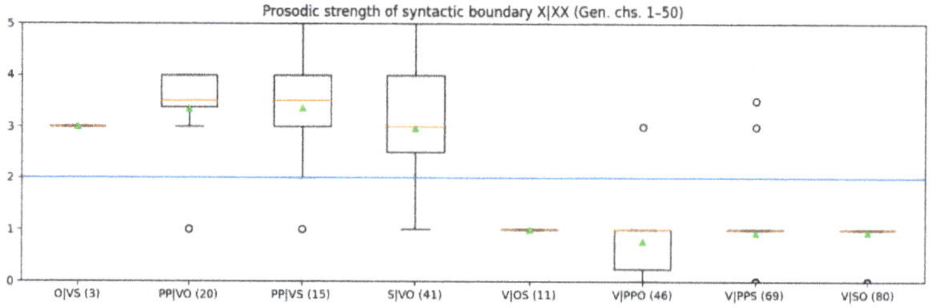

Figure 16: Exod. 1–40 X|XX

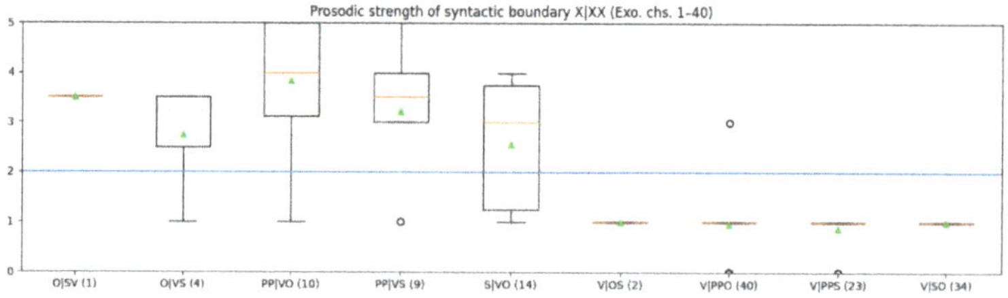

[12] Sequences included were: SVO, OVS, VOS, OVS, OSV, PPVS, SOV, SPPO, VPPS, VPPO, PPVS and PPVO. However, not all sequences were found in all books.

Figure 17: 1 Kgs 1–22 X|XX

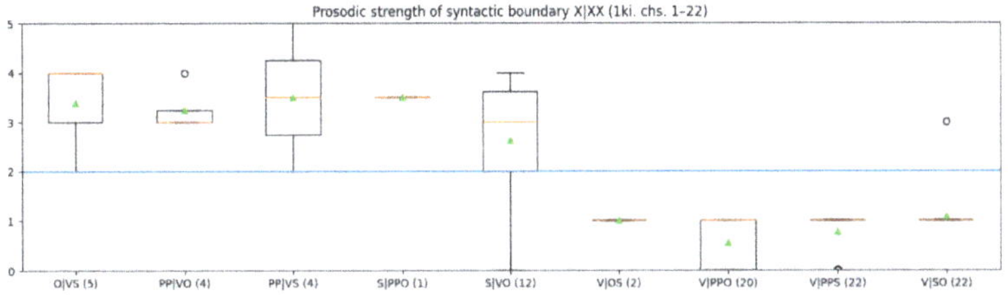

All three plots show a remarkable distinction in the prosodic structure of the first two constituents in VXX sentences, versus XVX or XPPX sentences: in VXX sentences a prosodic phrase boundary is rarely if ever present between V and the constituent that follows it; by contrast there is almost always a prosodic phrase boundary after the first constituent of XVX sentences.

6.2.3. Prosodic Boundary after Second Syntactic Constituent

The distribution of prosodic strengths after the second functional phrase are given in the form of box plots in Figures 18–20.

Figure 18: Gen. 1–50 XX|X

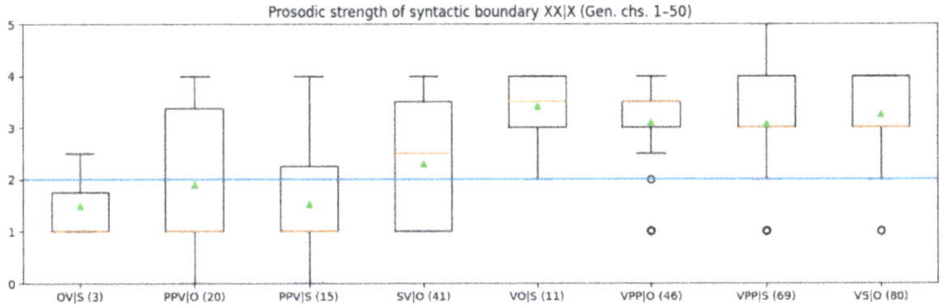

Figure 19: Exod. 1–40 XX|X

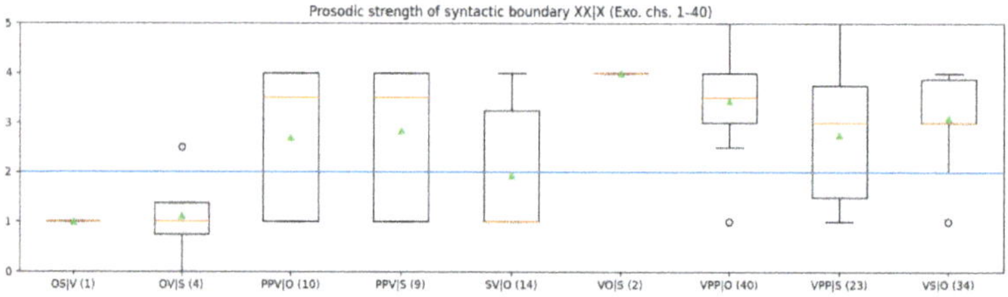

Figure 20: 1 Kgs 1–22 XX|X

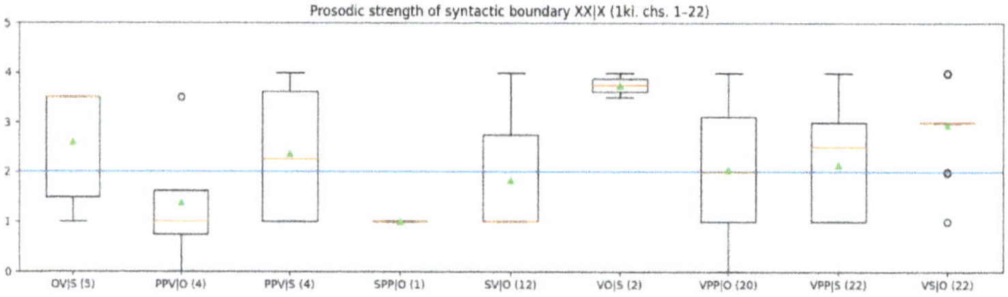

At the boundary between constituents two and three we find almost the reverse distribution of that found in the prosodic structure of the boundary between constituents one and two, although the distinction between VXX and XVX sentences is not quite as clear as in the case of the boundary after the first constituent. In VXX sentences, there is usually a prosodic phrase boundary between X and X, whilst there is much more variation in the nature of the boundary between V and X in XVX sentences: the median accent is often conjunctive, i.e., the boundary is characterised by the lack of a prosodic boundary. However, the interquartile range often straddles both disjunctive and conjunctive accents, showing that in an important number of cases a prosodic phrase boundary occurs between V and X.

6.2.4. Differences between Books

It is regrettably beyond the scope of the present contribution to go into detail regarding the similarities and differences between Bible books. While the broad picture is remarkably consistent across the corpus analysed, it is worth noting some interesting differences, to be pursued in future work. In particular the boundary between V and X in XVX sentences in Exodus is much stronger than in the other books considered, although we also see median disjunctive boundaries in Genesis (SVO) and 1 Kings (OVS, PPVS). The number of instances in each case is small: further investigation is needed.

6.3. Discussion

In what follows the particular behaviour of SVO, VSO, V + X and ADV + X sequences are discussed. The guiding question at issue is to determine what might help explain the apparent prosodic weakness of the Biblical Hebrew main verb. Owing to the limited scope of the present contribution, examples are furnished from Genesis only.

6.3.1. SVO Sentences

While not statistically predominant, SVO sentences have been argued to be the basic word order in (Classical) Biblical Hebrew (Holmstedt 2009). Consider the SVO sentence in Figure 21 (syntax) and Figure 22 (prosody) of Gen. 4.1a.

Figure 21: Gen. 4.1a (syntax)

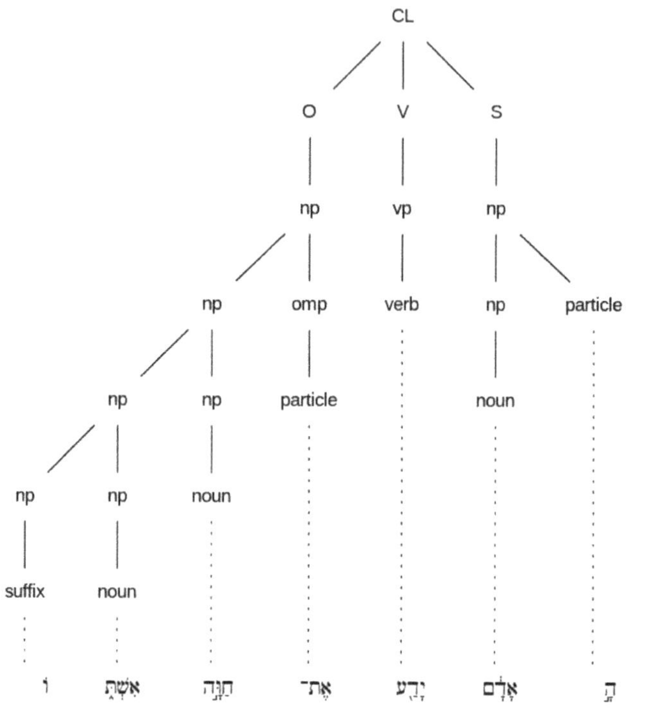

Figure 22: Gen. 4.1a (prosody)

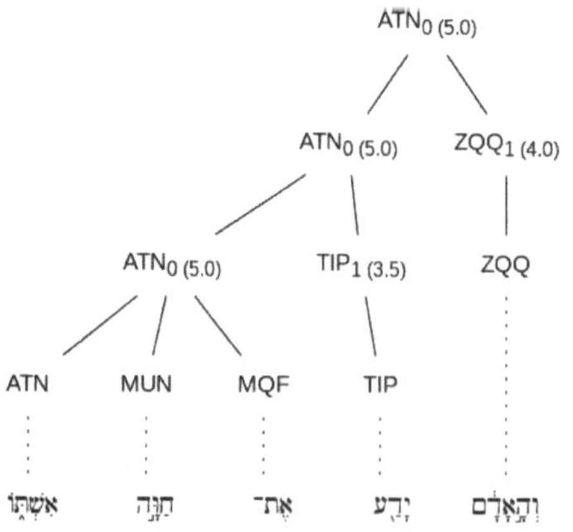

Comparison of the prosodic and syntactic trees shows that the prosodic structure closely mirrors the syntactic, in that prosodic phrase boundaries occur at major syntactic boundaries, namely, after S, הָאָדָ֔ם and after V, יָדַ֖ע.

Furthermore, although the disjunctive strength of the two accents, *little zaqeph* and *tifḥa* respectively, is the same (4 out of 5 on the scale used here), because disjunct strength is contextual (see above), the strength of the pause after the verb יָדַ֖ע is smaller than that after the subject הָאָדָ֔ם. This means that the deepest prosodic break in the sentence is after the subject, exactly where it is expected to be on syntactic grounds.

From the plots, it can be seen that there is a greater prosodic separation between subject and predicate than between verb and object. In 1 Kings and Exodus the median accent after the subject is a disjunctive, whereas between the verb and the object the median accent is conjunctive. In Genesis, in both cases, the median accent is a disjunctive, but the median strength of the disjunctive is lower. Here is evidence, therefore, that in Biblical Hebrew SVO sentences, syntax and prosody align as they would be expected to from a cross-/general-linguistic perspective. However, the difference is not very great, and in both cases the median accent is disjunctive.

6.3.2. VSO

As is well known, the statistically predominant word order in Biblical Hebrew is not SVO but VS(O) (Khan and van der Merwe 2020; for discussion of the 'basic' word order in Biblical Hebrew, see the discussion in Khan and van der Merwe 2020 and Holmstedt 2009).

The syntactically significant point is that the subject in VSO sentences stands between the verb and the predicate. On the level of surface syntax (leaving prosody aside briefly) the sentence cannot therefore be analysed straightforwardly into subject and predicate in cases where the predicate consists of more than a verb constituent.

The prosodic corollary of this is that in Biblical Hebrew we should obtain one or both of the following patterns: either (a) a prosodic divide occurs between the verb and the following constituents (S and O); or (b) a prosodic separation occurs between verb and subject, on the one hand, and the object, on the other.[13] Crucially, a prosodic boundary between subject and predicate (verb phrase) cannot be obtained, because the verb phrase is interrupted by the subject.

Figures 15–17 show that, in all three books considered, the first pattern, with a phrase boundary between V and S, is almost non-existent. Instead, all the examples are with a phrase boundary between S and O, e.g., Gen. 1.7a (Figure 23).

Figure 23: Gen. 1.7a (syntax)

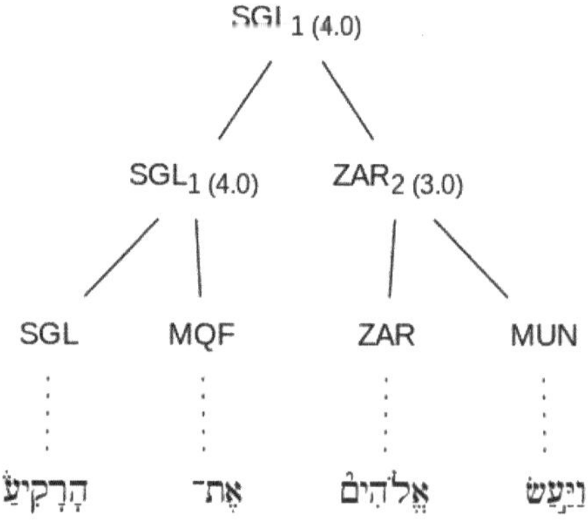

[13] The entire sentence could, of course, form a prosodic phrase. However, this is unlikely except in the very shortest of sentences, e.g., Gen. 23.9a.

6.3.3. V + X

A verb is not restricted to forming a prosodic phrase with a following subject constituent. When initial, V forms a prosodic phrase with *any* following nominal constituent, whether S, O or PP. This emerges clearly from perusal of the final four columns of Figure 15 and Figure 17, which show that only a handful of instances of (mostly V + PP sequences) are separated by a disjunctive; otherwise V forms a prosodic phrase with the following constituent.

When V is second, there is also a tendency for it to form a prosodic phrase with the following constituent, although, as already noted, the plots show that there is a greater range of attested behaviour.

6.3.4. ADV + X

The prosodic behaviour of adverb phrases in relation to following syntactic constituents shows similar features to that of verbs (see Figure 24 and Figure 25).[14] This is to say that adverbs frequently form a prosodic phrase (or word) with a following item.

---

[14] The search included ADVVS, ADVOV, ADVSV, SADVV, VADVS, ADVVS, SADVV, OADVV, ADVPPV, VSADV, ADVPPS, ADVPPO. Not all these sequences were found in Genesis.

Figure 24: Gen. 1–50 X|XX: Depth of prosodic division between constituents in sentences containing adverbs

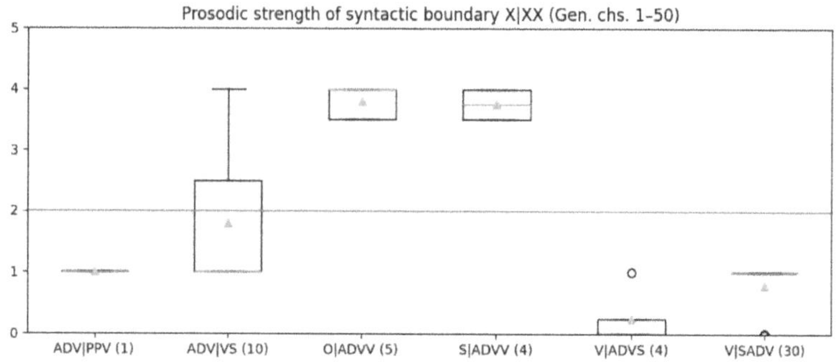

Figure 25: Gen. 1–50 XX|X: Depth of prosodic division between constituents in sentences containing adverbs

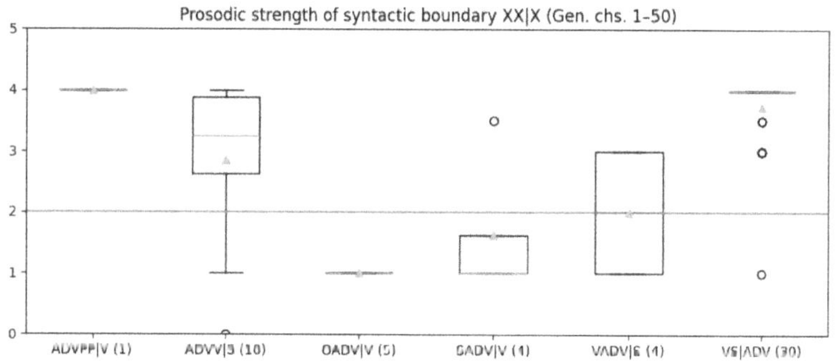

Closer inspection of the box plots reveals that in most cases the adverb forms a prosodic phrase with a following verb. This is perhaps not surprising, since adverbs typically modify verbs (hence the name).

6.3.5. (ADV + V) + X / (V + ADV) + X

Where an adverb is followed by a word of a class other than a verb, e.g., a noun phrase, there is typically a prosodic boundary, e.g., Gen. 45.21a (VADVS) in Figure 26 (syntax) and Figure 27 (prosody).

Figure 26: Gen. 45.21a (syntax)

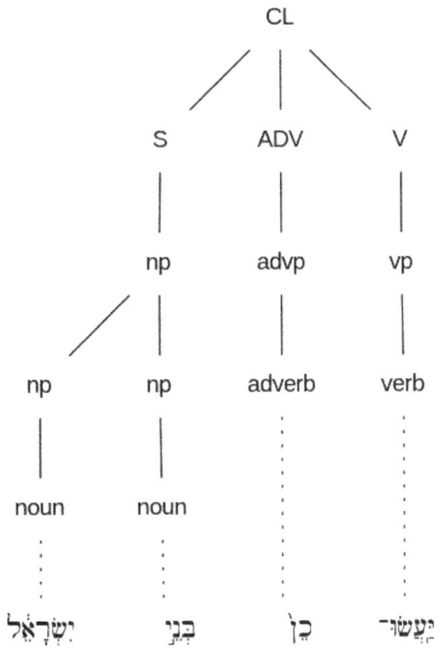

Figure 27: Gen. 45.21a (prosody)

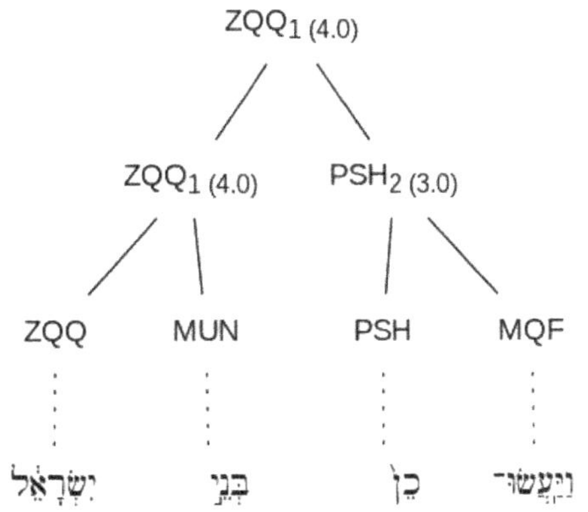

Note, however, that here the verb forms a prosodic word with the adverb. It is then after this verb-adverb complex that the prosodic phrase boundary falls.

Figure 25 shows that a prosodic phrase boundary also tends to fall after a verb if it is preceded by an adverb. This is an interesting exception to the general rule, observed above, that a verb tends to form a prosodic phrase with a following item. Consider Gen. 15.5e (ADVVS) in Figure 28 (syntax) and Figure 29 (prosody).

Figure 28: Gen. 15.5e (syntax)

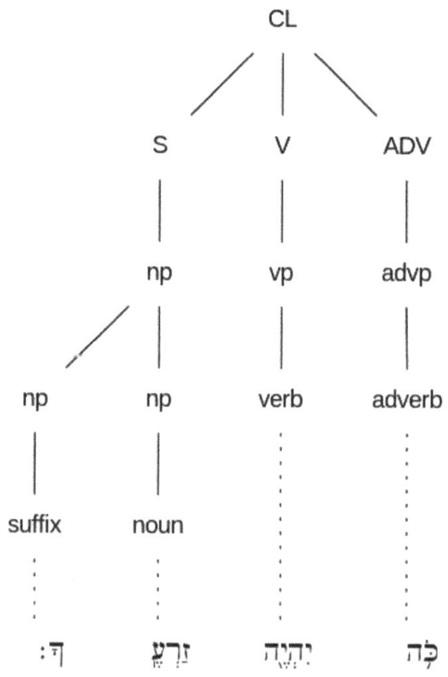

Figure 29: Gen. 15.5e (prosody)

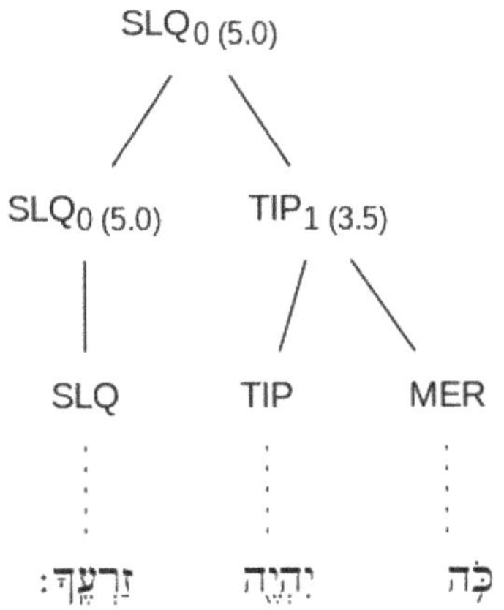

The important point is that, both in this case and in the previous one, the verb forms a (syntactic) phrase with the adverb; the boundary between the adverb-verb complex and the following item therefore follows the last word of this complex, whether it is the verb or the adverb. (Note that this point is not revealed in the Macula syntax tree, since adverbs, or adverb phrases, are presented as top level constituents.)

7.0. Accounting for the Prosodic Integration of Tiberian Biblical Hebrew Verbs

7.1. Are Biblical Hebrew Verbs Clitics?

The verb clearly shows a propensity to form a single prosodic phrase with a following constituent, especially when sentence-initial. We have seen that this phenomenon is largely unrelated to the syntactic role of the constituent following the verb: S, O and PP all show the same interaction with V in this position; the only exception to this is in SVO sentences, where a prosodic phrase boundary is present after V. In most syntactic contexts, therefore, it appears to be the fact of being a verb that drives the prosodic weakening of V. (I will return to the issue of SVO sentences at the end of the chapter.)

The propensity of V to become incorporated into the prosodic phrase of a following morpheme might be considered analogous to cliticization: in both cases a morpheme becomes prosodically integrated with a neighbouring one. Another similarity with cliticization is that the prosodic integration of V has a clear polarity (for a discussion of clitic polarity in connection with Ancient Greek, see Goldstein 2016, 60–68): it always forms a prosodic phrase with the following constituent, but rarely if ever with the previous one.

Indeed, the lack of accent on Hebrew verb forms, except *in pausa*, was already proposed by Kuryłowicz. In a discussion of the details of the system of Hebrew accentuation within the word (in comparison with Vedic), he states, "The above data suggest as their simplest explanation an original distribution of stressed and unstressed forms of simple verbs, viz. stressed forms *in pausa*, unstressed forms before another member of the sentence" (1959, 128).

However, the proposal that verbs are clitics in Biblical Hebrew suffers from two principal difficulties. First, the prosodic dependence of V differs from (prototypical) clitics in that the unit so formed is (for the most part) a prosodic *phrase*, not a prosodic *word*: phonological clitics (see introduction) do not carry their own accent (see e.g., Caink 2008, 491), whereas verbs in (Tiberian) Biblical Hebrew do. Exceptional are cases where the verb does form a prosodic word with the following item, such as Gen. 4.2b (see Figure 30):

Figure 30: Gen. 4.2b (prosody)

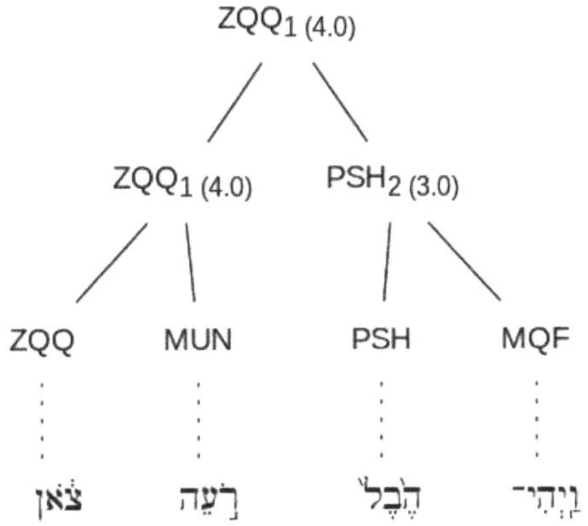

A further objection is that the verb is an open class, whereas, as we have seen, clitics are required (at least by some scholars) to belong to closed (functional) classes (Caink 2008, 491) In the following sections I set out to address these concerns in turn.

7.2. Excursus: A Parallel from Indo-European

The prosodic weakening of V in Tiberian Biblical Hebrew has a striking parallel in a feature of early Indo-European, namely the lack of accent on main clause verbs in Vedic Sanskrit (Kuryłowicz 1959; details and exceptions see Kuryłowicz 1959, 123; Hock 1982, 1; Hock 2014, 154; Hock 2015, 69). “As is well known, (simple) Vedic finite verbs are unaccented in main clauses (unless initial in the clause or poetic line), but accented in dependent structures” (Hock 2015, 69).

Wackernagel offered an explanation of this behaviour in terms of cliticization. "[W]e must expect that in the ancestor language the verb in the main clause was placed immediately after the first word in the clause because, and insofar as, it was enclitic" (quote 2020, 327; see also Hock 2015, 70). Wackernagel himself was equivocal (2020, 327):

> I do not wish to deny that the proposal put forward here could be made less general. For the law regarding the placement of enclitics (disregarding e.g., vocatives) we have only been able to adduce examples in which the enclitic is no larger than two syllables. It could therefore be said that the law was only valid for monosyllabic and disyllabic enclitics, and that those of more than two syllables remained in the position that the constituent in question would otherwise receive—or at least, to express the idea more carefully, that above a certain size threshold an enclitic was not bound by the positional law of the enclitics. Applying this to the verb would lead to the assumption that monosyllabic and disyllabic verb forms, or shorter verbal forms below a certain threshold, moved to second position in main clauses, and that the other verbal forms in main clauses kept to the position that was dominant in subordinate clauses.

Nevertheless, it was accepted for a number of years (see Hock 1982, 3 and Hock 2015, 52), although it has fallen out of favour more recently and other explanations adduced (Hock 2015, 69–71). For present purposes it is sufficient to note that a key part of the rejection of the verb-as-clitic proposal is that verbs are prototypically too prosodically heavy to have clitic status (Hock 1982, 1–4). Thus Fortson denies clitic status to the verb, except in limited circumstances (2008, 266):

It should also be emphasized that for the other Indo-European languages, even if verbs were atonic or lower in pitch, there is no evidence that they were clitics except for special instances, and, as in Latin, the strongest evidence of cliticization and/or weaker accentuation comes from the mono- and dissyllabic forms. In Greek, the only truly enclitic verbs are monosyllabic and dissyllabic forms of εἰμί and φημί.

7.3. Prosodic Word Clitics

A major difficulty with positing prosodic incorporation at the level of the prosodic phrase is, therefore, that clitics are usually defined as morphemes that are phonologically deficient at the level of the prosodic word (cf. Anderson 2005, 45–46). However, while most discussion of prosodic deficiency/dependency focuses on these sub-prosodic word clitics, the existence of sub-prosodic phrase clitics has also been observed (Anderson 2005, 32, 46; Goldstein 2016, 48–52). Anderson gives the examples of Italian *loro* 'to them' and Tagalog *tayo* 'we (dual)' as cases in point (2005, 32). These clitics, sometimes termed 'special clitics', are incorporated with their host to project a prosodic phrase (Anderson 2005, 46; Goldstein 2016, 48; see Figure 31).

Ancient Greek 'postpositives' have been analysed in these terms (Goldstein 2016, 48–52): these carry their own accent, but nevertheless have syntactic distributions that demonstrate dependence on a host (Goldstein 2016, 48–52). As the name suggests, they are placed immediately after their prosodic host (Figure 31). Morphemes in this category are all functional particles, such as γάρ, μέν, δέ (for further information see Goldstein 2016, 48, 51).

Figure 31: Prosodic word clitic: Ancient Greek postpositive (per Goldstein 2016, 51, fig. 3.16)

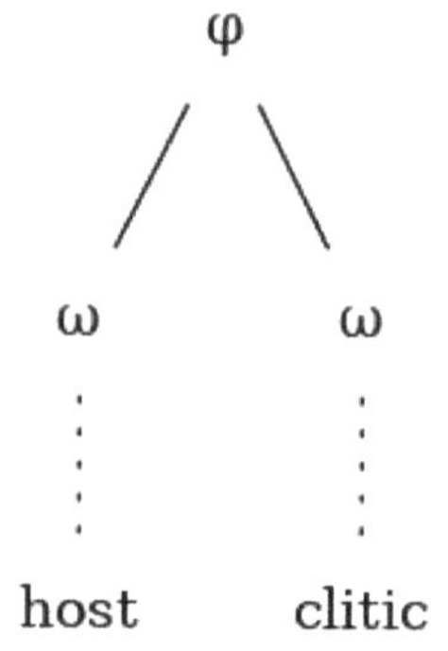

An analysis of Biblical Hebrew verbs and adverbs as prosodic word clitics can account for the distribution we have observed: in our case, the verb is placed prior to the host, per Figure 32.

Figure 32: Prosodic word clitic: Hebrew verb

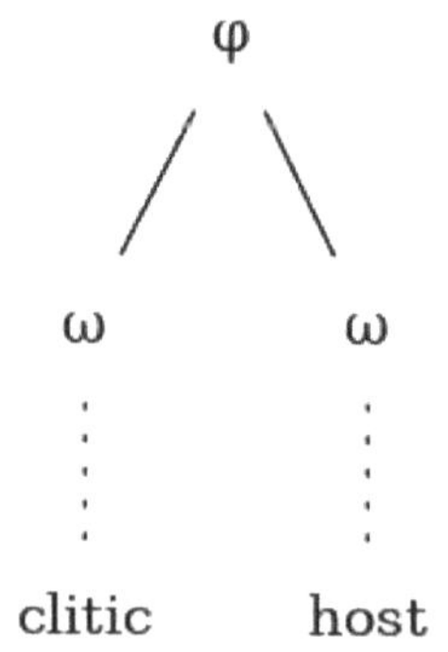

However, while this analysis works at the prosodic level, it remains the case that the examples from Italian, Tagalog and Greek discussed in this section involve unambiguously functional morphemes: in neither case are open class morphemes, such as verbs or nouns, involved. It is to the functional/lexical distinction that I therefore now turn.

7.4. The Functional/Lexical Distinction is a Continuum

The distinction between function and content classes is often presented as a hard-and-fast binary distinction. Such a distinction is presupposed in statements such as that of Caink, that "[i]tems that are clitic vary across languages but are always grammatical (or functional) words" (2008, 491). If clitics are always function words, it must be possible to be categorical about whether or not a word is a function word in the first place.

However, it has been argued that the lexical/functional distinction is better seen as a continuum. Klammer, Schulz and Della Volpe point out that some lexical items have very clear semantic content, giving the examples 'finger', 'tree', 'swim', 'humid', while the semantic content of items such as 'thing' and 'do' is much less clear (2007, 96).[15] Gelderen adduces the case of English prepositions: some, such as 'behind' and 'toward' have features of both function and lexical categories (2004). Developing this, let us consider the preposition 'behind'. This has a grammatical function, namely to relate two elements in the discourse to one another: in 'The cat sat behind the sofa', 'behind' grammatically relates 'the cat' to 'the sofa' in the discourse. However, 'behind' also carries semantic content: it refers to a relationship in

[15] Indeed, 'do' is (in part) an auxiliary verb in English.

the world outside the discourse, namely the relative geographical location of the cat and the sofa.

Much more grammatical is the preposition 'of', e.g., 'The house of friendship', where the grammatical function is clear, relating 'house' and 'friendship'. However, it is hard to detect any semantic content.

In this study we have found that verbs and adverbs show prosodic dependence at the level of the prosodic phrase. It is therefore relevant to point out that verbs and adverbs have characteristics that align with function words over against lexical words.

The verb is often seen as a prototypically open lexical class. (The major exception to this are auxiliary verbs, if present in the language under consideration, whose semantic content has typically been bleached to the extent that only the grammatical function is left.) However, it is less commonly observed that verbs by their nature are more grammatical than the other prototypically open lexical class, namely nouns. This is trivially the case with predicative verbs such as 'to be'. In 'The cat is on the sofa', the verb 'is' structures the predication. It does not refer to anything concrete outside the discourse.

However, verbs with much greater semantic content, such as 'walk', are also more grammatical than a noun, such as 'station'. Consider the sentence 'I walked to the station'. Here the verb 'walk' has semantic content: it refers to the activity of stepping so as to make progress relative to the ground. Language users will recognise this activity based on their experience of living in the world. However, in addition to its semantic role, 'walk' here has the function of describing a relationship of movement between the subject and the object: 'I walked to the station' predicates a 'walking to the station' event of the subject. This is to say, 'walk' structures the predication, in addition to its lexical function.

Adverbs are similar. Like verbs, adverbs vary in the degree of their lexical content. Some adverbs, such as the negative adverb 'not', are entirely functional. By contrast, an adverb like 'slowly' has both lexical and grammatical content: lexically it refers to 'slowness'; grammatically, it attributes 'slowness' to the event described in the sentence.

Nouns fundamentally do not have the same potential for grammaticality that verbs and adverbs do: even semantically bleached nouns, such as 'thing'—as in 'I saw an interesting thing yesterday'—do not relate items within the discourse to one another, even though the referent in the world outside the discourse is very ill-defined. Word classes can therefore be arranged on a grammaticalisation cline:

nouns < verbs, adverbs < prepositions, particles

The order of the elements of word classes on the grammaticalisation cline closely parallels that of the prosodic strength cline (see above). I therefore suggest that a relationship exists between the prosodic status of a morpheme, and its position on the lexical/functional cline, a connection that extends beyond the prosodic word to the prosodic phrase, enabling, in principle, morphemes that meet the requirements for prosodic wordhood to be prosodically dependent on a host at the level of the prosodic phrase.

7.5. What Motivates the Cliticization of V?

In the previous section I argued that there are grounds for seeing the verb as more functional than is often recognised. The fact, remains, however, that in the literature prosodic word clitics are words that belong unambiguously in the functional category, rather than verbs, which share both lexical and functional characteristics. It is therefore worth considering what might be motivating the cliticization of verbs in Biblical Hebrew.

We observed that verbs in Biblical Hebrew have a strong tendency to become incorporated into a following prosodic phrase in all word orders except SVO. V is also prosodically weakest when fronted to first position in the sentence, i.e., VXX. We also saw that SVO has been proposed as the basic word order in Biblical Hebrew, albeit not attested as frequently as VSO (Holmstedt 2009). One route to the observed distribution is, therefore, the following: Biblical Hebrew underlying word order is SVO, but in contexts of movement, and especially where V moves to first position, V loses prosodic independence and cliticises to a following element, whatever that may be. Note that a reversed explanation, where the basic word order is VSO, cannot explain why V should also be prosodically weak before all other elements in that position, i.e., O and PP.

The implication of this is that verb-first word orders in Biblical Hebrew may be in part at least phonologically driven. Compare the proposal that non-SVO word orders are cases of phonological movement in Ancient Greek (Agbayani and Golston 2010).

This hypothesis is presented tentatively: it needs to be tested by looking in detail at individual cases, and developed further in the light of crosslinguistic evidence. Whatever the correct explanation turns out to be, it is clear that there is something special about SVO sentences that leads V to be prosodically stronger in that position.

8.0. Conclusion: Biblical Hebrew Verbs are Prosodic Word Clitics

We have seen that verbs have a marked propensity to form a prosodic phrase with a following element, regardless of the syntactic role of that element. We observed that this behaviour is analogous to cliticization: both cases involve the incorporation of an element (the verb or the clitic) into a neighbouring prosodic unit (prosodic phrase or prosodic word, respectively). I raised two objections to this analysis: (1) cliticization is generally regarded as a phenomenon operating at the level of the prosodic word, rather than at the level of the prosodic phrase; (2) clitics are generally required to belong to closed functional classes, whereas the Hebrew verb (and the verb more generally) is an open lexical class;

I addressed the first objection by pointing out that, while most discussion of cliticization focuses on its manifestation at the level of the prosodic word, cliticization at the level of the prosodic phrase has also been observed to exist. It is therefore typologically acceptable for a prosodic word to depend prosodically on a neighbouring prosodic word to form a prosodic phrase, in a way analogous to a sub-prosodic word morpheme becoming integrated into a neighbouring prosodic word.

This analysis necessitates a loosening of the requirement for clitics to belong to a closed, viz. functional, word class. Further, I have argued that such a loosening is justified: the functional/lexical distinction is itself a continuum, not binary; verbs (and adverbs) occupy a position on this continuum somewhere between the (prototypically lexical) nouns and the (prototypically grammatical) object marker and prepositions. It is consistent with this that verbs (and adverbs) should sit between these two groups on the continuum of prosodic strength as well, that is, able to constitute their own prosodic words, but dependent on a host at the level of the prosodic phrase.

Biblical Hebrew verbs have sufficient prosodic weight (for the most part) to be able to stand as their own prosodic word, viz. carry their own accent. They do not in general have sufficient prosodic weight, however, to bound a prosodic phrase on the right, that is, to carry a disjunctive accent. The major exception to this is in SVO sentences, where a disjunctive is much more liable to occur at the boundary between V and O than between V and X in other word orders. I suggested that this is because in all word orders other than SVO, the verb is fronted and thereby loses prosodic independence. I leave it to further research to pursue this suggestion.

Acknowledgements

The present contribution was completed as part of ongoing research on the CROSSREADS project. This project has received funding from the European Research Council (ERC) under the

European Union's Horizon 2020 research and innovation programme (CROSSREADS: Grant agreement No. 885040).

I wish to thank the other participants of the InterSAME workshop, the editors and anonymous reviewers, as well as Randall Tan, James Cuénod, and Ryder Wishart, for their helpful questions and comments. As ever, any deficiencies remain my responsibility.

Trees are drawn on the basis of analyses in the Macula and TanakhML trees. The syntactic data was taken from the MACULA Hebrew Linguistic Datasets, available at https://github.com/Clear-Bible/macula-hebrew. The trees used were those as of 22nd May 2022. The TanakhML Project (https://www.tanakhml.org/) was founded by Alain Verboomen and is hosted by Emmanuel Dyan. The trees were downloaded between August 2022 and March 2023. The analyses are conducted using software written by the present author in Python. The software converts the XML of these treebanks into DOT (see https://graphviz.org/doc/info/lang.html). The resulting DOT file is compiled to PNG format using the Graphviz compiler in *Dependency2Tree* (https://github.com/boberle/dependency2tree/, last commit 2020) and *Graphviz* (https://graphviz.org/).

References

Agbayani, Brian. and Chris Golston. 2010. 'Phonological Movement in Classical Greek'. *Language* 86: 133–167.

Anderson, Stephen R. 2005. *Aspects of the Theory of Clitics*. New York: Oxford University Press.

Aronoff, Mark. 1985. 'Orthography and Linguistic Theory: The Syntactic Basis of Masoretic Hebrew Punctuation'. *Language* 61: 28–72.

Caink, Andrew D. 2008. 'Clitics'. In *Encyclopedia of Language and Linguistics*, edited by Keith Brown, 491–495. Oxford: Elsevier Science.

Crellin, Robert S. D. 2022a. *The Semantics of Word Division in Northwest Semitic Writing Systems: Ugaritic, Phoenician, Hebrew, Moabite and Greek*. Oxford: Oxbow.

———. 2022b. 'Word-level Punctuation in Latin and Greek Inscriptions from Sicily of the Imperial Period'. In *Writing Around the Ancient Mediterranean: Practices and Adaptations*, edited by Philippa M. Steele and Philip Boyes, 195–219. Oxford: Oxbow.

Devine, Andrew M., and Laurence D. Stephens. 1994. *The Prosody of Greek Speech*. Oxford: Oxford University Press.

Dresher, B. E. 1994. 'The Prosodic Basis of the Tiberian Hebrew System of Accents'. *Language* 70: 1–52.

Evertz, Martin. 2018. *Visual Prosody: The Graphematic Foot in English and German*. Berlin, Boston: De Gruyter.

Fortson, Benjamin. 2008. *Language and Rhythm in Plautus: Synchronic and Diachronic Studies*, vol. 3. 1st ed. Berlin, Boston: De Gruyter.

Fries, Charles C. 1952. *The Structure of English: An Introduction to the Construction of English Sentences*. London: Harcourt, Brace and World.

Gelderen, Elly V. 2004. 'Function Words'. In *Encyclopedia of Linguistics*, edited by Philipp Strazny. New York: Taylor and

Francis. https://www.proquest.com/encyclopedias-reference-works/function-words/docview/2137931488/se-2.

Goldstein, David M. 2016. *Classical Greek Syntax: Wackernagel's Law in Herodotus*. Leiden, Boston: Brill.

Haug, Dag T. T. 2009. 'Does Homeric Greek have Prepositions? Or Local Adverbs? (And What's the Difference Anyway?)'. In *Grammatical Change in Indo-European Languages*, edited by Vit Bubenik, John Hewson and Sarah Rose, 103–120. Amsterdam: John Benjamins.

Hock, Hans H. 1982. 'Clitic Verbs in PIE or Discourse-based Verb Fronting? Sanskrit Sá Hovaca Gárgyaḥ and Congeners in Avestan and Homeric Greek'. *Studies in the Linguistic Sciences* 12 (2): 1–38.

———. 2014. 'Vedic Verb Accent Revisited'. In *Vedic and Sanskrit Historical Linguistics*, edited by Jared Klein and Elizabeth Tucker, 153–178. Delhi: Motilal Banarsidass.

———. 2015. 'Proto-Indo-European Verb-finality: Reconstruction, Typology, Validation'. In *Proto-Indo-European Syntax and its Development*, edited by L. I. Kulikov and Nikolaos Lavidas, 51–78. Amsterdam, Philadelphia: John Benjamins.

Holmstedt, Robert D. 2009. 'Word Order and Information Structure in Ruth and Jonah: A Generative-typological Analysis'. *Journal of Semitic Studies* 54 (1): 111–139.

Hornkohl, Aaron D. 2018. 'Biblical Hebrew Tense-aspect-mood, Word Order and Pragmatics: Some Observations on Recent Approaches'. In *Studies in Semitic Linguistics and Manuscripts: A Liber Discipulorum in Honour of Professor Geoffrey*

Khan, edited by Nadia Vidro, Ronny Vollandt, Esther-Miriam Wager and Judith Olszowy-Schlanger, 27–56. Uppsala: Uppsala Universitet.

Hunter, Jonathan D. 2007. 'Matplotlib: A 2D Graphics Environment'. *Computing in Science & Engineering* 9: 90–95. https://doi.org/10.1109/MCSE.2007.55

Janis, Norman. 1987. 'A Grammar of the Biblical Accents'. PhD dissertation, Harvard University.

Khan, Geoffrey. 2020. *The Tiberian Pronunciation Tradition of Biblical Hebrew*. Cambridge: University of Cambridge and Open Book.

Khan, Geoffrey, and Christo H. J. van der Merwe. 2020. 'Towards a Comprehensive Model for Interpreting Word Order in Classical Biblical Hebrew'. *Journal of Semitic Studies* 65 (2): 347–390. https://doi.org/10.1093/jss/fgaa025.

Klammer, Thomas P., Muriel Schulz, and Angela Della Volpe. 2007. *Analyzing English Grammar*. 5th ed. New York: Pearson, Longman.

Kuryłowicz, Jerzy. 1959. 'The Accentuation of the Verb in Indo-European and in Hebrew'. *WORD* 15: 123–129. https://doi.org/10.1080/00437956.1959.11659688.

Nespor, Marina, and Marina Vogel. 2007. *Prosodic Phonology: with a New Foreword*. Berlin: Mouton De Gruyter.

Park, Sung J. 2020. *The Fundamentals of Hebrew Accents: Divisions and Exegetical Roles Beyond Syntax*. Cambridge: Cambridge University Press. https://doi.org/10.1017/9781108801782.

Payne, Thomas E. 1997. *Describing Morphosyntax: A Guide for Field Linguists.* Cambridge: Cambridge University Press.

Sapir, Edward. 1921. *Language: An Introduction to the Study of Speech.* London: Oxford University Press.

Selkirk, Elisabeth. 1996. 'The Prosodic Structure of Function Words'. In *Signal to Syntax: Bootstrapping from Speech to Grammar in Early Acquisition*, edited by J.L. Morgan and K. Demuth, 187–214. New York, NY: Psychology Press.

Tan, Randall, and Andi Wu. 2022. *MACULA Hebrew Treebank for Open Scriptures Hebrew Bible (OSHB) Initial Release Documentation.* Biblica. https://github.com/Clear-Bible/macula-hebrew/blob/main/doc/MACULA%20Hebrew%20Treebank%20for%20Open%20Scriptures%20Hebrew%20Bible.pdf.

Truckenbrodt, Hubert. 1999. 'On the Relation between Syntactic Phrases and Phonological Phrases'. *Linguistic Inquiry* 30: 219–255.

———. 2007. 'The Syntax–phonology Interface'. In *The Cambridge Handbook of Phonology*, edited by Paul d. Lacy, 435–456. Cambridge: Cambridge University Press. https://doi.org/10.1017/CBO9780511486371.019.

Wackernagel, Jacob. 2020 [1892]. *On a Law of Indo-European Word Order: Über ein Gesetz der Indogermanischen Wortstellung.* Translated by George Walkden, Christina Sevdali, and Morgan Macleod. Berlin: Language Science Press. 10.5281/zenodo.3978908.

Yeivin, Israel. 1980. *Introduction to the Tiberian Masorah.* Missoula: Scholars Press.

THE CONVERGENCE OF THE TRANSMISSION OF JEWISH AND MUSLIM SACRED SCRIPTURES REFLECTED BY THE MEDIEVAL KARAITE TRANSCRIPTIONS OF THE HEBREW BIBLE

Geoffrey Khan

1.0. The Use of Arabic Script by Karaites

In the Middle Ages the Rabbanite Jews of the Middle East wrote Arabic predominantly in Hebrew script. The first such Judaeo-Arabic manuscripts are datable to the ninth century CE. Thereafter Judaeo-Arabic in Hebrew script continued to be used as a written language of Rabbanite Jews down to modern times. In the early Judaeo-Arabic texts from the ninth and tenth centuries the orthography of the Hebrew script was essentially that of Rabbinic Hebrew and Aramaic. By the eleventh century, however, the orthography came to replicate in Hebrew script the spelling practices of Classical Arabic. The use of Hebrew script was taken over from the Hebrew and Aramaic literary tradition of the Jews. The language was changed but the traditional script continued. The different degrees with which the orthography of Arabic was

 https://doi.org/10.11647/OBP.0498.06

adopted reflects the different degrees of convergence with Muslim literature and culture at the various periods. This convergence was at its greatest in the High Middle Ages (approximately tenth–thirteenth centuries) (Blau and Hopkins 1984; Khan 2016). A large proportion of Arabic literary and documentary texts that have been preserved in medieval Jewish collections of manuscripts such as the Cairo Genizah collections and the Second Firkovitch collection are, therefore, written in Hebrew script.

At this period, however, Jewish scholars and scribes belonging to the Karaite movement of Judaism frequently used Arabic script to write Arabic. The main reason for the use of Arabic rather than Hebrew script by the medieval Karaites seems to be that they did not feel themselves to be so rooted in the rabbinic literary tradition as the orthodox rabbanite Jews and were, consequently, more open to adopting literary and linguistic practices from the surrounding non-Jewish environment.[1] It is important to note that there was not a complete assimilation to the literary Arabic culture by the Karaites,[2] since during the High Middle Ages the Karaites wrote many of their Arabic manuscripts in Hebrew script. Indeed, manuscript copies of the same text are sometimes extant in both scripts. There seems to have been a degree of free variation in the use of the two scripts at this period, which reflects an intermediate stage of cultural assimilation to the Islamic environment that had not reached completion (Khan 1992; 1993a).[3]

---

[1] For this phenomenon see Drory (1988; 2000, 127–29).

[2] Cf. the remarks of Stroumsa (2009, 56–57).

[3] This free variation is clearly reflected by a letter published by Khan (1993a) written by the assistant of a Karaite scholar to a merchant who

In the High Middle Ages many Karaite scribes in the Middle East used Arabic script not only to write the Arabic language but also to write the Hebrew language. Such Hebrew texts in Arabic transcription were predominantly Hebrew Bible texts. These were sometimes written as separate manuscripts containing continuous Bible texts. Some manuscripts in Arabic script contain collections of Biblical verses for liturgical purposes. Arabic transcriptions of verses from the Hebrew Biblical or individual Biblical Hebrew words were in many cases embedded within Karaite Arabic works, mainly of an exegetical nature, but also in works of other intellectual genres. Several Karaite Arabic works also contain Arabic transcriptions of extracts from Rabbinic Hebrew texts (Tirosh-Becker 2011). The Karaites transcribed into Arabic script only texts with an oral reading tradition, as was the case with the Hebrew Bible and Rabbinic texts in the Middle Ages. The transcriptions reflect, in principle, these oral traditions. It is for this reason that the transcription of the Hebrew Bible represents the *qere* (the orally transmitted reading tradition of the text) rather than the *ketiv* (the written tradition). Other types of Hebrew texts that were written by Karaites during the Middle Ages without an oral tradition, e.g., documents, commentaries, law books, were always written in Hebrew script (Khan 1992).

Most of the known manuscripts containing Karaite transcriptions of Hebrew into Arabic script are found in the British

---

commissioned a copy of this scholar's work. The main purpose of the letter is to ask the addressee whether he would prefer his copy of the work to be written in Hebrew script or Arabic script.

Library (Hoerning 1889; Khan 1987, 25–33; 1993b), the Firkovitch collections of the National Library of Russia in St. Petersburg (Harviainen 1993a; 1993b; 1994; 1995; 1996a), and in the Cairo Genizah collections (Khan 1990).[4] These manuscripts emanate from Palestinian circles of Karaites or Karaites in Egypt who had migrated to Egypt from Palestine after the capture of Jerusalem by the Crusaders in 1099. The majority of them were written in the tenth and eleventh centuries. One of the transcriptions in the British Library (Or. 2554) has a colophon which states that it was written in Ramle in 395 AH (1004–5 CE). Several of the other manuscripts of the British Library corpus are written with the same form of script and orthography. These include Or 2548. Or 2550, Or 2551 fol. 31–56, Or 2551 fols 57–101, Or 258IA fols 31–46. It would appear that these manuscripts all come from the pen of the same scribe. The manuscripts were preserved down to modern times mainly in Egypt. This applies, of course, to the material from the Cairo Genizah. The British Library corpus comes from a collection of mainly Karaite manuscripts that were purchased by the library from the bookseller M. W. Shapira of Jerusalem in 1882. The main source of Shapira's manuscripts and also the manuscripts acquired by Abraham Firkovitch appears to have been the Karaite community of Cairo. A number of transcription fragments preserved in the Cairo Genizah were originally parts of manuscripts acquired by Shapira and now in the British Library, which shows that these British Library manuscripts must

[4] Gottheil (1905, 647) mentions the existence of an Arabic transcription of part of the book of Daniel in the Khedevial Library of Cairo (now the Egyptian Library).

have come from Cairo (Khan 1990, 3–4). Some of the transcriptions in the British Library and Firkovitch collection may have been acquired also from the Karaite community of the Iraqi town of Hīt on the Euphrates (Hoerning 1889, v; Harviainen 1991; 1996b; 1998).

Most of the transcriptions of Biblical Hebrew reflect the Tiberian reading tradition, which is what is represented by the Tiberian vocalisation signs that were created by the Tiberian Masoretes. The transcriptions, therefore, are an important source for the reconstruction of this reading tradition of Biblical Hebrew.[5] Many of the manuscripts are vocalised with Tiberian Hebrew vowel signs and accents. These conform on the whole to the standard Tiberian notation system. Various sporadic deviations from the Tiberian standard are, however, found in the vocalisation and accents of some of the manuscripts. More systematic deviation is found in only a small number of manuscripts. Moreover only in rare cases does the orthography of the transcriptions reflect deviations from the standard Tiberian tradition of pronunciation.

2.0. The Motivation for the Karaite Transcriptions

2.1. The *Rasm* and the Authority of the Reading Tradition

The Arabic transcriptions of the Hebrew Bible reflect a remarkable degree of rapprochement of the Karaites with the Muslim environment. They represent a convergence with the external form

[5] For a description of our current knowledge of the Tiberian reading tradition based on the Karaite and other sources see Khan (2013; 2020).

of the Muslim Arabic Qurʾān and also with the concepts of authority associated with the transmission of Muslim scripture. Unlike the Masoretic Bible codices, which were used by both Rabbanites and Karaites, these transcriptions were exclusive to the Karaites.

The authoritative written form of Muslim scripture was fixed in the early Islamic period. This was known as the Uthmanic text, since it was based on a codex (*muṣḥaf*) authorised by the caliph Uthman in the first century AH/seventh century CE. To be precise, what was authorised was the *rasm* of the Uthmanic text, i.e., the letters, though not the diacritical points. In early Qurʾān manuscripts, the diacritical points of the Arabic letters are, in fact, only sporadically added. Although the *rasm* became fixed, this could potentially be read in various ways and a variety of reading traditions (*qirāʾāt*) existed. The *qirāʾa* was regarded as the authoritative core of the text of scripture, which was based on the matrix of the *rasm*. It was crucially important, therefore, to establish principles for determining which *qirāʾāt* were authoritative.

The early generations of Qurʾān readers felt a considerable amount of freedom in determining the reading of the Uthmanic fixed consonantal text. They often adopted one reading of the consonantal text rather than another on the basis of their judgment of its grammatical 'correctness', unconstrained by any other criteria (Nöldeke, Bergsträsser, and Pretzl 1938, 120; Beck 1946, 188). By the time of the Abbasid period, however, in the middle of the second century AH, the freedom allowable in the choice of Qurʾānic readings began to be narrowed down. This was achieved by the introduction of two conditions for the selection of a reading, in addition to the requirement that it be grammatical and in conformity with the fixed consonantal text: the condition that the reading must be based on the normative usage of prestigious readers of earlier times, and that the reading must be agreed upon by a majority of readers. The two conditions were not necessarily mutually exclusive; they were both aspects of the concept of a generally agreed practice. The sources of authority for establishing the correct reading of the consonantal text of the Qurʾān which are recognised by Sībawayh (d. 180 AH/796–797 CE) are those of the majority (*qirāʾat al-ʿāmma*) and the model of former authoritative sources (*al-sunna*). He, in fact, identifies the one with the other, as is shown by his statement: *al-qirāʾa lā tuḵālaf liʾannahā al-sunna* 'The reading [of the majority] is not to be disputed, because it is the normative usage.'[6] This expresses the view that the majority reading has religious sanction, since it is the normative ideal usage of the community. This notion of *sunna* and its merging with consensus is found also in the doctrine of the ancient schools of Islamic jurisprudence before al-Shāfiʿī (d. 204 AH/820 CE) (Schacht 1950, 58–81). Al-Farrāʾ (d. 207 AH/822 CE) also regards the agreement of the majority of the readers and the traditions of the ancients as sources of authority for establishing the correct reading. When referring to these, he generally uses the terms *ʾijtimāʿ* and *ʾāṯār*.

Throughout the third century AH, the so-called 'majority principle' was widely used to establish the authoritative *qirāʾa* of

[6] *Kitāb*, ed. H. Derenbourg (Paris, 1881), 1:62.

the Qurʾānic text. This was due mainly to the work of ʾAbū ʿUbayd (d. 224/834) and ʾAbū Ḥātim (Sahl ibn Muḥammad) al-Sijistanī (d. 255/ 869). The application of the 'majority principle' in the selection of readings excluded those of small minorities. In cases where there was no agreement by a clear majority, ʾAbū ʿUbayd, ʾAbū Ḥātim and others restricted their notion of 'majority' to that of the readers of specific centres, such as Medina and Kūfa, or Medina and Mecca, or to that of specific readers, such as Nāfiʿ and ʿĀṣim.

By the fourth century AH, under the instigation of Ibn Mujāhid (d. 324/936), the 'tradition principle', whereby authority was given to the tradition of specific readers, began to replace the 'majority principle.' Ibn Mujāhid established seven canonical traditions of reading, which were endorsed by the ruling ʿAbbāsid régime.[7] These still fulfilled the requirements that they should conform to the *rasm* of the authoritative text, that they should be grammatically correct, and that they should be broadly authenticated. At a later period, the seven canonical traditions came to be accepted on the basis of their authoritative pedigree alone, in the manner of the principles of establishing the authority of *ḥadīth* (traditions of the sayings of the prophet Muḥammad). Ibn Mujāhid himself applied some degree of critical assessment of the content of the traditions, notably in their degree of grammatical correctness (Nasser 2015).

We find eloquent evidence for the Karaites' convergence with Muslim thought regarding the transmission of scripture in

---

[7] Ibn Mujāhid, *Kitāb al-Sabʿa fī al-Qirāʾāt* (ed. Cairo, 1972).

the writings of the Karaite author al-Qirqisānī (first half of the tenth century CE). In a number of passages in his work *Kitāb al-ʾAnwār wa-l-Marāqib*, he expresses his opinion about the basis of authority of Hebrew scripture. He makes it clear that the authority lies in the text represented by the reading tradition (*qere*) and not in that represented by the written tradition (*ketiv*). Moreover the reading tradition derives its authority from the agreement of the entire community (*ʾijmāʿ*) and not from the authority of the sages or that of any specific group of people. The *ketiv* of the Hebrew Bible can be read in several different ways and the correctness of one reading rather than another can only be established by *ʾijmāʿ*. Furthermore in many cases reading the text on the basis of the written tradition blatantly results in the wrong meaning (ed. Nemoy 1939, II.23.6). For example, the frequent word נַעֲרָ in the Pentateuch would be read as 'boy' rather than 'girl' if the ketiv is followed. The word שברתי in שִׂבַּ֣רְתִּי לִֽישׁוּעָתְךָ֣ (Ps. 119.166) would have to be read with a *šin* as שִׁבַּרְתִּי if the *ketiv* is the basis of the reading and the meaning would be 'I have broken' rather than 'I hope'.[8]

Al-Qirqisānī was aware of the fact that there were some differences in reading between the communities of Palestine and Iraq (*ʾahl al-Šām wa-ʾahl al-ʿIrāq*). In such cases the reading of the community of Palestine must have the supreme authority, even though the community of Iraq was larger. By the term *ʾahl al-Šām* al-Qirqisānī was referring to the Tiberian tradition of reading.

---

[8] In Rabbinic tradition the *ketiv* of the letter ש was regarded as being */š/* and its reading as */s/* was considered to be the *qere* of this *ketiv*, i.e., the letter *sin* did not exist in the *qere* (Steiner 1996).

The position of al-Qirqisanī with regard to the biblical text, therefore, is as follows. The authoritative text of the Bible was represented by the reading tradition, which was validated by the *ʾijmāʿ* of the entire nation (*al-ʾumma*) in most of its details. Where there was no overriding consensus in the nation as a whole with regard to certain aspects of the tradition, it is the reading (*qirāʾa*) of the Palestinians (*ʾahl al-šām*) that was the correct and authoritative one. That is to say, the correct tradition in all its details is established by the *ʾijmāʿ* of the *ʾahl al-šām* rather than that of the nation as a whole. This has clear parallels to the overriding authority attributed to orally transmitted reading traditions (*qirāʾāt*) of the Qurʾān and also to the notion that *ʾijmāʿ* was a key determinant of the authority of a reading tradition.

Al-Qirqisānī's advocacy of *ʾijmāʿ* as a source of authority may have been further reinforced by the influence of by Muʿtazilī thought, which had a major impact on medieval Karaite thought in general at this period.[9] The Muʿtazila rejected tradition as a source of law but accepted the validity of *ʾijmāʿ*.[10] The Muʿtazilī theologian ʿAbd al-Jabbār (320/932 to 414–16/1023–25) considered traditionalism (*taqlīd*) to be an unsatisfactory way of acquiring

---

[9] It is well known that the Karaites were influenced by many doctrines of Muslim Muʿtazilī theologians. For Muʿtalizī ideas elsewhere in al-Qirqisānī's *Kitāb al-ʾAnwār*, cf. Ben-Shammai (1984, 27ff.).

[10] al-Shāfiʿī, *Kitāb al-ʾUmm* (Bulaq, 1321–25/1903–07), VII:252–253; cf. Schacht (1950, 41, 258–59). Also Ibn al-Murtaḍā, *Kitāb Ṭabaqāt al-Muʿtazila*, ed. Susanna Diwald-Wilzer (Beirut, 1961), p. 81, line 9, 95, lines 2–4; ʿAbd al-Jabbār, *Kitāb Faḍl al-ʾIʿtizāl wa-Ṭabaqāt al-Muʿtazila*, ed. Fuʾād Sayyid (Tunis, 1393/1974), p. 186.

knowledge, since it involved the uncritical acceptance of a report without demanding proof or evidence.[11] He maintained that *ʾijmāʿ*, on the other hand, had probative value (*ḥujjiyya*). The probative value followed from the existence of *ʾijmāʿ*. It does not require any proof that the information it conveys is true.[12]

The adoption of the reading tradition as the overriding basis of authority had the consequence that the Hebrew Bible could not be considered to offer two sources of authority, one on the basis of the way it is read and the other on the basis of the way it is written. The interpretation of the Scripture on two levels, one according to the *ketiv* and one according to the *qere* was a practice that is found in Rabbinic sources. As shown by Naeh (1992; 1993), this was a phenomenon that developed in the Talmudic

---

[11] *Al-Muġnī fī ʾAbwāb al-Tawḥīd wa-l-ʿAdl* (Cairo, 1380–89/1960–69), XII:123–126; *Šarḥ al-ʾUṣūl al-Ḵamsa*, ed. ʿAbd al-Karīm ʿUṯmān (Cairo, 1384/1965), p. 61.

[12] *Muġnī*, XVII:199 (*fa-ʾammā istidlāl ʿalā ṣiḥḥat al-ʾijmāʿ min jihat al-ʿaql fa-baʿīd* 'As for the demonstration of the validity of *ʾijmāʿ* by reason, [this] is unconvincing/far-fetched.). Cf. Bernand (1969; 1972). A similar fideistic acceptance of the probative validity of *ʾijmāʿ* and the rejection of traditions is expressed by ʾAbū al-Ḥusayn al-Baṣrī, who was the pupil of ʿAbd al-Jabbār, cf. *Kitāb al-Muʿtamad fī ʾUṣūl al-Fiqh* (Damascus, 1384/1964), pp. 457–540. Elsewhere ʿAbd al-Jabbār states that *ʾijmāʿ* is supported by the Qurʾān and *sunna*, cf. *Šarḥ*, p. 89. The extreme rationalist Muʿtazalī al-Naẓẓām and his school, however, had misgivings about the reliability of *ʾijmāʿ*, on the grounds that information has to be supported and ascertained before it can form the basis of *ʾijmāʿ*, i.e., *ʾijmāʿ* is only the consequence of truth, not the source of truth, cf. ʿAbd al-Qāhir ibn Ṭāhir al-Baġdādī, *Kitāb ʾUṣūl al-Dīn* (Istanbul, 1928/1346), pp. 19–20.

period. It is reflected by the Talmudic dictum יש אם למקרא ויש אם למסורת 'The reading has authority and the traditional text has authority'. The details of the spelling of the written text, in particular the distribution of full and defective orthography, were used as a source for interpretation in various Rabbinic texts (Goldberg 1990). According to the Midrash Genesis Rabbah, for example, there is exegetical significance as to why the second instance of the name Efron is spelled without a *waw* in the verse Gen. 23.16 whereas the first instance of the name in the verse and elsewhere in Gen. 23 has a *waw*:

> וַיִּשְׁמַ֣ע אַבְרָהָם֮ אֶל־עֶפְרוֹן֒ וַיִּשְׁקֹ֤ל אַבְרָהָם֙ לְעֶפְרֹ֔ן אֶת־הַכֶּ֕סֶף אֲשֶׁ֥ר דִּבֶּ֖ר בְּאָזְנֵ֣י בְנֵי־חֵ֑ת אַרְבַּ֤ע מֵאוֹת֙ שֶׁ֣קֶל כֶּ֔סֶף עֹבֵ֖ר לַסֹּחֵֽר׃
>
> Abraham agreed with Ephron; and Abraham weighed out for Ephron the silver which he had named in the hearing of the Hittites, four hundred shekels of silver, according to the weights current among the merchants (Gen. 23.16).

The lack of *waw* (*ketiv ḥaser*) indicates that Efron will suffer want because he was envious and mean in accordance with the verse:

> נִֽבְהָ֥ל לַה֗וֹן אִ֭ישׁ רַ֣ע עָ֑יִן וְלֹֽא־יֵ֝דַע כִּי־חֶ֥סֶר יְבֹאֶֽנּוּ׃
>
> A miserly man hastens after wealth, and does not know that want will come upon him (Prov. 28.22).

In some cases such Midrashic texts exhibit a terminology and style of presentation that constitute embryonic Masoretic notes regarding differences in orthography of similar words (Martín-Contreras 1999; 2002; 2003b; 2003a; 2014). As has been remarked above, exegetical comments based on differences in orthography are indeed found embedded within the Masoretic notes in some of the Tiberian codices, e.g., the comment on the orthography of רִישׁוֹן (Job 8.8) in the Masorah of the Aleppo codex discussed by Zer (2003).

If the *qere* is the only source of authority, as is the opinion of al-Qirqisānī, then variations in orthography cannot be a legitimate source of authoritative exegesis, as in the comment on Job 8.8 in the Aleppo codex. So the representation of only the *qere* in the transcriptions reflects this polemical stance of the Karaites against this Midrashic style of exegesis. Furthermore, convergence with the Islamic model of scriptural authority would logically have resulted in the inconsistency between the *ketiv* and the *qere* being considered problematic. One of the key requirements of authoritative Qurʾānic reading traditions at that period was that they conform to the *rasm* of the written text. This was clearly not the case in Hebrew scripture, in which the difference between *ketiv* and *qere* is sometimes very substantial, including reading whole words that are not written and writing whole words that are not read. The Hebrew Bible required a written *rasm* that corresponded to the reading tradition. The Karaite transcriptions of Hebrew Bibles represent the resolution of this tension by the abandonment of the traditional Hebrew written text and the provision of an acceptable *rasm*. The new *rasm* was created on the model of Islamic scripture in Arabic script.[13]

[13] Sporadic cases of lack of correspondence between the *rasm* and the vocalisation signs reflecting the reading tradition are attested in some early Qurʾān manuscripts. These, however, are rare exceptions to the general conformity of the vocalisation with the *rasm* and are restricted to a few specific Qurʾān manuscripts (Alba Fedeli, personal communication).

2.2. Convergence with Codicological Features of Qurʾān manuscripts

In addition to the use of Arabic script, the manuscripts of the transcribed Bibles exhibit a convergence with the Arabic Qurān in codicological features, such as a single column format (in contrast to the three–column format of model Bible manuscripts in Hebrew script), the use of coloured ink to mark vocalisation and accent signs, the occasional use of Arabic vocalisation signs and the insertion of sigla and ornamentation at various points on the page that resemble what is found in contemporary Qurʾān manuscripts.

Examples of the use of coloured ink are found, for example, in the manuscripts BL Or 2540, Or 2541 and Or 2542. BL Or 2540 uses red ink for Hebrew vowel signs and the diacritic of *šin* and *sin*, and green ink (often browned by oxidation) for accents. The scribe uses an Arabic *ḍamma* vowel sign in red above a *wāw* transcribing *ḥolem* and an Arabic *šadda* sign in green:

Figure 1: BL Or 2540, fol. 18v. Exod. 7.2–4

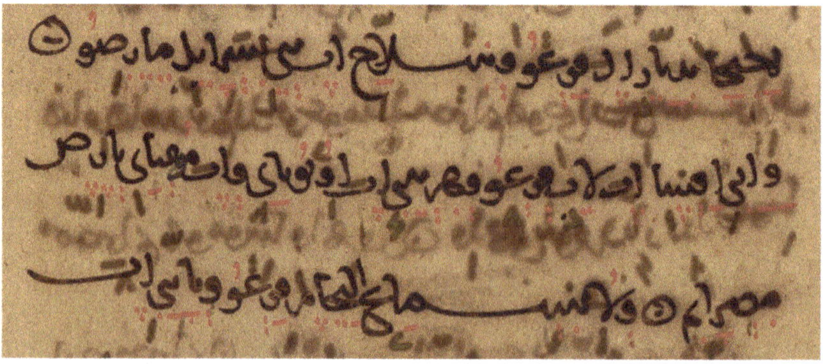

אָחִ֫יךָ יְדַבֵּ֣ר אֶל־פַּרְעֹ֔ה וְשִׁלַּ֥ח אֶת־בְּנֵֽי־יִשְׂרָאֵ֖ל מֵאַרְצֽוֹ׃ וַאֲנִ֥י אַקְשֶׁ֖ה אֶת־לֵ֣ב פַּרְעֹ֑ה
וְהִרְבֵּיתִ֧י אֶת־אֹתֹתַ֛י וְאֶת־מוֹפְתַ֖י בְּאֶ֥רֶץ מִצְרָֽיִם׃ וְלֹֽא־יִשְׁמַ֤ע אֲלֵכֶם֙ פַּרְעֹ֔ה וְנָתַתִּ֥י אֶת־

Manuscript BL Or 2541 uses red ink for Hebrew vowel and accent signs:

Figure 2: BL Or 2541, fol. 24r. Exod. 14.29

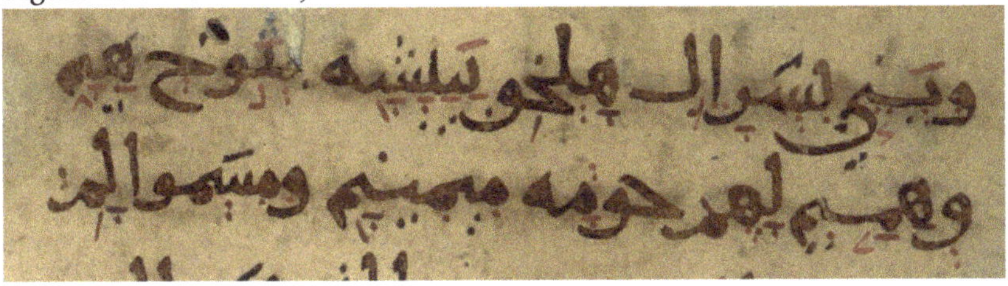

וּבְנֵ֧י יִשְׂרָאֵ֛ל הָלְכ֥וּ בַיַּבָּשָׁ֖ה בְּת֣וֹךְ הַיָּ֑ם וְהַמַּ֤יִם לָהֶם֙ חֹמָ֔ה מִֽימִינָ֖ם וּמִשְּׂמֹאלָֽם

Manuscript BL Or 2542 uses red for Hebrew vowel and accent signs, and uses an Arabic *šadda* sign in black:

Figure 3: BL Or 2542, fol. 47v. Exod. 4.27–29

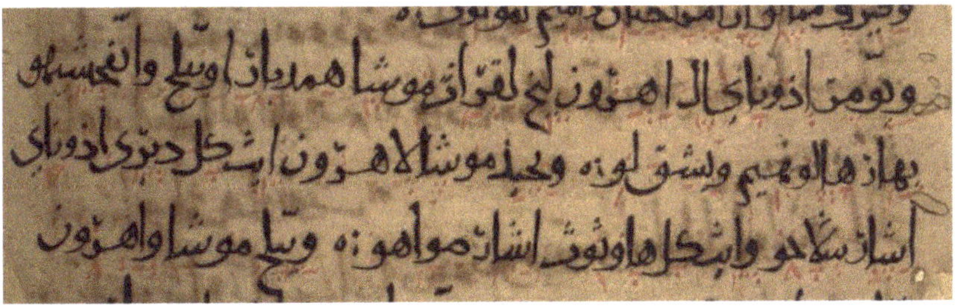

וַיֹּ֤אמֶר יְהוָה֙ אֶֽל־אַהֲרֹ֔ן לֵ֛ךְ לִקְרַ֥את מֹשֶׁ֖ה הַמִּדְבָּ֑רָה וַיֵּ֗לֶךְ וַֽיִּפְגְּשֵׁ֛הוּ בְּהַ֥ר הָאֱלֹהִ֖ים
וַיִּשַּׁק־לֽוֹ׃ וַיַּגֵּ֤ד מֹשֶׁה֙ לְאַהֲרֹ֔ן אֵ֛ת כָּל־דִּבְרֵ֥י יְהוָ֖ה אֲשֶׁ֣ר שְׁלָח֑וֹ וְאֵ֥ת כָּל־הָאֹתֹ֖ת אֲשֶׁ֥ר
צִוָּֽהוּ׃ וַיֵּ֥לֶךְ מֹשֶׁ֖ה וְאַהֲרֹ֑ן

Divisions between verses are in some manuscripts marked by a circular siglum. In BL Or 2542 MS B the circular siglum has a dot in its centre, e.g.,

Figure 4: Or 2542 MS B

In BL Or 2540 this siglum has a dot or line in its centre, e.g.,

Figure 5: BL Or 2540, sigla marking verse divisions

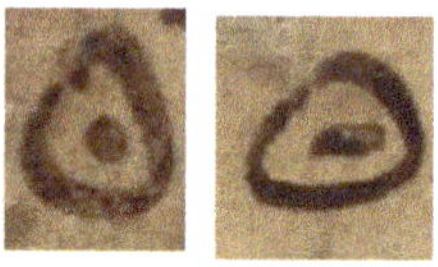

In BL Or 2542 MS A a circular siglum is combined with the siglum consisting of two dots arranged vertically, which is used in Hebrew Bible manuscript to mark verse divisions:

Figure 6: BL Or 2542, sigla marking verse divisions

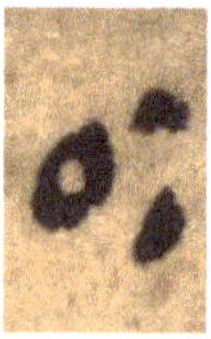

The small circular siglum appears to be modelled on the independent form of the Arabic letter *hāʾ*. In BL Or 2543 MS A a siglum in the form of an independent Arabic *hāʾ* (small circle) or an initial form of Arabic *hāʾ* is placed at *paraša* divisions, e.g.,

Figure 7: BL Or 2543 MS A. Fol. 5r. *Paraša petuḥa* before Jer. 25.1.

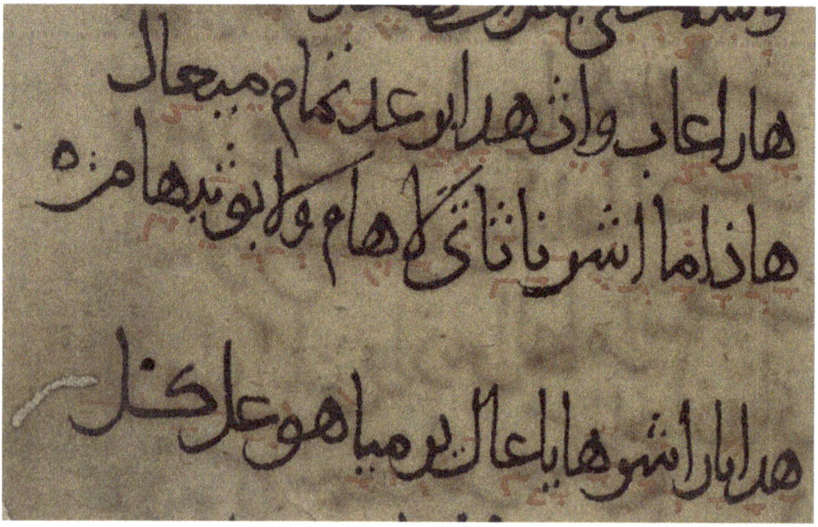

Figure 8: BL Or 2543 MS A, fol. 3v. *Paraša setuma* before Jer. 24.3.

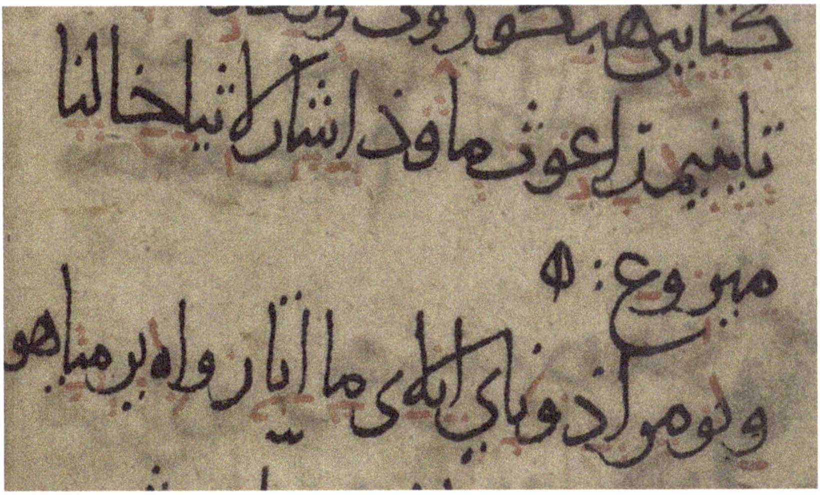

In BL Or 2540, coloured decorative shapes are used to fill space and mark divisions of various kinds in the texts. These occasionally fill spaces on both sides of a final centred line, e.g.,

Figure 9: BL Or 2540, fol. 7r. Exod. 2.20–21.

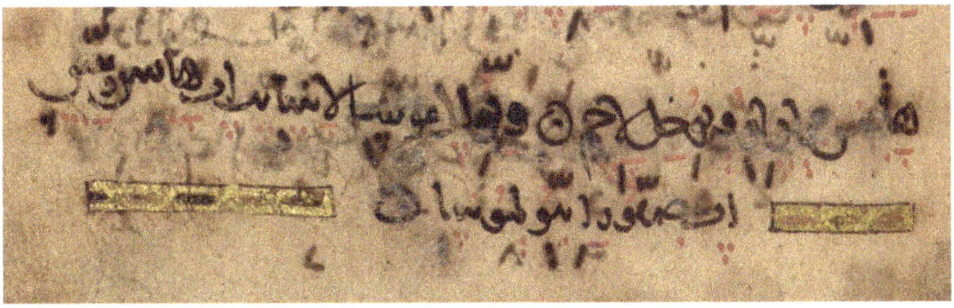

הָאִ֔ישׁ קִרְאֶ֥ן ל֖וֹ וְיֹ֥אכַל לָֽחֶם׃ וַיּ֥וֹאֶל מֹשֶׁ֖ה לָשֶׁ֣בֶת אֶת־הָאִ֑ישׁ וַיִּתֵּ֛ן אֶת־צִפֹּרָ֥ה בִתּ֖וֹ לְמֹשֶֽׁה׃

Parašiyyot divisions are marked by spaces in the text filled by decorative shapes and floral work with gold and various other colours. These divisions do not always correspond to Codex Leningradenis (L), e.g.,

Figure 10: BL Or 2540, fol. 4r, 1. *Paraša petuḥa* after Exod. 1.7 (= L).

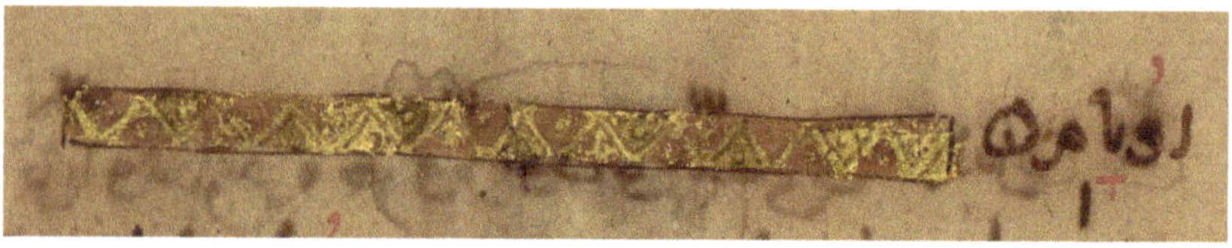

Figure 11: BL Or 2540, fol. 7v, 1. *Paraša petuḥa* after Exod. 2.22 (= L)

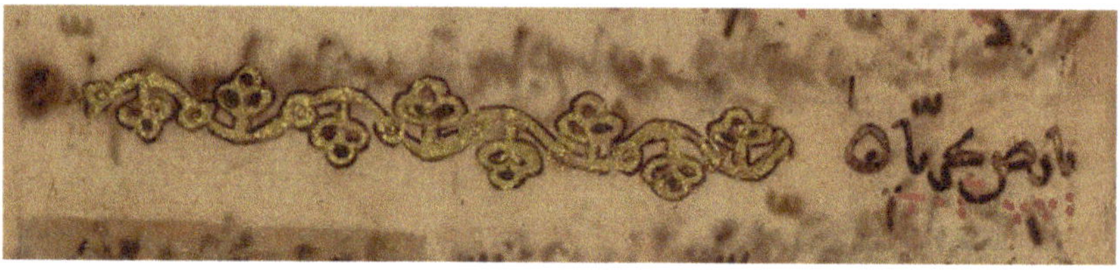

Figure 12: BL Or 2540, fol. 12r, 5. *Paraša petuḥa* after Exod. 4.17 (=L).

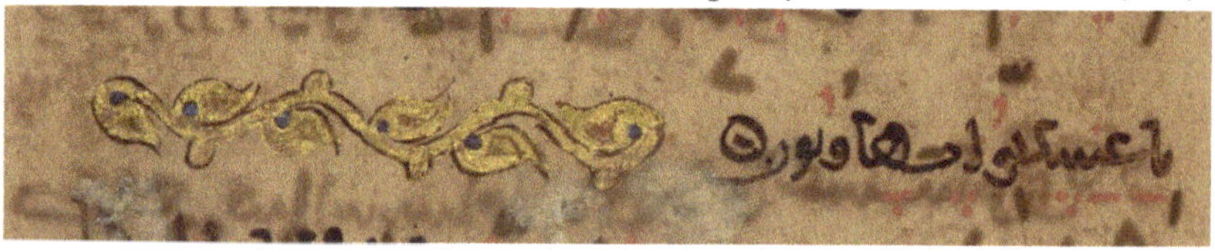

Figure 13: BL Or 2540, fol. 12v, 3. *Paraša petuḥa* after Exod. 4.20 (not in L)

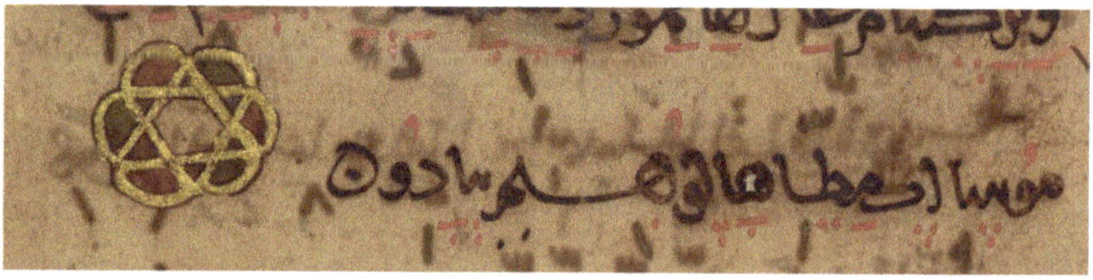

Figure 14: BL Or 2540, fol. 5v, 2. *Paraša setuma* after Exod. 1.22 (=L)

Figure 15: BL Or 2540. *Parаša setuma* after Exod. 2.25 (=L)

The beginning of the pericope וָאֵרָא at Exod. 6.2. is marked by decorative shapes and the word فراشه (i.e., פָּרָשָׁה) is written in the margin in gold in a Kufic-type of script. The phrase فذلك مائة واربعة وعشرون 'and that is [i.e., the total is] one hundred and twenty-four' indicates the number of verses of the previous pericope (שמות), which conforms to the figure given in Masoretic sources (Ginsburg 1880, II:465) and the Masoretic note in L קכ֗ד֗:

Figure 16: BL Or 2540, fol. 15v. The beginning of the pericope וָאֵרָא at Exod. 6.2.

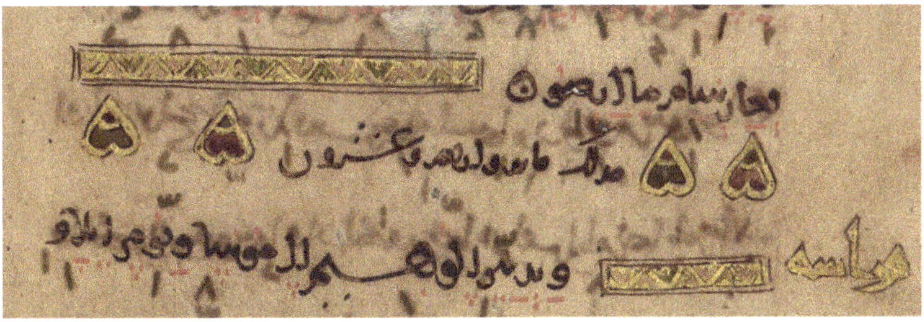

In some manuscripts various types of Masoretic annotations are written in Arabic script in red ink. This is found in BL Or 2542 MS A, e.g.,

Figure 17: BL Or 2542 MS A, fol. 203v. Beginning of Deuteronomy

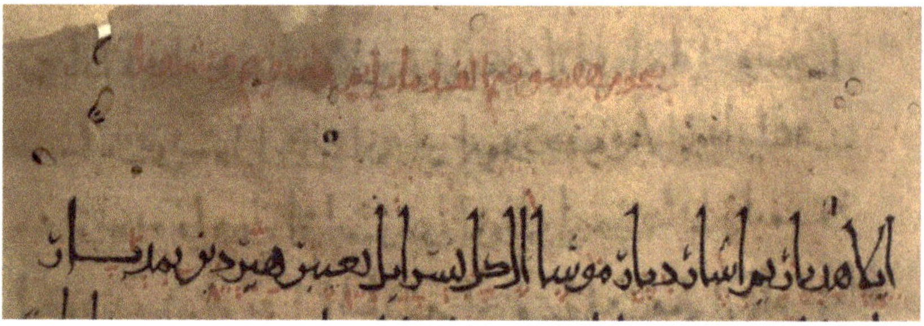

At the top of fol. 203v in this manuscript (Figure 17), there is an Arabic transcription in red ink of the Hebrew Masoretic note סכום הפסוקים אלף ומאתים שמונים ושמונה 'The number of verses is one thousand, two hundred and eighty-eight,' which indicates the number of verses of the book of Numbers. This corresponds closely to the Masoretic note in L: סכום הפסוקים שלספר אלף ומאתים שמונים ושמונה.

At the division of pericopes, the number of verses in the preceding pericope is indicated by transcribing into Arabic script the Hebrew alphabetical numeral that is customarily written in the Tiberian Masoretic codices, e.g.,

Figure 18: BL Or 2542 MS A, fol. 3v, 5.The beginning of the pericope תלדת at Gen. 25.19 with the numeral قه (= קה̇ 105)

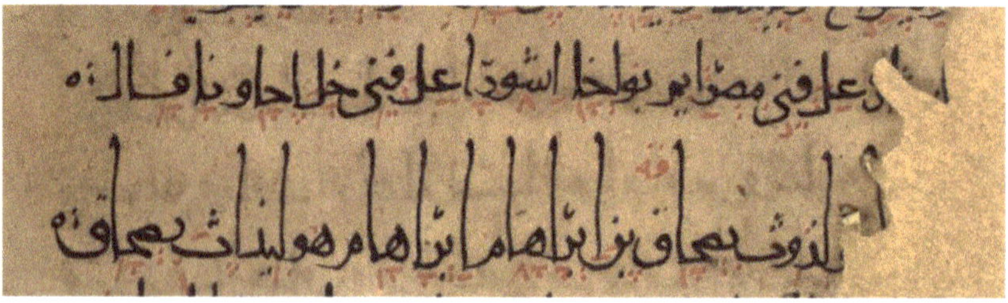

Figure 19: BL Or 2542 MS A, fol. 61r. The beginning of the pericope בשלח at Exod. 13.17 with the numeral قو (= קוֹ 106)

Parallels to these various codicological features of the manuscripts of Karaite transcriptions, i.e., single-column format on a page, vocalisation and annotations in coloured ink, verse divisions marked by circular sigla and decorative shapes marking text divisions, are found in Qurʾān manuscripts datable to roughly the same period, i.e., the Fatimid period, and earlier, as can be seen in the images below.[14]

The use of coloured ink for vowel signs was a feature of the vowel dots in so-called Kufic Qurʾāns as was the insertion of decorative bands to mark divisions in the text (Figures 22 and 23). These two features of the manuscripts of the Karaite transcriptions, therefore, had their roots in early Qurʾān manuscripts. Indeed decorative bands containing zig-zag patterns appear already in the Mingana-Lewis palimpsest (CUL Or.1287),[15] which is datable to the seventh century, before the appearance of vocalisation signs. Floral bands such as seen in Figures 11 and 12 are common in Qurʾān manuscripts from the Abbasid period, e.g., Figure 24.

The later type of Arabic vocalisation signs are also marked in coloured, generally red, ink and in some Qurʾān manuscripts

---

[14] I am grateful to Alba Fedeli, who drew my attention to many of the features of Qurʾān manuscripts that I discuss below.

[15] https://cudl.lib.cam.ac.uk/view/MS-OR-01287-LARGE/2

written in more rounded script types (Figures 25, 29). In some manuscripts in rounded script, red ink tends to be restricted to annotations relating to features such as prosodic divisions, pauses and liaisons (Figures 20–21). Note also the high vertical extension of the *hastae* of letters in the manuscript in Figure 25, which is feature of some Karaite transcriptions, e.g., BL Or 2542 MS A (Figures 17–19). The extended *hastae* in BL Or 2542 MS A (Figures 17–19) occur, in particular, at the top of pages or the beginning of sections. This is a feature of some Qurʾān manuscripts (Figures 26–28). The use of decorative bands continues in such Qurʾān manuscripts in rounded scripts.

Figure 20: Qurʾān, 1050–1150 CE, fols 127b–128a. Al-Naḥl 127–Al-ʾIsrāʾ 15. Khalili collection (James 1992, no. 2)

Figure 21: Qurʾān. 582 AH/1186 CE. Al-ʾIkḻāṣ 4–Al-Nās 6. Khalili collection (James 1992, no. 6)

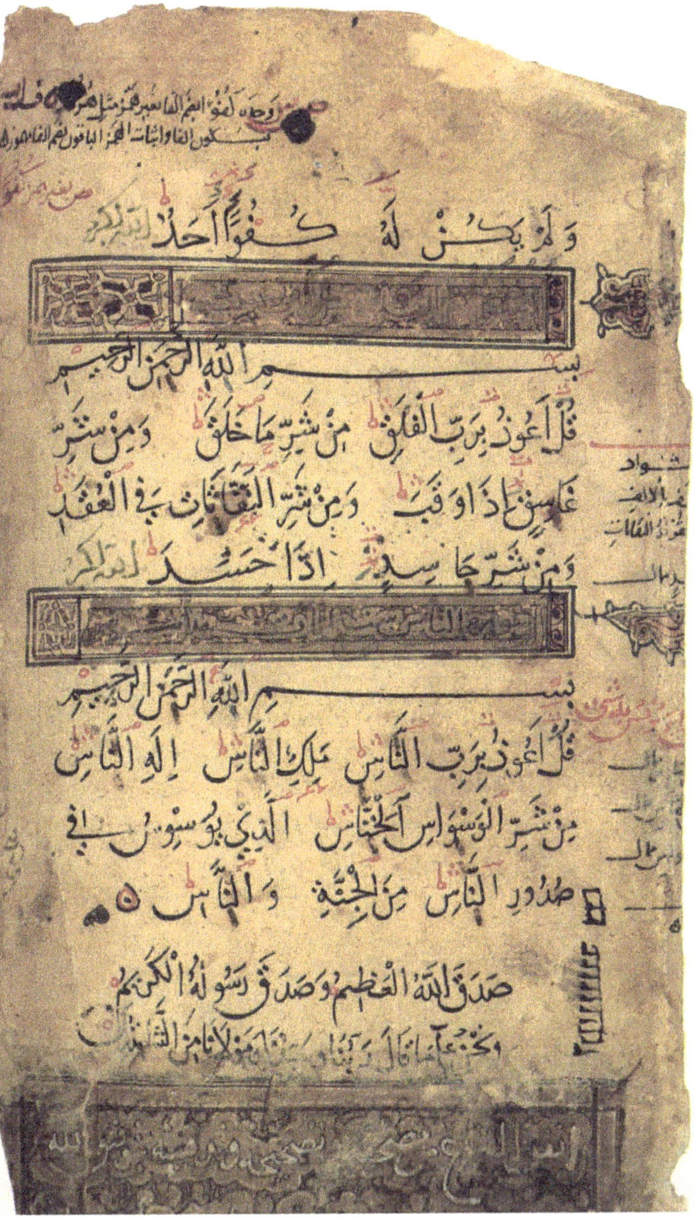

Figure 22: Kufic Qurʾān. Iraq (?), before 911 CE. Beginning of Al-ʿAnkabūt. The Morgan Library and Museum, New York, MS M.712. (https://smarthistory.org/quran-arabic-scripts/)

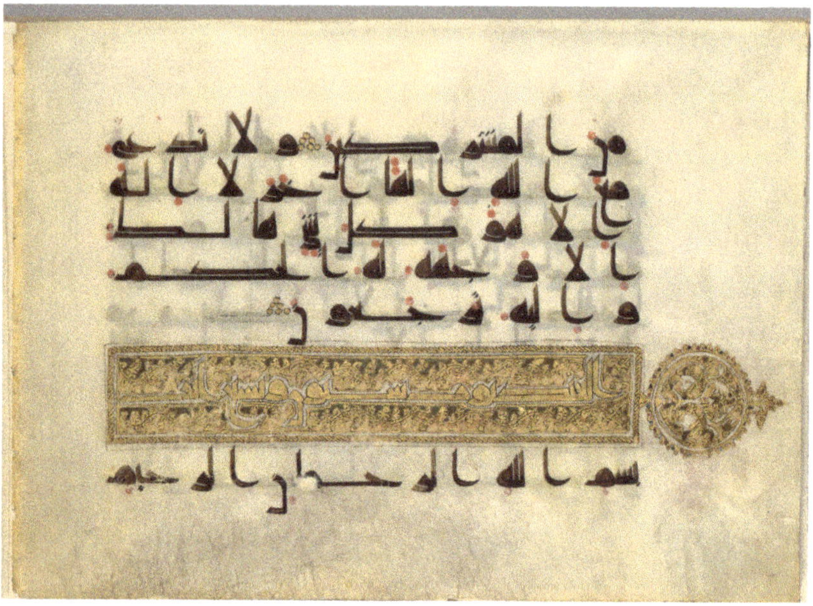

Figure 23: BnF. ar. 379c, fol. 33r. tenth century (?)

Figure 24: BnF ar. 5178h, fol. 12v. ninth century (?)

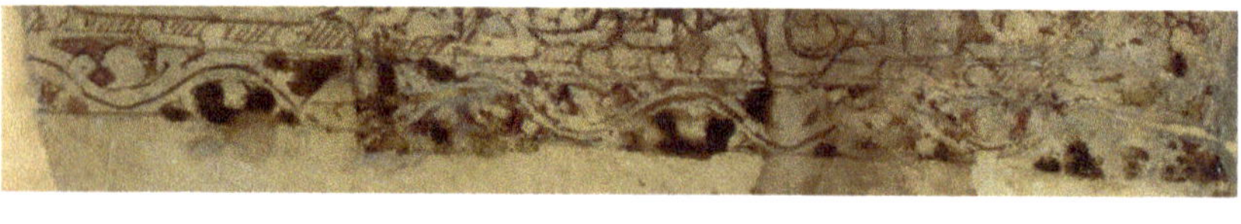

Figure 25: Qurʾān. Al-Māʾida 20–21. C. 1180 CE. Iran or Afghanistan. The Metropolitan Museum of Art. (https://smarthistory.org/quran-arabic-scripts/)

Figure 26: Qur'ān. Al-'Anbiyā' 105–107. BnF ar. 364, fol. 32r. ninth century (?)

Figure 27: Qur'ān. Al-Nisā' 148–151. BnF ar. 338b, fol. 14r. ninth century (?)

Figure 28: Qurʾān. Al-Ḥajj 19–23. Gotha (Erfurt) MS orient A 453, fol. 1r. ninth–tenth century (?)

Figure 29: Qurʾān. Al-Nāziʿāt 40–ʿAbasa 9, ʿAbasa 10–37. Cambridge University Library T–S Ar. 38.64 (Connolly and Posegay 2020, 347; 2021)

The drop-shape siglum resembling the Arabic letter *hāʾ* that appears in the Karaite manuscript BL Or. 2540 (Figures 14, 15, 16) is used in Qurʾān manuscripts to indicate a five-verse division (*hāʾ* = 5 in *ʾabjad*), e.g., James (1992, 26), Déroche (1992, 161, 165) (see Figure 30). In Qurʾān manuscripts these drop-shape sigla are not combined with oblong bands, as is the case in the Karaite manuscript (see Figure 16).

Figure 30: Khalili collection QUR 89A, fols 9r, 103v (Déroche 1992, no. 84), eleventh century (?)

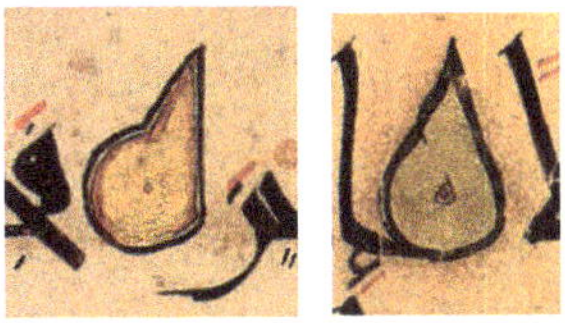

The circular sigla with a dot in their centre that mark verse divisions in some Karaite manuscripts (see Figures 4 and 5), can be compared to sigla of the same form that commonly occur in Qurʾān manuscripts to mark divisions of ten verses (see Figure 21 above, twelfth century, and Figure 31 below).

Figure 31: BnF ar.329b, fol. 7r. ninth century (?)

Regarding the use of red ink to mark the number of verses at the end of biblical books in the Karaite manuscripts (Figure 17), this can be compared to lines in red ink inserted between sūras in Qurʾān manuscripts to indicate the name of the sūra and the number of verses in words, e.g.,

Figure 32: BnF ar. 329b, fol. 14r. ninth century (?)

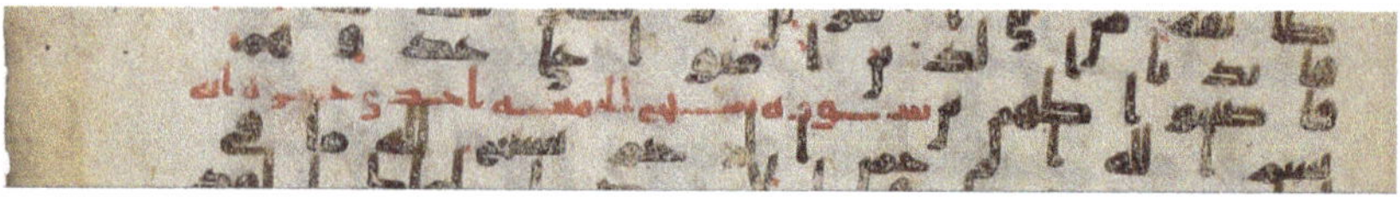

The use of letters to indicate the number of verses of pericopes at the end of the pericopes in the Karaite manuscripts, which is also a feature of Bible manuscripts in Hebrew script, can be compared to the use of numerical letters to mark the ends of groups of ten verses in Qurʾān manuscripts.

The marking of a *paraša* division by the insertion of the word فراشة in the margin written in Kufic script in gold that is a practice found in the Karaite manuscript BL Or 2540 (see Figure 16) can be compared to the marking of five verse divisions by writing the word خمس in Kufic script in gold in the margin of Qurʾān manuscripts, e.g.,

Figure 33: Khalili collection QUR 89A, fol. 103v (Déroche 1992, no. 84), eleventh century (?)

2.3. Transcription of the Tetragrammaton

Another feature that reflects the convergence of the Karaite transcriptions with the model of Arabic Qurʾāns is the use in some of the manuscripts of the Arabic word الله to represent the reading of the Tetragrammaton,[16] e.g.,

[16] For a more detailed study of the ways of representing the Tetragrammaton in the transcriptions, see Khan (2024).

(1) الله (BL Or 2539 MS A, fol. 92v, 1 || L יְהוָ֣ה Deut. 7.19 'the Lord').

(2) الله (BL Or 2552 MS B, fol. 128v, 10 || L יְהוָ֔ה Lam 4.11 'the Lord').

In some cases it has Hebrew vocalisation and accents, e.g.,

(3) الله (BL Or 2539 MS A, fol. 76r, 9 || L יְהוָֽה׃ Gen. 24.51 'the Lord').

In the manuscript BL Or 2539 MS B it often occurs with accents but not vocalisation, e.g.,

(4) الله (BL Or 2539 MS B, fol. 115v, 8 | L יְהוָ֖ה Num. 7.4 'the Lord')

(5) الله (BL Or 2539 MS B, fol. 115r, 13 | L יְהוָ֥ה ׀ Num. 6.25 'the Lord')

The writing الله is found used also to represent the word אֲדֹנָי when it is an appellation of God, e.g.,

(6) هايا الله (BL Or 2552 MS B, fol. 123r, 4 || L הָיָ֨ה אֲדֹנָ֤י ׀ Lam. 2.5 'the Lord was').

The phrase לַיהוָה is represented by corresponding Arabic orthography لله, e.g.,

(7) لله (BL Or 2539 MS B, fol. 115r, 8 || L לַֽיהוָ֑ה Num. 6.21 'to the Lord')

The representation of the Tetragrammaton by الله reflects the adoption of the *rasm* (i.e., written consonantal skeleton) of the divine name in the Qurʾān and Muslim writings for the Jewish divine name. This is not the Arabic word اللّٰه (*allāh*), since it is read as אֲדֹנָי, as is shown by its vocalisation in some manuscripts. It is not, therefore, a case of code-switching into Arabic. Nor is it an Arabic translation. Indeed medieval Karaites generally translated the Tetragrammaton into Arabic by the terms *al-rabb* 'the Lord' or *rabb al-ʿālamīna* 'the Lord of the Universe' rather than by the Arabic word *allāh* (Polliack 1997, 70, 153). It is a hybrid form consisting of the *rasm* of the Muslim Arabic divine name and the oral reading of the Jewish Hebrew divine name. One may say it is a form of logographic writing.

The question arises as to why many of the Karaite scribes of the transcriptions avoided a direct representation of the oral reading (*qere*) of the divine name and used these various substitutes. It would appear that although the *qere* of the Tetragrammaton was originally intended as a means of avoiding uttering the divine name יהוה through a taboo on its use due to its holiness, the *qere* itself, at least the default *qere* אֲדֹנָי, was regarded by some Karaite scribes as too holy to be represented directly in written transcription.

2.4. Features of the Orthography of the Transcriptions

A few of the extant Karaite Bibles in Arabic script exhibit what is essentially a letter-for-letter transliteration of the Hebrew orthography rather than a phonetic transcription in Arabic orthography. It is likely that these are among the oldest manuscripts. The

Hebrew *matres lectionis*, for example, are reproduced in Arabic script where they would not be appropriate according to Arabic orthography, e.g.,

(8) لَامُور (BL Or 2541, fol. 18v, 11 || L לֵאמֹר׃ Ex. 13.1 'saying').

(9) رَاش (BL Or 2541, fol. 30v, 13 || L רֹאשׁ־ Ex. 17.9 'top of')

(10) هلْيِله (BL Or 2541, fol. 16v, 9 || L הַלַּ֗יְלָה Ex. 12.29 'the night').

Conversely Arabic *matres lectionis* are not used when they are lacking in the Hebrew text even where they would be required in Arabic orthography to represent long vowels, e.g.,

(11) هعْم (BL Or 2541, fol. 17r, 9 || L הָעָ֖ם־ Ex. 12.33 'the people').

(12) حن (BL Or 2541, fol. 17r, 2 || L חֵן־ Ex. 12.36 'favour')

It is important to note, however, that such texts represent the *qere* in places where there is a conflict of *qere* and *ketiv*, e.g.,

(13) وِيَلونو (BL Or 2541, fol. 26v, 4 || L *ketiv* וילינו, *qere* וַיִּלּ֨וֹנוּ Exod. 16.2 'and they murmured')

(14) ثلينو (BL Or 2541, fol. 29r, 8 || L *ketiv* תלונ, *qere* תַלִּ֖ינוּ Exod. 16.7 'you will murmur').

Moreover, there is a tendency to eliminate the inconsistency that is found in the distribution of the *matres lectionis waw* and *yod* of the Hebrew *ketiv*, to which exegetical significance was attached in Rabbinic sources. This is seen in the fact that in many contexts where *waw* and *yod* are inconsistently used in the Hebrew *ketiv*, the Arabic text more regularly uses the corresponding Arabic *mater lectionis, wāw* and *yāʾ*. This results in the Arabic *matres lectionis* being used in many cases where the Hebrew *ketiv* has defective orthography, e.g.,

(15) غذوله (BL Or 2541, fol. 17r, 2 || L גְּדֹלָה Exod. 12.30 'great' [fsg])

(16) بسملوثم (BL Or 2541, fol. 17r, 12 || L בְּשִׂמְלֹתָם Exod. 12.34 'in their garments')

(17) وشليشيم (BL Or 2541, fol. 21v, 5 || L וְשָׁלִשִׁם Exod. 14.7 'officers')

(18) مايليم (BL Or 2541, fol. 26r, 13 || L מֵאֵילִם Exod. 16.1 'from Elim')

These early Karaite Bibles, therefore, attempted to produce a *rasm* that corresponded to the reading tradition and had an internal consistency.

The majority of extant Karaite Bibles in Arabic script, however, use a transcription system that is based essentially on the orthographic practices of Classical Arabic. These use *matres lectionis* to represent all long vowels, as is the practice in Arabic orthography. This appears to be a later development. Indeed a few manuscripts exhibit a hybrid system of orthography, which include features both of Hebrew orthography and Arabic orthography. These represent a transitional stage of development between the Hebrew type of orthography and the Arabic type of orthography, e.g.,

(19) اساه (BL Or 2551 fol. 34v, 13 || L אִשָּׁה Deut. 21.7 'wife')

(20) رواش (BL Or 2539 MS B, fol. 115r, 1 || L רֹ֣אשׁ Num. 6:18 'head')

2.5. Social Status of the Transcriptions

In general the written transcription in the Karaite Bibles could not be read correctly without a knowledge of the reading tradition. This is shown by the fact that they often omit crucial details, such as diacritical points on the Arabic consonants. Moreover, the spelling is often ambiguous. Each Arabic *mater lectionis*, for example, represents more than one quality of Hebrew vowel.

The transcription manuscripts appear to have been produced for private use. Bible manuscripts that have colophons indicating that they were deposited in Karaite synagogues for public liturgical reading are all large monumental codices in Hebrew script. The innovative use of Arabic script for Hebrew Bible manuscripts seems to have been restricted to private copies. This distinction in script between private and public copies of works is found also in medieval Karaite works written in Arabic language. A good example is the work on Hebrew grammar known as *al-Kitāb al-Kāfi* 'The Sufficient Book', which was written in Arabic in the first half of the eleventh century by the Karaite ʾAbū al-Faraj Hārūn. This is extant in numerous manuscripts. The manuscripts are almost exclusively written in Hebrew script. The surviving manuscripts include the autograph draft of the work by the author himself. It is significant that this private autograph manuscript is written in Arabic script. The other manuscripts appear to be published copies of the work (Khan, Gallego, and Olszowy-Schlanger 2003, xlvii–li).

In principle the traditional *ketiv* of Hebrew scripture could have been adjusted to conform to the *qere* without changing the script. Indeed this is found in some fragments of Bible manuscripts from this period that were written for private use and have been preserved in the Cairo Genizah.[17] The adoption of the Arabic script in the Karaite transcriptions reflects a convergence with the external form of the Qurʾān, which was facilitated by the assignment of exclusive authority to the reading tradition.

2.6. Grammatical Integrity of the Reading Tradition

The Islamic model required not only conformity of the reading to the *rasm* of the written text but also conformity of the reading to Arabic grammar. It was important for the Karaites, therefore, to legitimate the grammatical integrity of the Tiberian reading tradition. In the tenth century a tradition of Karaite Hebrew grammatical thought emerged. The main source of our knowledge of this Karaite grammatical tradition in its early stages of development in the tenth century is the grammatical commentary on the Bible by Yūsuf ibn Nūḥ known as the *Diqduq* (Khan 1998; 2000).

[17] Goshen-Gottstein (1962, 39ff.), Díez-Macho (1971, 92), Yeivin (1980, 30–31).

Ibn Nūḥ does not offer a systematic description of Hebrew grammar but rather concentrates on points that he believed may be problematic for the reader or concerning which there was controversy. One of the central concerns was to show that apparent inconsistencies in similar words can be explained as conforming to rational rules of grammar. This was often achieved by arguing that similar forms differing in small details were derived from different morphological bases. In the class of verbs which we refer to as final geminates, for example, there is variation in the position of stress in the past forms, e.g., קוּמָ֣ה 'arise!' (Ps. 9.20) vs קֻ֫מָה (Judg. 18:9). According to Ibn Nūḥ, this is not an arbitrary variation, but rather the forms with the penultimate stress are derived from a verbal base whereas the forms with final stress have a noun base (Khan 2000, 58). The Karaite grammarians were concerned only with the Tiberian reading tradition and did not take into account of the *ketiv*. Their work vouchsafed the grammatical integrity of the reading tradition.

3.0. Concluding Remarks

The Arabic transcriptions of the Hebrew Bible represent an extreme case of convergence with the Islamic environment. As has been remarked, there was variation in the Karaite community as to the degree of convergence. During the period in which the transcriptions were made, Karaites used also Hebrew script for both Arabic and Biblical Hebrew. Likewise there is evidence that some Karaites maintained the Talmudic principle of יש אם למקרא ויש אם למסורת. The Karaite lexicographer David ben Abraham al-Fāsī (second half of the tenth century), for example, cites this as a legitimate principle of exegesis in the introduction to his lexicon *Kitāb Jāmiʿ al-ʾAlfāẓ* (ed. Skoss, I:1–13).[18]

Of course, convergence with the culture of the Islamic environment was not unique to the Karaites. Rabbanites scholars of the tenth and eleventh centuries adopted the Arabic language in their writings and many elements of the Islamic intellectual tradition. This included a preference for the *qere* of the Hebrew Bible. Saadya Gaon, for example, in principle follows the *qere* in his Arabic translations of the Bible and exegesis. The extent of the convergence, however, was to a lesser degree and this is reflected by the fact that they maintained Hebrew script in their writings (Habib 2019).

The use of the *rasm* الله to avoid the representation of the *qere* of the Tetragrammaton in written form is a remarkable reflection of the adoption of the *rasm* of Arabic Muslim Scripture to represent the Jewish oral reading tradition of the Hebrew Bible. The very fact, however, that many Karaite scribes used الله as a substitute for the Jewish name of God can be interpreted as an expression of Jewish communal identity. One of the functions of taboos that are exclusive to a particular social group is to reinforce communal identity and distinctiveness. The substitution of a transcription of the *qere* of the Tetragrammaton by an alternative graphic form, in this case a graphic representation imported from the Islam environment, is a reification of the community-building taboo. The use of the Islamic model of Arabic script for Scripture and the graphic form of the Islamic God

[18] It was also accepted by the Byzantine Karaite scholar Judah Hadassi (twelfth century); cf. Bacher (1895, 113).

should not be interpreted as a reflection of the Islamification of the Karaites and a convergence with Islamic identity. On the contrary, the Karaites adopted features from the Islamic cultural environment in order to put them to functional use within Judaism to enrich the internal Jewish culture and enhance communal identity.

References

Bacher, Wilhelm. 1895. 'Jehuda Hadassi's Hermeneutik Und Grammatik'. *Monatsschrift für Geschichte und Wissenschaft des Judentums* 40:109–26.

Beck, Edmund. 1946. "ʿArabiyya, Sunna und ʿĀmma in der Koranlesung des zweiten Jahrhunderts'. *Orientalia* 15:180–224.

Ben-Shammai, Haggai. 1984. 'The Attitude of Some Early Karaites towards Islam'. In *Studies in Medieval Jewish History and Literature*, edited by Isadore Twersky, II:3–40. Cambridge, MA: Harvard University Press.

Bernand, Marie. 1969. 'L'iğmāʿ chez ʿAbd al-Ğabbār et l'objection d'an-Naẓẓām'. *Studia Islamica* 30:27–38.

———. 1972. 'Nouvelles remarques sur l'iğmāʿ chez le qāḍī ʿAbd al-Ğabbār'. *Arabica* 19:78–85.

Blau, Joshua, and Simon Hopkins. 1984. 'On Early Judaeo-Arabic Orthography'. *Zeitschrift für Arabische Linguistik* 12:9–27.

Connolly, Magdalen M., and Nick Posegay. 2020. '"An Arabic Qurʾān, That You Might Understand": Qurʾān Fragments in the T-S Arabic Cairo Genizah Collection'. *Journal of Islamic Studies* 11:292–351.

———. 2021. ‘A Survey of Personal-Use Qur’an Manuscripts Based on Fragments from the Cairo Genizah’. *Journal of Qur’anic Studies* 23:1–40.

Déroche, François. 1992. *The Abbasid Tradition: Qur’ans of the Eighth to the Tenth Centuries A.D.* London, Oxford: Nour Foundation.

Díez Macho, Alejandro. 1971. *Manuscritos hebreos y arameos de la Biblia: Contribución al estudio de las diversas tradiciones del texto del Antiguo Testamento*. Rome: Institutum patristicum Augustinianum.

Drory, Rina. 1988. *The Emergence of Jewish-Arabic Literary Contacts at the Beginning of the Tenth Century*. Literature, Meaning, Culture 17. Tel-Aviv: Tel-Aviv University. [Hebrew].

———. 2000. *Models and Contacts: Arabic Literature and Its Impact on Medieval Jewish Culture*. Leiden: Brill.

Ginsburg, Christian D. 1880. *The Massorah, Compiled from Manuscripts, Alphabetically and Lexically Arranged. Vol. I. Aleph-Yod.* London, Vienna: G. Brögg.

Goldberg, Arnold. 1990. ‘The Rabbinic View of Scripture’. In *A Tribute to Geza Vermes. Essays on Jewish and Christian Literature and History*, edited by Philip R. Davies and Richard T. White, 153–66. Sheffield: JSOT Press.

Goshen-Gottstein, Moshe. 1962. ‘Biblical Manuscripts in the United States’. *Textus* 2:28–59.

Gottheil, Richard. 1905. ‘Some Hebrew Manuscripts in Cairo’. *Jewish Quarterly Review* 17:609–55.

Habib, Joseph. 2019. 'The Interpretation of Biblical Passages with Qere-Kethiv Conflicts by Saadya and Karaites'. In *Semitic Vocalization and Reading Traditions*, edited by Geoffrey Khan. Cambridge: University of Cambridge and Open Book Publishers.

Harviainen, Tapani. 1991. 'Abraham Firkovitsh, Karaites in Hīt, and the Provenance of Karaite Transcriptions of Biblical Hebrew Texts in Arabic Script'. *Folia Orientalia* 28:179–91.

———. 1993a. 'Karaite Arabic Transcriptions of Hebrew in the Saltykov-Shchedrin Public Library in St. Petersburg.' In *Estudios Masorericos. En Memoria de Harry M. Orlinsky*, edited by Emilia Fernandez Tejero and María Teresa Ortega Monasterio, 63–72. Xtos y Estudios «Cardenal Cisneros» de La Biblia Políglota Matritense (TECC 55). Madrid: Consejo Superior de Investigaciones Cientificos.

———. 1993b. 'Karaite Bible Transcription with Indiscriminate Use of Tiberian Pataḥ and Segol Vowel Signs'. In *Semitica. Serta Philologica Constantino Tsereteli Dicata*, edited by Riccardo Contini, Fabrizio Pennacchietti, and Mauro Tosco, 83–97. Pubblicazioni del Gruppo di Ricerca «Lessicografia Semitica e Lessico Ebraico» Finanziato dal C.N.R. 6. Torino: Silvio Zamorani Editore.

———. 1994. 'A Karaite Bible Transcription with Indiscriminate Counterparts of Tiberian Qameṣ and Ḥolam (Ms. Firkovitsh II, Arab.-Evr.1)'. In *Proceedings of the Eleventh Congress of the International Organization for Masoretic Studies (IOMS), Jerusalem June 21–22, 1993*, edited by Aron Dotan, 33–40. Jerusalem: The World Union of Jewish Studies.

———. 1995. 'A Karaite Letter-for-Letter Transliteration of Biblical Hebrew—MS Firkovitsh II, Arab.-Evr. 355'. *Textus* 18:196–177.

———. 1996a. 'MS Arab.-Evr. 2 of the Second Firkovitsh Collection, A Karaite Bible Transcription in Arabic Script'. In *Studies in Hebrew and Jewish Languages Presented to Shelomo Morag*, edited by Moshe Bar-Asher, *41–*59. Jerusalem: Bialik Institute.

———. 1996b. 'The Cairo Genizot and Other Sources of the Firkovich Collection in St. Petersburg'. In *Proceedings of the Twelfth International Congress of the International Organization for Masoretic Studies*, edited by E. John Revell, 25–36. Atlanta, GA: Scholars Press.

———. 1998. 'Abraham Firkovich and the Karaite Community in Jerusalem in 1864'. *Manuscripta Orientalia* 4 (2): 66–70.

Hoerning, Reinhart. 1889. *British Museum Karaite MSS. Descriptions and Collation of Six Karaite Manuscripts of Portions of the Hebrew Bible in Arabic Characters; with a Complete Reproduction... of One, Exodus I. 1 – VIII. 5, in... Facsimiles*. London: Williams and Norgate.

Ibn Mujāhid, ʾAḥmad ibn Mūsā. 1972. *Kitāb al-Sabʿa fī al-Qirāʾāt*. Edited by Shawqi Ḍayf. Cairo: Dār al-Maʿārif.

James, David. 1992. *The Master Scribes. Qurʾans of the tenth to fourteenth Centuries AD*. New York: The Nour Foundation and Oxford University Press.

Khan, Geoffrey. 1987. 'Vowel Length and Syllable Structure in the Tiberian Tradition of Biblical Hebrew'. *Journal of Semitic Studies* 32 (1): 23–82.

———. 1990. *Karaite Bible Manuscripts from the Cairo Genizah.* Cambridge University Library Genizah Series 9. Cambridge: Cambridge University Press.

———. 1992. 'The Medieval Karaite Transcriptions of Hebrew in Arabic Script'. *Israel Oriental Studies* 12:157–76.

———. 1993a. 'On the Question of Script in Medieval Karaite Manuscripts: New Evidence from the Genizah'. *Bulletin of the John Rylands University Library of Manchester* 75:133–41.

———. 1993b. 'The Orthography of Karaite Hebrew Bible Manuscripts in Arabic Transcription'. *Journal of Semitic Studies* 38 (1): 49–70.

———. 1998. 'The Book of Hebrew Grammar by the Karaite Joseph Ben Noaḥ'. *Journal of Semitic Studies* 43 (2): 265–86.

———. 2000. *The Early Karaite Tradition of Hebrew Grammatical Thought: Including a Critical Edition, Translation and Analysis of the Diqduq of ʾAbū Yaʿqūb Yūsuf Ibn Nūḥ on the Hagiographa.* Studies in Semitic Languages and Linguistics 32. Leiden: Brill.

———. 2013. *A Short Introduction to the Tiberian Masoretic Bible and Its Reading Tradition.* 2nd ed. Piscataway, NJ: Gorgias.

———. 2016. 'Judeo-Arabic'. In *Handbook of Jewish Languages*, edited by Lily Kahn and Aaron Rubin, 22–63. Leiden, Boston: Brill.

———. 2020. *The Tiberian Pronunciation Tradition of Biblical Hebrew: Including a Critical Edition and English Translation of the Sections on Consonants and Vowels in the Masoretic Treatise Hidāyat al-Qāriʾ 'Guide for the Reader'.* 2 vols. Cambridge

Semitic Languages and Cultures 1. Cambridge: University of Cambridge and Open Book Publishers.

———. 2024. 'The Representation of the Tetragrammaton in the Medieval Karaite Transcriptions of Hebrew into Arabic Script'. In *Religious and Intellectual Diversity in the Islamicate World and Beyond. Essays in Honor of Sarah Stroumsa*, edited by Omer Michaelis and Sabine Schmidtke, 2:1001–12. Leiden, Boston: Brill.

Khan, Geoffrey, María Ángeles Gallego, and Judith Olszowy-Schlanger. 2003. *The Karaite Tradition of Hebrew Grammatical Thought in Its Classical Form: A Critical Edition and English Translation of al-Kitāb al-Kāfī fī al-Luġa al-ʿIbrāniyya by ʾAbū Al-Faraj Hārūn Ibn Al-Faraj*. Studies in Semitic Languages and Linguistics 37. Leiden: Brill.

Martín-Contreras, Elvira. 1999. 'Terminología masorética en la exégesis de Génesis Rabbâ (secciones «Běre'šîṯ» y «Noaḥ»)'. *Sefarad* 59 (2): 343–52.

———. 2002. 'Noticias masoréticas en el midrás "Lamentaciones Rabbâ"'. *Sefarad* 62 (1): 125–41.

———. 2003a. 'Comments on Textual Details: Relationships between Masorah and Midrash'. *Journal of Jewish Studies* 54:62–70.

———. 2003b. 'Noticias masoréticas en los midrasim halákicos más antiguos y su comparación con los midrassim exegéticos'. *Sefarad* 63 (1): 119–39.

———. 2014. 'Rabbinic Ways of Preservation and Transmission of the Biblical Text in the Light of Masoretic Sources'. In *The Text of the Hebrew Bible. From the Rabbis to Masoretes,* edited by Elvira Martín Contreras and Lorena Miralles Maciá, 79–90. Journal of Ancient Judaism Supplements. Göttingen: Vandenhoeck & Ruprecht.

Naeh, Shlomo. 1992. 'Did the Tannaim Interpret the Script of the Torah Differently from the Authorized Reading?' *Tarbiz* 61:401–448. [Hebrew].

———. 1993. 'En Em Lammasoret – Second Time'. *Tarbiz* 62:455–462. [Hebrew].

Nasser, Shady Hekmat. 2015. 'Revisiting Ibn Mujāhid's Position on the Seven Canonical Readings: Ibn ʿĀmir's Problematic Reading of Kun Fa-Yakūna'. *Journal of Qur'anic Studies* 17 (1): 85–113.

Nöldeke, Theodor, Gotthelf Bergsträsser, and Otto Pretzl. 1938. *Geschichte Des Qorans, Part 3.* 2nd ed. Leipzig: Dieterichsche Verlagsbuchhandlung.

Polliack, Meira. 1997. *The Karaite Tradition of Arabic Bible Translation: A Linguistic and Exegetical Study of Karaite Translations of the Pentateuch from the Tenth and Eleventh Centuries C.E.* Études Sur Le Judaïsme Médiéval 17. Leiden: Brill.

Qirqisānī, Yaʿqūb ibn Isḥāq. 1939. *Kitab Al-ʾAnwār w-al-Marāqib*, edited by Leon Nemoy. New York: The Alexander Kohut Memorial Foundation.

Schacht, Joseph. 1950. *The Origins of Muhammadan Jurisprudence.* Oxford: Clarendon Press.

Steiner, Richard. 1996. 'Ketiv-Ḳerē or Polyphony: The שׁ-שׂ Distinction According to the Masoretes, the Rabbis, Jerome, Qirqisānī, and Hai Gaon'. In *Studies in Hebrew and Jewish*

Languages Presented to Shelomo Morag, edited by Moshe Bar-Asher, *151–*179. Jerusalem: Bialik Institute.

Stroumsa, Sarah. 2009. 'The Muslim Context of Medieval Jewish Philosophy'. In *The Cambridge History of Jewish Philosophy: From Antiquity through the Seventeenth Century*, edited by Steven M. Nadler and Tamar Rudavsky, 39–59. Cambridge: Cambridge University Press.

Tirosh-Becker, Ofra. 2011. *Rabbinic Excerpts in Medieval Karaite Literature*. 2 vols. Jerusalem: Bialik Institute and the Hebrew University. [Hebrew].

Yeivin, Israel. 1980. *Introduction to the Tiberian Masorah*. Masoretic Studies. Missoula: Scholars Press.

Zer, Rafael Isaac. 2003. 'Was the Masorete of the Aleppo Codex of Rabbinite or Karaite Origin?' *Sefunot* 8:573–87.

A JEWISH TRANSLATION OF GENESIS IN 10TH-CENTURY EGYPTIAN ARABIC

Nick Posegay

1.0. Introduction: The Manuscript

MS Firkovitch Yevr. II B 1526 comes from a Judaeo–Arabic translation of the biblical book of Genesis produced no later than the tenth century. It consists of two parchment folios containing most of Gen. 13.10 through 17.1. In total, 146 lines of text survive at least partially intact. They contain a significant number of Tiberian Hebrew vowel signs—uncommon for a Judaeo–Arabic manuscript this old—which record precise Arabic vocalisation. This article presents an edition of Firkovitch Yevr. II B 1526 and analyses the linguistic features preserved by its non-Classical orthography and vocalisation. It shows that, despite the relative prestige of a biblical manuscript of this scale, the scribe who copied it did not transcribe a linguistic register that matches what might be expected of a 'Classical Arabic' reading tradition. Instead, they recorded phonetic variations, apparently from their own Arabic dialect, which can be extracted from the extant text to reconstruct a medieval variety of spoken Arabic.

 https://doi.org/10.11647/OBP.0498.07

The extant fragments of MS Yevr. II B 1526 are in the second Firkovitch Collection at the Russian National Library,[1] gathered during Abraham Firkovitch's efforts to collect Karaite manuscripts from the Middle East in the 1860s. Some—probably most—of the manuscripts in this collection ultimately come from the Karaite genizah of Cairo's Dar Simḥa Synagogue, which Firkovitch visited in 1864 (Harviainen 1996, 31–32; Ben-Shammai 2010, 45). This provenance is also likely for Yevr. II B 1526, although this article makes no arguments either for or against a Karaite being the one who translated the biblical text in Yevr. II B 1526.

Each folio of Yevr. II B 1526 originally measured about 25.5 x 25.5 cm.[2] They belonged to a codex that likely contained a full Arabic translation of Genesis, if not more. Each page has two columns with 19 lines of well-executed Judaeo–Arabic text, for a total of eight columns in the extant leaves. Most verses begin with a one-word Hebrew incipit in the same hand as the Judaeo-Arabic scribe and end with a vertical pair of diacritic dots.

---

[1] I first encountered this manuscript while digitally sorting Firkovitch material for Ludwig Maximilian University of Munich's MAJLIS project. Subsequent work was funded by a Leverhulme Early Career Fellowship at the University of Cambridge under the project title, "Interfaith Exchange in the Intellectual History of Middle Eastern languages." Thank you to Magdalen M. Connolly for her comments on an earlier draft of this paper.

[2] This estimation is imprecise. The extant fragments are square-ish but missing substantial portions of their edges, and the measurement label digitised by the Russian National Library is unclear. I would measure the fragments myself, but they are in Russia.

Throughout this article, citations of individual lines from the manuscript take the form: 1r.1.1 (folio 1 recto, column 1, line 1). Refer to the edition below for the full context of each example.

The text of Yevr. II B 1526 contains numerous features of early phonetic Judaeo–Arabic orthography (see Blau and Hopkins 1984; Khan 2018, 150–51). They include *plene* spellings for most short *i*- and *u*-vowels (2r.2.2, אלמליך *al-malik*, 'the king'; 2r.1.11, והום *wa-hum*, 'and they'), the use of the Hebrew *dalet* to represent Arabic *ḍād* and *ẓāʾ* (see below), and an absence of the *lām* of the definite article before coronal consonants ('sun letters') (1v.2.13, אשמס *aš-šams*, 'the sun'; 2r.2.12, אסמא *as-samāʾ*, 'heaven').[3] These features suggest a date for Yevr. II B 1526 no later than the tenth century (Blau and Hopkins 1984; Ackerman-Lieberman 2014, 162–66; Khan 2018, 150; van Putten 2020, 51). It is also likely that the manuscript predates Saʿadiya Gaon's translation of the Pentateuch, which used the later Classical Judaeo–Arabic orthography prior to 942 (see Ackerman-Lieberman 2014). If this is the case, then Yevr. II B 1526 is among the oldest extant Jewish translations of the Bible into Arabic (compare Blau 1992) and one of the longest samples of a pre-Saʿadianic translation of the Pentateuch (see Vollandt 2014, 64–69, esp. fn. 25).

2.0. Writing System

The orthography of Yevr. II B 1526 follows an early phonetic Judaeo–Arabic writing system that transcribes Arabic sounds but does not conform to the orthography of Classical Arabic. Such

[3] There is one instance where a sun letter appears when we would expect it to be elided (2r.2.9, אלנפוס *al-nufūs*, 'souls').

writing systems are often generalised as Early Phonetic Judaeo–Arabic Spelling (EPJAS), although there can be significant orthographic variation between the writing systems of different EPJAS texts.

2.1. Vocalisation

The manuscript's vocalisation is sporadic, but the scribe used every Tiberian vowel sign at least once.[4] *Pataḥ* typically represents a short /a/ where we would expect to find Arabic *fatḥa*. *Ḥireq* and *qibbuṣ* represent /i/ and /u/, equivalent to *kasra* and *ḍamma*.

2v.2.12, אלְבַר *al-bar*, 'the wilderness'
2v.2.11, גִּבֶאל *gibɛ̄l*, 'mountains'
1v.2.10, תֻקבר *tuqbar*, 'you will be buried'

Šureq represents /u/ or /ū/, but it appears only at the ends of two plural verbs and in two other places:

2v.2.7, כַּלְעוּ *k̲alaʿū*, 'they broke away'
2v.2.13, וֹדרבוּ *wa-ḍarabū*, 'they struck'
1r.2.12, אֲתֻּום *ʾa-ṯumm*, 'then' [interrogative]
2v.2.13, עַיְן אלְחוּכְם *ʿAyn al-Ḥukm*, 'the Spring of Judgement'[5]

Segol usually indicates an Arabic *a*-vowel that has been contextually raised towards /i/ (i.e., a form of *ʾimāla*), approximating /ɛ/ or /æ/. For this discussion, I assume that the scribe intended

[4] There are no Arabic vowel signs in this manuscript, but on Arabic vocalisation in Judaeo–Arabic texts, see Vidro (2018).

[5] *ʿAyn al-Ḥukm* is a literal translation of the biblical place name *ʿEyn Mišpɔṭ* in Gen. 14.7.

for the *segol* sign in Judaeo–Arabic to record a vowel similar to that which the standard Tiberian Hebrew *segol* represented (i.e., /ɛ/; see Khan 2020, I:259–60), and I transliterate it as such below. *Ṣere* appears once, presumably indicating a stronger form of *imāla* approximating /e/:

1v.1.1, מותּדׄהיב *mutaḏɛhib*, 'going on'
2r.1.10, סיֵכין *sēkin*, 'dwelling'

Qameṣ appears once, indicating /ɔ/, though it is in a Hebrew loan rather than a native Arabic word. *Ḥolem*, /o/, may also occur twice, but both instances are dubious, and their phonetic value is unclear:

1r.1.9, הָגר *Hɔgar*, 'Hagar'
2r.2.2, אלאׄסתְּוא *al-ʾostawā*(?)[6]
1v.2.12, דׄנבְ אלאמרי *ḏanbo*(?) *l-ʾamurī*, 'the sin of the Amorites'[7]

Šewa seems to follow its default Tiberian quality /a/ (Khan 2020, I:305), appearing frequently in places where we would expect Classical Arabic *fatḥa*, although its use instead of *pataḥ* may imply some reduction in length or change in quality of that

[6] The word *al-ʾostawā*(?) corresponds to the Hebrew place name שָׁוֵה *Šaveh* from Gen. 14.17, as in "the Valley of *Šaveh*, which is the Valley of the King."

[7] It is slightly tempting to read the two dots on the *bet* of דׄנבְ as the Babylonian dot sign for /ɔ/ (see Khan 2013, 954), but more likely I suspect it is acting as a sort of conjunctive accent connecting the two elements of the construct phrase "sin of the Amorites" (Gen. 15.16). It could also just be a random ink splatter.

vowel.[8] Elsewhere it behaves as 'silent' *šewa*, marking the lack of a vowel, equivalent to Arabic *sukūn*:

2v.1.13, תְּרֶי *tarē̄*, 'you see'
2v.2.15, מְלִיךְ *malik*, 'king'
2v.1.19, אֻעְטִיהַא *ʾuʿṭīhā*, 'I give it'

Finally, several *ḥatef pataḥ* signs also mark short /a/. They are functionally equivalent to vocalic *šewa* when it represents /a/ elsewhere in the manuscript, but follow the Masoretic Hebrew scribal tendency to not write a vocalic *šewa* on glottal or pharyngeal consonants:

1r.2.13, אֲכִיר *ʾaḵīr*, 'back'
2v.2.11, חֲתֶּי *ḥattē̄*, 'up to'
2v.2.11, אַלְחֲוֶרִייִן *al-ḥawɛriyyīn*, 'the Horites'
2v.2.14, אלְאֲמֻרִי *al-ʾamurī*, 'the Amorites'

2.2. Consonantal Diacritics

In addition to vowel signs, the scribe used several diacritic marks to signal other features of the Arabic text. Most notable is the system of dots and strokes to differentiate between fricative and plosive forms of a single Hebrew consonant. Within this system, the intralinear Hebrew *dageš* dot indicates the Arabic plosives *gīm*, *dāl*, *kāf*, and *tāʾ*:

---

[8] In other vocalised Judaeo–Arabic manuscripts, *šewa* in unstressed, open syllables sometimes represents a short epenthetic vowel that corresponds to /i/ or /u/ in Classical Arabic, but I have not observed this phenomenon in Yevr. II B 1526. See Khan (1992, 110–11), Posegay (2020, 46), and Posegay and Arrant (2021, 266–67).

2v.2.14, אלגֶ֯אליס *al-gēlis*, 'dwelling'
2v.1.3, אלארדון *al-ʾurdun*, 'Jordan'
2v.1.10, עיניך *ʿaynayk*, 'your two eyes'
2v.1.11, אנתּ *ʾant*, 'you'

By contrast, a supralinear dot or oblique stroke with no *dageš* denotes the corresponding Arabic fricatives *ġayn*, *ḏāl*, *ḵāʾ*, and *ṯāʾ*:

2r.2.16, אלגׄלמאן *al-ġulmān*, 'the young men'
2v.1.13, אלדׄי *allaḏī*, 'that'
2r.1.6, ואכׄדׄו *wa-ʾaḵaḏū*, 'and they took'
2r.1.14, ותׄלתׄ *wa-ṯalāṯ*, 'and three'

Additionally, a Hebrew *dalet* with a supralinear dot can indicate *either* the Arabic *ḍād* or *ẓāʾ*, with no graphical distinction between these letters and *ḏāl*:

2v.1.18, אלארדּׄ *al-ʾarḍ*, 'the land'
2v.1.10, ואנדׄור *wa-ʾunẓur*, 'and look'

Dageš can also indicate Arabic gemination, just as it does in Hebrew:[9]

---

[9] There are also four places where *dageš* unexpectedly marks an ungeminated consonant that does not typically take *dageš lene* (2v.1.7 twice, סדום *sadom*; 'Sodom'; 2v.1.18, אלארדּׄ *al-ʾarḍ*, 'the land'; 2v.1.1, מצר *miṣr*, 'Egypt'). This feature resembles Tiberian Masoretic practices that employ *dageš* to orthoepically reinforce a Hebrew consonant at the end of a syllable or onset of a word (Khan 2020, I:542–44). Such a *dageš* ensures that the reciter clearly enunciates the consonant and does not elide it with the preceding syllable. This practice is not common in Judaeo–Arabic, nor is it clear that it is what is happening with the unexplained *dageš* dots in Yevr. II B 1526.

2v.1.9, וארבּ *war-rabb*, ‘and the Lord’

1r.2.6, אִנִּיך *ʾinnik*, ‘indeed you’

A supralinear stroke resembling the Hebrew *rafe* sign appears in several places. It sometimes seems to mark a *mater lectionis* letter that stands for a vowel sound, but other times it indicates a fricative consonant or its meaning is unclear. Whether the original scribe, or other users, added all these signs is not certain:

2v.2.5, אלמֶאלִיֿח *al-mɛ̄liḥ*, ‘salty’

2v.2.7, כַלְֿעוּ *k̲alaʿū*, ‘they broke away’

2v.2.3, עַֿמְקְ *ʿamaq*, ‘valley’

The Hebrew *mappiq* dot also occurs often in the letter *heʾ*, usually at the end of words, both when it represents an Arabic *tāʾ marbūṭa* and when it represents a pronominal suffix:

1v.1.17, תׄלתׄהּ *t̲alāt̲a*, ‘three’

2v.1.6, באכׄביתוהּ *bi-ʾak̲biyatuh*, ‘in his tents’

3.0. Edition of MS Yevr. II B 1526

Note that the manuscript has been photographed and digitised the wrong way round.[10] The extant text begins on the verso of folio 2 and ends on the recto of folio 1.

---

[10] Images and further description available here: https://www.nli.org.il/en/discover/manuscripts/hebrew-manuscripts/.

Firkovitch Yevr. II B 1526, f2 verso:

Column 1	Line
(Gen. 13.10) {...}ארד̇ מצ̇ר מות{...}	1
(11) ואכתַ̇אר לוה̇ לוט א{...}וד א{.}	2
אלארד̇ון וארת̇חל {לוט} מן אשרק	3
ואפת̇רקו אמר מן א{כ}וה̇: (12) אברם:	4
קעד פי א{רד כנ}ען ולוט קעד̇ פי	5
קורֶי אלג̇ו{ר..} באכ̇ביתוה̇ אלי	6
ס̇דום: (13) (ואנשי): ואוניסי ס̇דום רד̇יין	7
וכ̇ייב̇ין לרב{ג..}עני בינד̇י אלרב:	8
(14) (ויוי): וארב̇ קאל לאברם מן בעד̇ אפת̇רק	9
לוט מינוה אסני יֶא עיניך̇ ואנד̇ור	10
מן אלמוד̇יע אלד̇י אנת̇ ת̇ם שֶמְיַ̄א ו̇	11
וקבלי וְשַׂרְקַא ובחרַא: (15) (כי): לאן	12
איי כ̇ול אלארד̇ אלד̇י אנת̇ תְרֶי לך̇	13
אֶעטיה̇א ולולד̇ך̇ אלי אלאבד̇: (16) (ושמתי):	14
ואוצייר איי ולד̇ך̇ כ̇תורב̇ אלארד	15
אלדי אן יסת̇טִיע אנסין ליחצי איי	16
ת̇וראב אלארד̇ הם ולד̇ך̇ יוחצא:	17
(17) (קום): אסלוך̇ פי אלארד̇ לטולהא	18
{.}ד̇הא אן לך̇ אֶעְטִיהַ̄א: (18) (ויאהל):	19

Firkovitch Yevr. II B 1526, f2 verso:

Column 2	Line
(14.1) סדׄום ואיי {...} (2)	1
מליךׄ אדׄמה {...}	2
ומליךׄ בלע {...}	3
(3) אצטחבו אלי עַמְקְ א{...}	4
אלמֶאלִיׄח: (4) (שתים): אתׄנעשר{...}	5
איי כדרלעמר ותׄלתׄ{...}	6
כַּלְעוּ: (5) ובארבעתׄעשׂר סנה גַּא{...}	7
ולמלוךׄ אלדי מעוהׄ ודׄרבו איי אלגבא{...}	8
פי אצנמין ואיי אַלְוַזְוְיֶהׄ אלדי פי אלח{...}	9
אלחייבין אלדי פי מְ{סֶאן.} קְ{נ.א..} (6)	10
ואיי אַלְחֲוֶרִיין פי גִּבֶּאל שְׂרֶאָהׄ חַתֶּי אלב{...}	11
קנְטְרתְ אלחיגֶּאז אלדי עְלַא אלְבַּר: (7) (וישוב) {...}	12
וְגוו אלי עַיין אלְחוּכְּם היא רקם ודׄרבוּ {...}	13
חקל אלעְמַאלִקַהׄ וְהַם אלְאֲמֻרי אלגֶּאליס {בעיין}	14
גְדׄי: (8) (ויצא): וְכׄרג מְלִיךׄ סדׄום וְמ{...}	15

Firkovitch Yevr. II B 1526, f2 recto:

Column 1	Line
(14.9) {...} אלכמסה:	1
(10) {...}בַיאר חומר	2
{...ר}ה ווקעו תם	3
{...}אל: (11) (ויקחו):	4
{...} סד̇ום ועמרה	5
{...אַכ}להום ואנ̇טלקו: (12) ואכ̇ד̇ו	6
וסרחוה איבן אכי אברם	7
{..לק..}א ג̇אליס פי סדום: (13) (ויבא):	8
{...} אלמֻנפלית̇ וכ̇בר לאברם אלעִברי	9
{...}א סיֵכין בבלוט ממרי אַלאמורי אכו	10
{..}ול ואכו ענר והום אֶכ̇דִאן עהד̇	11
{..ר}ם: (14) (וישמע): וסמיע אברם אִד̇: סובי	12
אכוה וג̇רד̇ איי תֶאד̇יבוה̇ א'ולַד̇[11] ביתוה	13
{י}עני ת̇לאמיד̇וה ת̇מנתעשר ות̇לת̇	14
{מ}ייה וכ̇לב אלי בַאניאַס: (15) (ויחלק): וקסם	15
{ע}ליהום אליל הוא ועִביד̇וה וקת̇להום ו̇	16
{...}הום אלי. אלדי מִן שמאל ד̇משק: (16) ורד̇	17

[11] A later hand inserted the first *vav* in א'ולַד̇.

Firkovitch Yevr. II B 1526, f2 recto:

Column 2	Line
(14.17) {...} כדרלעמר ואיי אל{מלוך אל}די	1
מעוה א{ל ... } אלאֿסתְּוא הוא עמק אלמליךּ:	2
(18) (ומלכיצֿ): ומ{לכי}צדּק מליךּ סֶאלים אכֿר{ג}	3
טעַאם ומַא{..}א אימַאם לטאיק א{.}אדם	4
(19) ובּרכּוה וקַאל מובּרך {...}לטַאיק אלעאלי	5
קני אסמא ואלאר{ד}: (20) (וברוךּ) ומוברךּ אטייק	6
אלעאלי אלדי חיין אעדא{...}יךּ ודּפע אליה	7
אלעושר מן כול: (21) (ויא) וקאל מליך סדום	8
לאברם אדּפע לי אלנפוס יעני אלקווּם	9
אלדי אכֿדֿו ואסרח כֿודֿ לך : (22) (ויאמר):	10
וקאל אברם למליךּ סדום דפעתּ יד{י} אלי	11
ארב אטַייק אלעאלי קני אסמא ואלארדֿ:	12
(23) (אם): אמין שמע ואלי שרַאךּ נעל אן	13
אַכֿודֿ מן כול אלדֿי לךּ ולא תּקול אנא	14
אגֿניתּ איי אברם: (24) (בלעדי): כֿלא אלדי	15
אכּלו אלגֿלמאן וקסמת אלאוניסי אלדי	16
סלכּו מעי ענר אשכל וממרא הום	17
יַכֿדֿון אנצבּתּהום: (15.1) (אחר): מן {בעד ...}	18
דֿליךּ אלכלַאם כַּאן כּ{טב} ארב{...}	19

Firkovitch Yevr. II B 1526, f1 verso:

Column 1	Line
(15.2) לי {ו}אני מותּדׄהיב עקים ו{...}קד ביתּי	1
הוא דׄמשקי אליעזר: (3) (ויא) וקאל אברם	2
הודׄא לי לם תֶּעטי ולדׄ והודׄא איבן	3
אהלי יריתׄ אייי: (4) (והנה): והודׄא כיטַאב	4
ארב אליה קַ{אל} לא לַא יריתׄךּ דׄא אילא	5
אלדי יכׄרוגּ מן א{מ}עַאדׄ יריד צֱלבוה	6
הוא יריתׄך (5) (ויוצא): ואכׄרגּ אייה כׄ	7
כׄארגּא וקאל אלתּפיתּ יא אסמא ואחצי	8
אלכואכּיב אן תּסתּטיע לתּחצי איהום	9
וקאל לוה כּדׄא יכון ולדׄךּ: (6) (והא): ואמין	10
ברב וחסבּהא לוה עידׄאלה: (7) ויאמר:	11
וקאל לוה אנא ארב אלדי אכׄרגּתּךּ מן	12
אדוהא לאדׄפע איליךּ איי תּיךּ אלארדׄ	13
לתּריתׄהא יעני ארדׄ כנען: (8) ויא: וקאל	14
יאִרב יא אילאהּ בִמאדׄא אעריף איני	15
{אר}יתׄהא: (9) ויא: וקאל לוהּ כׄודׄ לי מן אלעוגול	16
תׄלתׄהּ ומן אלמעזא תׄלתׄה ומן אלכיבאש	17
{...}ה {..}וקטי וגוזל: (10) ויקח: ואכׄד̄ לוה	18
{...} פי אלוסט וצנע	19

Firkovitch Yevr. II B 1526, f1 verso:

Column 2	Line
(15.11) וירד: {...}	1
(12) וקע עלא {...}	2
כּבירה וקע{ת} {...}	3
(13) עִלם תעלִם {...}	4
ארד ליס לה{ום} {...}	5
ויעדׄיבוהום ארבע מייה {...}	6
(14) והם איי אשעבֿ אלדׄי יסתֿ{...}	7
אנא מודין ומִן בעדֿ דׄאליךֿ יכׄר{...}	8
כּביר יעני אכׄריגֿהום: (15) ואתה: ואנתֿ	9
תֿנטליק אלי אַבאךֿ בסלַאם תֱקבר	10
בשׄייבה גֿיידֿה: (16) ודור: וגֿיל ראַבִיע	11
ירגֿעו הונא לאן לם יכּמול דׄנבֿ אלאמרי	12
חתי אלאן: (17) ויהי: וכאנתֿ אשמס גֱילה {..}:	13
ודֿוהֿמהֿ כַאנתֿ ואידׄי תֿנור דֿוכׄאן ופל{.}ל{..}	14
נַאר אלדי גַֿאזביין אוליךֿ אלקסַאם: (18) ביום:	15
פי דׄליךֿ אליום קטע ארב מע אברם ע{הד}	16
קַאיל לולדֿךֿ דֿפעתֿ איי הידׄיה אלארד מִן	17
ניל מצר אלי אנהר אלכּביר נהר אלפורַאתֿ:	18
(19) את: איי אלקיני ואיי אלקניזי ואיי אלמשר{ק}	19

Firkovitch Yevr. II B 1526, f1 recto:[12]

Column 1	Line
(16.1) {...}הא הגר:	1
(2) {...אב}רם ה'ודא אנא	2
{...}ליא אלי אמתי לעל	3
{...} אברם לקוול שרי:	4
(3) {...מ}רת אברם איי הַגר	5
{...} אמתהא מן אנקידא עשר	6
{...}קעוד אברם פי ארד כנען ודפעת	7
{..}א לאברם ז'וגהא לוה לְמרה: (4) ויבא	8
וגא אלי הָגר וחבילת ונדׄרת איד	9
חבילת וסתכׄפת מולתהא פי עייניהא:	10
(5) ותא וקאלת שרי לאברם דולמי עליך	11
ואִיני דפעת אמתי פי חיגרך ונדרת	12
איד חבילת ואסתכפת פי עיניהא י	13
יחכום ארב בייני ובינך: (6) ויא וקאל	14
אברם לשרי ה'ודא אמתיך בידיך	15
אִעמלי להא אלדי יחסון פי עיניך ו	16
{.}עדבתהא שרי והרבת מן בינדיהא:	17
(7) וימצ ווגידהא מלַאך ארב עלי עין	18
אלמא פי אלבר עלא אל{...} פי טריק	19

[12] A later hand inserted the first *vav* in ה'ודא (ll. 2, 15) and ז'וגהא (l. 8).

Firkovitch Yevr. II B 1526, f1 recto:

Column 2	Line
(16.8) אנא {...} (9) {מ}לאךּ	1
ארב ארג{ע...} ואתעדבי	2
תחת ידיהא: (10) ויא וקאל להא מלאך	3
ארב כתרה אוכתיר איי ולדיך ולא	4
יוחצא מן אלכּתרהּ (11) ויא וקאל להא מלאך	5
ארב אִנִּיךּ חובִלא ותלידי איבן ואדעי	6
אסמוה אסמעיל תפסי{ר..} סמיע אטייק	7
אד סמיע ארבֿ אלי שקאד: (12) והוּא יכון	8
וחשי אלאדמי ידוהּ פי כול ויד כול ביה	9
ועלא וגּה כֻּל אכותּוה יסכון: (13) ותקרא	10
ודעת אסם ארב אלמוכטיב אליהא אנת	11
טייק נדֿרי איד קאלתֿ אֱתֿוּם הונא ראיתּ	12
אֱכִֿר נדרי: (14) על כן: עלא דליך דועי לְלבר	13
ביר לחין נדרת הודא ביין אלמַוְעַדּ ובין	14
ברדּ: (15) ותלד וולידת חגר לאברם איבן ודעא	15
אברם אסם אבנוה אלדי ולידת הגר	16
אסמעיל: (16) ואברם איבן תמאנין סנה וֹ	17
וסית סנין בולדה הגר איי אסמע{יל}	18
(17.1) ויהי וכאן אברם {א...}	19

4.0. Linguistic Analysis

The writing system employed in this manuscript records several features of the scribe's Arabic dialect, including variations in the realisation of consonants and vowels like /g/ and /ɛ/. The translator's vocabulary and syntax provide further data for reconstructing their Arabic dialect while also revealing influences from their Hebrew source text. The following discussion is only a partial analysis and notes that further examination is needed to do justice to all the non-Classical patterns of pronunciation, vocabulary, and morphosyntax in this manuscript.

4.1. *Gimel* and *Gīm*

The scribe systematically deployed the Hebrew letter *gimel* with *dageš* and supralinear dots to signify the Classical Arabic consonants *jīm* and *ġayn*. *Gimel* with a supralinear dot and no *dageš* indicates *ġayn*, graphically mimicking the diacritic dot on the Arabic character (غ):

2r.2.15, אגׄנית *ʾaġnit*, 'I have made rich'
2r.2.16, אלגׄלמאן *al-ġulmān*, 'the young men'

By contrast, a *gimel* with *dageš* invariably represents *jīm*—or rather, the scribe's dialectal reflex of Classical Arabic *jīm*. Most medieval Judaeo–Arabic scribes distinguished *jīm* by placing a diacritic dot above or below a *gimel* (Connolly 2019, 157), so this scribe's choice to use *dageš* instead is somewhat irregular. It suggests that they pronounced *jīm* the same way as Tiberian Hebrew *gimel* with *dageš*; that is, as a voiced velar stop /g/:

1v.1.6, יכׄרוגְ *yak̲rug*, ‘he goes out’
1v.1.8, כׄארגְא *k̲ārig*^{an}, ‘outwards’
1r.2.10, וגְה *wagh*, ‘face’
2v.2.12, אלחיגֶאז *al-ḥigēz*, ‘the Hijaz’
2v.2.13, וְגוו *wa-gāwū(?)*, ‘and they came’

This dialectal *gīm* reflex is best known from modern varieties of Egyptian Arabic, but some Judaeo–Arabic papyri suggest it may have existed in Egypt as early as the ninth century (Connolly 2019, 167–68), and it is present in Classical Judaeo–Arabic manuscripts dating to approximately the eleventh century (Posegay 2020, 49; Posegay and Arrant 2021, 270–71). Since Yevr. II B 1526 was produced no later than the tenth century and most likely belonged to Karaites in Cairo,[13] it seems to be an early witness to this Egyptian feature. *Gimel* with no dot at all is rare in the manuscript, but it also indicates *gīm*:

1r.1.12, חיגרך *ḥigrak*, ‘your embrace’
2v.2.15, גְדי *gadi*, ‘[ʿAyn] Gedi’[14]

---

[13] A further hint of an Egyptian provenance comes from the manuscript’s translation of Gen. 15.18. The original Hebrew states that God will give Abram’s descendants land “from the river of Egypt to the great river, the River Euphrates.” The Arabic translator amends this verse with the name of the Egyptian river, writing “from the Nile of Egypt to the great river, the River Euphrates” (1v.2.17–18, מן ניל מצר אלי אנהר אלכביר נהר אלפורַאת).

[14] Compare discussion of unpointed *gimel* in Connolly (2019, 157), particularly fn. 3–5.

4.2. Interdental Consonants

The regular uses of *dageš* and supralinear diacritic dots suggests that the scribe made some distinction between the Arabic interdental plosives and fricatives, but they do not mark both types in every case. They clearly recorded the voiceless interdental *tāʾ* /t/ with *dageš*, in contrast to marking the fricative *ṯāʾ* /ṯ/ with a supralinear dot, more than a dozen times each (e.g., 2r.1.14, ת̇מנתעשר *ṯamantʿašr*, 'eighteen'). Furthermore, *tav* with neither supralinear dot *nor dageš* usually represents /t/, but there are three exceptions where we expect to find /ṯ/ in Classical Arabic:

1r.2.4, כתרה *kaṯra*, 'multitude'
1r.2.5, אלכתרה *al-kaṯra*, 'the multitude'
1r.2.17, תמאנין *ṯamānīn*, 'eighty'

The scribe also distinguished the voiced Arabic interdentals *dāl* /d/ and *ḏāl* /ḏ/ using these diacritics, although they are less consistent than with their voiceless counterparts:

1v.2.11, גיידה *gayyida*, 'good'
2v.1.17, ולדך *waladak*, 'your son'
2r.1.17, דמשק *dimašq*, 'Damascus'
2v.1.11, אלד̇י *ʾallaḏī*, 'that'
2r.1.6, ואכ̇ד̇ו *wa-ʾaḵaḏū*, 'and they seized'
1v.1.10, כד̇א *kaḏā*, 'like, as'

Notably, it is not clear that the scribe consistently differentiated an emphatic interdental fricative *ẓāʾ* /ẓ/ from the non-emphatic *ḏāl* /ḏ/, as both letters can appear as a Hebrew *dalet* with a single supralinear dot or stroke:

1v.1.16, כֹּוד *kuḏ*, 'take, bring'
1r.1.9, ונדׄרת *wa-naẓarat*, 'and she saw'

The typical early phonetic Judaeo–Arabic practice of transcribing both Arabic *ḍād* and *ẓāʾ* with *dalet* and a supralinear dot further complicates this conflation. Both are graphically identical to *ḏāl* when they appear with a supralinear dot:

2r.1.14, תלאמידׄוה *talāmīḏuh*, 'his students, his disciples'
2v.1.11, אלמודׄיע אלדׄי *al-mawḍīʿ ʾallaḏī*, 'the place which'
2v.2.13, ודׄרבו *wa-ḍarabū*, 'and they struck'[15]

They can also appear as a *dalet* with no dot, in which case they are identical to *dāl*. This fact means that the Hebrew *dalet* with no diacritic dots can stand for four different consonants, distinguished only by context, and we cannot be sure that the scribe or the manuscript's readers 'correctly' differentiated them in every place:

1r.1.12, דפעת *dafaʿt*, 'I handed over'
1r.1.13, איד *ʾiḏ*, 'when, then'
1r.1.11, דולמי *ẓulmī*, 'my iniquity'
1r.1.7, ארד *ʾarḍ*, 'land'

This lack of distinction suggests that the consonantal phonemes typically represented by *ẓāʾ* and *ḍād* in Classical Arabic may have lost their emphatic character and merged with *ḏāl* and

---

[15] The word ודׄרבו might be pointed וּדְרָבוּ, but the vocalisation marks are partially illegible. It is also a clear example where the mark on the *dalet* representing Arabic *ḍād* looks more like a horizontal stroke than a point (i.e., דֿ). The variation between dots and strokes on בגד כפ"ת letters often appears to be random, perhaps reflecting the work of multiple pointers.

dāl, respectively, in the scribe's Arabic dialect. That dialect was then in the process of losing the voiced interdental fricative /ḏ/, such that *ḏāl*, *ẓāʾ*, and *ḍād* could all be conflated with the voiced alveolar stop /d/ represented by Hebrew *dalet* with *dageš*. Other explanations are possible (perhaps two pointers with different dialects, or two pointers at different times in the chronology of a single dialect), but it appears that the scribe heard the same sound when pronouncing the Arabic letters *ḍād*, *ẓāʾ*, and *ḏāl*.[16]

4.3. Non-Standard Vocalisation

Most of the vocalised words in Yevr. II B 1526 are either non-Arabic loans or Arabic words that match the expected vowels of Classical Arabic. However, of note are places where the scribe recorded an *e*-vowel in place of an expected Classical Arabic /a/ or /ā/. This phenomenon is usually known in Arabic as *ʾimāla* 'bending down' (Hopkins 2005; Levin 2007; Khan 2018, 150–51; van Putten 2020, 62–64; Posegay 2020, 44–45). In such cases, the scribe of Yevr. II B 1526 preferred the Hebrew *segol* sign, approximating /ɛ/. This sign often appears where Classical Arabic would have *ʾalif* indicating long medial /ā/ or *ʾalif maqṣūra* indicating long final /ā/:

2v.1.13, תְרֶי *tarɛ̄*, 'you see'
2v.1.6, קוּרֶי *qurɛ̄*, 'villages'

---

[16] On a related note, see discussion of the (lack of) merger between *ẓ and *ḍ in the variety of Arabic recorded by the early phonetic Judaeo–Arabic text of MS Cambridge University Library, T-S 13J8.7 (van Putten 2020, 68).

2v.1.10, יֶא *yɛ̄*, 'O, now'[17]
2v.2.11, חַתֶּי *ḥattɛ̄*, 'up to'
2v.2.11, גִבֶּאל שַׁרֶאה *gibɛ̄l šarɛ̄*, 'the Mountains of Šarat'[18]
1v.2.13, גֶּילה *gɛ̄la*, 'revolved, set' [of the sun after setting]

It is notable that several of these words, specifically those with II- and III-weak roots (i.e., תַּרֶי *tarɛ̄*; קורֶי *qurɛ̄*; and גֶּילה *gɛ̄la*), seem to preserve a phonemic long *e*-vowel known from early medieval reports by Arabic grammarians (see discussion in van Putten 2022, 24–28 and Rabin 1951, 113).

As mentioned above, the Hebrew *ṣere* sign appears in only one Arabic word, approximating long /ē/ where Classical Arabic would have /ā/. It is not clear what makes *sēkin* in this context phonologically distinct from other *fāʿil* patterns like *sɛ̄lim* or *gɛ̄lis* that are marked with *segol*.

2r.1.10, סֵיכִין 'dwelling'
2r.2.3, מליך סֶאלים *malik sɛ̄lim*, 'a perfect king'[19]
2v.2.14, אלגֶּאליס *al-gɛ̄lis*, 'dwelling'

There are also a few examples of *segol* with short medial vowels:

[17] The particle *yɛ̄*, which looks like the Classical Arabic vocative particle *yā*, is a translation of the Hebrew word נָא *nɔ* ('please, now') from Gen. 13.14.

[18] 'Mountains of Šarat' refers to the southern mountainous region of Jordan with the same name. It is a translation of the Biblical 'Mount Seir' from Gen. 14.6.

[19] Equivalent to מֶלֶךְ שָׁלֵם *mɛlɛḵ šɔlem* ('the King of Salem') from Gen. 14.18, but the translator appears to interpret *šɔlem* as an adjective (cognate with Classical Arabic *sālim*) rather than a place name.

2r.1.11, אֶכּ֗דִאן *ʾɛḵḏān* or *ʾɛḵḏīn*, ‘they two held’

2r.1.13, תֶאדִיבוּהִ *tɛʾdībuh*, ‘his educated/disciplined [ones]’[20]

The *plene* orthography of Yevr. II B 1526 also preserves vowels that diverge from expected Classical Arabic vocalisation, including further evidence of *a*-vowels vowels raised towards /e/ or /i/. One example is the contrast between the Arabic prepositions *ʿalā* ‘upon’ and *ʾilā* ‘to’. The scribe consistently spells *ʿalā* with final *aleph*, but *ʾilā* with final *yod*:

1r.2.13, עלא *ʿalā*, ‘on’

2v.1.14, אלי *ʾilā*, ‘to’

In Classical Arabic, both particles are typically spelled with *alif maqṣūra* representing final /ā/, but the Judaeo–Arabic orthography implies that the scribe heard their vowels differently, more

[20] *Tɛʾdībuh* is an odd form that artificially conforms to the Hebrew morphology of this verse. Gen. 14.14, which relates Abraham’s call for 318 men to aid him in battle, includes the phrase חֲנִיכָיו יְלִידֵי בֵיתוֹ ‘his trained [ones] who were born in his house’. The Judaeo–Arabic translator renders it with the longer תֶאדִיבוּהִ אולַד ביתוה {י}עני תלאמידוה ‘his educated [ones], the boys of his house, that is, his students’. This interpretation seems to stem from a Talmudic explanation which holds that the 318 men were Torah scholars and Abraham’s disciples (Nedarim 32a:14). In what I cannot quite believe is a coincidence, this depiction of Abraham as the leader of a group of scholars corresponds with a passage in a letter by Dawid bar Pawlos, a late eighth–century West Syriac abbot. Dawid writes that his great, great grandfather Sabroy founded a miaphysite school near Mosul and links his students to Abraham’s followers, stating “He gathered 318 men for a school, and he set his son over them as a leader, and he resembled the head of the patriarchs, Abraham” (Dolabani 1953, 48, lines 11–13; Posegay 2021, 146, 148).

like *ʿalā* and *ʾilē* or *ʾilī*. Other orthographic differences from the expected vocalisation of Classical Arabic can be found throughout the edition (e.g., 1v.2.17, הידֿיה אלארד *hīḏihi al-ʾarḍ*, 'this land').

4.4. Pronouns and Pronominal Suffixes

Both the independent and suffixed forms of the Arabic pronouns in Yevr. II B 1526 differ from the expected orthography and morphology of Classical Arabic. Most obvious are the *plene* spellings of the independent third-person pronouns *huwā* and *hiyā*, which happen to share the same orthography as the equivalent pronouns in Hebrew:

2r.1.16, הוא *huwā*, 'he, it'
2v.2.13, היא *hiyā*, 'she, it'

Meanwhile, the definite relative pronoun *ʾallaḏī* appears without inflection for gender or number. Blau and Hopkins have argued that this invariable relative pronoun is a 'classicised' archaic feature of early phonetic Judaeo–Arabic (1987, 125), but it persists even in modern Arabic dialects (van Putten 2020, 63, 66). The invariable relative pronoun is thus more likely to be a dialectal evolution of an older inflected pronoun, rather than a 'classicism'.

In contrast to *ʾallaḏī*, the translator does inflect demonstrative pronouns, including the Classical masculine singular *ḏālik*, a vaguely Classical masculine plural *ʾulāʾik* or *ʾulayk*, and a non-Classical feminine singular *tik*.

1v.2.8, בעד דֿאליך *baʿd ḏālik*, 'after that'
1v.2.16, דֿליך אליום *ḏālik al-yawm*, 'that day'

2v.2.15, אוליך אלקסאם *ʾulāʾik al-q*[*i*]*sām*, 'those portions'
1v.1.13, תיך אלארד *tik al-ʾarḍ*, 'that land'

Several pronominal suffixes also take non-Classical forms throughout the text. For the third-person masculine singular suffix (equivalent to Classical *-hu*), the scribe instead gives *-uh*, following a practice known from other vocalised, early phonetic and classical Judaeo–Arabic manuscripts (Blau and Hopkins 1987, 151; Posegay 2020, 39, fn. 30; van Putten 2020, 57; Posegay and Arrant 2021, 166). For the second-person feminine singular, they give *-ik*, the same as numerous modern Arabic dialects. The second-person masculine singular suffix may also match the *-ak* ending of such dialects and other vocalised Judaeo–Arabic manuscripts (compare Khan 2010, 210; Posegay 2020, 47), but the scribe spells it defectively with no vowel signs:

2r.1.16, ועִבידוה *wa-ʿibīduh*, 'and his servants'
1r.1.15, אמתיך *ʾamatik*, 'your maidservant'
1v.1.12, אכׄרגתך *ʾak̠ragtak(?)*, 'I sent you out'
2r.1.15, ולדך *waladak*, 'your son'

4.5. Particles Influenced by Hebrew Forms

Other features are best explained as the translator's artificial attempts to match the Hebrew of their source text, rather than natural features of spoken Arabic. For example, they apply the Arabic particle *ʾiyyā* (perhaps *ʾiyyē*) as a one-to-one equivalent of the Hebrew direct object marker *ʾet*, including with pronominal suffixes:

1v.1.13, איי *ʾiyyā* [direct object marker]
1v.1.4, אייי *ʾiyyāy*, 'me'

1v.1.7 אייה *ʾiyyāh*, ‘him’
1v.1.9, איהום *ʾiyyāhum*, ‘them’

It is unlikely that this particle was equally productive in the translator’s dialect. Similarly, the Arabic *huwaḏā* translates the Hebrew particle *hinne* ‘indeed, behold’ (1v.1.3, הוֹדא; 1r.1.15, הודא). The translator also invariably renders the Hebrew tetragrammaton with ארב (*ar-rabb*), rather than the more common Judaeo–Arabic אללה (*allāh*), as well as אטַייק (2r.2.12, *aṭ-ṭayyiq*?) for Hebrew *El*.

5.0. Conclusion: Arabic Reading Traditions and Vernacular Phonology

MS Firkovitch Yevr. II B 1526 comes from an early medieval Arabic translation of Genesis produced no later than the tenth century CE. It employs an early phonetic Judaeo–Arabic writing system that preserves distinct phonological features of the variety of Arabic spoken by the scribe who wrote it. This scribe was well-trained in Hebrew calligraphy and they (or someone shortly after them) also vocalised the text using Tiberian signs that would make difficult portions easier to read aloud. These signs recorded vocalic variations not typically represented in Classical Arabic writing, but which the vocaliser nevertheless perceived as discrete vowel qualities that corresponded to sounds in their pronunciation tradition of Biblical Hebrew. There is still much more to be learned about the linguistic features of this text. In particular, the Arabic vocabulary that the translator used to render Hebrew place names and people groups, many of which appear in the extant chapters, may enable more precise identification of their geographic context.

The careful execution and professional character of the scribal work raises questions about the cultural status of this biblical translation for an Arabic-speaking Jew in the medieval world. Where would this book have been read? Was it strictly for private use, or was the Arabic also recited in more public settings, akin to the Aramaic Targumim? It belongs to a growing corpus of Judaeo–Arabic biblical and ritual texts with precise Tiberian vocalisation,[21] a phenomenon which suggests that some Jews were reciting such texts in Arabic. More research is needed to better understand both the function of Arabic in the recitation traditions of early medieval Jews and the position of Judaeo–Arabic manuscripts like this one in the broader study of Arabic historical linguistics.

References

Ackerman-Lieberman, Phillip I. 2014. 'The Disappearance of the Early Phonetic Judeo–Arabic Spelling (EPJAS) and Saʿadya Gaon's Translation of the Bible'. *Jerusalem Studies in Arabic and Islam* 41: 137–72.

Ben-Shammai, Haggai. 2010. 'Is "The Cairo Genizah" a Proper Name or a Generic Noun? On the Relationship between the Genizot of the Ben Ezra and the Dār Simḥa Synagogues'. In

[21] These texts include the present translation of Genesis, a translation glossary to the book of Samuel (Posegay 2020, esp. fn. 23), a translation of Ecclesiastes (Posegay and Arrant 2021), and an Arabic *siddur* by Saʿadya Gaon (Khan 2010, 202–10; 2017, 296–402).

'From a Sacred Source': Genizah Studies in Honour of Professor Stefan C. Reif, 43–52. Leiden, Boston: Brill.

Blau, Joshua. 1992. 'On a Fragment of the Oldest Judaeo–Arabic Bible Translation Extant'. In *Genizah Research After Ninety Years: The Case of Judaeo–Arabic*, edited by Joshua Blau and Stefan C. Reif, 31–39. Cambridge: Cambridge University Press.

Blau, Joshua, and Simon Hopkins. 1984. 'On Early Judaeo–Arabic Orthography'. *Zeitschrift für Arabische Linguistik* 12: 9–27.

———. 1987. 'Judaeo–Arabic Papyri: Collected, Edited, Translated and Analysed'. *Jerusalem Studies in Arabic and Islam* 9: 87–160.

Connolly, Magdalen M. 2019. 'Revisiting the Question of Ǧīm from the Perspective of Judaeo-Arabic'. *Journal of Semitic Studies* 64 (1): 155–83. https://doi.org/10.1093/jss/fgy033.

Dolabani, P.Y. 1953. *Egroteh d-Dawid bar Pawlos d-Metidaʿ d-Bet Rabban*. Mardin: The Syriac Printing Press of Wisdom.

Harviainen, Tapani. 1996. 'The Cairo Genizot and Other Sources of the Second Firkovich Collection in St. Petersburg'. In *Proceedings of the Twelfth International Congress of the International Organization for Masoretic Studies 1995*, 25–36. Masoretic Studies 8. Atlanta: Scholars Press.

Hopkins, Simon. 2005. 'On Imāla of Medial and Final ā in Early Judaeo–Arabic'. In *Sacrum arabo-semiticum: homenaje al profesor Federico Corriente en su 65 aniversario*, edited by Jordi Aguadé, Ángeles Vicente, and Leila Abu-Shams, 195–

214. Zaragoza: Instituto de Estudios Islámicos y del Oriente Próximo.

Khan, Geoffrey. 1992. 'The Function of the Shewa Sign in Vocalized Judaeo–Arabic Texts from the Genizah'. In *Genizah Research after Ninety Years: The Case of Judaeo–Arabic*, edited by Joshua Blau and Stefan C. Reif, 105–11. Cambridge: Cambridge University Press.

———. 2010. 'Vocalized Judaeo–Arabic Manuscripts in the Cairo Genizah'. In *'From a Sacred Source': Genizah Studies in Honour of Professor Stefan C. Reif*, 201–18. Leiden, Boston: Brill.

———. 2013. 'Vocalization, Babylonian'. In *Encyclopedia of Hebrew Language and Linguistics*, edited by Geoffrey Khan. https://doi.org/10.1163/2212-4241_ehll_EHLL_COM_00000449.

———. 2017. 'Orthography and Reading in Medieval Judaeo–Arabic'. In *Arabic in Context: Celebrating 400 Years of Arabic at Leiden University*, edited by Ahmad Al-Jallad, 89:395–404. Studies in Semitic Languages and Linguistics. Leiden, Boston: Brill.

———. 2018. 'Judaeo–Arabic'. In *Arabic Historical Dialectology: Linguistic and Sociolinguistic Approaches*, edited by Clive Holes, 148–69. Oxford Studies in Diachronic and Historical Linguistics 30. Oxford: Oxford University Press.

———. 2020. *The Tiberian Pronunciation Tradition of Biblical Hebrew*, vol. 1. Cambridge Semitic Languages and Cultures 1. Cambridge: University of Cambridge and Open Book Publishers.

Levin, Aryeh. 2007. 'ʾImāla'. In *Encyclopedia of Arabic Language and Linguistics*, edited by Lutz Edzard and Rudolf de Jong, II:311–15. Leiden: Brill. https://doi.org/10.1163/1570-6699_eall_EALL_SIM_vol2_0022.

Posegay, Nick. 2020. 'A Judaeo–Arabic Biblical Glossary as a Source for Arabic Historical Dialectology'. *Journal of Arabic and Islamic Studies*, 20: 33–52. https://doi.org/10.5617/jais.7863.

———. 2021. 'Men of Letters in the Syriac Scribal Tradition: Dawid Bar Pawlos, Rabban Rāmišoʿ, and the Family of Beṯ Rabban'. *Hugoye: Journal of Syriac Studies* 24 (1): 127–86.

Posegay, Nick, and Estara J. Arrant. 2021. 'Three Fragments of a Judaeo–Arabic Translation of Ecclesiastes with Full Tiberian Vocalisation'. *Intellectual History of the Islamicate World* 9 (3): 259–96. https://doi.org/10.1163/2212943X-bja10001.

Rabin, Chaim. 1951. *Ancient West Arabian*. London: Taylor's Foreign Press

van Putten, Marijn. 2020. 'A Judaeo–Arabic Letter in Early Phonetic Judaeo–Arabic Spelling: T-S 13J8.7'. *Jerusalem Studies in Arabic and Islam* 48: 49–73.

———. 2022. *Quranic Arabic: From Its Hijazi Origins to Its Classical Reading Traditions*. Studies in Semitic Languages and Linguistics 106. Leiden: Brill.

Vidro, Nadia. 2018. 'Arabic Vocalisation in Judaeo–Arabic Grammars of Classical Arabic'. In *Semitic Linguistics and Manuscripts: A Liber Discipulorum in Honour of Professor Geoffrey*

Khan, edited by Nadia Vidro, Ronny Vollandt, Esther-Miriam Wagner, and Judith Olszowy-Schlanger, 341–51. Uppsala: Uppsala University Library.

Vollandt, Ronny. 2014. 'Whether to Capture Form or Meaning: A Typology of Early Judaeo–Arabic Pentateuch Translations'. In *A Universal Art: Hebrew Grammar across Disciplines and Faiths*, edited by Nadia Vidro, Irene E. Zwiep, and Judith Olszowy-Schlanger, 58–83. Leiden: Brill.

PATTERNS OF SELECTIVE VOWEL-DOTTING IN EARLY QURʾĀNIC MANUSCRIPTS[1]

Alba Fedeli

1.0. Introduction

The Arabic writing system consists of basic characters and optional signs that function as diacritics. In early Qurʾānic manuscripts, the optionality of vowel signs—visually represented by round, coloured dots—gave rise to 'partially dotted' manuscripts. The term 'partially' views the phenomenon from its end point but there were no fully-dotted manuscripts at this stage. Early manuscripts contained a system that did not have vowel signs. Manuscripts were selectively dotted and dot positions were context-

[1] This research is part of the InterSaME project, which ran from 2020 to 2023 and was funded by the Deutsche Forschungsgemeinschaft (DFG, German Research Foundation). Project number: 428993887.

My heartfelt thanks are due to Shady H. Nasser and Geoffrey Khan for their comments on my work, to Carolin Kinne-Wall for her help in handling the data I produced after the edition of the manuscript. I am indebted to Johan Lundberg who offered suggestions for improvements to the initial version of my article.

 https://doi.org/10.11647/OBP.0498.08

dependent. These early manuscripts are a source that can be explored to answer questions such as: which positions were marked or not, and why might the dotter mark one position and not another? These answers can shed light on the function of vowel dots at this early stage, and elucidate the development of the diacritic system of Arabic Qurʾānic manuscripts. These patterns reveal traces of the intentions of dotters and point to aspects of their educational and professional backgrounds. General rules can be detected, describing the overall distribution of dots in the early manuscripts from the eighth to the tenth century. Some patterns are characteristic of single manuscripts, while others characterise a group of manuscripts.

This chapter focuses on the development and use of vocalisation in early Arabic writing. Each part of the system is relationally defined and can be understood only as part of the whole system. A system—according to Russell L. Ackoff, a pioneer of systems thinking—is not the sum of its parts but the product of the parts' interactions.

Each manuscript, or each dotter in each manuscript, can exhibit its idiosyncrasy by marking certain letters and leaving other letters unmarked. In all partially dotted manuscripts, from the eighth century onwards, the absence may mean its inhibited and non-manifest presence, the powerful presence of the absence (Ohnuki-Tierney 1994b). The manuscript vocalisation system is the result of a process of generally accepted conventions and personal strategies intentionally applied by dotters. The investigation of conventions and patterns of marking is of the utmost importance for reconstructing the context of the development of the vocalisation system and the context in which anonymous dotters worked.

This chapter is a part of a larger survey of partially dotted manuscripts. The analysis focuses on the mechanisms of dotting in MS Bibliothèque nationale de France (BnF) ar. 340c, and specifically on the dots that mark vowels. For example, the word {*ḍll*} /ḍalāl/ occurs four times in the manuscript, and only the final letter of the inflectional suffix is dotted while the body of the noun remains undotted. The unmarked body {*ḍll*} does not have a meaning per se but takes on its significance when inserted into the whole dotting system. The undotted {*ḍll*}—and all undotted nouns—derive significance from and give significance to dotted nouns. In another example, the complete dotting of the word {*ẓulumt*} /ẓulumāt/ has meaning only when compared to the rest of the manuscript's system, where nouns are never internally dotted (see below).

The analysis of the vocalisation system of this manuscript provides insights into the dotter's professional and educational background.[2] This, therefore, contributes to the ongoing discussions of the relationship between manuscript variation and *qirāʾāt*, i.e., the canonical and non-canonical oral reading traditions that are documented in special manuals.

---

[2] The observations reported here are the result of my manual analysis based on a dataset in tabular format that merged my edition of the manuscript text with the morphosyntactic tagging and tokenisation provided by the Leeds project (Dukes 2009–2017). Carolin Kinne-Wall assisted in building the dataset to allow a powerful visualisation and on-the-fly analysis and filtering.

2.0. Manuscript BnF ar. 340c

The manuscript analysed in this study is one of the ten units gathered under the shelf mark of the manuscript Bibliothèque nationale de France (BnF), Département des Manuscrits, Arabe 340, from folio 31 to 46. It belongs to the Asselin de Cherville collection (1772–1822), from the Mosque of ʿAmr ibn al-ʿĀṣ in Fusṭāṭ. The collection was acquired by the Royal Library in Paris (now, Bibliothèque nationale de France) from Asselin's heirs in 1833. The 16-leaf fragment examined here contains two continuous sections of the Qurʾānic text, from Q.13:14 to Q.15:88 (nine leaves) and from Q.21:67 to Q.22:68 (seven leaves).

In order to understand the dotting, three aspects of the manuscript must be considered: first, the size of the parchment leaf and text area; second, the palaeographic style of the first layer of script; and third, the layers and mechanisms of the writing process, identifying the stage(s) of dotting.

Size and layout. The 16 parchment leaves measure 140 × 210 mm and the text is laid out in 16 lines occupying 100 × 155 mm (Déroche 1983, 72, no. 32). The distance between two lines, and the height of *ʾalif*, is approximately 6 mm. Manuscripts written in this style have an average line spacing distance of 5 to 6 mm and 14 to 16 lines per page (see Déroche 1990, 61). There are no signs of ruling, and the scribe did not respect the baseline concept but apparently followed several imaginary baselines on a given line: ascenders and descenders do not intersect, and letters are adjusted, where possible, to create visual effects. For example, on f.40r, a series of the letter *ʾalif* are placed on the left margin to form a column.

Script style and palaeographic dating. The script style is classified, by Déroche, as the B II type: a small hand with upward strokes always vertical, with no traces of slanting ascenders. This style is present in manuscripts from the four main deposits of stored Qurʾānic manuscripts in the mosques of Cairo, Damascus, Kairouan, and Ṣanʿāʾ. Other examples in the same script style give three dates: AH 22[9] (843–4 CE) and AH 249 (863 CE) in two Damascus manuscripts and AH 270 (883–4 CE) in a Cairo manuscript (Déroche 1992, 36, n. 16). The radiocarbon dating results of Qurʾānic manuscripts written in the script style of the B II type—as part of the recent systematic approach to dating early Qurʾānic manuscripts conducted by 'Corpus Coranicum'—gave a time span between 680 and 798 CE for MS Leiden Or. 6814 and between 653 and 766 CE for Papyrus Leiden Or. 8264, in a style close to the B II type (Marx and Jocham 2019, 216).

Stages of production, dotting and relative chronology. The text contains elements that may indicate copying from a written exemplar, e.g., the metathesis of the group *šīn* + *jīm* into *jīm* + *šīn* in *ka-šajaratin* (f.35v, l.4), which was not amended. On the same page a few lines below (f.35v, l.7), the same word *ka-šajaratin* (i.e., 'as a tree') is written with the sequence *šīn* + *jīm*. The possible metathesis was not amended during the life cycle of the manuscript. Other points of the manuscript testify to the role played by similar passages of the Qurʾānic text when copied, e.g.:

Q.22:26: *wa-ṭahhir baytiya lil-ṭāʾifīna wa-l-qāʾimīna wa-l-rukkaʿi l-sujūdi* ('And do thou purify My House for those that shall go about it and those that stand, for those that bow and prostrate themselves').[3]

Q.2:125: *ʾan ṭahhirā baytiya lil-ṭāʾifīna wa-l-ʿākifīna wa-l-rukkaʿi l-sujūdi* ('Purify My House for those that shall go about it and those that cleave to it, to those who bow and prostrate themselves').

The manuscript BnF ar 340c has *wa-ṭahhir baytiya lil-ṭāʾifīna wa-l-ʿākifīna wa-l-rukkaʿi l-sujūdi* in Q.22:26 (f.44r, ll.6–7). The word *wa-l-ʿ(ā)kifīna*, which is not attested in the overall majority of the early manuscripts,[4] has not been amended. The dotter marked it with a rounded dot above the final *nūn* according to the rules applied in the manuscript.

Identifying possible traces of the stage in which a dot was added, e.g., after or before an amendment, is crucial: it can help establish a relative chronology in the absence of an absolute chronology of the dotting of a manuscript. The visual inspection of

---

[3] The translated sections of the Qurʾān quoted in this chapter are from Arberry (1964).

[4] See, among other examples, MS Staatsbibliothek zu Berlin (SBB), Petermann I 38, f.24v, l.7; MS Cambridge University Library (CUL), MS Add. 1136, f.1v, ll.6–7; MS CUL, MS Or. 771, f.19v, l.7; MS BnF ar. 328c, f.83v, l.21. MS SBB, Ms. or. oct. 1819, f.24r, l.12 shows traces of an earlier layer which appears to have the same reading as MS BnF ar. 340c (*lil-ṭāʾifīna wa-l-ʿākifīna*). The manuscript section was searched and accessed via Manuscripta Coranica (MC), published by the Berlin-Brandenburgische Akademie der Wissenschaften, edited by Michael Marx (accessed on 09 December 2023).

the manuscript using digital images revealed at least two stages of added red dots that mark vowels. It is unclear whether the first layer of dotting is contemporaneous with the writing of the consonantal text, sometime between the eighth and ninth century CE. The parts of the *rasm* that have been amended appear to have dots added after the amendment. An example can be found on f.32v, l.10, where the first layer of the *rasm* has *wa-ṣaddun ʿani l-sabīli,* which was later amended as *wa-ṣuddū ʿani l-sabīli*, i.e., '[A]nd they are barred from the way' (Q.13:33).[5]

Figure 1: BnF.ar.340c, f.32v, l.10, detail of dot to mark /i/ in *ʿani* added at the right of final *nūn* after the amendment (Source: gallica.bnf.fr / Bibliothèque nationale de France)

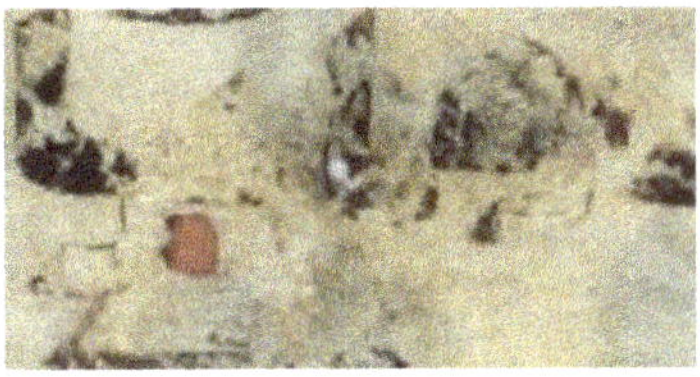

---

[5] The reading of MS BnF ar. 340c can be compared with MS SBB Wetzstein II 1913, f.96r, l.6, where Q.13:33 is marked with a dot above the *ṣād* to read *wa-ṣaddū* (the active form of the verb), which is the reading of Nāfiʿ, Abū ʿAmr, Ibn ʿĀmir, and Ibn Kaṯīr (Nasser 2020, 507). The focus of this chapter does not allow for full consideration of all the features of the manuscript and its readings such as this non-canonical reading *wa-ṣaddun* (EVQ), which corresponds to the reading of ʿAbdallāh b. Abī Isḥāq al-Ḥaḍramī (d. 736); see *Variae Lectiones Coranicae* (VLC), accessed on 09 December 2023.

The original *ʿan* has been cancelled to make space for the writing of the final *wāw* and *ʾalif* of the amended *wa-ṣuddū*. Then, *ʿan* has been rewritten in the empty space between letter-blocks. The preposition has been dotted with a dot at the right of the descender of the newly written *ʿan*. This suggests that the dotting took place after the first amendment stage, i.e., not immediately after the initial step of the writing of the *rasm* and probably not during the process of the initial production project (see Figure 1).

It is likely that a further amendment of the *rasm* took place after the dotting phase, as suggested by the dotting of *fī-hā* (Q.21:91:5) in *fa-nafaḵnā fīhā min rūḥinā*, 'so We breathed into her of Our spirit [and appointed her and her son to be a sign unto all beings]'. The first layer has the masculine suffix *fī-hu*, 'into him' (in the syntactical structure, it would refer to Jesus), which the dotter marked with the u–dot placed at the very left of final *hāʾ*. The final *hāʾ* was reshaped into its medial form and the final *ʾalif* was added to read *fīhā* (i.e., 'into her', referring to Mary). The dotter operated before this amendment stage (see Figure 2).[6]

---

[6] In the manuscript, all eight occurrences of {fyh} are marked with a dot to the left of the final *hāʾ* (in f.36r, l.1, f.36v, l.8, f.37v, l.10, f.38r, l.11, f.39r, l.10, f.40v, l.1, f.44r, l.3 and l.4).

Figure 2: BnF.ar.340c, f.41r, l.7, detail of the word *fī-hu* dotted before being adjusted into *fī-hā* (Source: gallica.bnf.fr / Bibliothèque nationale de France)

The process of writing, amending the *rasm* and dotting, and dotting and amending can be visualised by the reconstruction proposed in Figure 3 with a hypothetical splitting of strata. The layers are traced and drawn based on their logical sequence.[7]

Regarding stages and authors of changes pertaining to the *rasm*, there are some internal elements for establishing a relative chronology. There do not seem to be any changes made *in scribendo*, but at the second stage, e.g., in Q.22:18:16–18, the empty space left after the erasure of a (now illegible) word indicates the stage of the intervention. There are traces of different stages of correction, reflected by the appearance of coloured inks (brown and black), and logical sequences of changes. However, while the material evidence clearly indicates successive interventions, it remains difficult to determine precisely who changed the

[7] The *rasm* of **qālat rusulu-hum* has been traced on the basis of *rusulu-hum* on f.34r, l.10. The first layer in Figure 3 is a hypothetical reconstruction. In the first layer of **wa-saddun ʿan-i l-sabīli*, the preposition *ʿan* is drawn on the basis of its model on f.33v, l.10. The dotting of the ending of *ʾummatin* is considered to be the production of a different stage of vocalisation because of the vertical position of the pair of dots below the final *tāʾ marbūṭah*. This is a different pattern, as the dots are placed horizontally below a letter without a descender.

rasm or to reconstruct the various agencies and processes involved in each stage of correction. Based on the evidence, it would seem there are at least three groups of actors, although the relation and time between them is uncertain: the original scribe, the amender(s) of the *rasm*, and the dotter(s). The dotter is different from that of the person who amended the *rasm*, as the dotter did not care about the *rasm*, and those who amended the *rasm* did not revise the whole text. Therefore, it is unlikely the dotting is the work of the first hand, or the possible later hands.

However, only a material analysis of the ink composition of red dots can confirm whether these dots were added to the *rasm* in a first or second stage, and whether they are the work of a single dotter. The first and second layers of the *rasm*, with first writing and amendments, could have been dotted by the same person in a single session or they could have been added in two separate sessions.

As previously mentioned, this chapter explores possible patterns in the dotting system of MS BnF ar. 340c, which may provide insight into the function of dots during the development of the vowel dot system.

Figure 3: Drawing with separated stages of writing and dotting based on images of BnF.ar.340c (Source: gallica.bnf.fr / Bibliothèque nationale de France)

First layer: the *rasm*	**Amendment** before the first dotting	**First Dotting**	**Amendment** after the first dotting	**Second dotting**
 **fa-nafaknā fī-hu* (*reconstructed)		 **fa-nafaknā fī-hu* (*reconstructed)	 *fa-nafaknā fī-hā* Q.21:91 (f.41r, l.8)	
 **qālat rusulu-hum* (*reconstructed *rasm*)			 *qālat lahum rusuluhum* Q.14:10 (f.34r, l.13) undotted	
 **wa-saddun ʿan-i l-sabīli* (*reconstructed *rasm*)	 *wa-ṣuddū ʿan-i l-sabīli* Q.13:33 (f.32v, l.10)	 *wa-ṣuddū ʿan-i l-sabīli* (dotted after the amendment)		
[illegible]			 *ʾummatin* Q.15:5 (f.37r, l.16)	 *ʾummatin* (dots placed vertically for *tanwīn kasra*)
eighth/ninth century (after script style)		ninth/tenth century? (phase of change in vocalisation)		date?

3.0. The Dots and the Writing System as the Product of the Interactions between Its Parts

3.1. Writing System of 'Partially Dotted' Manuscripts: Which Parts are Dotted?

Previous studies of dotting have explored the meaning of marked positions as reflections of a particular reading traditions (*qirāʾāt*) (e.g., Dutton 1999 and 2000; van Putten 2019; and Ince 2023). The relationship between regional habits, described in al-Dānī's treatise, and patterns in Qurʾānic manuscripts sheds light on the grouping of manuscripts (George 2015a and 2015b), enabling an examination of individual dots as distinct signs of a system. Cellard (2015) investigates the whole range of the diacritical layer, connecting the richness of manuscripts with habits described in treatises, and readings transmitted in the *qirāʾāt* literature. In summary, all previous studies have focused solely on the vowels. In contrast, I have considered where vowel markings are present and where they are absent in the writing system of each dotter—that is, in each manuscript—as well as the exact spatial position of the dots in relation to their associated letters. The individuality of each manuscript in terms of readings (i.e., *qirāʾāt*), as suggested for example by Nöldeke and Cellard, cannot be abstracted from the physicality of the writing system and the internal relationship between the signs. The individuality of the readings might go hand in hand with the individuality of the choices made in dotting the manuscript text.

A search for consistently dotted 'parts' can shed light on the function of vowel dots and possibly on the perspective of the dotter, who marked certain positions of the script's skeleton. According to treatises, the original dotting was not intended to fully vocalize a word but rather to clarify different grammatical features. The main dots to be used are *rafʿ*, *naṣb*, *ḵafḍ*, *šadda*, *tanwīn*, *madd*, and *qaṣr*. Some dotters preferred to add more dots in their own codices by using for example red for *rafʿ* and *ḵafḍ*, green for *hamza*, and yellow for *šadda* as this system makes it easier for the reader to differentiate between different grammatical and linguistic phenomena.[8] The marking of grammatical categories is a general feature of partially dotted manuscripts, to which MS BnF ar. 340c belongs. However, it does not explain the whole system of patterns applied in each manuscript.

Let us start with a simple example that clarifies how the absence of dots can have a graphemic significance. The word 'MN'[9] illustrates the relationally defined signs of the system in BnF ar. 340c. The final *nūn*, like all other homographs in all positions in this manuscript, is never marked with a consonantal diacritic. The final /n/ is *musakkan*, i.e., vowelless, except when it is followed by a word starting with a vowelless letter. The word may be ambiguous without optional vowel signs, signs marking either the preposition *min* or the pronoun *man*. This ambiguity and the non-transparent phonemic coding of the word make the Arabic system a deep orthography (Frost et al. 1987). Context and background knowledge provide the reading of *min* or *man*. In the early dotting system, the addition of optional signs would

---

[8] In al-Dānī's *Muḥkam*.

[9] We use an elaborated version of the archigraphemic system introduced by Milo (2013), as described in Fedeli (2024).

disambiguate the word, placing the i-dot below the *mīm* and the a–dot above.

In reality, the concept of ambiguity has to be approached differently. The sign مں may be ambiguous, generally speaking, in a system where vowel signs are not mandatory. In manuscript culture, there are concrete instances of written artefacts, not just homographs, that are ambiguous in the same abstract way. For example, there are 164 occurrences of *min* and 45 occurrences of *man* in the Qurʾānic text of manuscript BnF ar. 340c. The preposition *min* is unmarked in 163 out of 164 occurrences, while the pronoun *man* is marked in 43 out of 45 occurrences; for example, see Figure 4.[10]

Figure 4: Examples of unmarked and marked {MN} to express *min* and *man* (Source: gallica.bnf.fr / Bibliothèque nationale de France)

Example of unmarked *min* in BnF.ar.340c, f.32r, l.6 (Q.13:27:8) 163 out of 164 occurrences of *min* are unmarked

Example of marked *man* in BnF.ar.340c, f.32r, l.7 (Q.13:27:14) 43 out of 45 occurrences of *man* are marked

[10] The preposition *min* is marked in Q.15:60:5 (f.39r, l.8) when it is preceded by the preposition *la-*, i.e., *la-min-a-*, the preposition *la-* being marked. The preposition *li-* prefixed to *man* is always marked (3 out of 3 occurrences). *Man* is not marked in Q.13:23:4 (f.31v, l.13) and Q.22:40:30 (f.45r, l.9). When both *man* and *min* end with a euphonic vowel before a following vowelless letter, the vowel is always marked (40 out of 40 occurrences of an a–dot after *min* and 2 out of 2 occurrences of an i-dot after *man*).

This shows that *min* (undotted) is defined in relation to *man* (dotted), although at first sight it might be interpreted as unmarked (i.e., undotted and vowelless) and ambivalent. {MN} and {MaN} would seem to be a personal habit of some dotters, as it is not governed by a general rule described in manuals. Thus, the absence of a grapheme can represent a phoneme or the reading of an entire word, i.e., an entity (Ohnuki-Tierney 1994b, 70).

Borrowing the image of *kanji* characters and their empty brushstrokes, partially dotted Qurʾānic manuscripts can be seen as 'the background emptiness' (Ohnuki-Tierney 1994a, 305–306). The *rasm* is 'imbued with additional meaning' because dots do not only contribute the immediate meaning of /a/, /i/, and /u/, but together with their absence they construe a web of relational meanings within the writing system. The vocalisation system of Qurʾānic manuscripts from the eighth to the tenth century (i.e., partially dotted manuscripts), is based on the principle that 'the absence of any explicit signifier functions by itself as a signifier' (Barthes 1979, 77).

In the early Arabic writing system, vowel-dots are not represented in the materiality of the script. The birth of vowels is a gradual development, so in early vocalised manuscripts, only certain vowels are deliberately represented by means of red, round dots.[11] Since the original system lacked vowel signs, it is likely

[11] Early Qurʾānic manuscripts from the seventh century have *ʾiʿjām* diacritics executed in a stroke-like shape, while later they developed a more rounded shape. Early Arabic documents do not provide complete diacritical pointing, and previous scholarship has proposed some possible explanations for their distribution and motivation. For example,

that the introduction of round dots was intended to mark certain positions, not to 'complete' the *rasm*, or 'background emptiness'. Dotting was likely a personal choice, a tentative initiative to create a system and mark some features. The dotting of early manuscripts was not yet rule-governed but rather context-dependent. This suggests a situation that differs from the accepted idea that dots are used to solve ambiguities.

If "the unmarked is assigned the absence of a specific property that characterizes the marked counterpart" (Ohnuki-Tierney 1994b, 61), the unmarked is a mechanism of the writing system. In the newly developed dotting system, too many dots would have eliminated their meaning and value. They were not intended to indicate the complete reading of whole words in all their details, but likely something else (Ohnuki-Tierney 1994b, 66).[12] My analysis suggests that the initial dotting system had three functions:

1) to mark the ending of words (reflecting morphological distinctions), as well as prefixes, suffixes, and infixes
2) to indicate boundaries between words

Kaplony (2008) observed that most diacritics, in a corpus of Arabic papyri, mark affixes and particles. In other words, they are used to distinguish between grammatical categories.

[12] The same concept is emphasised in al-Dānī: "There is no need to make *šakl* for every consonant; it is only done when there is confusion. If all letters were dotted consonantally, it would darken the word," whereas the addition of diacritics should have the opposite effect, i.e., to lighten the words.

3) to clarify the reading of words, where different readings are preserved in the *qirāʾāt* literature (see below)

3.2. Conveying Morphosyntactic Information

The initial stages of vocalising Qurʾānic manuscripts suggests that morphosyntactic information is privileged over phonological information. Over time, this preference shifted towards a system that privileged phonological information.[13] If we exclude dots marking vowels associated with *hamzas* (on *ʾalif*, *yāʾ* and *wāw*), the majority of vowel–dots in BnF ar. 340c are associated with morphological positions, i.e., endings and derivational and inflectional affixes on verbs and nouns. The manuscript contains 3,605 words (linguistic units made of verbs, nouns and particles with their affixes)[14] and a total of 3,782 dots, both single and in pairs. Of these, 108 instances are uncertain due to the condition of the parchment and ink, while 3,674 are clearly legible. Specific patterns are exhibited, respectively, with monosyllabic particles, endings of past and imperfect verbs, prefixes of imperfect verbs, and the ending of nouns. The results of the investigation are detailed below.

---

[13] The same shift was observed for Punic in Crellin (2019, 173); see also Kerr (2010 and 2013).

[14] We have adopted the word count of the Leeds project as we have imported its morphosyntactic information into our tabular format, which includes the edited manuscript and its details.

3.2.1. Monosyllabic Particles

The following monosyllabic particles are undotted (see Appendix A):

bi- (115 out of 115)
fa- (116 out of 119)
wa- (458 out of 468)
ka- (6 out of 6)
sa- (1 occurrence)
yā- (5 out of 6)

The following monosyllabic particles are dotted:

lan (4 out of 4)
lam (14 out of 14)
ʾa- (19 out of 20)[15]

3.2.2. Affixed *Lām* Representing *li-* or *la-*

The particle *lām* occurs 237 times in the manuscript. Five instances are illegible because the manuscript has a lacuna. It is marked with a dot below the baseline 57 times (representing *li-*); a dot above the baseline 86 times (representing *la-*); and undotted

[15] Note that the interrogative particle *ʾa-* is undotted in Q.22:65:1 (f.46v, l.9), before the dotted particle lam in *ʾa-lam tara ʾanna llāha.* It is likely that the missing a–dot is due to the intention to avoid interfering with the space reserved for the ending of the previous verse, *al-ḥamīdu*, and the ending of the word *al-sam(ā)w(ā)ti* on the line above. There is no space for a careful execution of three proportionally spaced dots.

94 times (*li-* or *la-*). In some cases, it is possible to observe a pattern behind the dotting of the particle, but it is unclear if there is a set rule governing its application (see Appendix B).

3.2.3. Dotting Endings of Past Verbs

As mentioned above, the dots are added mainly to mark the ending of verbs. The following endings of past forms are dotted:

/a/ marking the 3sg.m form (97 out of 106)[16]
/a/ in /ta/ marking the 2sg.m form (5 out of 5)
/u/ in /tu/ marking the 1sg (13 out of 17)[17]
/a/ in /na/ marking 3pl.f (only 1 occurrence: Q.14:36:3)
/u/ in /mu/ marking the 2pl.m as -t(u)mu (13 out of 13)[18]

---

[16] Whether there is a pattern in the nine undotted endings of the 3sg.m is unclear. In some cases, such as Q.15:18:5 (f.37v, l.14), the undotted letter *ʿayn* touches the tail of the final *nūn* of the previous line, making it difficult to confirm the absence of dots. The endings of the two occurrences of *razaqa-humu* (Q.22:28:12 and 22:34:10) are not marked. In Q.13:42:2 (*makara*, in *wa-qad makara -llaḏīna min qabli-him* 'those that were before them devised'), the ending /a/ is not dotted, possibly due to the assimilation of /r/ into the following /l/. It should be noted that the eight other occurrences of 3sg.m ending in /ra/ and followed by a word beginning in /la/ are marked by an a–dot (Q.13:21:4; 13:25:10, 14:32:16; 14:32:23; 14:33:1; 14:33:6; 22:35:3 and 22:65:5).

[17] The unmarked endings are found in the two occurrences of *ʾaḵaḏtu-hum(u)* (Q.13:32:10 and Q22:44:8); in *fa-ʾaḵlaftu-kum(u)* (Q.14:22:12) and *ʾamlaytu* (Q.22:48:4).

[18] This phenomenon is known as *ḍamm mīm al-jamʿ* and *ṣilat mīm al-jamʿ* (Nasser 2020, 191–192). None of the 13 dotted *-t(u)mu* are followed by

The following past form endings are undotted:

/a/ before the *tāʾ* marking 3sg.f (31 out of 32)[19]

nūn marking 1pl both when it is followed by *ʾalif* and when it stands alone (39 unmarked cases of *nūn* out of 41 occurrences and 64 unmarked *nūn-ʾalif* sequences out of 64 occurrences);[20] and the long vowels for the ending /ā/ in 3sg.m (19 out of 19 occurrences)

/ū/ spelled with *wāw-ʾalif* and *wāw* only before a pronominal suffix marking 3pl.m (107 out of 107) and *-t(u)mu* marking 2pl.m spelled with *wāw* when there is a pronominal suffix (4 out of 4)

The writing system, including the vocalisation system, guarantees an unambiguous marking of past form endings. The 3sg.f is marked by the letter *tāʾ*, which is unambiguously /at/, since the other forms ending in *tāʾ* are dotted, i.e., *-ta* and *-tu*. As with *man* and *min*, the absence of a dot indicates a specific reading, /at/, as opposed to dotted, /ta/ and /tu/. The same strategy is used in marked vs unmarked *nūn*. Undotted *nūn* marks the 1pl, even when it is not followed by *ʾalif*. The undotted letter acquires its value in relation to the *nūn* of 3pl.f, which is marked by the a–dot.

ʾalif al-waṣl. The habit of marking the *ṣilat mīm al-jamʿ* is discussed in the section below.

[19] The only marked ending is *jāʾat-humu*, which is marked with a dot to the upper left of *ʾalif* (Q.14:9:18).

[20] There are two occurrences of dotted *nūn* out of a total of 105 forms in the 1pl, i.e., Q.14:21:25 *la-hadayna-kumu* and Q.21:71:1 *wa-najjaynā-hu*, the dot in the latter case being unclear.

There are special cases where dots do not follow the aforementioned rules. In Q.22:42:4, the 3sg.f form *kaḏḏabat* ends with a dot:

> *fa-qad kaḏḏabat qabla-hum qawmu nūḥin wa-ʿādun wa-ṯamūdu*
> 'so too before them the people of Noah cried lies, and Ad and Thamood'

Reading the red dot, placed above the final denticle, as /ta/ (**kaḏḏabta*) makes no sense in this context (see Figure 5). It is therefore possible that the dotter of BnF ar. 340c marked the following positions, and two possible readings:

> *fa-qad *kḏḏbt qabla-humu qawmu nūḥin wa-ʿādin [wa-]ṯamūda.*

Since the subject is *qawm*, followed by three proper nouns in the genitive, the dot could mark the final /a/ of the 3sg.m form *kaḏḏaba*, marking the whole word without changing the *rasm*. Alternatively, the final dot could mark the vowel of the last syllable, /bat/. These readings are not exclusive, and perhaps the dot marked both readings.

Figure 5: Detail of the dotting of *kaḏḏabat* likely to be read as *kaḏḏaba* (BnF.ar.340c, f.45r, l.14) Source: gallica.bnf.fr / Bibliothèque nationale de France

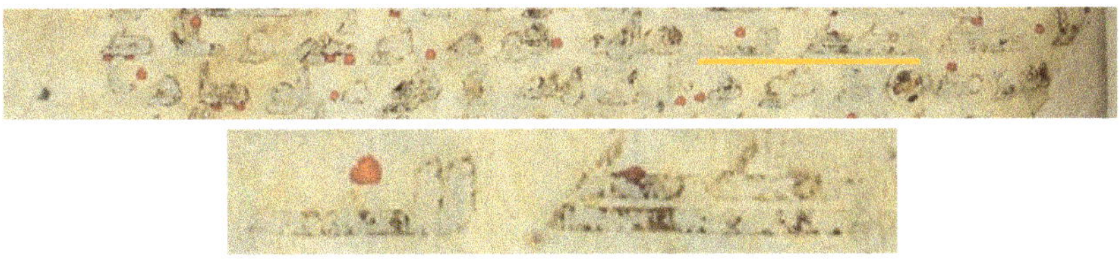

3.2.4. Dotting Endings of Imperfect Verbs

The 355 imperfect forms follow this rule: endings are marked when the form ends with a short vowel: 224 dotted out of 240 endings. The endings are unmarked in forms with *sukūn*: 19 occurrences of unmarked *sukūn* of the jussive. The same holds for long vowels: 75, marked by *ʾalif*, *yāʾ* and *wāw*, are undotted out of 79 occurrences. In some instances, dots mark long vowels (4 out of 79) and the ending /a/ of the energic *nūn* (9 out of 17) (see Appendix C).

3.2.5. Dotting Prefixes of Imperfect Verbs

The above pattern, marking endings, takes on a particular importance when compared to the marked vs unmarked prefixes of the imperfect forms: 91 imperfect prefixes are dotted, out of 354 occurrences.[21] The patterns observed in the dotting of 82 prefixes are significant: 62 dots marking /u/ and 29 dots marking /a/ (see Appendix D).

3.2.6. Dotting Endings of Nouns

The pattern of dotting imperfect forms can also be observed in the dotting of nouns. There are 1,428 nouns with case inflection, and the dotter mainly marked the case inflection of nouns when the word's ending—nominative, accusative, and genitives—is not

[21] The numbers for endings and prefixes in imperfect verb forms may differ, because the total number of prefixes excludes any forms with a lacuna in the prefix, even if the ending of the same verb is fully legible.

marked by *ʾalif, yāʾ*, and *wāw*. Out of the 1,428 words, 175 endings are undotted because they are marked at the *rasm* layer. These include:

53 nouns ending in *ʾalif, yāʾ* and *wāw*

14 occurrences of undotted *yāʾ* marking the pronominal suffix of the 1sg[22]

two dual forms ending in *-āni* and *-ayni* that are marked by the *ʾalif* and *yāʾ*; their final *nūn* is dotted (a dot above the baseline and a dot at the left of the descender respectively)

one accusative plural in *status constructus*

81 plural suffix *-īna*

24 plural suffix *-ūna*

It should be noted that the long vowels of the suffixes *-īna* and *-ūna* are undotted according to the system observed in this manuscript, while the dotter added a dot above the final *nūn* in 78 and 24 cases respectively (see below about the function of dotting at the word boundary level). All the other 1,253 words—those not ending in *ʾalif, yāʾ* and *wāw*—are dotted with a final

---

[22] The suffix *yāʾ*, which marks the first singular pronominal suffix, is undotted according to the rules because it marks the long /i/. The dotter also did not mark *yāʾ* in the following two examples: Q.14:31:2 (f.35v, l.15), *li-ʿibādiya* ('to my slaves'), and in Q.22:26:12 (f.44r, l.6) *baytiya* ('my house'). When final *yāʾ* is undotted, it marks the long /i/, thus corresponding to the other known reading *li-ʿibādī* (in Ibn ʿĀmir, Ḥamza and al-Kisāʾī) and *baytī* (in Ibn Kaṯīr, Abū ʿAmr, Ibn ʿĀmir, ʿĀṣim, Ḥamza and al-Kisāʾī), respectively (EVQ and VLC in Q.14:31:2 and Q.22:26:12).

single dot (869) or a final pair of dots (304), except for 80 occurrences. These 80 undotted include 9 nominative, 57 accusative, and 14 genitive occurrences, which represent 5.6% of the total number of nouns with case inflection.

Out of the 57 undotted accusative nouns, the majority are indefinite forms ending in *ʾalif*. The dotter added a pair of dots to all nominative (96 out of 96) and genitive forms (171 out of 172). For the accusative forms, the pair of dots is always placed above *tāʾ marbūṭah* (in all 20 occurrences) while out of the 69 accusative forms ending with *ʾalif*, the dotter only marked 17 cases and did not mark the remaining 52 final *ʾalif* cases. For example, *jamīʿan* is marked with a final pair of dots at the right of *ʾalif* once out of 6 occurrences (in Q. 13:31:18, f.32r, l.16) and *ḥukman* is dotted once out of 3 occurrences (in Q.13:37:3, f.33r, l.4).

The dotter follows a phonological rule that applies only to nouns ending in simple *ʾalif*, and not those ending in *tāʾ marbūṭah*, *ʾalif maqṣūra*, or *ʾalif* or *wāw* followed by *hamza*.[23] When the final *ʾalif* in the accusative form is followed by *ʿayn* (in the manuscript fragment occurring as *ʿa-*, *ʿi-*), *ḥāʾ* and *ʾalif* (dotted with /a/ and /i/),[24] it is marked by a pair of dots, while in all the other contexts it is undotted. This corresponds to what al-Dānī transmitted,

---

[23] The manuscript has no specific sign to mark *hamza*, but its presence is implied, for example, when words such as *jufāʾ* and *šayʾ* are marked by a pair of dots placed to the left of the ascender of *ʾalif* to express *jufāʾan* and *šayʾan*, as opposed to a hypothetical form with the pair of dots to the right of *ʾalif*, expressing *jufan* and *šayan* respectively. See the section on *hamza* below.

[24] *Tanwīn fatḥa* followed by *ʾalif* dotted with /u/ applies a different phonological rule, e.g., *ʿiwajan* followed by *ʾulāʾika* in Q.14:3:12–13 is not

namely that Kūfans and some dotters dot the *manṣūb* when followed by pharyngeals (*al-ḥurūf al-ḥalqiyya*), otherwise they do not dot the *manṣūb* (Muḥkam 2004, 47).

The dotting of the noun endings (93.6% of the 1,253 occurrences of inflected nouns) carry a stronger meaning compared to the undotted body of words. This is similar to the observed behaviour of dotting imperfect forms. If we exclude the 192 participles and 28 verbal nouns from the count,[25] the dotter added 288 dots in the internal position of 1,336 words. Their distribution is as follows. Three quarters of the internal dots (212 single dots and 4 pairs) mark the vowels attached to *hamza* with *ʾalif*, *yāʾ*, and the groups *rāʾ*+*wāw*.[26] Only 54 words have 68 internal dots not related to *hamza*. The percentages of internally dotted

---

dotted (f.33v, l.10). All occurrences of indefinite accusative followed by *ʿayn* (5 of 5), *ḥāʾ* (1 of 1), *ʾalif* followed by short vowel /a/ (1 of 1), and long vowel /a/ (2 of 3) and *ʾalif* followed by /i/ (2 of 2) are dotted with a pair of dots. In a few cases there appears to be only one dot to the left of the *ʾalif*, but the difficulty of reading due to the materiality of the ink does not provide a solid basis for observing possible patterns. In Q.22:23:19 (f.43v, l.15), *wa-luʾluʾan* and *šayʾan* in Q.22:5 (f.42v, l.6) appear to have only one dot to the left of *ʾalif*. Further material analysis of the inks would likely help to solve the problem.

[25] They behave similarly to the imperfect form, i.e., the dotter marked /i/ in the fourth form active participle, /a/ in the fourth form passive particle, or the affix *-ta-* in the sixth form, and /i/ in the ninth form active participle.

[26] E.g., *ruʾūs* (piercing *wāw* at its right in f.36v, l.9 and f.43v, l.8 likely marking *ruʾūs*) and *raʾūf* (at the left of *wāw* in f.46v, l.12 likely marking *rūf*) and *fāʾ*+*dāl* in *ʾafʾidatan* (Q.14:37:17).

words (6.4%) and dotted endings of inflected nouns (93.6%) help us understand the relational nature of the dotting system in early manuscripts. It is noteworthy that endings of inflected nouns are dotted both when they are followed by a pronominal suffix and when they occupy a word boundary position.

3.3. Conveying Phonological Information

3.3.1. Dotting to Convey Phonological Information

The use of dots, marking the case inflection of nouns and the prefixes and suffixed of imperfect forms, appears to support the hypothesis that dots mark morphological functions. This hypothesis is consistent with the results of Kaplony's analysis of the function of consonantal diacritics in early papyri (2008). A closer analysis of the relational dotting system of MS BnF ar. 340c shows that the dots also have a phonological function. This can be seen by observing these habits:

marking *tanwīn fatḥa* with a pair of dots only when certain sounds follow (see section 3.2.6)

adding dots to mark vowels associated with *ʾalif*, *wāw* and the unmarked denticle for *yāʾ* (see section 3.3.2)

expressing euphonic vowels that have no morphological function (see section 3.3.3)

adding /a/ to *nūn* at the end of the plural *-ūna* and *-īna* (see section 3.3.4)

3.3.2. Dotting *ʾAlif*, *Wāw* and *Yāʾ* Independently of their Morphological Function

The manuscript has a particular habit of marking vowels associated with *ʾalif*, *wāw* and the unmarked denticle for *yāʾ*. In the base text, used for our digital edition (i.e., the Medina edition), there are 838 *hamza* signs, while in the manuscript these positions are dotted 785 times and undotted 53 times (including 21 cases of *hamza* that are marked with *sukūn* in the base text). Since there is no special sign for *hamza* in the early manuscripts, it is difficult to assume that the dotting has the value of a *hamza* sign when it is on letters which were later marked with the special sign for *hamza* (see Figure 6).[27]

---

[27] Imbert (2012, 123–125) identified signs used to mark a 'proto-hamza' in an inscription dated 692 CE (in the form of two vertical strokes placed above *wāw* in al-*muʾminīna*); in a graffito at al-ʿUlā (in the form of two dots placed vertically to the left of *wāw* in *al-muʾminīna*); in a graffito at Qaṣr al-Kharānah dated 710 CE (in the form of two dots placed vertically to the left of *ʾalif* in *qaraʾa-hu*); and in a graffito at Qāʾ Banī Murr (in the form of a dot to the left of *ʾalif* in *lā ʿazāʾa*). In a sixth- or seventh-century rock inscription discovered near Qaṣr Burquʿ in northeastern Jordan, a dot above *ʾalif* in the *lām-alif* ligature of the Christian Arabic formula *dkr ʾl-ʾlh* was interpreted as a *hamza* sign (al-Shdaifat et al. 2017, 316–318). Puin and Cellard explored the patterns of dotting that reveal the presence of *hamza* (Puin 2011; Cellard 2015, 156–163). Before the introduction of the special sign indicating *hamza*, manuscripts exploited the dot symbol through its position and colour. They also used semicircles, which were added at the same time as the introduction of miniature letters, the origin of modern vowel symbols (e.g., in MS BnF ar. 330f).

Figure 6: Details of different mechanisms used to mark *hamza* in early manuscripts (Source: gallica.bnf.fr / Bibliothèque nationale de France and Dār al-Maḵṭūṭāt, San‘a’)

BnF.ar.340c, f.31v, l.11: *[wa-]yadraʾūna*

BnF.ar.330f, f.31v, l.13: *bi-ʾaḥsana*

BnF.ar.330f, f.33v, l.7: *li-muʾminin*

BnF.ar.329d, f.22r, l.1: *ʾummatin*

BnF.ar.6982 f.79v, l.3: *ʾa-ʾiḏa*

DaM, unclassified: *al-maʾwā*

The peculiar behaviour of the dotter is interesting in regards to *ʾalif*, *wāw*, and *yāʾ*. For example, the dotter marks imperfect prefixes with /u/ in the second, third, and fourth forms. By contrast, prefixes with /a/ are left unmarked, and the body of the verb is undotted if the ending is marked. However, *ʾalif*, *wāw*, and *yāʾ* follow specific rules that fall outside the morphological patterns of the verbs, and dotting these here conveys phonological information. Looking at the manuscript as a system, we can see that the initial *ʾalif* of *hamzah al-qaṭʿ* is always dotted, unlike *ʾalif al-waṣl*. The dotter marked 641 out of 657 occurrences of the initial *ʾalif* at the beginning of words. The dotter placed:

285 dots to the right of the ascender of the initial *ʾalif*
67 dots to the left of it
13 dots in the middle of it
30 dots to the bottom left of it (marking /u/)
246 dots below the baseline level (marking /i/)

The dotter left initial *ʾalif* undotted only 12 times, where we assume a reading of /a/; three cases where we assume a reading of

/u/; one case where we assume a reading of /i/. It is interesting to note that the value of the vowel /a/, usually expressed by a dot to the right of the ascender of *ʾalif*—in contrast to the long vowel /ā/, which is expressed by a dot to the left—is not consistently applied in the manuscript, e.g., Q.15:22:10 has a dot to the left of *ʾalif* in *ʾantum.*[28]

3.3.3. Dotting the Position before *ʾAlif al-Waṣl*

The dotter is consistent in marking the vowel-dots between two words to indicate the exact way of reading the boundary between two words. Notably, the overall majority of euphonic vowels are marked. In the 559 (readable) occurrences of *ʾalif al-waṣl* at the beginning of a word, the dotter always marks the letter at the end of the previous word when the vowel is short, including 4 out of 4 occurrences of the energic *nūn* and 71 out of 72 occurrences of euphonic vowels:

qul-i (2 out of 2)
hum-u and *kum-u* (23 out of 23)
min-a (40 out of 41)
man-i (2 out of 2)
ʿan-i (3 out of 3)
ʾin-i in *wa-la-ʾin-i* (1 out of 1)

---

[28] Discussions of the presence of *hamza* in early Arabic is beyond the scope of this chapter, but some interesting remarks have emerged from this manuscript, contributing to this discussion (see Appendix E for a few examples).

The reason for the undotted ending of the euphonic vowel after *min* in *min-a l-ẓulumāti* (Q.14:5:8–9, f.33v, ll.14–15) is unclear. If the vowel preceding *ʾalif al-waṣl* is long, it is not dotted but only marked by *ʾalif*, *yāʾ*, and *wāw* + *ʾalif*. The undotted short vowel before *ʾalif al-waṣl* in *makara llaḏīna* (Q.13:42:2–3 on f.33r, l.15) is likely due to the assimilation of /ra/ into /lla/ mentioned above. In *ʿan-i llaḏīna* it is unclear (Q.22:38:4–5 on f.45r, l.3). It is also unclear why the ending of *(i)sma*, before *(a)llāhi*, was left unmarked (Q.22:34:6–7, f.44v, l.7). In the first part of the line there are traces of two stages of writing. In one case the dotter marked *ʾalif al-waṣl* of *ištahat* with a dot to its right: *fī-mā (a)-štahat* (Q.21:102:5–7 on f.41v, l.7). In another, the dot marking the /i/ of the first word is placed below the *ʾalif al-waṣl* of the second word: *bil-bayti l-ʿatīqi* (Q.22:29:7–8 on f.44r, l.13). A different rule is observed when *ʾalif al-waṣl* is not at the beginning of a word, namely when it follows the particles *wa-*, *fa-*, *la-* and *bi-*. Out of 100 (readable) occurrences, 95 particles are not dotted.[29] The evidence that the dots carry a phonological function at the word-boundary level, likely relating to the recitation of the text, may be seen in the following: 1) the habit of dotting the endings before *ʾalif al-waṣl* and the euphonic vowels (as in *min-a llāhi*); but 2) leaving the vowel before *ʾalif al-waṣl* unmarked when it is word internal, e.g., *wa-llāhu*.

---

[29] See the five occurrences of dotted particles when preceding *ʾalif al-waṣl* in section 3.2.1.

It is interesting to note that the mysterious letters at the beginning of Q.15 are dotted, namely *ʾalif* is marked with an a–dot (at its top right); the *lām* is not dotted and the final *rāʾ* is marked with an a–dot (above the letter, in the middle). The dotting of the initial *ʾalif* and the final letter, and the un-dotting of the central part of the word, follow the general pattern of dotting, although the mysterious letters have no morphosyntactic connotation. This also seems to suggest the phonological value of the dot with *ʾalif*, at the word-boundary level (see section 4.4).

3.3.4. Dotting *ūna* and *-īna*: Vowel Signs Expressing a Phonological or Grammatical Import

Recitation (i.e., the rules of *tajwīd*) and the focus of the dotter on word boundaries are the most likely explanation for the dotting of the final *nūn* (see Figure 7):

-*ūna* (91 out of 91 occurrences, i.e., 24 noun endings and 67 imperfect endings)
-*īna* (78 out of 81 occurrences)

The *nūn* is always marked, even though its presence does not convey any morphosyntactic information and the undotted form is not part of an ambiguous pair.

Figure 7: Examples of the dotted endings -*ūna* and -*īna* (Source: gallica.bnf.fr / Bibliothèque nationale de France)

Examples of dotted *nūn* to mark /na/ in -*ūna*
in BnF.ar.340c, f.37r, l.15 and f.39r, l.9

91 out of 91 occurrences of -*ūna* are dotted on the final *nūn*

Examples of dotted *nūn* to mark /na/ in -*īna*
in BnF.ar.340c, f.39v, l.2

78 out of 81 occurrences of -*īna* are dotted on the final *nūn*

The analysis of dotted and undotted positions suggests that the vocalisation system of BnF ar. 340c was mainly intended to mark the text according to the recitation rules at the word-boundary level. However, morphosyntactic information also plays an important role. In the majority of cases, the dotting of the particles *li*- and *la*- depends on the morphological category following the particles. This seems to indicate a developmental stage towards a vocalisation system that makes the morphological system explicit, as we see, for example, in the dotting of the case endings, but not -*īna* or -*ūna*. The next stage will be the 'complete' dotting of words and, after that, the complete marking of the text with vowel–symbols and other signs.

The distinction between phonological and grammatical import is not only exemplified by partially dotted manuscripts, but also applies to the terminology. Among comparative studies, Posegay (2020 and 2021) examines the development of the Semitic vocalisation systems and studies Arabic phonetic terminology in relation to Syriac. Versteegh (1993) notes that the terminology used in al-Kalbī does not distinguish between vowel names and declensional endings. Sībawayh (d. 180/796) introduced the distinction between phonological descriptors and *iʿrābī* declensional terms (vowels with grammatical import) (Posegay 2020, 207). The vowels defined as *ḍamma*, *kasra* and *tanwīn* are *ʾiʿrāb* and "the line between 'declension' and 'vocalisation' became blurred at the end of words where the Arabic case vowels occurred" (Posegay 2021, 132). The function of vowels expressed through their terminology has been interpreted as developing from a phonological to a morphological function. Not only the concepts changed over time, but also their embodiment in the manuscript vocalisation. Slowly the technology changed as well, from a dot system exploited to the maximum, to additional symbols representing not only the vocalisation but a whole set of recitation rules. The chronology attributed to the development of the terminology, i.e., from a relative phase by the end of the eighth century, to an absolute phase by the tenth century, and finally, a consolidation phase in the tenth/eleventh century, could be applied to the chronology of the development of the technology and the system used to vocalise the text.

The dotting of BnF ar. 340c seems to belong to the ninth/tenth century, when the system changed. This possible dating is of particular importance as it would also date the awareness of *qirāʾāt* literature, which can be observed through the analysis of the dotting system (see below).

4.0. The Dots in the Manuscript Space: Abstract Model and Concrete Dots

4.1. Positions of Dots around Their Letter and Word

The mechanism of the dotting system is based on the position of the dots in relation to their letter: before, after/inside, and below the letter. According to the treatises, there are some variations within this model, related for example to the length of the vowel or the phonetic context. Dots placed to the right or left of the letter *ʾalif* marks a short or long /a/ respectively. According to al-Dānī, the two dots marking the *tanwīn* are always placed horizontally, except when they are followed by guttural letters (*hamza*, *ḥāʾ*, *ḵāʾ*, *hāʾ*, *ʿayn* and *ġayn*). In the latter case, the two dots may be placed vertically when the *tanwīn* is clearly enunciated or horizontally when the *tanwīn* is not clearly pronounced. This is another mechanism that enhances the meanings expressed by the positioning of the dots.

In this manuscript, the two dots marking *tanwīn fatḥa* are placed horizontally or vertically (according to the available space) and the shape of the letter to which the *tanwīn* is attached, not according to the phoneme that follows the *tanwīn* sign. The phonological rule is marked by dotting or leaving the *ʾalif* undotted, as described above. The *tanwīn fatḥa* with *ʾalif* is always placed vertically (17 out of 17 occurrences), while it is placed horizontally with *tāʾ marbūṭah* (20 out of 20 occurrences) and *ʾalif maqṣūra* (4 out of 4 occurrences). The 96 occurrences of dots placed after a final letter, to mark *tanwīn ḍamma,* are all vertical except in one case. On f.32r, l.5, the dotter marked *matāʿun* at the end of Q.13:26 by placing two horizontal dots, the left one piercing the *wāw* of the following *wa-yaqūlu.*

The vertical placement of two dots to mark *tanwīn ḍamma* is likely due to the physical space to the left of the letter where the u–dot is placed, which would hardly accommodate two horizontal dots, considering the small script and the size of the text area (100 × 155 mm). The 167 occurrences of the pair of dots below the baseline level on the Y axis and at the centre or right of the letter on the X axis, to mark *tanwīn kasra,* are placed vertically or horizontally depending on the shape of the letter in its final or isolated form. The pair of dots is placed vertically when attached to letters with a vertical descender, i.e., *sīn, ṣād/ḍād, qāf, lām, nūn* and *yāʾ* (with its s-like descender). There are only two exceptions, namely in *ḍal(ā)lin* (at the end of Q.13:14, before a five-verse marker, f.31r, l.1) and *ḥīnin* (at the end of Q.21:111, before a ten-verse marker, f.42r, l.4). In the latter case, the pair of dots is placed slightly obliquely below the baseline, and the dot on the right pierces the top of the *ʾalif* on the following line. In all other cases, when the letters do not have a vertical descender but a round tail that develops horizontally below the baseline (i.e., *jīm/ḥāʾ, ʿayn, yāʾ* with its retroflex horizontal tail) or no descender at all (i.e., *ʾalif, bāʾ/tāʾ, dāl, rāʾ/zāy, ṭāʾ, fāʾ, kāf, mīm, tāʾ marbūṭah, wāw*), the dots for the *tanwīn kasra* are placed horizontally.[30]

Pairs of dots appear to have been placed horizontally or vertically according to the graphic layout of the letters and the available space between letters, without following the phonological rules in al-Dānī. The graphic layout and the space on the whole page seem to be the general principle for the placement of all the dots in MS BnF ar. 340c. Its dotter has a very peculiar habit of placing dots on the manuscript page that do not correspond to the abstract model of dot positions known from treatises. Their positions do not correlate with the overall dotting behaviour of early manuscripts. Taking as an example the pair *min/man* and the euphonic vowel added to *min* (*min-a*) and to *man* (*man-i*), some spatial collocations of the dots attributed to *min* and *man* create the visual impression of equivalent signs (see Figure 8). This is a peculiarity of this manuscript and is probably related to the fact that the dot marks the whole syllable or word.

---

30 There are three exceptions: in *munīrin*, at the end of Q.22:8 (f.42v, l.13), the dots are placed vertically and the lower one pierces the denticles on the following line; *ka-ramādin* in Q.14:18:6(f.34v, l.16) and *ʾummatin* in Q.15:5:4 (f.37r, l.16). The latter two occurrences are cases of dotting a second layer of the *rasm* after the *rasm* has been amended. This seems to indicate that there are at least two stages of dotting, probably produced by two different dotters who were active before and after the second stage of amending the *rasm*.

Figure 8: Example of ambiguous placement of red dots above the body of the letter (Source: gallica.bnf.fr / Bibliothèque nationale de France)

man (man-i-[staraqa])

- in BnF.ar.340c, f.37v, l.14 (Q.15:18:2)
- the a–dot is attributed to *mīm*

man

- in BnF.ar.340c, f.42v, l.11 (Q.22:7)
- ambiguous position of an a–dot attributed to *mīm* that produces a position similar to an a–dot attributed to *nūn* in *min-a*

min (min-a-[l-nāsi])

- in BnF.ar.340c, f.42v, l.11 (Q.22:7)
- the a–dot is attributed to *nūn*

4.2. Web of Dots in the Manuscript Page

A closer look at the positions of the dots shows that they can sometimes be contextually placed. The position depends on the placement of the dots on the whole manuscript page and the *rasm* in brown ink. There are two apparently contrasting dynamics, which are linked to the skeleton of the letters:

i) The dotter does not attach a dot to a single letter, but rather to its syllable or word, or even to the larger space around the word on the line (the horizontal axis of the layout of the script).
ii) There is a general effort not to attach a dot to the ascenders and descenders of the line below and above, when they are also marked by dots. This effort resulted in puzzling dot positions, as in Figure 9.

The positioning of the dots is free on the x-axis of the single line, but depends on the other letters and dots on the y-axis.[31]

Figure 9: Examples of contextually positioned dots to avoid overlapping or intersection of two dots belonging to words on two lines (Source: gallica.bnf.fr / Bibliothèque nationale de France)

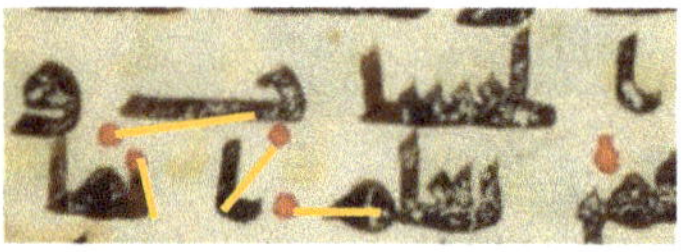

Fig. 9a. BnF.ar.340c, f.31v, ll.3–4 (Q.13:18:23 and Q.13:19:2–3) *al-ḥisābi wa-* and *[ʾa-fa-man] yaʿlamu ʾannamā*

Fig. 9b. BnF.ar.340c, f.31v, ll.9–10 (Q.13:21:13 and Q.13:22:5–6) *al-ḥisābi* and *rabbi-himu wa-ʾaqāmū*

The dotter is careful to maintain a minimum distance between two dots—if possible—and to place them in the form of lines or geometric figures, regardless of the vowel that may be associated with that contextually positioned dot, as the examples in Figure 10 show.

[31] For example, in Q.13:18 and Q.13:19 (f.31v, l.3 and l.4,) the dot marking the ending of *al-ḥisābi* has been contextually placed to the far left of the tail of the isolated *bāʾ* so as not to overlap with the dot marking the /a/ associated with *ʾalif* of *ʾannamā* on the line below. This gives a first impression of a dot placed below the baseline to the far left of the *bāʾ* as associated to it (see Figure 9a). A few lines below on the same page (see Figure 9b), the dot marking the ending of the same word has been placed in the middle of the isolated *bāʾ*, as the second letter block of *ʾaqāmū* on the following line is not dotted and does not create any possible intersections of letters and dots.

On f.42v, l.1 and l.2, two pairs of dots, placed below the last and second-last letters, mark the endings of *nuṭfatin* and *mukallaqatin* (Figure 10a).

On f.42v, l.3, the pair marking the ending of *musamman* is positioned so that it is at the same distance from the following pair of /u/ and /a/ in *ṯumma*, regardless of the position of their letters, and the u–dot is at the same point of /a/ on the y-axis (Figure 10b).

On f.42v, l.9 and l.10, the dot marking the ending of *al-ḥaqqu* is contextually positioned below the baseline to form a sequence with the pair of dots marking the ending of *qadīrun* on the line below (Figure 10c).

On f.43r, l.9 and l.10, the dots are placed to form three pairs of vertically dots in *ʾinna llāha* and [*yanṣu*]*ra-hu llāhu*, regardless of the position of the dots in relation to their letters—the dot marking the ending of *yanṣura* is positioned to the left of *rāʾ*, which is the model position for /u/, and the two dots marking the endings of *ʾinna* and *allāha* are positioned relatively far from their letter in order to be on the same y-axis as the u–dot s in *-hu* and *allāhu* on the line below (Figure 10d)

The dotter seems to prefer adding single dots as if they were part of a pair, placed horizontally, vertically and diagonally (from bottom-to-top and from top-to-bottom). The effect produced is similar to the variety of the combinations of Syriac dots.[32] The analysis of the shapes produced by the dots did not

---

[32] See the chapter by Lundberg.

lead to the identification of any patterns in them. The graphic and aesthetic result of the dotter's approach to dotting does not apply to all the dots in the manuscript, but explain the majority of the puzzling positions. These shapes and effects do not provide a strong argument in favour of dot positions as expressions of phonetic phenomena in the recitation of the text at a word-boundary level, e.g., liaison before *ʾalif al-waṣl* and assimilation.

Figure 10: Examples of contextually positioned dots that form lines and shapes regardless of the meaning usually associated with the dot's position (Source: gallica.bnf.fr / Bibliothèque nationale de France)

Fig. 10a. BnF.ar.340c, f.42v, ll.1–2 (Q.22:5:15 and Q.22:5:24) *nuṭfatin* and *mukallaqatin*

Fig. 10b. BnF.ar.340c, f.42v, l.3 (Q.22:5:34–35) *musamman thumma*

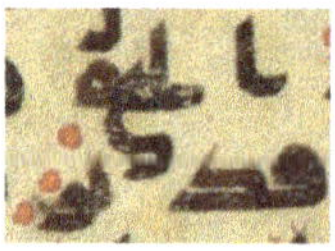

Fig. 10c. BnF.ar.340c, f.42v, ll.9–10 (Q.22:6:5 and Q.22:6:13) *l-ḥaqqu* and *qadīrun*

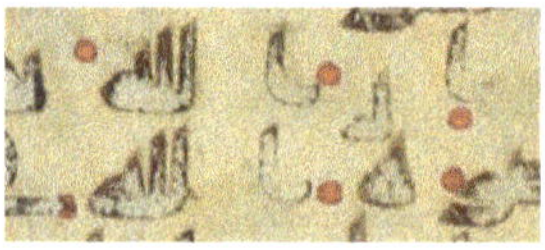

Fig. 10d. BnF.ar.340c, f.43r, ll.9–10 (Q.22:14:13–14 and Q.22:15:6–7) *ʾinna llāha* and *[yanṣu]ra-hu llāhu*

4.3. Dots in Positions Marking the Liaison between Words

Analysis of the 412 occurrences of *ʾalif al-waṣl* preceded by a single dot or a pair of dots (excluding unmarked long vowels or unclear and unmarked cases of short vowels) revealed no pattern in the placement of the dots. Some dots seem to pierce the letter *ʾalif* to visually express assimilation, but the behaviour is never consistent. For example, the dotter placed a dot piercing the *ʾalif* in *wa-yaqūlu -llaḏīna* (Q.13:27:1–2 in f.32r, l.5, see Figure 11a) and *l-ġafūru l-raḥīmu* (Q.15:49:5–6 in f.38v, l.14, see Figure 11b). This position may suggest a function where the dot marks not only the liaison between the two words but also their assimilation.

Figure 11: Examples of *ʾalif al-waṣl* preceded by /u/ marked by a dot suggesting possible assimilation (Source: gallica.bnf.fr / Bibliothèque nationale de France)

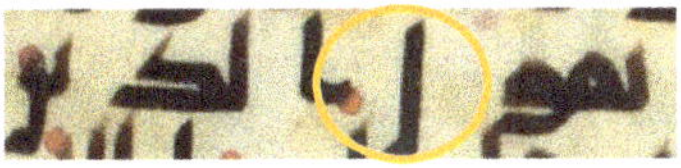

Fig. 11.a BnF.ar.340c, f.32r, l.5
(Q.13:27:1–2)
*[wa-]yaqū**lu -lla**ḏīna*

Fig.11.b BnF.ar.340c, f.38v, l.14 (Q.15:49:5–6)
*l-ġafū**ru l-ra**ḥīmu*

The hypothesis of positioning the dot to mark the liaison with *ʾalif al-waṣl* does not seem to be a rule for the dotter. Out of 123 dots marking /u/, only 21 dots pierce the following letter *ʾalif* and only in five cases the last and first syllables before and after *ʾalif al-waṣl* could be affected by assimilation. However, the liaison at the word boundary level is suggested by the 59 cases of u–dot s placed closer to *ʾalif al-waṣl* and further from the preceding letter.

The liaison function at the word boundary level seems to be supported by further dot placements, as for example in *qul ʾinna -llāha* (Q.13:27:10–12 in f.32r, l.6). The dot referred to the beginning of *ʾinna* is placed in an unusual position, to the right of the letter *ʾalif* at its baseline level, probably to mark the liaison with the previous word *qul*, likely to be read as *qulinna* (see Figure 12).

Figure 12: Example of unusual placement of i-dot at the baseline level in *ʾinna* (Source: gallica.bnf.fr / Bibliothèque nationale de France)

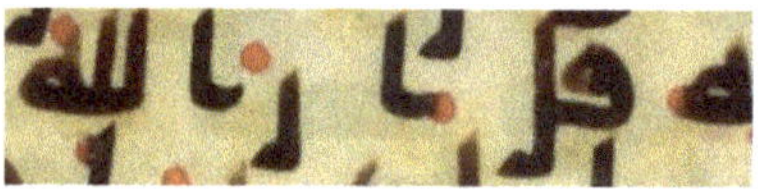

BnF.ar.340c, f.32r, l.6
(Q.13:27:10–12)
qul-inna (rather than *qul ʾinna*)

When the last vowel dot of the word before *ʾalif al-waṣl* is attached to the *ʾalif*, its position on the y-axis is variable and puzzling. The same position, e.g., a dot below the letter *ʾalif* or to the right of it at the baseline level, can represent different phonemes (see Figures 13, 14, and also 19).

Figure 13: Example 1. The same dot position before *ʾalif al-waṣl* marks different phonemes (Source: gallica.bnf.fr / Bibliothèque nationale de France)

Dot to the left of *ʾalif*, baseline level, marking /a/ in *ʾinna* ***-llāhu***
BnF.ar.340c, f.43r, l.7 (Q.22:14:1–2)

Dot to the left of *ʾalif*, baseline level, marking /u/ in *[lan] yanṣurahu* ***-llāhu***
BnF.ar.340c, f.43r, l.10
(Q.22:15:6–7)

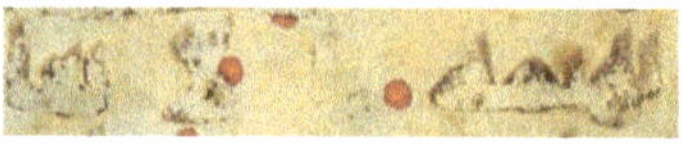

Dot to the left of *ʾalif*, baseline level, marking /i/ in *[min] bahīmati* ***-l-ʾa[nʿā]mi***
BnF.ar.340c, f.44r, l.11
(Q.22:28:14–15)

In the three examples shown in Figure 13, the dot is placed at the same point on the x- and y-axes and closer to the initial *ʾalif* of the following word. From the morpho-syntactic context and the analysis of the network of dots on the whole page, the three dots cannot be anything other than three different phonemes.[33]

Figure 14: Example 2. The same dot position before *ʾalif al-waṣl* marks different phonemes (Source: gallica.bnf.fr / Bibliothèque nationale de France)

Dot below the *ʾalif* marking /u/ in *wa-yaqūl***u** *-llaḏīna* BnF.ar.340c, f.33v, l.1 (Q.13:43:1–2)

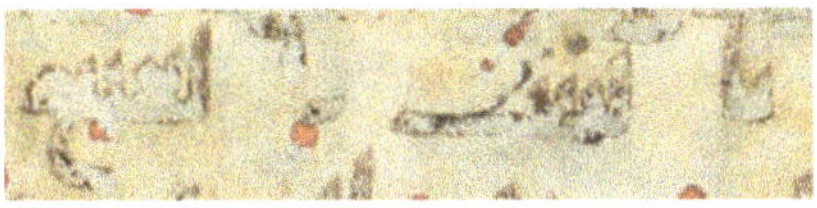

Dot below the *ʾalif* marking /i/ in *bi-l-bayt***i** *-l-ʿatīqi* BnF.ar.340c, f.44r, l.13 (Q.22:29:7–8)

The same combination of two identical words can be dotted differently, e.g., the expressions *ʾinna llāha* and *ʾanna llāha*, which occur 34 times in the manuscript (see Figure 15). The dotter placed a dot above the isolated *nūn* 12 times (piercing or detaching it on the y-axis) and to its left 22 times (far from the letter *nūn* or piercing the following *ʾalif*). My analysis did not reveal any system that the dotter may have followed to mark the endings of *ʾinna* and *ʾanna* before *allāha*.

[33] In *[min] bahīmati -l- ʾanʿāmi*, a possible harmonisation that could lead to the reading **[min] bahīmatu -l- ʾanʿāmi* is not present, as for example in the reading *li-l-malāʾikatu -sjudū* by Abū Jaʿfar in Q.2:34:3–4 (EVQ), where *[u]sjudū* begins with a *ḍamma* related to the *ʾalif*. I thank Shady Nasser for bringing this case to my attention.

Figure 15: Example of final -*na* marked with a dot in different positions (Source: gallica.bnf.fr / Bibliothèque nationale de France)

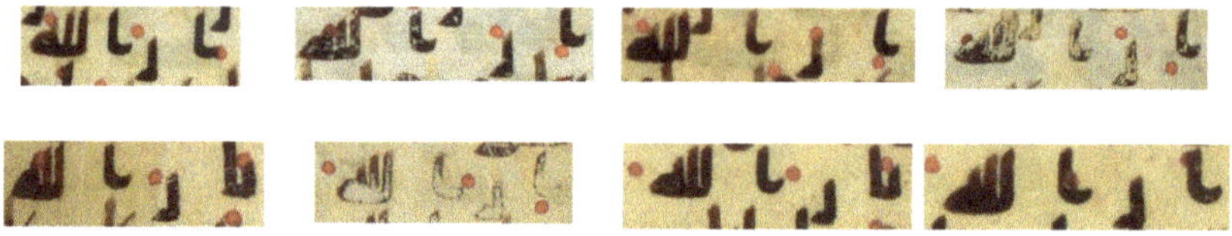

MS BnF.ar. 340c, f.32r, l.6; f.32v, l.4; f.35r, l.10; f.37r, 13; f.37v, l.8; f.43r, l.9 and f.46v, ll.4 and 6 (left-to-right, top row, then bottom)

4.4. Recitation and the Dot Placement on the Page

The dotter's artistic commitment, placing dots in relation to the other dots on the page, hampers the identification of possible patterns related to recitation. It is likely that the dotter already had an initial plan for the page overall, otherwise it would have been difficult to position a dot on a line without knowing the placement of the dots on the following line. This would imply that the dotter had a knowledge of the positions to be marked, and the positions not to be marked, already at the start of the dotting process. Moreover, the puzzling positions of the dots, created by the artistic and geometric plan of the page, suggest that the basis of the dotting system was unimportant to the dotter (i.e., the position of the dots below, above or in front/inside the letter). In this manuscript, the real aim of the dotting was not to disambiguate the reading of the *rasm* skeleton by placing dots in /a/, /u/, and /i/ positions, but rather to mark the positions of vowel-dots in a text that was most likely known by heart. This is confirmed, for example, by the ambiguous position of the dot to the right of *ʾalif* at the baseline level (see Figure 13 above); therefore, the function of a dot in the same position to mark /a/, /i/ and /u/ cannot be to disambiguate the reading of its syllable.[34]

5.0. Relational System, Interaction of Parts and the Power of Absence

5.1. Intentionality

In his 1974 book *The Freudian Slip*, Timpanaro warns of the dangers of deciding what is in a scribe's mind and suggests caution in applying psychoanalysis to explain the mistakes of scribes/editors/readers. The same caution must be emphasised when suggesting the rationale behind a partially dotted manuscript and the perspective of its dotter. This warning is important when scholars seek to establish the reading of a manuscript through its dotting, but also through its *rasm* skeleton, by connecting the manuscripts to the *qirāʾāt*.

Recently, Hilali offered an overview of this ongoing discussion. She pointed out that "[i]n most studies of Qurʾānic manuscripts, the Qurʾānic variants are assumed to be those recorded in canonical collections such as that of Ibn Mujāhid (d. 936)" while "[t]he classical collections of variants should be viewed as the end result of multiple stages of canonization that entailed multiple actors and processes" (Hilali 2021, 239–240). Hilali considers it ahistorical to assume that the canonised list of variants

---

[34] Some preliminary reconstructed visualisations of the dot position in MS BnF ar. 340c in comparison with MS BnF ar. 334c show the idiosyncrasies of the dotter in the former manuscript. See the chapter in this volume co-authored by Fedeli, Kinne-Wall, and Sidky.

in the classical collections of variants corresponds to the actual content of the original codices. This view seems to correspond to the hypothesis of 'mixed text types', i.e., Qur'ānic manuscripts have a mixture of readings when compared to canonised lists of Qur'ānic variant readings. The third volume of the *Geschichte* drew up some hypotheses about the provenance of the manuscripts, taking into account their attribution to particular readers, and emphasising the methodological problem of identifying the location of a manuscript on the basis of single variants (Nöldeke et al. 2013, III:270).[35] This led to a typology of textual mixture and the research question of text type of Qur'ānic manuscripts.

The same conclusions were drawn by Jeffery and Mendelsohn in their analysis of Pissareff's reproduction of the Samarqand Codex. According to them, the manuscript contains "Iraqi readings as well as Medina readings thus expressing a mixed textual type" (Jeffery and Mendelsohn 2011, 401–402). More recently, Cellard suggested that dotters intended to indicate "not seven, ten or fourteen canonical readings, but two readings: one pertaining to the Norm and the other pertaining to a variant" (Cellard 2015, 175). Interestingly, Cellard mentioned Nöldeke and his view of certain manuscript variants as the expression of a single reader/scholar. Another way of looking at the content of

---

[35] The manuscript described as an example of textual mixture is MS Saray 50386 (see Déroche 2009, 148). Similar problems regarding the location of manuscripts and readings have been highlighted by Déroche (2014, 34), e.g., codex Parisino-petropolitanus, which, according to Dutton, originated in Syria because of the Syrian readings in the manuscript.

early manuscripts—in terms of readings and lists of variants in canonical collections—is to define the former as a fluid or flexible situation.

A painstaking analysis of the marked and unmarked positions in each manuscript, and not only the marked ones that may be labelled with a reader's name, can give an indication of the dotters' view on possible reading systems. Manuscript BnF ar. 340c provides an interesting example of the application of one reading system and the awareness of the existence of other systems. Moreover, if we look at the readings of MS BnF ar. 340c, expressed only by means of red dots, and if we assume that they were added around the ninth/tenth century as suggested above, these readings are likely to be contemporary with Ibn Mujāhid's period. Before comparing the dot readings with "the end result of multiple stages of canonization that entailed multiple actors and processes" (the *qirāʾāt* system established from the tenth century onwards), this analysis will focus on the internal evidence provided by the dotting system (Hilali 2021, 240). This partial dotting system has readings that cannot be attributed to a known reader in the *qirāʾāt* literature, but at the same time—by being partially dotted—it is intended to mark only certain sections of the text. The analysis and its implications are described in the following section.

5.2. Internally Dotted Nouns

In my analysis, I have focused on the unmarked internal positions of nouns because they are not affected by the rules of pattern morphology related to verbs (e.g., passive forms). For the same reason, I have analysed participles and non-participle forms separately in order to highlight how the dotter marked forms with a certain phonological pattern in contrast to forms that do have a specific pattern (see Appendix F for the schema of derivational morphology of participles). In the following analysis, I do not include the presence or counting of dots related to *hamza* with *ʾalif*, *wāw* and the denticle for *yāʾ* (although they also convey phonological information).

Considering verbal nouns forms, 28 out of 28 occurrences are internally undotted, including forms I, II, III, IV and VIII, while their endings are all dotted according to the rule (i.e., those ending in long /ā/ are not dotted).

The difference between internally dotted/undotted forms and dotted/undotted endings is clear from the description above. Internally dotted forms show a consistent dotting of the same lemma, e.g., the four internally dotted passive participles in pattern IV are all forms of *mursal* and all its occurrences are internally dotted, while the other lemmata *munẓar*, *muḵraj*, *munkar* (twice), *mubʿad*, and *mudḵal* are internally undotted.

In the group of nouns, 1,278 out of 1,331 are internally undotted, excluding dots associated with *hamza* on *ʾalif*, *wāw*, the denticle for *yāʾ*, and cases of *hamza* without graphical support (e.g., the dotting of *rāʾ* in *ruʾūs*). The 53 internally dotted nouns represent the 4.1% of the total number of occurrences. The analysis of this very small percentage, focused on possible patterns, yields the following:

Some dots mark long vowels: /ī/ is dotted in *al-mīṯ(ā)q*; /ā/ is dotted in *warāʾi-hu* (1 occurrence in Q.14:16:2, while in

Q.14:17:14 *ʾalif* is not dotted). In *salām* (Q.15:52:5) the dot is associated with the second radical. A dot above the first radical marks the diphthong /ay/ in *ḵayr(ā)t* and *ṭayr*.

Some lemmata are dotted consistently:

jahannam (dotted on the first or second radical to mark /ja/ or /ha/ in 4 out of 5 occurrences)
sirr (dotted in 2 out of 2 occurrences)
šakk (dotted in 2 out of 2 occurrences)
ʿ(ā)lamīna (dotted on the second radical to mark /la/ in 4 out of 4 occurrences)
ʾajmaʿīna and *ʾajmaʿūna* (dotted on the second radical to mark /ma/ in 4 out of 5 occurrences, although the reading of the undotted *ʾajmaʿīna* is unclear)
ṣudūr (dotted on the first radical to mark /u/ in 2 out of 2 occurrences)
rusul (dotted on both the first and second radicals or only on the first radical to mark /u/ in 7 out of 8 occurrences, where the undotted *rusul* is a later amendment)

The dotting of the plural *rusul* is interesting when compared to its singular form *rasūl*, which is always undotted (4 out of 4). Similarly, the plural *ʾajmaʿīna/-ūna* can be compared to the form *jamīʿ*, which is never dotted (6 out of 6). In other cases, singular and plural forms are always dotted, e.g., *sirr* as mentioned above and *surur* (only one occurrence). Comparing the internally dotted nouns with the available information about their readings from the *qirāʾāt* literature, the analysis shows that in 20 of the 53 internally dotted nouns, the dotter marked a reading where the *qirāʾāt* literature attests to more than one reading. In two instances they marked a reading that is not known from the literature. This suggests that the 41% of internally dotted words are probably motivated by the existence of different ways of reading the text. These 22 internally dotted nouns are:

rusul – It is marked in 7 out of 7 occurrences for which the seven and fourteen Readings also report the reading *rusl* (EVQ).[36] The word is either dotted on both the first and second radicals (f.32v, l.5; f.33r, l.6; f.34r, l.10; f.36v, ll.12–13) or only on the first radical (f.34v, l.2 and l.8; f.37r, ll.2–3). As the manuscript system does not utilise the sign for the *sukūn*, it is unclear whether the former four occurrences mark *rusul* while the latter three occurrences mark *rusl*.

ẓulum(ā)t – It is marked in its first and second /u/ (3 out of 4 occurrences, noting that one undotted occurrence is of uncertain reading, on f.40v, l.16); the reading al-*ẓulm(ā)t* is known from the fourteen Readings for all four occurrences, see Figure 16 (EVQ). The other forms *ẓalūm*, *ẓallām* and *ẓulm* are not dotted and other readings for these are currently unattested.

lisān – It is marked in the first radical to read /li/ (1 occurrence); the fourteen Readings also report the reading *lasn*; and the *šawāḏḏ* Readings include *lusun*, *lisn*, and *lusn* (EVQ).

---

[36] I follow the convention of capitalising 'Reading' to denote a collection of readings attributed to an eponymous Reader, as in Nasser (2013: 5, n. 1). For discussion of the status of the collections associated with the seven and fourteen eponymous Readers, see Nasser (2013).

subul – It is marked in the first and second radicals to read *subul* (1 occurrence) and the seven Readings also know *subl* (EVQ). All 5 occurrences of the singular *sabīl* are internally undotted.

kalimat – It is marked in the first and second radical to read *kalimat* (2 out of 2 occurrences); the *šawāḏḏ* Readings also report the reading *kilmat* (EVQ).

surur – It is marked in its first and second radical as /u/ and /u/ (1 occurrence) and the *šawāḏḏ* Readings also have *surar* (EVQ).

buyūt – It is marked /u/ in its first radical (1 occurrence); the seven Readings also have the reading *biyūt* (EVQ).

raġab – It is marked in its first and second radical as /a/ and /a/ (1 occurrence); the fourteen Readings include *ruġb* while the *šawāḏḏ* Readings have *raġb* and *ruġub* (EVQ).

ḥaṣb – It is marked in its first radical as /a/ (1 occurrence), whereas the *šawāḏḏ* Readings also have *ḥaḍab* and *ḥaḍb* (EVQ). As there is no sign for *sukūn*, it is unclear whether the dotting is meant to convey the reading *ḥaṣb* with *sukūn*.

kutub – It is marked in its first radical as /u/ (1 occurrence), whereas the seven Readings also have the singular *kitāb* and the *šawāḏḏ* Readings have *kutb* (EVQ). The singular form *kit(ā)b/kitāb* is always undotted (8 out of 8 occurrences) and the *qirāʾāt* literature consulted so far, knows no other readings for it.

suk(ā)rā – It is marked in its first radical as /u/ (1 out of 2 occurrences), whereas the seven Readings also have *sakrī* and the *šawāḏḏ* Readings have *sakrā*, *sakārā*, *sukrā* and *sukārā* (EVQ). Both dotted and undotted occurrences are difficult to read because of the layers of ink and the degradation of the ink. The form of the noun *sakrat* (only 1 occurrence in the manuscript) is undotted, and the *qirāʾāt* literature consulted so far knows no other readings for it.

barūj – It is marked in its first radical as /a/ (1 occurrence), whereas the seven Readings include *burūj* (EVQ).

labās – It is marked in its first radical as /a/ (1 occurrence), whereas the seven Readings only have *libās* (EVQ). The scheme *labūs* (1 occurrence) is unmarked and the *qirāʾāt* literature consulted so far has no other readings for it.

Figure 16: Examples of nouns consistently dotted and undotted in internal position (Source: gallica.bnf.fr / Bibliothèque nationale de France)

ẓulum(ā)t) is always dotted (3 out of 4 occurrences, one unclear)
BnF.ar.340c, f.31r, l.7 (Q.13:16:27)

53 out of 1,331 occurrences of nouns are internally dotted in BnF.ar.340c

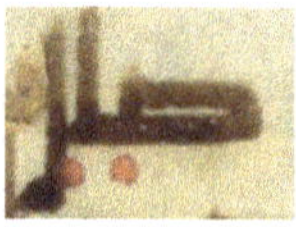

ḍal(ā)l is always undotted (4 out of 4 occurrences)
BnF.ar.340c, f.31r, l.1, Q.13:14:27

1,278 out of 1,331 occurrences of nouns are not internally dotted in BnF.ar.340c

The nouns that have only one reading in the widely known *qirāʾāt* works are mostly unmarked (all except the 22 cases listed above in addition to eight other single occurrences, i.e., *duʿāʾ*, *ḏunūb*, *wujūh*, *ḥukm*, *turāb*, *ṭifl*, *ḥurum(ā)t*, *kaṯīr*). This pattern of dotting the skeleton of words is a specific behaviour of the dotter of BnF ar. 340c. Other manuscripts with the same section of text do not follow these patterns.

In the present case study, dots add further clarification to words (e.g., *rusul* is not *rusl*). The internal dotting of nouns represents a perfect subsystem. The bodies of nouns, which have a huge number of possible patterns, are unmarked or marked according to a personal strategy. Dots are mainly used to confirm a specific reading of the noun, in opposition to other known readings (see Figure 16). Internally dotted nouns are part of a system and as such have meaning only in relation to the whole and not in isolation. To interpret a word independently would be misleading and would not represent the complexity of the system.

6.0. Idiosyncrasies of the Dotter of BnF ar. 340c: Professional and Educational Experience

6.1. Geographical Area and Time

The system of dots in the manuscript provides the dotters' perspective, and adds a possible cultural and scholarly context for their activity. I did not find any internal clue as to the geographical origin of the dotting layer. I have therefore compared the characteristics and mechanisms of the system with the description given by al-Dānī (d. 1053), regarding the regional habits of marking the *rasm* with dots and symbols. There are features that point to a vocalisation system attributed to Iraq and the Mashriq, namely the presence of only red dots; the absence of green, yellow or blue dots; the absence of special symbols, e.g., for *shadda* or *sukūn*; the absence of a special code for marking different readings, for example, with green dots (George 2015a and 2015b).

The terminus *post quem* for the addition of red dots is a possible date for the writing of the *rasm*. This probably took place between the eighth and ninth centuries CE, the period to which scholars attribute the introduction of the dotting system. The material traces of different strata of dots, such as words whose *rasm* skeleton has been amended (see Section 1 and Figure 1), suggests that dotting is an activity that did not take place immediately after the first writing. This is consistent with what is known from treatises about the role of the dotter as a separate, specialised task (George 2015a, 9), commissioned by scholars and readers. It is also likely that the dots of BnF ar. 340c are the work of two dotters in two different periods (see above and Figure 3). Finally, when looking at the development from phonological to morpho-syntactic values attributed to dots, the dotting of BnF ar. 340c seems to belong to a point of transition from one phase to the other in the ninth/tenth century.

6.2. Intentionality

The interpretation of the dotting system as a co-ordinated system shows the point of view of the dotter and the mechanisms chosen and implemented to convey different types of information. Some mechanisms are common to the majority of the corpus of early Qurʾānic manuscripts, such as the marking of endings. Other mechanisms are common to a subset of manuscripts, e.g., the use of the opposition zero/dot to mark *min* and *man*; others are peculiar to the person who dotted MS BnF ar. 340c. The dotter of this manuscript was deliberate in the placement of the dots not only in relation to their letters, but in relation to the other dots on each page. The result is an idiosyncratic placement of dots that I have not observed in other manuscripts. The phonological, grammatical, and recitational function of certain dots has been described above, as well as the number of internally dotted nouns and their probable correlation with *qirā'āt* literature.

6.3. Correlation between *Qirā'āt* and Variance in the Manuscripts

It is not the purpose of this chapter to enter into the details of the ongoing debate on the interrelationship and overlap between variant readings in manuscripts and *qirā'at* documented in medieval treatises. At the heart of that debate is the different status and value attributed to readings that in manuscripts appear without explicit reference to the system of a reader, whereas in treatises, readings are explicitly ascribed to individual readers. A common scholarly approach is to compare manuscript readings with the attributed readings in treatises in order to assign a label retrospectively.[37] Although this case study includes such a comparison, the main focus is to understand the internal patterns of

[37] Over the last two decades, there has been a growing interest in Qur'ānic manuscripts and their variant readings, leading to discussions on the topic. A significant milestone in this conversation was the simultaneous publication of facsimiles by Déroche and Noja Noseda, and Rezvan in the 1990s. The reproduction of manuscript images, prior to the introduction of digitisation and open access, generated works such as those by Dutton in 2001 and 2004. From 2005 onwards, there has been a turning point in scholarship with regards to readings (canonical and

vowel marking in the manuscript. The analysis seeks to identify features that may indicate the existence of a system of readings independent of explicit ascription. An example of comparison with the readings in treatises is the interpretation of *all(ā)hu* in Q.14:2:1 with a red dot placed to the left of the final *hāʾ* at the baseline level. There are no physical constraints justifying the positioning of a dot representing /i/ on the baseline level, e.g., intersection of letters or minimum distance from another dot (as described above). *All(ā)hu* corresponds to the reading of Nāfiʿ and Ibn ʿĀmir, while *all(ā)hi* is the reading of Ibn Kaṯīr, Abū ʿAmr, ʿĀṣim, Hamza, al-Kisāʾī and Nāfiʿ from al-Aṣmaʿī from Naṣr b. ʿAlī from ʿUbayd Allāh b. ʿAlī from Ibn Mujāhid (EVQ and Nasser 2020, 508). However, the word dotted with the final /u/ is a reading not accompanied by the explicit or encoded name of its reader.

An example of an internal element that may indicate the existence of a system of readings is the proportion of nouns that are dotted compared to those left undotted, which might provide insight into the perspective of the dotter regarding a system of reading. It is quite unlikely that the dotter internally marked 53 out of 1,331 nouns without attributing a specific function to their addition. It is even more unlikely that the dotter accidentally marked the words that have more than one reading according to the *qirāʾāt* literature, being unaware of the existence of a diversity of oral readings. Since there are readings that are not attested

non-canonical) in manuscripts: whereas previously, readings were only considered from the perspective of treatises, readings from manuscripts have now become equally important.

in widely known treatises (2 of the 53 internally dotted nouns), the range of oral reading traditions known to the dotter probably do not fully overlap with those known today. The dotter worked (in placing vowel dots) in relation to a system of oral readings. Moreover, when the *rasm* was different from what is attested in treatises on *qirāʾāt* and the overall majority of early manuscripts, the dotter added the dots to the *rasm* without correcting it (e.g., the word *wa-l-ʿ(ā)kifīna* on f.44r, l.6 mentioned above).

If we want to catalogue the specific readings of the manuscript according to the way they correspond to the different reading traditions (*qirāʾāt*), in the light of the hypothesis that the dotter was aware of an existing system of oral readings, we see that some readings and names of readers are known from the *qirāʾāt* literature (27 affecting the vowel dot layer) and other readings are unknown (62 affecting the vowel dot layer, a third of which are probably a misplacement of the dot). Considering the readings as a relational system, an interesting example is the dotting of the particle *ʾin/ʾan/ʾinna/ʾanna*.

In Q.22:62:6, the dotter marked the *rasm* of *wāw*, *ʾalif* and the single letter-block of denticle, *mīm* and *ʾalif* as *wa-ʾinna-mā*, placing a dot below the *ʾalif*. This corresponds to the reading of al-Ḥasan al-Baṣrī (d. 728/729), known from the treatise *al-Baḥr al-muḥīṭ* by Abū Ḥayyān al-Ġarnāṭī (d. 1255): *wa-qaraʾa l-jumhūru (w-a-n m-a) bi-fatḥi l-hamzati, wa-qaraʾa al-Ḥasan bi-kasri-hā* (al-Ġarnāṭī 1993, 6, 355). The dotting of the manuscript seems to reflect readings attributable not only to al-Ḥasan al-Baṣrī but also to several other readers, both canonical and non-canonical. The manuscript also has readings which are not known from the widely known *qirāʾāt* works:

ʾinna l-arḍa instead of *ʾanna l-arḍa* in Q. 21:105:8
wa-ʾinna llāha instead of *wa-ʾanna llāha* in Q. 22:16:5
ʾinna [sic] *lā tušrik* instead of *ʾan lā tušrik* in Q. 22:26:6
ʾinna-hu l-ḥaqqu instead of *ʾanna-hu l-ḥaqqu* in Q. 22:54:5
wa-ʾinna llāha instead of *wa-ʾanna llāha* in Q. 22:61:12

The dotter also marked *ʾin* in Q.10:25 where only the reading *ʾan taṣuddūnā* is known; *ʾinna* in Q.14:19:9 where only the reading *ʾin yašaʾ* is known; and *ʾanna* in Q.15:85:9 and Q.22:38:8 where the only known reading is *ʾinna*. Were all these readings part of a cluster of diverse oral readings, or were they associated with a single reading tradition known to the dotter, or the source used by the dotter? Is it an individual habit of the dotter rather than a reading? In any case, the identification of al-Ḥasan al-Baṣrī's reading in Q.22:62:6 does not adequately account for the complex situation of the dotted text.

When we focus on the readings that tell us something about the dotter's point of view and the original function of the dots, we observe the following. The dotter marked the *rasm* without adjusting it to the reading expressed by the dots, e.g., (Figure 17):

In the first layer of the *rasm* (i.e., *all(ā)h*) of Q.13:16:7, *li-llāli* is marked by a dot below the final *hāʾ* and the *ʾalif* is left.

In Q.13:31:16, the *rasm* reads *bal li-llāhi* without *ʾalif*, while the dotter marks *bal-i llāhu* with a dot to the left of the *hāʾ* at the baseline level and the euphonic dot vowel /i/ without modifying the *rasm*.

In Q.22:40:27, *kathīran* is not marked according to the rules as it is followed by */wa/* and the *ʾalif* has not been added.

In the latter example, the correlational system indicates the reading of *tanwīn ʾalif* expressed by the zero signifier, as all *tanwīn ḍamma* and *kasra* are marked.

Figure 17: Examples of readings marked by the dots without adjusting the *rasm* (Source: gallica.bnf.fr / Bibliothèque nationale de France)

qul li-llāhi in Q.13:16:7
the *rasm* has *qul-i llāhu* (with *ʾalif*)
BnF.ar.340c, f.31r, l.4

bal-i llāhu in Q.13:31:16
the rasm has *bal li-llāhi* (without *ʾalif*)
BnF.ar.340c, f.32r, l.16

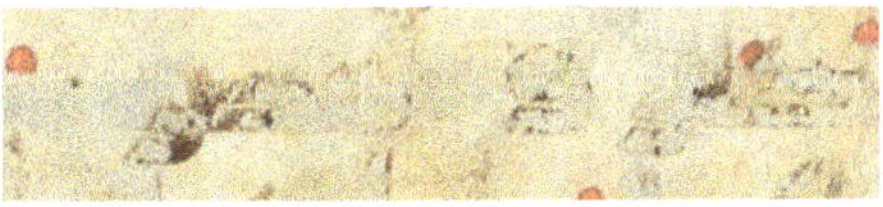

kaṯīran wa-la-yanṣuranna in Q.22:40:27
the *rasm* does not have the *ʾalif* for the *tanwīn*
BnF.ar.340c, f.45r, l.9

In Q. 22:60, the *rasm* reads *wa-man ʿāqaba bi-miṯli mā ʿūqiba bi-hi* with the first occurrence of the active form marked by *ʾalif* and the second passive form marked by *wāw*, i.e., 'and whosoever chastises after the manner that he was chastised'. The dotter in f.46r, l.16, marked the *ʾalif* of *ʿāqaba* with a dot to its left at the baseline level to mark it as the following passive form in /u/, i.e., *ʿūqiba* (see Figure 18). The *rasm* was not modified.

Figure 18: Examples of the reading /ū/ in *ʿūqiba* based on a different *rasm* with *wāw* and *ʾalif* (Source: gallica.bnf.fr / Bibliothèque nationale de France)

Reading *ʿūqiba bi-hi* in Q.22:60:7–8
BnF.ar.340c, f.46v, l.1

Reading *wa-man ʿūqiba bi-miṯli mā* in Q.22:60:3–6; the *rasm* has *ʿāqaba*
BnF.ar.340c, f.46r, l.16

The dotter always accepted the *rasm*, including cases already mentioned, such as *fī-hu* in Q.21:91:5 (Figure 2) and *wa-l-ʿākifīna* in Q.22:26:14, where the known *rasm* has *fī-hā* and *wa-l-qāʾimīna* respectively.

There are some uncertain cases where the dots appear to have been placed by mistake. There are no physical constraints that would have led the dotter to place them in a particular position, and there is no known explanation. However, if the same position occurs more than once, it deserves special attention. For example, the dot marking the ending of *bahīmat* in Q.22:28:14 is placed to the left of *tāʾ marbūṭa* as if it was /u/ in *bahīmatu* after *min* in *min bahīmati l-ʾanʿāmi*. The same situation occurs in Q.22:34:12 (see Figure 19). This suggests that the dot was not positioned to mark the vowel /u/, but probably to mark the liaison between *bahīmat* and *al-ʾanʿām*, the sound being unimportant and known by heart.

Figure 19: Example of ambiguous dot placement (Source: gallica.bnf.fr / Bibliothèque nationale de France)

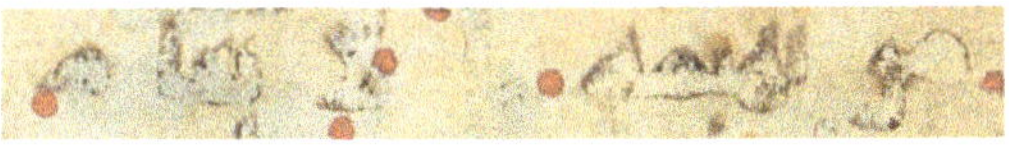

min bahīmati l-ʾanʿāmi
Q.22:28:14
BnF.ar.340c, f.44r, l.11

min bahīmati l-ʾanʿāmi
Q.22:34:12
BnF.ar.340c, f.44v, l.7

6.4. Who Placed the Dots in BnF ar. 340c?

The dotter was probably a reader, or a person working for a reader, who applied the expertise of a collection of reading traditions to the *rasm*. Most likely, the dotter knew the Qurʾān by heart and had extensive experience in dotting, as suggested by his mapping dots in relation to the other dots on the page. That the manuscript's dotting reveals the dotter's awareness of a cluster of different readings—while maintaining a degree of creativity in deciding what to mark and what to leave unmarked—is indicative of the stage of development in which the dotter was operating, the possible learning or working context, and the community of readers in which dotter operated (Nasser 2020, 167–168). Further, the dotter of MS BnF ar. 340c seems to be skilled in the art of dotting, to have knowledge, to be aware of, different readings for some words, and to have solid grammatical knowledge. The dotter pays some attention to the physical placement of the dots, not only with regard to their phonological and grammatical meaning, but also with the aim of achieving a carefully executed network of dots on the page.

The first layer of the artefact may have been produced in the eighth/ninth century, following the subdivision system of the text attributed to Baṣra alone, e.g., marking a five-verse group at the end of Q.13 (f.33v, l.3), where the Baṣra system alone counts 45 verses in Q.13. The manuscript shows three possible layers of vowel-dotting whose techniques seem to be part of the developmental stage of the vowel system, with some traces of a relative and relational system from the ninth/tenth century, not yet perfected into an absolute system. It is not intended to disambiguate the reading. It is rather a work with an educational or professional purpose for reciting the text and making explicit the pronunciation of specific words within a given system of readings. The system based on dots is inefficient as a means of disambiguating the text, as the same dot position can express different values, while the same value can be expressed by different dot positions. The *rasm* does not conform to the uniform consonantal text of the Qurʾān, and the dotter did not amend it, but marked the *rasm* without adapting it. The dotter did not follow a single reader known from the canonical collections of the time, but applied a unique marking to the text using the potentialities of the undotted positions of the writing system.

The inefficiency of the system created ambiguities, especially in a manuscript with a small script. These ambiguities reveal the original nature of the system (i.e., to indicate positions or functions and not sounds), but also the reason for abandoning the dot layer only when the system was changed to answer the need to mark sounds and the details of recitation.

Appendix A. Undotted Monosyllabic Particles

- **The conjunction *fa-*** is dotted in three cases when preceding *ʾalif waṣla* (3 dotted cases out of 17 occurrences of contextual *ʾalif waṣla* among the 119 *fa-*), i.e., Q.14:22:22, *fa-stajabtumu* (f.35r, l.13); Q.21:90:1, *fa-stajabnā* (f.41r, l.4) and Q.21:92:8, *fa-ʿbudūni* (f.41r, l.10). It is unclear what the rationale is behind the dotting of 3 out of 17 *fa-* followed by *ʾalif waṣla*. In *fa-ʾasqayna-kumū-hu*, the dotter placed the red dot above the letter *fāʾ*, but this could be due to the idiosyncrasies of the dotter in placing the round dots. The red dot piercing the top head of *fāʾ* is likely related to the following letter *ʾalif* which, according to the observed rules, should be dotted (Q.15:22:8 in f.38r, l.4).
- **The conjunction *wa-*** is undotted in the overall majority of cases (458 out of 468 occurrences). Three cases are illegible; six conjunctions are marked with a dot above the baseline (*wa-*) and one conjunction is marked with a dot piercing the letter *wāw* below the baseline (*wi-*). In Q:13:15:11, the dotter (f.31r, l.3) placed a dot inside the second *wāw* denoting the conjunction rather than attaching it to the first *wāw* that marks the genitive case in the expression *bi-l-ġuduwwi **wa**-l-ʾaṣāli* ('in the mornings and the evenings'). This is likely due to the habit of the dotter of placing dots between words beyond the boundary space.[38] Three occurrences of the conjunction *wa-* in the context of *ʾa-wa-lam* (3 out of 3) are dotted. In f.37r, l.10, the dotter added three dots to *wa-li-yaḏḏakkara* in Q.14:52:11 (*wa-li-yaʿlamū ʾannamā huwa ʾilāhun wāḥidun wa-li-yaḏḏakkara ʾulū l-ʾalbābi*, i.e., 'and that they may know that He is One God, and that all possessed of minds may remember'): one dot above the conjunction *wa-*; one dot below the particle *li-*

38 Note the non-canonical variant *bi-l-ġuduwwi wa-l-ʾīṣāli* (EVQ in Q.13:15).

and one dot above *rāʾ* to mark the ending of the imperfect subjunctive form.[39] The two remaining occurrences of dotted *wa-* precede *ʾalif waṣla*, i.e., *wa-ttaqū* (Q.15:69:1, f.39r, l.16) and *wa-bna-hā* (Q.21:91:9, f.41r, l.8) which amounts to two dotted *wa-* out of 66 occurrences of *wa-* before *ʾalif waṣla*.

- **The particle *yā-***: the only dotted vocative particle *yā-* (out of 6 occurrences) is in Q.22:49:2 (f.45v, l.11), *yā-ʾayyuhā l-nāsu*, which does not follow the patterns as the letter block *yāʾ* + *ʾalif* has two dots and there is a dot between *hāʾ* and *ʾalif* whereas the long vowel /ā/ is very rarely dotted.

Appendix B. Dotting of Affixed *Lām*

Out of 232 occurrences, the particle *lām* is marked as *li-* 57 times, as *la-* 86 times, and it is undotted (*li-* or *la-*) 94 times.
The particle *li-* is consistently dotted when prefixed to:

- *allaḏīna in li-llaḏīna* (6 out of 6)
- nouns (25 out of 33, with a clear rule for nouns with the prefixed article, i.e., 14 dotted nouns out of 16 occurrences)

It is consistently undotted when prefixed to:

- *allāh* in *li-llāhi* (9 out of 9 occurrences)
- the pronominal suffix of 1sg (4 out of 4 occurrences according to the general rule of the unmarked long vowel)

---

[39] In the whole sentence (and page) only this occurrence of the conjunction *wa-* is dotted. It should be noted that the first layer of the *rasm* has been adjusted at a later stage. There are two denticles after the initial particle *li-* probably expressing the fifth form affix /ta/, which is probably missing in the script due to assimilation (*wa-li-yataḏakkara* > *wa-li-yaḏḏakkara*). Then *wa-* is preceded by *tanwīn ḍamma*, i.e., *ʾilāhun wāḥidun wa-li-yaḏḏakkara*.

The particle *la-* is consistently dotted when prefixed to:

- pronominal suffixes (74 out of 79 occurrences)

But it is consistently undotted when prefixed to:

- pronouns in their independent form (4 out of 5 occurrences)
- nouns (25 out of 26 occurrences)
- *qad* in *la-qad* (11 out of 11 occurrences)

Appendix C. Dotting Endings of Imperfect Verbs

The patterns for dotting the ending of the imperfect are as follows.

- **3sg.m**: out of 152 occurrences of the 3sg.m, 21 forms end in a long vowel (18 undotted forms marked by *yā'* or *wāw* only and 3 dotted forms, i.e., the letter *yā'* is preceded twice by the i–dot in *ya'tī-hu* and once by /a/ in *yūḥā*). Among the remaining 131 forms, 107 dots mark forms ending in a short vowel. The ending of the imperfect is always unmarked when followed by the energic *nūn* (6 out of 6 occurrences), and the *nūn* is marked reading /*na*/ in three cases. Of the remaining 18 undotted forms, 11 are likely marking the imperfect jussive, and 7 ending in an unmarked short vowel (one of the 7 occurrences being difficult to read). In *li-yaġfira* (Q.14:10:11), the dotter marked only /i/ below initial *lām* and left the rest of the expression unmarked. The presence of *li-*, which is marked, clarifies the reading of the ending of the subjunctive form. However, this is not the rule for the dotter, who almost always marked the endings in this system. It is possible that the dotter did not mark the final /a/ due to the major assimilation of final *-ra* into the following initial *la-* in *li-yaġfira* + *la-kum(u)*. All five undotted endings are followed by a pronominal suffix.[40]

[40] No other occurrences of imperfect 3sg.m ending in *-ra* and followed by a word beginning with *la-* were found in the manuscript to establish

- **3sg.f**: out of the 33 occurrences of the 3sg.f, 18 forms ending in a short vowel are marked with dots. All 13 forms ending in a long vowel are undotted and marked only by *yāʾ*. One undotted form likely corresponds to the jussive, and there is only one undotted form that likely corresponds to /u/ in the indicative, although the script is rather unclear at this point.
- **2sg.m**: out of the 23 occurrences of the 2sg.m, 5 forms end in *yāʾ* that mark a long vowel (4 undotted forms marked by *yāʾ* only, and one dotted form, i.e., the letter *yāʾ* is preceded by an i–dot in *taʾtī-nā*) and one form (*li-tatluwa* in Q. 13:30:10) ends in an unmarked *wāw* followed by *ʾalif*. Among the remaining 17 forms, there are 4 forms that likely express the jussive form, 10 dotted forms, and 3 undotted forms when followed by an energic *nūn* that is dotted (3 out 3 occurrences).
- **1sg**: out of 10 occurrences of the 1sg, there are 3 undotted forms ending in a long vowel marked by *yāʾ* and *wāw* only; 3 undotted forms followed by an emphatic *nūn* (which is dotted in two occurrences); one undotted form likely corresponding to a jussive. There are three dots marking forms ending in a short vowel.
- **1pl**: out of 33 occurrences of the 1pl, 5 forms end in a long vowel marked by *yāʾ* only. Out of the remaining 28 occurrences, 16 are marked with a dot. Among the 12 unmarked endings, 2 forms are likely in the jussive form; 6 forms are followed by an emphatic *nūn*, which is dotted to read /na/ when it ends the word and when the emphatic *nūn* assimilates with the *nūn* of the root (s-k-n) also in the rasm.

In the suffixes of the imperfect form, only short vowels are marked, namely:

---

a rule regarding possible assimilation and the system of leaving the first syllable *-ra* unmarked before the second syllable *-la*. However, the unique case of the perfect mentioned above supports this hypothesis.

- **3pl.m**: /a/ is marked in *-ūna* (54 dotted nūn out of 54 occurrences), while the 22 jussives and subjunctives are expressed by *wāw* only as long vowels are unmarked.
- **2pl.m**: /a/ is marked in *-ūna* (13 out of 14 occurrences). The undotted /na/ in *tadʿūna-nā* in Q.14:9:35 is likely related to the assimilation of /na/ into the following pronominal suffix /nā/, which is also attested as a non-canonical reading (i.e., *tadʿūna-nā* and *tadʿūn-nā*). The single occurrence of emphatic *nūn* in Q.14:13:9, *la-taʿūdun*-na, shows two stages in the manuscript: a first layer with two *nūn* characters and a second layer with one single *nūn* character vowelled with an a–dot. The 10 subjunctive and jussive forms ending in *wāw* are undotted.
- **3pl.f**: /a/ is marked in *-na* (2 dotted endings out of 2 occurrences).
- **3d.m**: /i/ is marked in *-āni* (1 dotted ending out of 1 occurrence).

Appendix D. Dotting Prefixes of Imperfect Verbs

The dotter marked with an a–dot the prefixes of the imperfect forms of the verbs:

- *ʾatā* (9 occurrences of *naʾtī-kumu, yaʾtī-kumu, yaʾtī-hu, yaʾtī-humu, yaʾtū-ka, yaʾtiya, taʾtiyu-kum*, and *yaʾtiya-humu*)
- *ʾakala* (1 occurrence of *yaʾkulū*)
- *šāʾa* (9 occurrences of *yašāʾu* and *našāʾu*)
- *kāna* (1 occurrence of *takun*)
- *wajila* (1 occurrence of *tawjal*)
- *saqā* (1 occurrence of *wa-yasqī* in Q. 14:16:4)[41]

[41] The dot is placed above the first denticle, piercing its top, probably indicating the reading *wa-yasqī*, while the base text reads *wa-yusqā* and no variants are known (EVQ in Q.14:16:4).

The 1sg starting with *ʾalif*, which is dotted according to the observed patterns (see section 3.3.2.).

The strategy of the dotter is to mark the prefixes in /u/ that characterize the beginning of the second, third, and fourth forms (11 out of 19, 3 out of 6, and 42 out of 72 occurrences, respectively), as well as the passive voice in the first form (5 occurrences) and in the fifth form (1 occurrence). He dotted 62 occurrences of *yu-*, *tu-*, *nu-*, *ʾu*. It is unclear why the dotter sometimes dotted the prefix and sometimes left it unmarked in the same lemma (e.g., *yušrik* marked in Q. 22:31:7 and *tušriku* unmarked in Q.22:26:8 or *yuʿaẓẓim* marked in Q. 22:32:3, f.44v, l.3 and unmarked in Q. 22:30:3, f.44r, l.13). In some cases, such as the latter example, the brown ink of the *rasm* may have faded and the absence of a dot could be an accident of the materiality of the script.

When considering the whole dotting system of the manuscript, it is evident the consistency in marking the ending of the imperfect in its forms with short vowel, and the general tendency to mark prefixes when vocalised in /u/ and—in some contexts—when vocalised in /a/. This consistency contrasts with the dotting of the body of the imperfect form. The body of the imperfect is undotted, except for 55 cases that include 10 dots for marking short vowels attached to *ʾalif*,[42] *wāw* and *yāʾ* and 2 dots in the groups *rāʾ*+*wāw* and *zāy*+*wāw* in *wa-yadraʾūna* in Q.13:22:13 and *yastahziʾūna* in Q.15:11:8. Out of the total 355 imperfect forms, only 43 dots mark the vocalisation of the imperfect in its

[42] The count includes the manuscript spelling of *yastaʾkirūna* with *ʾalif* in Q.15:11:8.

body: 14 dots in the first form; 6 dots in the second form to mark the geminated letter (and also /a/ in the fully dotted *yukaḏḏibū-ka* in Q.22:42:2);[43] 2 dots mark the characteristic /i/ in the third form; 17 dots mark the characteristic /i/ in the fourth form and 1 dot marks the passive *tujab* (f.36v, l.12);[44] 3 dots mark /a/ for the geminated *kāf* in the occurrences of the imperfect of *tawak-kala*.

Appendix E. Examples of Dotting *ʾAlif*, *Wāw* and *Yāʾ*

- *maʾāb* (*maʾābin* and *maʾābi* in Q.13:29:8 and Q.13:36:25) and *qurʾān* (*qurʾānan*, *wa-qurʾānin*, and *wa-l-qurʾāna* in Q.13:31:3, Q.15:1:5 and Q.15:87:6) have a dot at the upper right and a dot at the left of the ascender of *ʾalif* in f.32r, l.10; f.33r, l.3; f.32r, l.14; f.37r, l.13 and f.39v, l.15. Given the habit of placing a–dots, the two dots make explicit the reading with the glottal stop and the long vowel /ā/, i.e., *maʾāb* and *qurʾān*, against the reading expressed by a single dot to the right or left of *ʾalif*, i.e., *māb* and *qurān*. Despite the absence of a *hamza* sign, there seems to have been an awareness of the glottal stop reading, and the mechanism designed to mark it within the dot system was the dot to the right of *ʾalif* in addition to the one to its left.
- *yayʾasi* (يَايْـَٔسِ) in *ʾa-fa-lam yayʾasi llaḏīna ʾāmanū ʾan* ('Did not the

[43] A form dotted to mark the geminate letter is *yuṯabbitu* in Q.13:39:5 (f.33r, l.9), which is also read as *yuṯbitu* by Ibn Kaṯīr, Abū ʿAmr and ʿĀṣim (EVQ and VLC in Q.13:39:5).

[44] In Q.14:44:14, *[y]ujab* is followed by the accusative *daʿwata-ka* (f.36v,l.12), while the structure *tujab* followed by the nominative *daʿwatu-ka* is known as a non-canonical reading by Abū Muʿāḏ (al-Faḍl b. Ḵālid an-Naḥwī al-Marwazī) (EVQ and VLC in Q.14:44:14).

believers know that [...]?' in Q.13:31:20) has been marked with a dot attached to *ʾalif* and a dot marking the ending *-i* (f.32r, l.16). The reading of the dot at the baseline level to the left of *ʾalif* may indicate the reading /i/ of *ʾalif*, later made explicit with the letter *yāʾ* (Puin 2011, 149), although the damaged ink and parchment prevent us from being certain about this. It is worth noting the alternative reading among the seven Readings, i.e., *yāyasi*.

- *wa-ʾafʾidatuhum* ('[and] their Hearts' in Q.14:43:8) has been marked with a dot attached to the initial *ʾalif* at the upper right and a dot after the final *mīm* (f.36v, ll.9–10). According to the rules of the manuscript's relational system, the reading is probably *wa-ʾafidatu-hum-u* (like in van Putten 2022, 257).

- *yastaʾḵirūna* ('they put [it] back' in Q.15:5:7) and *l-mustaʾḵirīna* ('the laggards' in Q.15:24:7) are spelled in the manuscript with *ʾalif* between *tāʾ* and *ḵāʾ*, which is not the usual spelling in other early manuscripts.[45] The dotter marked /i/ (below *ḵāʾ*), characteristic of the tenth form, and the ending /a/, but also marked *tāʾ* followed by *ʾalif* in f.37v, l.1 (the reading is likely *yastaʾḵirūna*) and left *tāʾ* unmarked in f.38r, l.6 (the reading is likely *l-mustāḵirūna*)—if we apply the rules observed in the manuscript. On the same page of the first example (f.37v, l.8), *yastahziʾūna* ('they mocked [at him]' in Q.15:11:8) is marked with its characteristic /i/ after the second radical letter and ending /a/ and the dotter has added a dot to the upper right of *wāw* to mark the reading of the *hamza*, i.e., *yastahziʾūna* rather than the reading /u/.

- The position of the dot attributed to *wāw* can reveal the reading. The dotter marks *wāw* in *muʾmin* ('believer') with a dot to the left, probably indicating *mūmin* (5 out of 5 occurrences); in

[45] See, for example, MS BnF ar. 334c, f.34v, l.21 (*yastaḵirūna* is spelled without *ʾalif* and dotted on *tāʾ* and *ḵāʾ*) and f.35r, l.20 (*al-mustaḵirīna* is spelled without *ʾalif* and dotted on *tāʾ* and *ḵāʾ*).

yuʾminūn/tuʾminūna, *wāw* is marked with a dot above the centre of the top of the *wāw* or to the upper right and a dot to the left, almost touching the following *mīm* in f.37v, l.9 and equidistant from *wāw* and *mīm* in f.39r, l.13) or only one dot to its left (f.46r, ll.5–6); in *tuʾtī* (Q.14:25:1) the dotter placed one dot to the left of the first denticle (/tu/) and one dot to the left of *wāw*, while in 14 of the 15 occurrences of the imperfect form vocalised in /a/, i.e., *yaʾt-*, *taʾt-* and *naʾt-*, the dot was attached only to the denticle or to the *ʾalif*. In the two occurrences of *yuʾaḵḵiru-hum-u*, only the initial denticle is marked by a dot, whereas the *wāw* is unmarked. The variability in the dotting of *wāw* in a closed syllable of the imperfect forms suggests a developmental stage in the dotting system.

- *fa-kaʾayyin* in Q.22:45:1 (f.45v, l.1) is dotted in its denticle only to mark /i/, and the absence of a dot associated with *ʾalif* seems to express the reading of a long /a/ after /k/ as in *fa-kāʾin* rather than *fa-kaʾayyin*, two ways of reading it according to the system of the Seven Readings (see EVQ).
- *ʾulāʾika* in Q.14:3:13 (f.33v, ll.10–11) is not dotted in its *ʾalif* probably due to the deterioration of the ink and parchment, as the other six dotted occurrences seem to suggest. The ending of the previous word in the accusative indefinite form (*ʿiwajan*) is undotted against the phonological rule that makes explicit the behaviour of *tanwīn* followed by hamza (see above). This may imply the different phonological value of *ʾalif* followed by *wāw* and *ʾalif* dotted with /a/ or /i/ e.g., in *jamīʿan* + *ʾa-fa-lam* (Q.13:31:18–19, f.32r, l.16) and *wa-nūḥan* + *ʾiḏ* (Q.21:76:1, f.40r, l.12).

Appendix F. Dotting of Participles

The manuscript has 192 occurrences of participles, of which only 32 are dotted as follows:

- 11 active participles in pattern I are dotted to mark the vowel /i/ below the second radical of the root (8 occurrences); the *ʾimāla* in the first radical of *al-kāfirīna* (3 occurrences) and in one case, the dotter also marked the vowel /a/ above the first radical in addition to the /i/ of the second radical.
- 1 active participle in pattern III, 11 in pattern IV, 1 in pattern VI and 2 in pattern X are dotted to mark the vowel /i/ below the second radical characterizing the active form.[46]
- 4 passive participles in pattern IV are dotted to mark the vowel /a/ above the second radical that characterises the passive form.
- 2 active participles in pattern V and 1 in pattern VI are dotted to mark the infix *-ta-* that characterises the pattern.

Considering the dotted forms of the participles in comparison to the undotted ones in internal position, the manuscript has the following:

- 95 out of 106 occurrences of pattern I are internally undotted, while only 5 of them are unmarked in their ending.
- 2 out of 2 occurrences of pattern II are internally undotted, whereas their endings are marked.
- 1 out of 2 occurrences of pattern III is internally undotted, while the endings are marked according to the rules listed above (i.e., undotted *tanwīn* in the accusative because of the phonetic rule in one occurrence and dotting of the plural suffix *-īna* in the other).
- 32 out 47 occurrences of pattern IV are not dotted internally, while they are all marked in their endings according to the rules listed above (e.g., phonetic rule applied to *tanwīn* in the accusative).

---

[46] In two instances of pattern II, the active form is marked by the dotter, whereas other manuscripts (and the base text) have the passive form.

- 2 out of 2 occurrences of pattern V are internally dotted and marked in their ending.
- 1 out of 1 occurrence of pattern VI is internally dotted and marked in its ending.
- 2 out of 2 occurrences of pattern VIII are internally undotted, while they are marked in their ending.
- 1 out of 1 occurrence of pattern IX is internally undotted, while it is marked in its ending.
- 4 out of 6 occurrences of pattern V are internally undotted, while they are all marked in their ending.

References

Ackoff, Russell L. 1989. 'From Data to Wisdom'. *Journal of Applied Systems Analysis* 16 (1): 3–9.

al-Dānī, Abū ʿAmr ʿUṯmān b. Saʿīd b. ʿUṯmān. 2004. *al-Muḥkam fī Naqṭ al-Maṣāḥif*, edited by Muḥammad Ḥasan Muḥammad Ḥasan Ismāʿīl. Beirut: Dār al-kutub al-ʿilmīyah.

al-Ġarnāṭī, Abū Ḥayyān. 1993. *Tafsīr al-Baḥr al-Muḥīṭ*, edited by ʿĀdil Aḥmad ʿAbd al-Mawjūd et al. 8 vols. Beirut: Dār al-kutub al-ʿilmiyya.

al-Shdaifat, Younis, Ahmad Al-Jallad, Zeyad al-Salameen, and Rafe Harahsheh. 2017. 'An Early Christian Arabic Graffito Mentioning "Yazīd the King"'. *Arabian Archaeology and Epigraphy* 28 (2): 315–324.

Arberry, Arthur J. 1964 [1955]. *The Koran Interpreted.* London: Oxford University Press.

Barthes, Roland. 1979. *Elements of Semiology*. Translated by Annette Lavers and Colin Smith. New York: Hill and Wang.

Cellard, Eléonore. 2015. 'La vocalisation des manuscrits coraniques dans les premiers siècles de l'islam'. In *Les origines du Coran, le Coran des origines*, edited by François Déroche, Christian Robin, and Michel Zink, 151–176. Paris: Académie des Inscriptions et Belles-Lettres.

Crellin, Robert. 2019. 'Writing Vowels in Punic. From Morphography to Phonography'. *Written Language & Literacy* 22 (2): 198–222.

Déroche, François. 1983. *Les manuscrits du coran. Aux origines de la calligraphie coranique. Catalogue des manuscrits arabes. Deuxième partie: manuscrits musulmans, Tome I-1*. Paris: Bibliothèque Nationale.

———. 1990. 'The Qurʾān of Amāǧūr'. *Manuscripts of the Middle East* 5: 59–66.

———. 1992. *The Abbasid Tradition: Qurʾans of the 8th to 10th Centuries AD*. The Nasser D. Khalili Collection of Islamic Art, vol. 1. London: Nour Foundation, in association with Azimuth Editions and Oxford University Press.

———. 2009. *La transmission écrite du Coran dans les débuts de l'islam. Le codex Parisino-petropolitanus*. Leiden: Brill.

———. 2014. *Qurʾans of the Umayyads. A First Overview*. Leiden: Brill.

Déroche, François, and Sergio Noja Noseda. 1998. *Le manuscrit arabe 328 (a) de la Bibliothèque nationale de France*. Sources de la transmission manuscrite du texte coranique. Les manuscrits de style ḥiǧāzī. vol. 1. Lesa, Paris: Fondazione Ferni Noja Noseda and Bibliothèque nationale de France.

———. 2001. *Le manuscrit Or.2165 (f.1 à 61) de la British Library.* Sources de la transmission manuscrite du texte coranique, I, Les manuscrits de style ḥiǧāzī, vol. 2, 1. Lesa, London: Fondazione Ferni Noja Noseda and British Library.

Dutton, Yasin. 1999 'Red Dots, Green Dots, Yellow Dots and Blue: Some Reflections on the Vocalisation of Early Qurʾanic Manuscripts, Part I'. *Journal of Qurʾanic Studies* 1 (1): 115–140.

———. 2000. 'Red Dots, Green Dots, Yellow Dots and Blue: Some Reflections on the Vocalisation of Early Qurʾanic Manuscripts, Part II'. *Journal of Qurʾanic Studies* 2 (1): 1–24.

———. 2001. 'An Early Muṣḥaf According to the Reading of Ibn ʿĀmir'. *Journal of Qurʾanic Studies* 3 (1): 71–89.

———. 2004. 'Some Notes on the British Library's 'Oldest Qurʾan Manuscript' (Or. 2165)'. *Journal of Qurʾanic Studies* 6 (1): 43–71.

Fedeli, Alba. 2024. 'Early Qurʾānic Manuscripts: Re-mediating Their Manuscript Page in the Most Recent Digital Form as Part of the InterSaME Project'. In *The Qurʾān and its Handwritten Transmission in Current Research*, edited by François Déroche, 53–104. Leiden: Brill.

Frost, Ram, Leonard Katz, and Shlomo Bentin. 1987. 'Strategies for Visual Word Recognition and Orthographical Depth: A Multilingual Comparison'. *Journal of Experimental Psychology: Human Perception and Performance* 13 (1): 104–115.

George, Alain F. 2015a. 'Coloured Dots and the Question of Regional Origins in Early Qurʾans (Part I)'. *Journal of Qurʾanic Studies* 17 (1): 1–44.

———. 2015b. 'Coloured Dots and the Question of Regional Origins in Early Qur'ans (Part II)'. *Journal of Qur'anic Studies* 17 (2): 75–102.

Hilali, Asma. 2021. 'The Qur'ān before the Book. History and Concepts of Qur'ānic Variants (*qirā'āt*)'. *Journal of College and Sharia and Islamic Studies* 38 (2): 233–245.

Imbert, Frédéric. 2012. 'Réflexions sur les formes de l'écrit à l'aube de l'Islam'. *Proceedings of the Seminar for Arabian Studies* 42: 119–128.

Ince, Barış. 2023. 'Arabe 330b: The Discovery of Two Canonical Readings'. *Journal of Islamic Manuscripts* 14 (2–4): 115–154.

Jeffery, Arthur, and Isaac Mendelsohn. 2011. 'The Orthography of the Samarqand Qur'ān Codex'. In *Which Koran? Variants, Manuscripts, Linguistics*, edited by Ibn Warraq, 367–403. New York: Prometheus Books.

Kaplony, Andreas. 2008. 'What are those few dots for? Thoughts on the Orthography of the Qurra Papyri (709–710), the Khurasan Parchments (755–777) and the Inscription of the Jerusalem Dome of the Rock (692)'. *Arabica* 55 (1): 91–112.

Kerr, Robert M. 2010. *Latino-Punic Epigraphy. A Descriptive Study of the Inscriptions*. Tübingen: Mohr Siebeck.

———. 2013. 'Phoenician–Punic: The View Backward—Phonology versus Paleography'. In *Linguistic Studies in Phoenician*, edited by Robert D. Holmstedt and Aaron Schade, 9–29. Winona Lake: Eisenbrauns.

Marx, Michael Josef, and Tobias J. Jocham. 2019. 'Radiocarbon (^{14}C) Dating of Qur'ān Manuscripts'. In *Qur'ān Quotations*

Preserved on Papyrus Documents, 7th–10th Centuries and the Problem of Carbon Dating Early Qurʾāns, edited by Andreas Kaplony and Michael Marx, 188–221. Leiden: Brill.

Milo, Thomas. 2013. 'Toward Arabic Historical Script Grammar through Contrastive Analysis of Qurʾān Manuscripts'. In *Writings and Writing: Investigations in Islamic Text and Script, in Honour of Dr Januarius Justus Witkam*, edited by Robert M. Kerr and Thomas Milo, 249–292. Cambridge: Archetype.

Nasser, Shady H. 2020. *The Second Canonization of the Qurʾān (324/936). Ibn Mujāhid and the Founding of the Seven Readings*. Leiden: Brill.

Nöldeke, Theodore, Friedrich Schwally, Gotthelf Bergsträsser, and Otto Pretzl. 2013. *The History of the Qurʾān*, edited and translated by Wolfgang H. Behn. Leiden: Brill.

Ohnuki-Tierney, Emiko. 1994a. Review of *The Empire of Signs; Elements of Semiology and Writing Degree Zero, by Roland Barthes. Semiotica* 96 (3–4): 301–308.

———. 1994b. 'The Power of Absence: Zero Signifiers and Their Transgressions'. *L'Homme* 34, 130: 59–76

Posegay, Nick. 2020. 'Connecting the Dots: The Shared Phonological Tradition in Syriac, Arabic, and Hebrew Vocalization'. In *Studies in Semitic Vocalisation and Reading Traditions*, edited by Aaron D. Hornkohl and Geoffrey Khan, 191–226. Cambridge: Open Book Publishers.

———. 2021. *Points of Contact: The Shared Intellectual History of Vocalisation in Syriac, Arabic, and Hebrew*. Cambridge Semitic Languages and Cultures. Cambridge: Open Book Publishers.

Puin, Gerd R. 2011. 'Vowel Letters and Ortho-epic Writing in the Qurʾān'. In *New Perspectives on the Qurʾān. The Qurʾān in Its Historical Context 2*, edited by Gabriel Said Reynolds. London: Routledge.

Rezvan, Efim A. 2004. *The Qurʾān of ʿUthmān (St.Petersburg, Katta-Langar, Bukhara, Tashkent), vol. I.* St. Petersburg: St. Petersburg Centre for Oriental Studies.

Timpanaro, Sebastiano. 1985 [1974]. *The Freudian Slip. Psychoanalysis and Textual Criticism*. London: Verso.

van Putten, Marijn. 2019. 'Arabe 334a. A Vocalized Kufic Quran in a Non-Canonical Hijazi Reading'. *Journal of Islamic Manuscripts* 10 (3): 327–375.

———. 2022. *Quranic Arabic. From Its Hijazi Origins to Its Classical Reading Traditions*. Leiden: Brill.

Versteegh, Cornelis H. M. 1993. *Arabic Grammar and Qurʾanic Exegesis in Early Islam*. Leiden: Brill.

Datasets

Dukes, Kais 2009–2017. *The Quranic Arabic Corpus*. Maintained by the quran.com team. School of Computing, University of Leeds. https://corpus.quran.com/, last accessed 1 January 2024.

Encyclopedia of the [Variant] Readings of the Qurʾan [EVQ], edited by Shady Hekmat Nasser. Harvard Digital Humanities. https://erquran.org/, last accessed 1 January 2024.

Manuscripta Coranica [MC], published by Berlin-Brandenburgische Akademie der Wissenschaften, edited by Michael Marx. https://corpuscoranicum.de/en/manuscripts/, last accessed 1 January 2024.

Variae Lectiones Coranicae [VLC], published by Berlin-Brandenburgische Akademie der Wissenschaften, edited by Michael Marx. https://corpuscoranicum.de/de/verse-navigator/sura/1/verse/1/variants, last accessed 1 January 2024.

NEW APPROACHES TO ANALYSING THE VOCALISATION OF EARLY QUR'ĀNIC MANUSCRIPTS[1]

Alba Fedeli, Carolin Kinne-Wall, and Hythem Sidky

1.0. The Early Arabic Vocalisation System

This paper aims at providing detailed descriptions of the methods used to create new approaches and tools to analyse the vocalisation of early Arabic that combines traditional philological approaches and new techniques afforded by digital imaging and encoding of datasets.

[1] This research is part of InterSaME project that ran from 2020 to 2023 and was funded by the Deutsche Forschungsgemeinschaft (DFG, German Research Foundation), project number: 428993887. The team was composed of its PI, Alba Fedeli, as a palaeographer, philologist and editor in collaboration with Carolin Kinne-Wall (from September 2022) as a developer, and Hythem Sidky, as an analyst. Initially, the project benefited from the contribution of Alicia González Martínez, as a computational linguist (until September 2022). Fedeli's proposal and then methodology designed during the project has been greatly influenced by the philosopher Dino Buzzetti with his ideas on text encoding (see, for example, Buzzetti 2002 and 2004). This article benefited from all these inputs and suggestions. Its writing and the results here presented are to be attributed solely to the three co-authors.

 https://doi.org/10.11647/OBP.0498.09

The early Arabic vocalisation system was most likely developed and introduced in Qurʾānic manuscripts in the eighth century. The system—based on a colour and position code of rounded dots and lines—was later replaced by vowel-symbols that correspond to the modern Arabic system. The new, developed system first appeared in non-Qurʾānic manuscripts in the ninth century, but the archaic dot system continued to be used in Qurʾānic manuscripts for a longer period (Abbott 1939, Posegay 2021a and 2021b). In the history of script scholarship, there are many cases of the disappearance of writing systems (Baines-Bennet-Houston 2008). What is rare, however, is the disappearance of only one component of the script, as found in the Arabic writing system. There was a replacement of vowel-dots with vowel-symbols, whereas the consonantal skeleton (*rasm*) and the consonantal diacritic system have been kept.

Studies of the vocalisation of Qurʾānic manuscripts have largely focused on the reading traditions they belong to. While this is an important part of understanding the context and history of the use of vocalisation, there are other aspects of this system that remain understudied. Beyond the values represented by the coloured dots (i.e., *a, u, i, an, un, in,* etc.), subtleties of dot placement can also encode other information, such as orthoepic elements of recitation. For example, much is known about the orientation of *tanwīn* dots which, in some instances, when oriented horizontally rather than vertically, denote *ʾik̲fāʾ*, i.e., partial assimilation or concealment of the nasal, as described in al-Dānī (2004, 49–52). Additionally, just as the study of palaeography can reveal much about manuscript chronology, scribal traditions, habits, and regional practices, there is potential for a palaeographic study of vocalisation to do the same. Finally, most vocalised manuscripts are only partially dotted. Understanding the context within which a letter is dotted can provide insight into implied and counterfactual readings and into morphology.

The first step in working towards understanding the aforementioned aspects of vocalisation is to develop an objective way of encoding vocalisation that is divorced from the phonetic value of the vocalisation itself. This is the focus of this article. We explore the development of vocalisation transcription methods and offer preliminary insights into the potential ways in which these methods can be used to study vocalisation in new ways. We also document our workflow, problems encountered, and possible directions of further development of the methodology and tools. The specific results produced by the analysis presented in this article are instrumental examples to illustrate the methodology and its development. They are not a comprehensive representation of the dotting system of the manuscripts.

Another important aspect of this study is to identify to what extent digital analysis can augment, validate, or otherwise evaluate insights identified through traditional philological work. A scholar who works with an object for an extended period of time will record observations, formulate hypotheses, and identify potential patterns in the data. Often those observations are not formally demonstrated or backed by systematic documentation. In the context of this project, we seek to demonstrate the viability of leveraging digital analysis of manuscript vocalisation patterns to gain new insights into scribal habits and validate independent observations made through traditional philological means. As part of an iterative process, the research questions concerning dot distribution and placement have shaped the methodology delineated here, and fostered the development of novel tools as discussed below.

2.0. Methodology and Tools to Encode the Dots

2.1. The Process of Digital Editing, Data Creation, and Analysis

The creation of digital editions of early Qurʾānic manuscripts are an important part of their analysis, that is ultimately shaped by an initial, traditional philological, and palaeographic analysis of the artefacts. Digital editions also enable shareability and reusability of data (Bechhofer et al. 2010; Aschenbrenner et al. 2013). The general structure of TEI markup has been the leading principle inserted in a scientific workflow and several formats. The editorial environment chosen to transcribe the manuscript text and features is Archetype, a software framework for palaeographic analysis and editing of manuscripts (Noël 2014–2024) that has been customised for Arabic Qurʾānic manuscripts vocalised with the early dotting system, named ArQuM, 'Archetype for Qurʾānic Manuscripts' (Fedeli 2023 and 2024).[2]

[2] The creation of digital editions is based on Fedeli's previous experience in editing Qurʾānic manuscripts during her PhD research at the Institute for Textual Scholarship and Electronic Editing at the University of Birmingham, and the challenges faced during the project of phylogenetic

2.2. Qualitative Description of Vowel-Dots

While transcribing Qurʾānic manuscripts, the editor observed some idiosyncrasies in the way in which dotters placed some dots, and a possible meaning expressed by that position (e.g., the /u/ dot at the left of a word final letter that pierces the initial letter of the following word). Hence, the first system we developed was designed to capture both the dot position (e.g., a u-dot piercing the following word) and the dot presence with its phonetic value (e.g., *ḍamma*). For the sake of clarity, the aim was to encode for example the position of /u/ dots marking the nominative or indicative ending of a word but piercing the first letter of the following word in comparison with the position of /u/ dots attached to the ending of a word (see Figure 1). The encoding creates structured data that is then processable and searchable.

Figure 1: Examples of /u/ dots attached to the ending of a word or piercing the first letter of the following word (Source gallica.bnf.fr / Bibliothèque nationale de France)

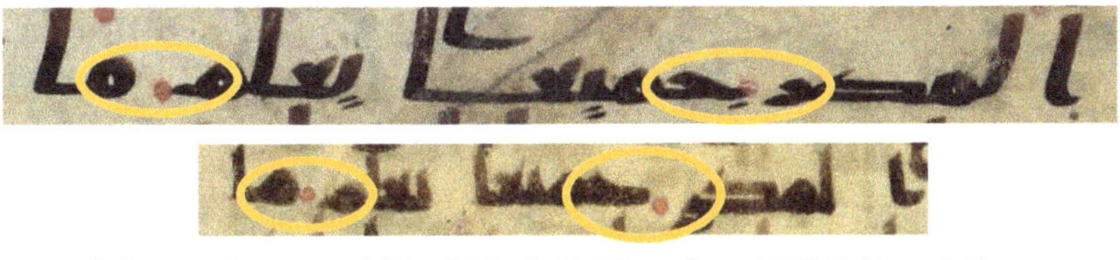

Detail from MS BnF.ar. 334c, f.32r, l.13 (above) and MS BnF.ar. 340c, f.33r, l.15 (below): *l-makru jamīʿan yaʿlamu mā* in Q.13:42

The transcription system uses Latin characters and symbols to transcribe the skeleton of the script and its diacritic layers building on the archigraphemic system developed by Thomas

analysis of several Qurʾānic manuscripts hosted at the Central European University in Budapest.

Milo (Milo 2013), i.e., capital Latin letters for the homographs and non-homographs (e.g., B for the denticle and M for *mīm*); apostrophes and commas for consonantal diacritics (e.g., B, for *bāʾ* with one comma and B'' with two apostrophes for *tāʾ*); miniature superscript and subscript vowels for transcribing a default majority position of dots (e.g., ^{a} for a dot above the letter at its centre on the x-axis and touching the outline of the body of the letter) specified by extra symbols when the dot is not at the centre and/or not touching the body of the letter (e.g., $^{a}\rightarrow$ for a dot above the letter, at its right). The dot syntax applies the following order:

$$\{^{u},^{a},_{i}\} \quad © \quad \{\rightarrow,\leftarrow,\leftrightarrow\}\ \{-,\neq\} \quad \{\uparrow,\updownarrow,\downarrow\} \quad !$$

- The copyright symbol (©) marking the piercing dot is placed in the first position, unless it is referred to the following or previous letter, i.e., when the dot is piercing the following/previous letter using the symbol $\neq$.
- The arrow symbols $\rightarrow$, $\leftarrow$ and $\leftrightarrow$ mark the dot position on the x-axis while the distance from the letter is marked by the hyphen symbol (–) when the dot is detached from the letter or the not equal to symbol ($\neq$) when the dot is close to the previous or following letter.
- The arrow symbols $\uparrow$, $\downarrow$ and $\updownarrow$ mark the dot position on the y-axis while the exclamatory mark refers to the dot detached from its letter on the y-axis.

The extra symbols are a more complex description and narrative of the dots that are not reduced to the symbols of *fatḥa*, *ḍamma* and *kasra*. The compromise of using the Latin alphabet offers not only a syntax for a qualitative description of the dots but also the possibility of tagging a specific layer of the writing system, e.g., to mark as unclear a single consonantal diacritic stroke or a single vowel dot in a pair.

2.3. Quantitative Description of Vowel Dots: A Pointer-based Encoding

In the editing process, the qualitative description of the dot's position by means of Latin characters and symbols is accompanied by a quantitative description by means of a pointer, a tool that describes the relationship between the letter and the dot in the manuscript image (see Figure 2). The palaeographic environment of Archetype/ArQuM enables the creation of the pointer, by linking images, dot position and transcription (see below).

Figure 2: Example of a manuscript page (MS BnF.ar.340c, f.33r) with dots' position described in relation to their letters by means of both a pointer (the vectors marked in yellow in the image) and extra symbol system (in the transcription below the image)

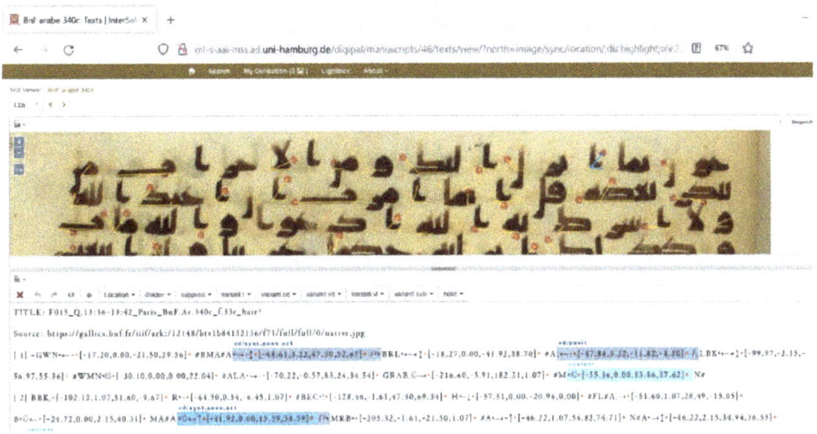

The pointer complements the qualitative description of the dots, solving its possible ambiguities.[3] This ambiguity inspired the development of a pointer-based transcription system. Each dot is described using a set of two vectors. The first vector defines the baseline and horizontal extent of a letter, and the second vector defines the position of the dot relative to the first vector. Together, both vectors can be used to determine the absolute placement of a dot relative to a letter in a manner that can adjust for variations in letter length and orientation.

Figure 3: Illustration of the pointer-based transcription system which uses two vectors to define the position of each dot relative to a letter. The vectors then go through a process of registration in order to normalise their positions and orientations to facilitate direct comparison.

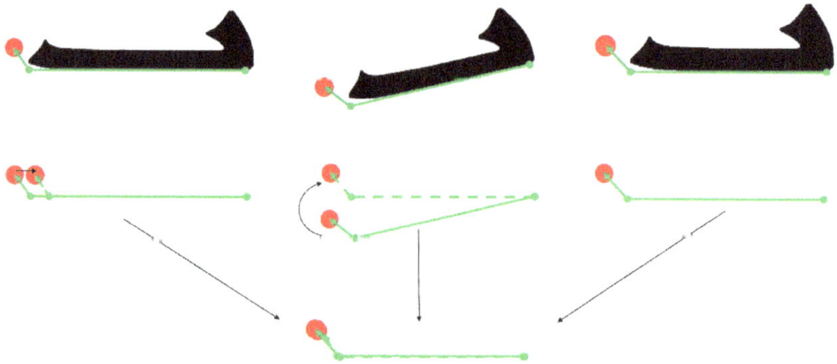

[3] For example, u-dot piercing the body of final *mīm* in its centre (i.e., ^{u}©↔) can coincide with a-dot piercing the body of the final *mīm* and placed inside its body (i.e., ^{a}©↕ or ^{a}©↓). The two qualitative descriptions are different (^{u}©↔ vs ^{a}©↕ or ^{a}©↓) but can indicate the same dot position.

This process is illustrated in Figure 3 using the homograph letter constituted by a single denticle in its final shape that can be disambiguated by means of diacritics as *bāʾ*, *tāʾ* and *ṯāʾ* (B in the transcription system based on archigraphemes). In this hypothetical example, there are three occurrences of final B with a dot placed to the left of each letter. In the first occurrence (top left), the scribe lengthened the letter compared to the other two instances. In the second occurrence (top middle), the body of the letter sits on a slightly oblique baseline compared to the other instances. The third occurrence (top right) represents an otherwise overall shape of the letter. Beneath each letter in the first row are two vectors marking both the baseline and the centre of the dot. These three sets then go through a process of registration to normalise their orientations and positions to facilitate direct comparison. This registration process proceeds in three steps. Using the horizontal axis as a frame of reference, the vectors are stretched and rotated such that the baseline lies along the horizontal axis and are of unit length. This optimisation process is shown in the central row of Figure 3. In this example, the first dot (left centre) is scaled to match the reference length but does not need any rotation. The second dot (middle centre) is rotated in order to match the reference orientation but does not need rescaling. The third dot (right centre) does not undergo any transformation as its scale and orientation already match the reference. In practice, every dot undergoes some degree of rotation and scaling due to natural variance against an abstract model.

The process described above is known in statistics as Procrustes analysis, and we implemented it using the Kabsch algorithm (Kabsch 1976). This type of analysis is commonly used in the fields of computer graphics and bioinformatics to align both point clouds and molecular structures. The final output of this process is shown in the bottom row of Figure 3, where the three dots are now optimally aligned.

In order for the pointer-based method to be practical, we developed an additional tool in Archetype/ArQuM. The pointer functionality was implemented through the OpenLayers API and TinyMCE editor, which are components used in the Archetype web application. The editor activates the tool and draws the initial line directly on the image of the manuscript page (see e.g., blue vectors in Figure 2). As previously stated, this initial line corresponds to the length of the body of the letter from its origin on the right and its end on the left at the baseline level. Then, the editor inserts an arrow starting from the end of the first line in the direction of the dot, up to its centre. This is all done in a single interaction for ease of use and, once the editor completes the third click, the information derived from the two vectors is automatically stored in the database as part of the manuscript transcription.

As described above, this pointer-based method accounts for scribal variation in the orientation and horizontal scale of a letter. What it does not account for is variation in the vertical scaling and skew of a letter. This decision was made as it is common for letters to have variable length and slight variations in orientation, while their height is consistent in the majority of the manuscripts.[4] Requiring the editor to enter a fourth point would accommodate this remaining issue but would also increase the burden and time required for transcription.

2.4. Digital Palaeography Performed through the Pointer

The pointer performs digital palaeography inasmuch it allows one to question the data collection and interpretation process in understanding the dots as part of the writing system. The vectors and visualisation produced are a metadata associated with each dot. The two vectors make explicit what the editor is transcribing. They make clear the scholar's decision in reading, for example, an unclear dot or connecting a dot to a word on the line above or on the line below.

In the example in Figure 4b, on the first line, the dot piercing the *ʾalif* at the right of its foot is attached to final *rāʾ* by the editor in reading *al-ḏikru*, while the dot touching the top of *ʾalif* on the line below is attached to the *ʾalif* after *al-ḏikru*, reading *ʾinna-ka*, all positions being marked by the dotter. In the example on the left (detail Figure 4a), on the first line, the lower dot of the pair marking the ending of *ʾajalin* was read by the editor after

---

[4] The rationale behind the decision of not including the height in the pointer encoding is the fact that a consistent height of letters is applied in the writing of Qurʾānic manuscripts as a consequence of fixed ruling. Ruling can be imaginary or materially executed (Gacek 2009, 203–204). On the contrary, the length of the body of a letter is never consistent but can be stretched or elongated to respect the justification of the text and the common rule of non-intersecting ascenders of a line with descenders of a previous line.

enhancement by filtering the image with a photo editing software; while the dot piercing the bottom right of the foot of *lām* is attached by the editor to the *lām* on the line below, reading *ʾa-wa-lam*. The pointer and the vectors enabled the editor both to make explicit her interpretation and determine the absolute placement of a dot relative to a letter.

The two representations of dots by means of characters and coordinates can be combined together in the analysis of the data from the manuscript editions thus reconciling qualitative and quantitative descriptions of the dots. This reconciliation proved to be successful in other fields (Robertson et al. 2017).

The digital data produced by the manuscript editions can be explored by performing different kinds of analysis that are shaped based on the initial palaeographical and philological observations of the editor. These observations have also been partially included in the manuscript editions as editorial notes. The investigation into the data depends on the granularity of the description and transcription of the manuscript text and features and by the way in which the data is enriched.

Figure 4: Examples of vectors that make explicit the interpretation of the editor in reading the dots (Source gallica.bnf.fr / Bibliothèque nationale de France)

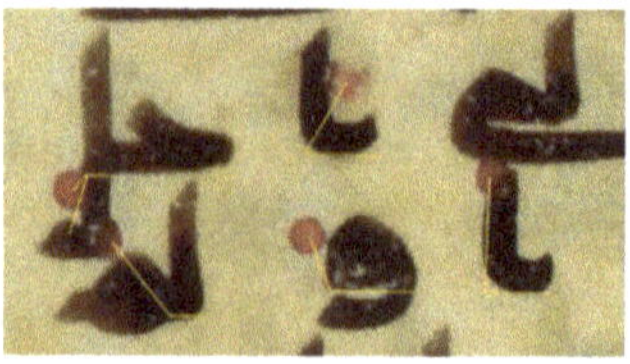

4a. Detail from MS BnF.ar. 340c, f.36v, ll.12–13: *[ʾi]lā ʾajalin and ʾa-wa-lam* in Q.14:44

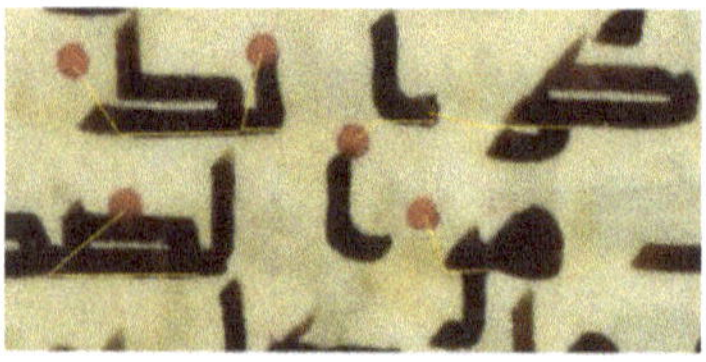

4b. Detail from MS BnF.ar. 340c, f.37v, ll.2–3: *[al-ḏi]kru ʾinna-ka and min-a l-ṣa[diqīna]* in Q.15:6–7

3.0. The Analysis

3.1. Analysis and Visualisation Using Pointer-based Transcription Data

To evaluate the potential of the pointer-based transcription system, we transcribed a selection of pages from a handful of manuscripts to test the tool. The criteria for the selection of the few pages was the peculiarity of the manuscripts and the creation of editions of overlapping sections of the Qurʾānic text. Dots have been encoded using the pointer in a few pages from the following:

- MS Bibliothèque nationale de France. Département des Manuscrits. Arabe 330 f (BnF ar. 330f, Déroche 1983, Posegay 2021a), ff.31r–33v, (Q.4:78–4:101), selected because of the presence of two layers of vocalisation by means of dots and miniature letters.
- MS Bibliothèque nationale de France. Département des Manuscrits. Arabe 340 c (BnF ar. 340c, Déroche 1983), ff. 32r–34v (Q.13:25–14:18), chosen because of its uniqueness in placing the dots contextually to the other dots and letters and paying attention to the shapes that dots formed together.

- MS Bibliothèque nationale de France. Département des Manuscrits. Arabe 334 c (BnF ar. 334c, Déroche 1983), ff.31r–33r (Q.13:17–14:21) because it is one of the rare examples of manuscripts written in *ḥijāzī* script style that have been marked with dots (Fedeli 2024).[5] Moreover, the selected pages and MS BnF ar. 340c share an overlapping portion of text spanning Q.13:25–14:18 that will produce a visualisation of the dots in the same section of text.
- MS Universitätsbibliothek Tübingen, Ma VI 165 (UbT Ma VI 165, Weisweiler 1930, Fedeli 2013), ff. 2v–6r (Q.17:64–18:21) because of its provenance. It comes from Damascus while all the other selected examples are from al-Fusṭāṭ. The different provenance could offer an interesting element of analysis of possible patterns connected with their cultural and social environment.
- MS Bibliothèque nationale de France. Département des Manuscrits. Arabe 330 b (BnF ar. 330b, ff.3r–4v and ff.9r–10v, Déroche 1983, Ince 2023) because it has two sections overlapping with the selected pages from MS BnF ar.330f (they share Q.4:81–101) and partially with the selected pages from MS UbT Ma VI 165 (they share Q.17:68–86 and Q.18:10–21).[6]

---

[5] Cellard identifies the script style of BnF ar 334c as part of group C (Cellard 2021, 462).

[6] The vocalisation of all the leaves of (BnF ar. 330b) was analysed in Ince (2023). The fact that "not all words have full vocalisation" has been noticed and explained with the general remark in Ibn Abī Dāwūd

Using the pointer-based transcription system enables a variety of novel analyses to be carried out on the vocalised text. Specifically, it provides a data-driven means of systematically describing patterns of dot placement in a text, which can then inform the identification of scribal habits. It can also produce a schematic representation of each individual dot placement using letter templates, which can serve as a direct visualisation of the manuscript itself, and as a basis of comparison against a base text. Since the main focus of this chapter is on methodology, we will illustrate the potential applications of this transcription method through examples.

Dot-placement patterns can be identified by superimposing all dots for a particular letter of interest in a single plot. A prototypical trace of that letter can be placed in the background to serve as a visual aid for the researcher. We demonstrate this by comparing vocalisation patterns of isolated *lām-ʾalif* (LA), final *lām-ʾalif* (-LA), final *bāʾ/tāʾ/ṯāʾ* (-B), and isolated *bāʾ/tāʾ/ṯāʾ* (B) across the pages of the five selected manuscripts.

---

that “dots are not used for all vowels, but always for either the grammatical case endings, *hamzahs*, or the vowels that would distinguish between two readings (e.g., *fa-mathaluhū* vs *fa-mithluhū*). This is generally also the case in Arabe 330b although medial consonants that do not necessarily differentiate between readings often appear vowelled as well” (Ince 2023, 117). The patterns of the vowelled consonants are not further investigated in the article as Ince focuses on the meaning of the dotting with reference to two canonical readings and the use of green and red ink to mark vowel dots.

Table 1 shows the distribution of single and double dots for isolated and final *lām-ʾalif* for the indicated manuscripts. The manuscripts broadly display four prominent positions for dot placement: right, centre top, left, and bottom. The right and centre positions generally correspond to *lām* followed by *hamzah* + short /a/ and *hamzah* + long /ā/ respectively. The left position typically marks the vowel attached to the *lām* and indicates *la-ʾ* and the bottom position marks the *i* vowel attached to the *ʾalif*. There may be a further distinction in the central position between dots that are to the right of the left ascender and dots to the left of the right ascender, but at this level, that distinction is not apparent. Dot pairs, particularly for final -LA, mark accusative *tanwīn* (*-lan*) to the right of the letter, or *hamzah* + nominative *tanwīn* following a long vowel (*-lāʾun*).

The visualisation of the distribution of dots for isolated and final *lām-ʾalif* may provide interesting insights to the scholar who can then verify and corroborate them with further arguments or disregard them in the process of understanding the dotting system. The insights are generated by the possibility of comparing the dots distribution in several manuscripts. Comparison of the extent to which dot positions are unique or identical makes it easier for the scholar to identify patterns and phenomena in the data. The understanding of possible patterns is the result of an iterative process as described above: data is observed and collected by the editor, processed by the analyst, tested by the editor and analysist, and then, again, observed and collected by the editor.

For example, cases where no dot is present, such as final -LA single dots in all but MS UbT Ma VI 165, may be informative under certain circumstances. In this case, we have not fully transcribed any of the manuscript texts in question with the pointer and the dots are sometimes connected to non-overlapping sections of the text. While in some instances implied readings may be obvious, in other cases, without more comprehensive coverage of the text, it is difficult to make categorical statements about potential implied readings in the absence of dots relying on the visualisation only. The editor can verify that MS UbT Ma VI 165 has two occurrences of final -LA that do not occur in the other manuscripts, not even in MS BnF ar. 330b that has a long lacuna in that point. The third unique dot attached to final -LA in MS UbT Ma VI 165 is the result of the deterioration of the ink used for the *tanwīn* in *tafḍīlan* (Q.17:70). The legible dot from the pair has been collocated in the row of the occurrences of single dots rather than in the row for the double dots.

The observations about single dots attached to the final -LA outlined above—and solved by the editor as caused by the materiality of the fragments—are not the only insights that can be derived from the visualisations. From a distribution perspective, what immediately stands out is the high degree of variance in dot placement for MS BnF ar. 340c and MS UbT Ma VI 165 compared to the remaining manuscripts. In particular, the position of dots at the right of *lām-ʾalif* for both manuscripts extends along the entirety of the lower diagonal.

Table 1: Comparison of the distribution of single and double dots for isolated and final *lām-ʾalif* for MSS BnF ar. 340c, 334c, 330b, 330f, and UbT Ma VI 165

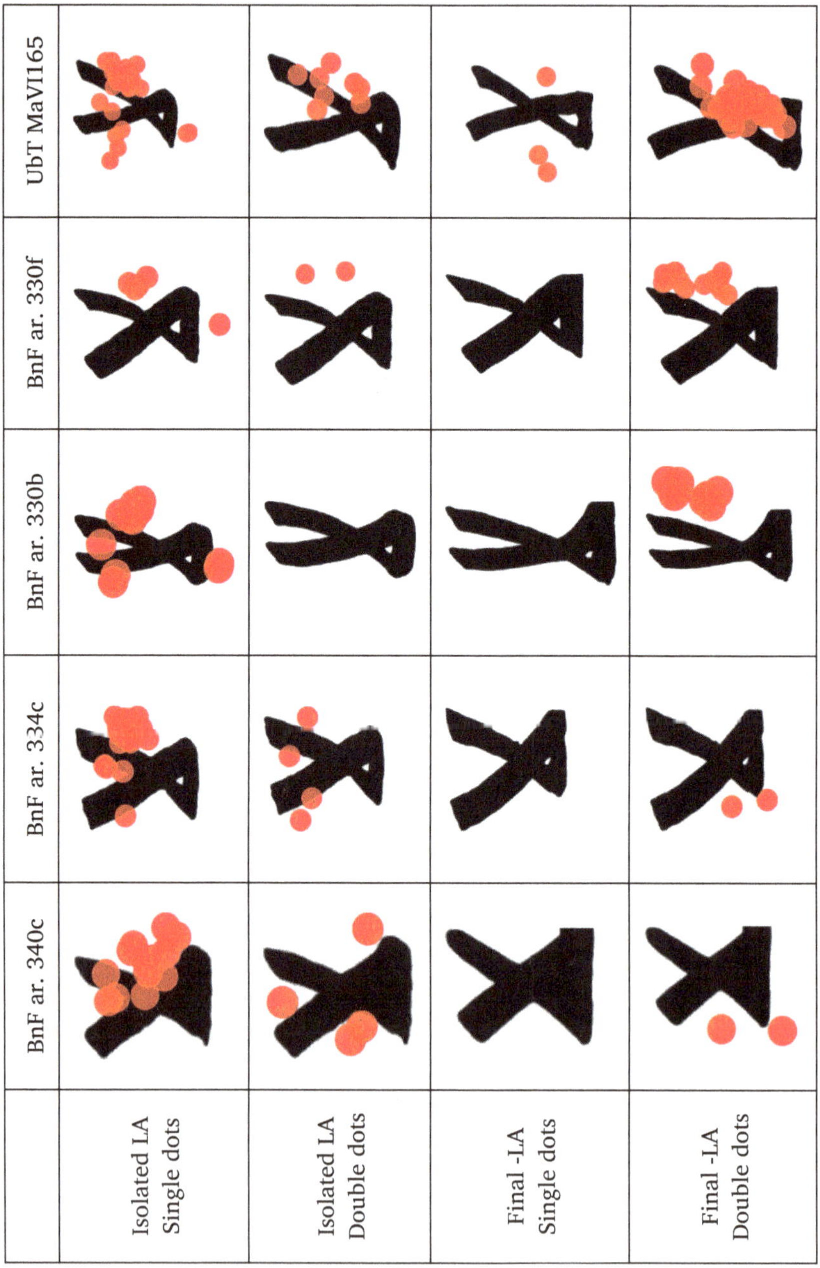

Table 2: Comparison of the distribution of single and double dots for isolated and final B for MSS BnF ar. 340c, 334c, 330b, 330f, and UbT Ma VI 165

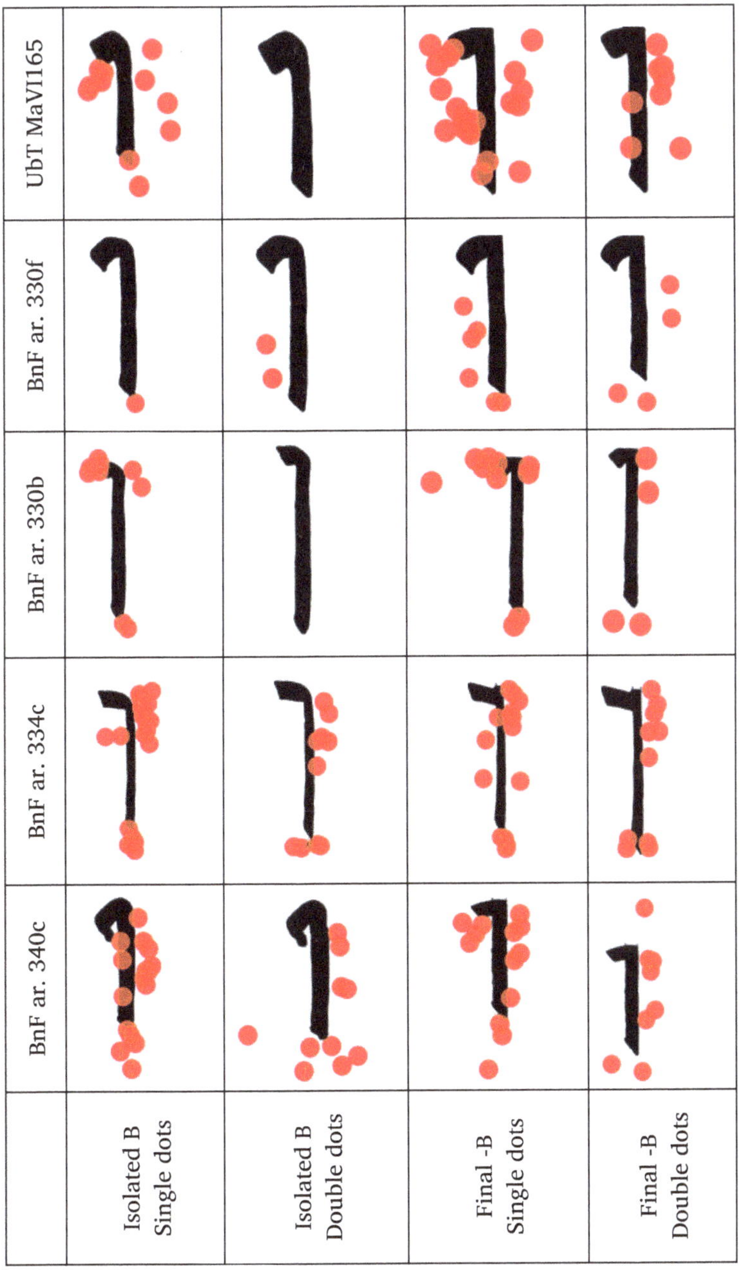
UbT MaVI165
BnF ar. 330f
BnF ar. 330b
BnF ar. 334c
BnF ar. 340c
Isolated B Single dots
Isolated B Double dots
Final -B Single dots
Final -B Double dots

There are a number of possible explanations for this observation that can be tested by scholars. For example, dotters may have simply been careless and not consistent with their dot placement, or they may aim at placing the dots according to geometric patterns.[7] Another possibility is that the original scribe did not reproduce the letter in a consistent manner. As previously discussed, variation in letter height and skew cannot be adjusted for with the existing pointer-based system.[8]

To determine which of those factors are responsible for the variance, and to what degree, we use MS BnF ar. 340c as a motivating example because of its idiosyncratic way of placing the dots as already observed at an early stage in the project before the implementation of the pointer.[9] We visualised each occurrence of reconstructed dotting independently, then compared it against the original manuscript, as shown in Figure 5. There is a noticeable degree of variation in the execution of the letter. For example, comparing the *lām-ʾalif* on f. 32v l. 14 to f. 34r l. 7, we observe that the former has a narrower aspect ratio and its first

---

[7] This is the hypothesis proposed for the behaviour of the dotter in MS BnF ar.340c (see contribution in this volume).

[8] See above, note 4. The variation in skew is rather problematic when working on manuscripts written in *ḥijāzī* script style, characterised by slanting ascenders. The majority of *ḥijāzī* style manuscripts are undotted. MS BnF ar. 334c is a rare case and its overall appearance of slanting vertical lines must be taken into consideration when trying to understand the distribution of dots.

[9] See the patterns in the relative contribution in this volume.

ascender is at less of an acute angle. Since the latter instance deviates more from the reference letter shape used as a model for the reconstructed dotting, the automatic reconstruction of the dot placement carried out by the algorithm is ultimately less accurate if compared against the actual instance of the manuscript. However, it is also clear that letter shape alone is not the only contributing factor to the increased variance between reconstructed and actual dotting displayed in Table 1. Once again, both examples cited above have a dot placed to the right of the letter. The dot on f. 32v l. 14 is piercing the letter and is vertically positioned at the intersection of the two ascenders. On the other hand, the dot on f. 34r l. 7 is located much higher, along the upper arm of the right ascender. Thus, although variation in letter shape and aspect ratio affects the accuracy of dot position reconstruction, the portrait presented in Table 1 reflects genuine variation in the underlying scribal practice.

Moving on to isolated and final *B*, we generated similar dot placement distributions as shown in Table 2. Once again, we observe a greater deal of variation in dot placement in MS BnF ar. 340c and MS UbT Ma VI 165 compared to the remaining manuscripts. We also observe two prominent outliers: one present among the isolated *B* double dots for MS BnF ar. 340c, and another among final *-B* single dots for MS BnF ar. 330b. Figure 6 reveals both instances to be a result of distortion due to a curving of the edge of the folio relative to the plane of the image.

Figure 5: Comparison between actual and reconstructed dotting for isolated *lām-ʾalif* for MS BnF ar. 340c. Blue line underneath the reference letter in reconstructions indicates the baseline used for calculating dot positions.

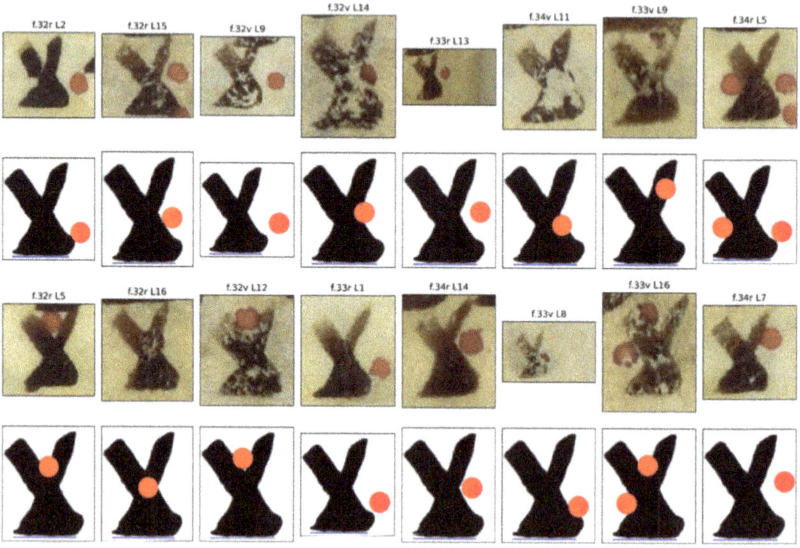

Figure 6: (left) BnF ar. 340c f. 34v l. 15, *ʿaḏābun*; (right) BnF ar. 330b f. 10v l. 5, *wa-la-muliʾta* (Source gallica.bnf.fr / Bibliothèque nationale de France)

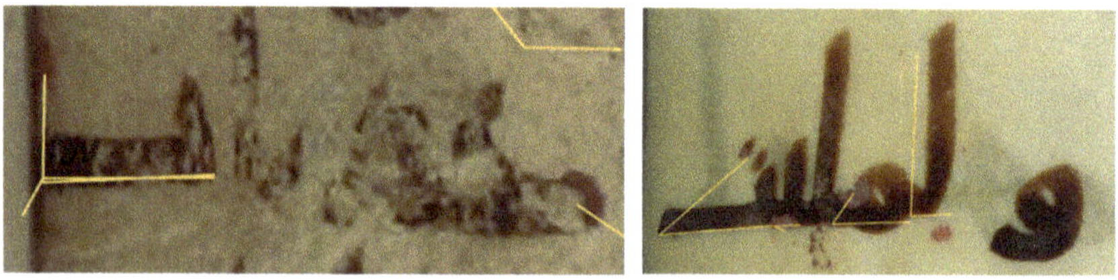

As for general patterns for isolated and final *B* among the manuscripts, we see stark variation in execution of the dotting by the dotters. For single dots, both MS BnF. ar. 334c and ar. 330b display relatively tight clusters which clearly isolate top, bottom, and left positions. Interestingly, there appears to be more latitude in the horizontal positioning of a dot, particularly in the bottom position, compared to the vertical positioning. For double dots, both manuscripts have a bottom right position with a horizontal arrangement, and a far-left position with a vertical arrangement. There is not enough data captured with the pointer for MS BnF ar. 330f to make a clear determination as to the execution by the dotter. As with LA, MS BnF ar. 340c and UbT Ma VI 165 both display a much larger degree of variability in dot placement, though those same positions are broadly applicable.

We emphasise that the distributions shown in this section are primarily for illustrative purposes, and the amount of data collected from encoding of dots by means of the pointer is insufficient to come to any definitive conclusions. Nonetheless, it demonstrates the possibilities enabled by leveraging the pointer-based transcription method and highlights some avenues for further investigation. One distinct advantage of collating dot distributions is that it allows us to begin characterising scribal habits and execution in comparison against each other. This can provide insight into the degree of training and the broader milieu in which a manuscript was vocalised and opens up a new area of investigation which has not previously been looked at.

3.2. Visualisation of Dotting for Collation

What turned out to be very effective in providing insights to the scholar working on the manuscripts is the visualisation of the reconstructed dotting of letters generated from data of fragments that have the same section of the Qurʾānic text. It constitutes a novel kind of collating manuscripts focusing on the dotting level. The collation can be visualized showing possible different readings of a letter (and word/s) marked by a different dot position. This visual collation that semi-automatically reproduces the same segment of the text and its dotting in different manuscripts is a secondary result coming from the pointer implementation and unforeseen at the beginning of the research project. Its possible use and further implementation opens new methods in textual analysis given the fact that the majority of the disagreements in early dotted manuscripts are expressed at the dot layer when comparing the number of disagreements affecting the *rasm*, the consonantal diacritics and the vowel-dots. Moreover, the visualisation of the mapping of the dotting in manuscripts that have the same section of text enables not only to visualise disagreements between manuscripts but also brings to the attention of scholars unmarked positions in contrast with marked position revealing insights into the meaning of the distribution of dots.[10]

[10] See the meaning of the absence of dots described in Fedeli's contribution in this volume.

3.2.1. The Iterative Process

The insights given by the reconstructed visualisation of the distribution of dots is a further step in the iterative process of the dots analysis developed during the InterSaME project:

i) The editor explored the manuscripts and encoded them in Latin characters making her first observations.
ii) She explored the manuscripts editions by means of tabular files enriched in collaboration with the developer; the editor formulated initial hypotheses about the distribution of dots.
iii) She encoded again (part of) the same manuscripts by means of the pointer, thus confirming or questioning her previous reading/edition.
iv) The analyst processed the encoding of the dots produced by the pointer, reconstructing the visualisation of the dots distribution and provided an initial set of independent insights.
v) The editor read the reconstructed visualisation questioning her interpretation: she could understand certain phenomena because of her previous analysis and interpretation of possible patterns in the dotting system, but also detected phenomena that she did not detect before.
vi) Thus, the editor went back to the manuscript images and edition (first step) and to the tabular files (second step); she could discuss unclear points or inconsistencies with the analyst.
vii) Finally, the editor could confirm or refine her previous interpretation.

3.2.2. Examples of Visualisation of Dotting for Collation

We will provide a few examples of insights offered by the 'visualised collation' of the overlapping sections of text in MSS BnF ar. 340c and 334c in Table 3; MSS BnF ar. 330b and 330f in Table 4; MSS BnF ar. 330b and UbT Ma VI 165 in Table 5.

The visualisation reproduced in Table 3 enabled the editor to detect the pattern observed in the dotting of MS BnF ar. 340c in a previous phase of the analysis.[11] These patterns emerged even more clearly in the visualisation in Table 3 when compared against the dotting of BnF ar. 334c. After a first palaeographic and philological analysis, the editor concluded that the dotting in the former case is highly dependent on the placement of other dots present on the whole page, and from the physical limitation imposed by the other letters on the previous and following line. This hypothesis is confirmed in the visualization isolated B in MS BnF ar. 340c in Table 3. The distribution of dots does not cluster neatly, unlike the three clusters of single dots attached to isolated B in MS BnF ar. 334c. Also, the small area respected by the dotter of MS BnF ar. 334c when placing the pair of dots at the left of isolated B in contrast with the dotter of MS BnF ar. 340c which uses a large area at the border with the previous and following line. The case of a pair of dots attached to final B is illuminating: the dotter of MS BnF ar. 340c placed a dot even below the previous letter while the dotter of BnF ar. 334c placed all the dots below the baseline inside the area of the letter (see Figure 7).

---

[11] See the contribution on BnF ar 340c in this volume.

The comparison between the distribution of single dots attached to isolated LA in the two manuscripts shows a disagreement in placing a dot at the left of the LA ligature (conveying /a/ attached to *lām*) in MS BnF ar. 334c while there are no dots at the left of the ligature in MS BnF ar. 340c. This suggested to the editor to investigate the possible reason behind the different habit of the two dotters in marking the prepositions *li*- and *la*-. Both prepositions are rather consistently dotted in MS BnF ar. 334c while they are subject to rules in MS BnF ar. 340c. A closer inspection shows that the dotted *la*- in MS BnF ar. 334c occurs at f.32r, l.6 in Q.13:37, *la-ʾin-i* and the particle *ʾin* is spelled with *ʾalif* in addition to the denticle while MS BnF ar. 340c has a spelling with a denticle only (see Figure 8). For this reason, the occurrence of Q.13:36 does not fall into the group of the ligature of isolated LA and in this case, both dotters marked the preposition *la*-.[12]

[12] In the section of text edited with the pointer for the comparison between MSS BnF ar. 340c and 334c, there are three occurrences of (*wa*)*la-ʾin*, namely in Q.13:37:5, 14:7:4 and 14:7:7 (respectively, MS BnF ar. 334c, f.32r, l.3, f.32v, ll.11 and 12 and MS BnF ar. 340c, f.33r, l.4, f.34r, ll. 5 and 6). All occurrences are spelled with a denticle only except the mentioned occurrence in MS BnF ar. 334c which has *ʾalif* and denticle. All positions in both manuscripts are dotted except the conjunction *wa*- which is consistently unmarked.

Figure 7: Example of dotting of the ending of *murībin* (Q.14:9), one dot of the pair being below the previous denticle in MS BnF ar.340c (Source gallica.bnf.fr/ Bibliothèque nationale de France)

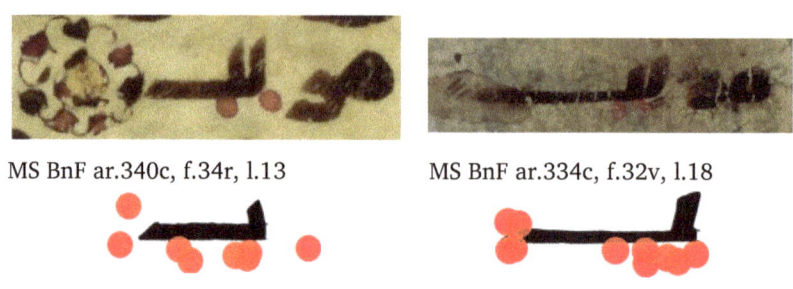

MS BnF ar.340c, f.34r, l.13

MS BnF ar.334c, f.32v, l.18

Reconstructed visualisation of final -B with pairs of dots in the same sequence of text in the two manuscripts (as in Table 3).

Figure 8: Different pattern in spelling *wa-la-ʾin-i* in Q.13:37 in two manuscripts that caused the visualisation of a different pattern in dotting the ligature *lām-ʾalif* (Source gallica.bnf.fr/ Bibliothèque nationale de France)

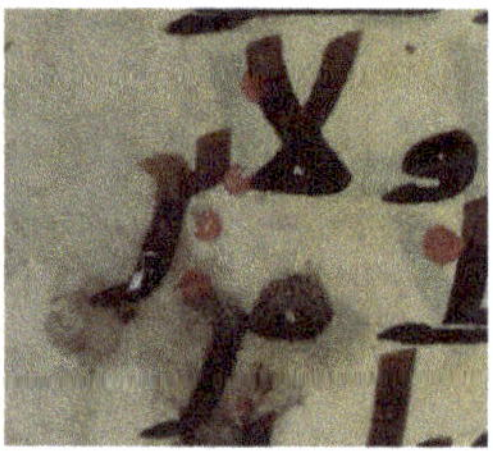

MS BnF ar. 334c, f.32r, l.3

MS BnF ar. 340c, f.33r, l.4

Table 3: Comparison of the distributions of single and double dots for isolated and final LA and B for BnF ar. 340c and 334c for Q.13:25-14:18

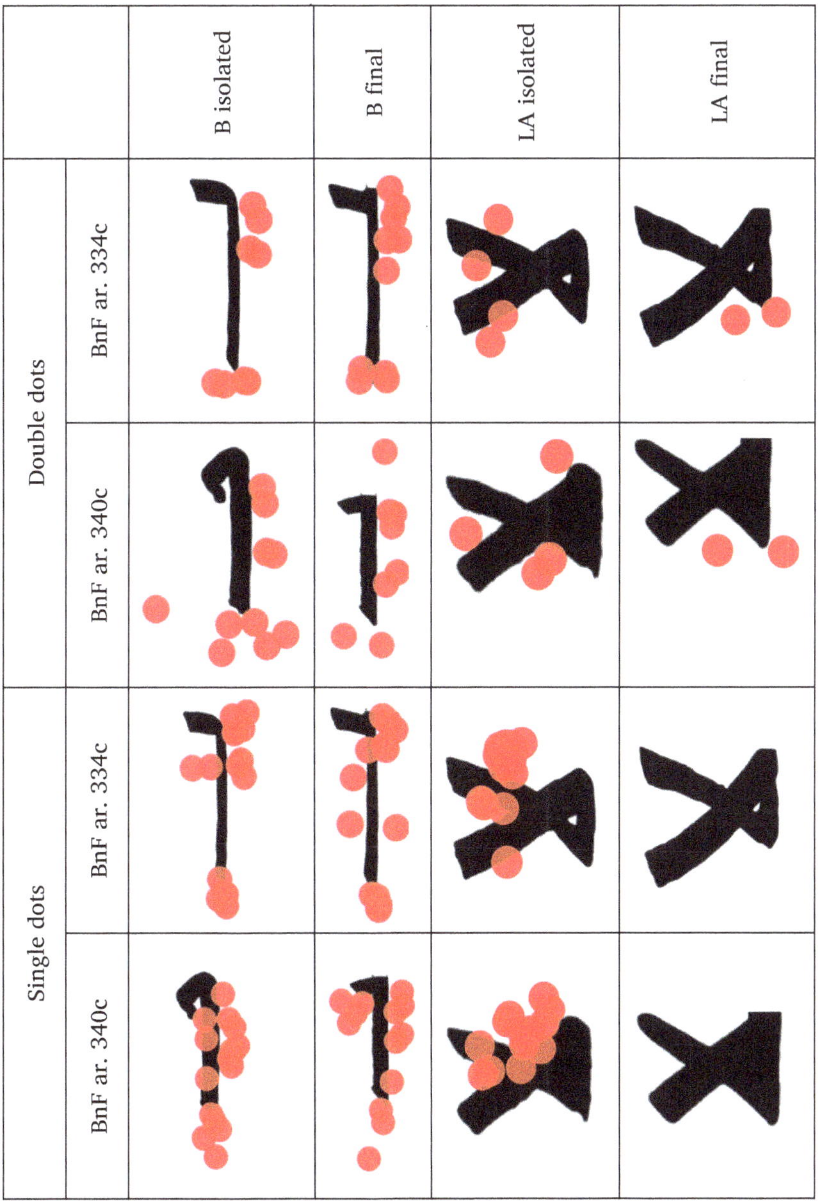

Table 4: Comparison of the distributions of single and double dots for isolated and final LA and B for BnF ar. 330b and 330f for Q:4:82–101

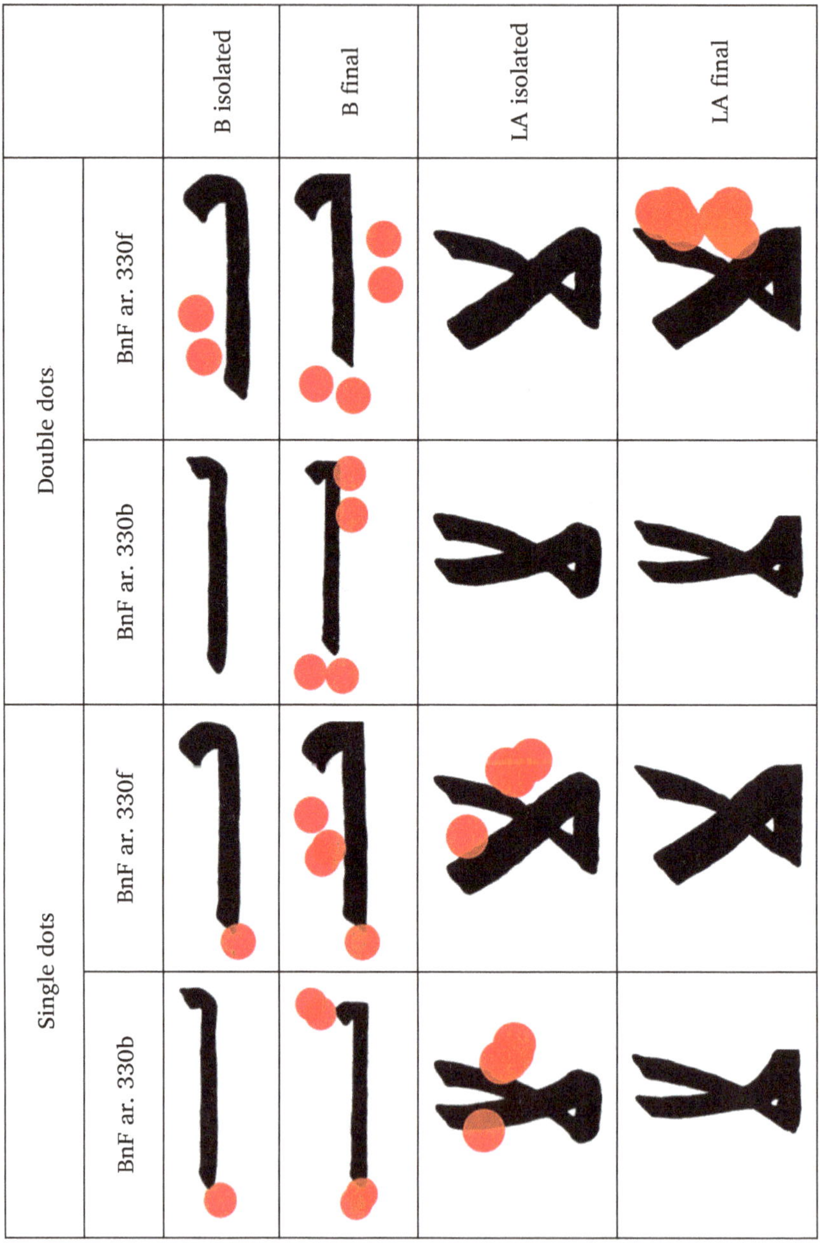
B isolated
B final
LA isolated
LA final
Double dots
BnF ar. 330f
BnF ar. 330b
Single dots
BnF ar. 330f
BnF ar. 330b

Table 5: Comparison of the distributions of single and double dots for isolated and final LA and B for BnF ar. 330b and UbT Ma VI 165 for Q:17:69–86, 18:10–21

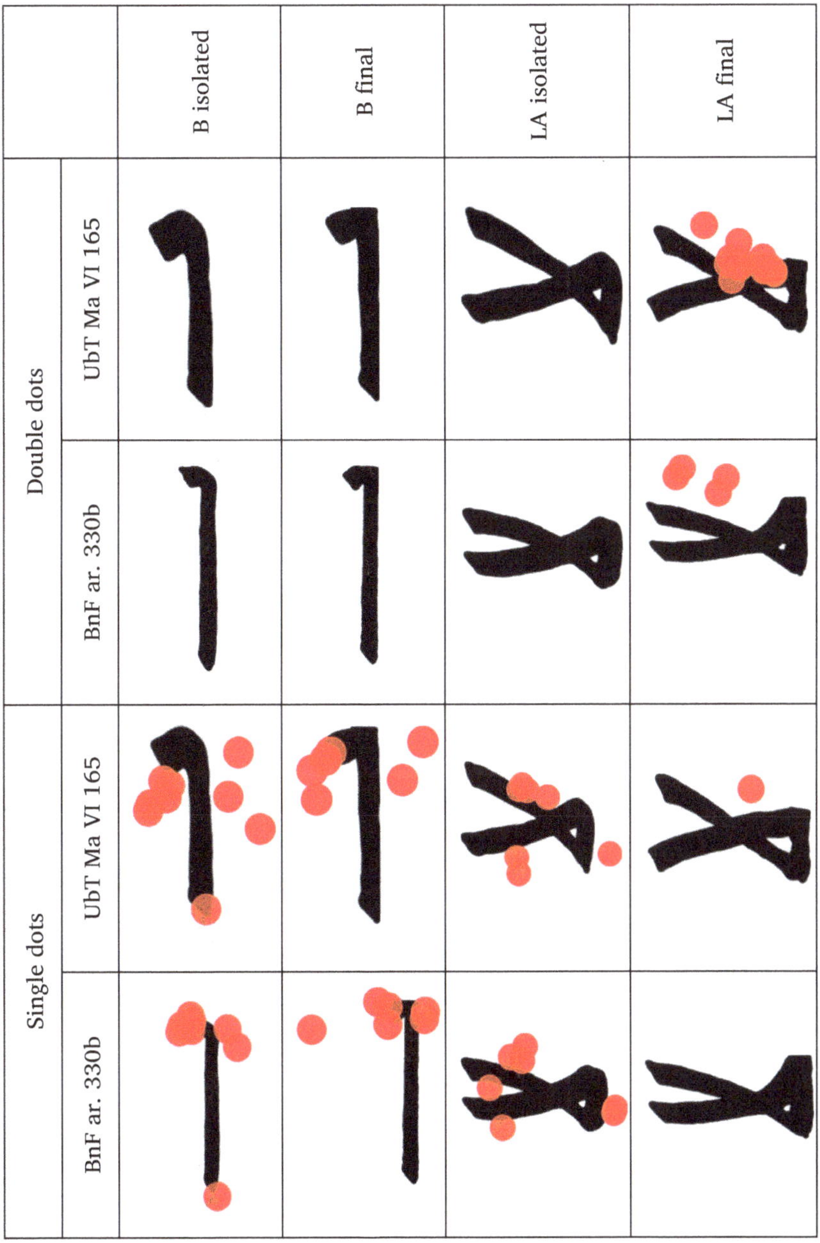
B isolated
B final
LA isolated
LA final
Double dots
UbT Ma VI 165
BnF ar. 330b
Single dots
UbT Ma VI 165
BnF ar. 330b

3.2.3. Example 1: Visualising the Patterns in Dotting *tanwīn fatḥa*

Another insight related to the marking of the ligature of final -LA with a pair of dots was provided for MSS BnF ar. 330b and 330f. Table 4 shows the model letter -LA without dots in the former and with pairs of dots in the latter. The dotters in the two manuscripts apply a different rule in marking the ending for the *tanwīn fatḥa*. Looking at the larger section of text in the two manuscripts, in MS BnF ar. 330f, the dotter marked all the accusative forms ending in *ʾalif* independently from the following letter, while the dotter of MS BnF ar. 330b dotted the final *ʾalif* in the accusative form when followed by *hamzah*, *ʿayn*, *ḥāʾ*, *hāʾ*, and *ḵāʾ*. This pattern corresponds to what we find in al-Dānī regarding the practice of the Kūfans in dotting the final *ʾalif* before the *ḥurūf ḥalqiyyah*, 'the pharyngeals' (2004, 47). As the overlapping section in MS BnF ar. 330f does not include occurrences of accusative forms with *hamzah*, the visualisation does not suggest the phonetic rule but gives insights about the different behaviour of the two dotters (see Figure 9).

Figure 9: Examples of the different patterns in dotting *tanwīn ʾalif* depending on the following phoneme in MSS BnF ar. 330b and 330f (as suggested by the visualisation in table 4) (Source gallica.bnf.fr/ Bibliothèque nationale de France)

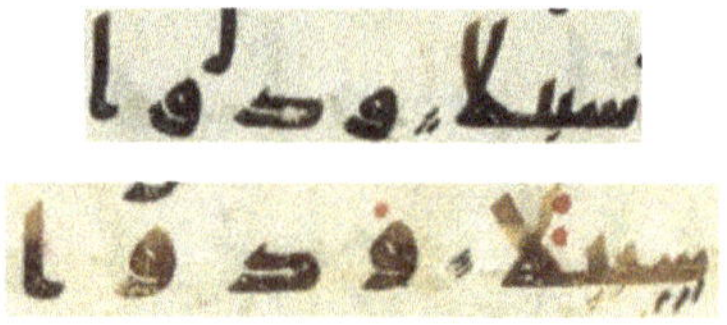

End of Q.4:88 and beginning of Q.4:89 (*sabīlan // waddū*) in BnF ar. 330b, f.3v, l.3 (top) and BnF ar. 330f, f.32r, l.4 (bottom)

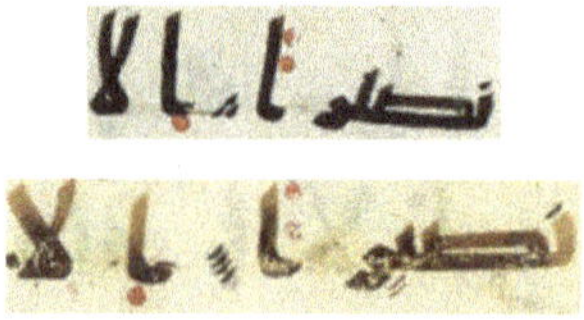

End of Q.4:89 and beginning of Q.4:90 (*naṣīran// ʾillā*) in BnF ar. 330b, f.3v, l.7 (top) and BnF ar. 330f, f.32r, l.10 (bottom)

Looking at the distribution of final -LA in MSS BnF ar. 330b and UbT Ma VI 165, in Table 5, it emerges immediately that for the same section of text, MS BnF ar. 330b has only two pairs of dots whereas MS UbT Ma VI 165 has several pairs of dots. At a glance, the visualisation suggests that the discrepancy in the number of occurrences is likely due to the application of the phonetic rule in one manuscript only (see Figure 10).

The phonetic rule for the accusative ending in *tanwīn ʾalif* is not represented in the occurrences of isolated or final -LA visualised in Table 3 for MSS BnF ar. 340c and 334c but the pattern has been observed by the editor in the whole section of the two manuscripts.

Figure 10: Examples of the different patterns in dotting *tanwīn ʾalif* depending from the following phoneme in MSS BnF ar. 330b and UbT Ma VI 165 (as visualised in Table 5) (Source gallica.bnf.fr/ Bibliothèque nationale de France)

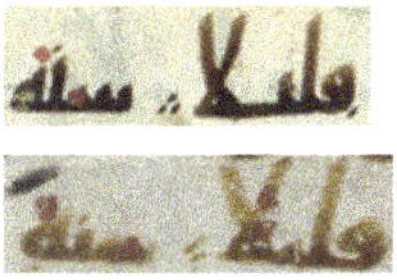

End of Q.17:76 and beginning of Q.17:77 (*qalīlan // sunnata*) in BnF ar. 330b, f.9v, l.1 (top) and UbT 165, f.3r, l.10 (bottom)

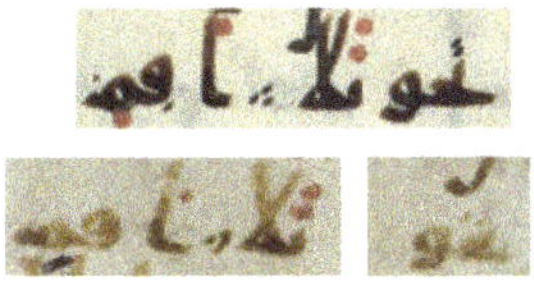

End of Q.17:77 and beginning of Q.17:78 (*taḥwīlan // ʾaqimi*) in BnF ar. 330b, f.9v, l.2 (top) and UbT 165, f.3r, ll.11–12 (bottom)

3.2.4. Example 2: Visualising the Patterns in Dotting *la-* Followed by *ʾAlif al-Waṣl*

An interesting suggestion to be considered in Table 4 is the distribution of single dots attached to isolated LA in MSS BnF ar. 330b and 330f. There are a few dots at the right of the ligature in both manuscripts whereas the former has a dot at the left of the ligature and the latter has a dot in the middle of the two ascenders. Searching for the word that coincides with such a situation, we find *la-ttabaʿtumu*, i.e., 'you would surely have followed [Satan]' in Q.4:83:27 (Arberry 1964). The different position of the dot—as suggested by the visualisation—might express a different reading of the word *la-ttabaʿtumu* i.e., *la-* with the dot referred to the *lām* in MS BnF ar. 330b and *ʾā* with the dot placed at the left of the *ʾalif* marking a long /a/ in MS BnF ar. 330f (see Figure 11). As the reading *la-ʾāttabaʿtumu* is grammatically incorrect, it is likely that the placement of the dot in the middle of the ascenders in the latter case is the result of the care of the dotter to avoid the contact of the dot at the left of the *lām* with the dot above the following denticle to mark its gemination.

Figure 11: Detail of a different dot placement in *la-ttabaʿtumu* (Q.4:83) as suggested by the visualisation in Table 4 (Source gallica.bnf.fr/ Bibliothèque nationale de France)

BnF ar. 330f, f.31v, l.4

BnF ar. 330b, f.3r, l.6

3.2.5. Example 3: Visualising the Patterns in Dotting the Assimilation

Another interesting case is the pair of dots placed above isolated B which occur in MS BnF ar. 330f only, and is absent in MS BnF ar. 330b. This is a case that was already known to the editor because of its peculiarity. Dots above isolated or final homograph letter B for *bāʾ*, *tāʾ* and *ṯāʾ* indicate /a/ according to the model. A pair of dots above a final letter is assumed to express the *tanwīn fatḥa* and have *ʾalif*. The peculiarity here is the pair of dots in the position associated to /a/ without *ʾalif*. Going from the visualisation back to the instance in the manuscript, the pair of dots occurs in MS BnF ar. 330f, f.32r, l. 12, *ḥaṣirat ṣudūru-hum* in Q.4:90:11–12. This code of two dots might be used for marking the assimilation (Fedeli 2020 and 2024). More likely, they are marking the reading *ḥaṣiratan ṣudūruhum* by Yaʿqūb and al-Ḥasan al-Baṣrī as reported in Ibn Ḵālawaih (Muḵtaṣar: 27–28, see EVQ). In our corpus, the assimilation or the reading are possibly marked by means of two dots in MS BnF ar. 330f only, but the mechanism is unknown in MS BnF ar. 330b where the dotter uses a horizontal red line to mark the phenomenon on f.3v, ll.8–9 (see Figure 12).[13]

Figure 12: Detail of a different pattern in marking the assimilation with a pair of dots (at the left) and a red horizontal line (at the right) (Source gallica.bnf.fr/ Bibliothèque nationale de France)

BnF ar. 330f, f.32r, l.12

BnF ar. 330b, f.3v, ll. 8–9

3.2.6. Visualisation of the Distribution of Dots as a Novelty and Its Potentialities

The visualisation of the distribution of dots resulting from the data produced by means of the pointer represents a novel instrument for representing the enormous richness of dot positions and

[13] The horizontal red line has already been noticed in Fedeli (2024) after a presentation at the colloquium, 'Current Research on Qurʾān Manuscripts', at the Collège de France on 2 and 3 June 2022, and in Ince (2023, 125).

the dotters' freedom in positioning dots. The visualisation also produced a novel way of representing disagreement between manuscripts at a dot level which are an instrument and a result at the same time. As a tool, it gives insight at a glance about the disagreement while as a result, it constitutes a visualised critical apparatus of the manuscript tradition's richness. Use of images is known for producing a direct link between text and images for an apparatus criticus made of images of the instances in the manuscript. Among the pioneer projects there is kleio IAS (Image Analysis System) developed at the Max-Planck-Institut für Geschichte in Göttingen (Germany) in the 1990s (Buzzetti and Tabarroni 1995). What is unique in the possibilities given by a future exploitation of the pointer and visualisation as conceived and developed in the InterSaME project is the intermediary step between images and text that the vectors and model letters represent.

A subsequent line of investigation that would build upon the visualisations shown above would be to map dots across various manuscripts at an individual level. This entails collating and aligning the transcribed text from several manuscripts at the level of individual letters. Then, for each letter or word of interest, comparative visualisations can show the individual vocalisations attested in each witness text. While we have not pursued this approach in this work, it is an open area of inquiry which has the potential to offer a scalable manner of comparing specific vocalisation decisions.

3.3. Analysing Vocalisation Context and Probability

The qualitative transcription method described in section 2.2 can also be used to synthesise a graph representing the morphological patterns which condition the presence of vocalisation. This can be accomplished by first aligning the letters of a transcribed text to a fully-vocalised base text. In this example those would be MS UbT Ma VI 165 and the Tanzil Qurʾan edition respectively. After alignment, the reference text is abstracted into a sequence of vowels and consonants, focusing on word morphology. For example, the word *ḥubuk* would be rendered as CuCuC. Note that since the base transcription incorporates orthographic elements, it is not straightforward to resolve all instances of *matres lectionis* and other orthographic conventions that are not phonetic. An instance of this limitation in the base transcription is the word *ʾulāʾika* which, though containing a *wāw* in writing, does not have a lengthened /u/ vowel. Thus, the letters *yāʾ*, *wāw*, and *ʾalif* were left as-is and not resolved into short or long vowels or consonants.

The next step is to select a particular vowel position from the base text. In our running example, we select word-final *a* (Figure 13). All occurrences of *-a* in the base text are identified and then, for each occurrence, the aligned transcription is checked for the presence of the *-a* vowel as well. This produces an overall probability of vocalisation for word-final *-a*.[14] Here, it is 81.6%, or 674 out of 826 occurrences. We can then unravel the conditional probability of vocalisation further by looking at the preceding context of the vowel. The four possible cases are *Ca*, *Wa*, *Ya*, and *Aa*. Once again as shown in Figure 13, this can be further unravelled for each four cases into a total of 22 possible conditions where *-a* can occur.

This graph can serve several functions. It can act as a starting point for further investigation into cases where certain patterns are dotted with high probability but not certainty. For example, final *-a* in CuCa is marked 30 out of 34 times. Instances where *-a* is not marked could indicate the presence of a variant in comparison with the base text.

In this case the dotter of MS UbT Ma VI 165 marked the ending of *t-f-j-r* in Q.17:90 with a dot after the *rāʾ* marking the indicative form, its prefix with /-u/, i.e., *tu-* and its body with a dot below the *jīm*, thus likely reading *tufjiru* or *tufajjiru* where ʿĀṣim, Ḥamza and al-Kisāʾī read *tafjura* (Nasser 2020, 537). Nāfi, Ibn Kaṯīr, Abū ʿAmr and Ibn ʿĀmir read *tufajjira* (Shāṭibiyya in EVQ and Nasser 2020, 537) and a non-canonical reading is *tufjira* (EVQ). The widely known readings works have the subjunctive form while the dotter of this manuscript marked the indicative

[14] This process assumes the reading of Ḥafṣ < ʿĀṣim. This is not an issue for two reasons. The first is that the reading traditions disagree over a minority of words in the Qurʾān, so there is still utility in using any reference text, regardless of the reason. The second, and more importantly, is that this process still enables us to identify deviations from Ḥafṣ. This is illustrated below.

form after *ḥattā* in 'till thou makest [a spring] to gush forth' (Arberry 1964). The indicative form in *-u* is also confirmed by the later stage of modern vowel symbols added in black ink. The second disagreement in the sequence CuCa is the dotting of the pronominal suffix *-ki* with a dot below the *kāf* in *rabbuki* vs *rabbuka* in Q.19:9. This is possibly an error where the scribe assimilated the reading in Q. 19:21, in which case this approach also provides a mechanism to detect those as well. The other two instances correspond to *kulla*, which is both geminated and may be unmarked due to it being a high frequency word.[15] A further check of the two instances into the manuscript shows a limitation of the analysis when dealing with damaged artefacts and the uncertainty of their interpretation. On f.2v, the ink of the last lines of the page is faded and thus, the unmarked final position of *kulla* (Q.17:71) could be an accidental result. The other instance occurs on f.16r, l.12. The faded script has been reinked with black ink at several point of the page, including *kulla*. The black ink may cover a red dot of an earlier layer. Both occurrences of *kulla* have been marked by a modern symbol of *fatḥa* in black ink. Only the analysis of the ink composition of the script might help detect the presence of red dots marking the ending of *kulla*.

---

[15] In principle, we would filter out geminated words to focus solely on ungeminated CuCa. However, achieving this using the current base transcription is difficult to limitations in the system used of the base text. As a result, we lose the ability to filter on all the elements of the text. This requires further investigation beyond this initial proof of concept and will be explored in future work.

The graph—like in the case of the visualisation of dot positions and distribution reconstructed after the data produced by the pointer—can give insights that the scholar can explore and validate. The graph is also an instrument for verifying patterns that the editor perceived during her work of editing and annotating the manuscript text and features. The perception of a possible model during the editing process is a kind of inferential intuition or guess that the graph can validate or reject in a few seconds. The prompt and rapid verification does not merely save time for the scholar but enables an immediate redefinition for making a possible pattern emerge and take shape.

During the collaborative work generated as part of the project, we experienced the utility of data analysis but also its limitations or, rather, the sometime overestimated expectations about the capabilities of the machine. In our work, detecting patterns and models or finding order in disordered data have never been the immediate result of data analysis by means of a piece of coding or similar. Indeed, the traditional palaeographic and philological analysis accompanied by a manual editing of the manuscript has produced ideas that the data analysis has transformed into hypotheses and new ideas by programming, programs and databases (intuition informed by data analysis).

Figure 13: Conditional probability graph showing vocalisation probabilities for word-final *-a* in MS UbT Ma VI 165

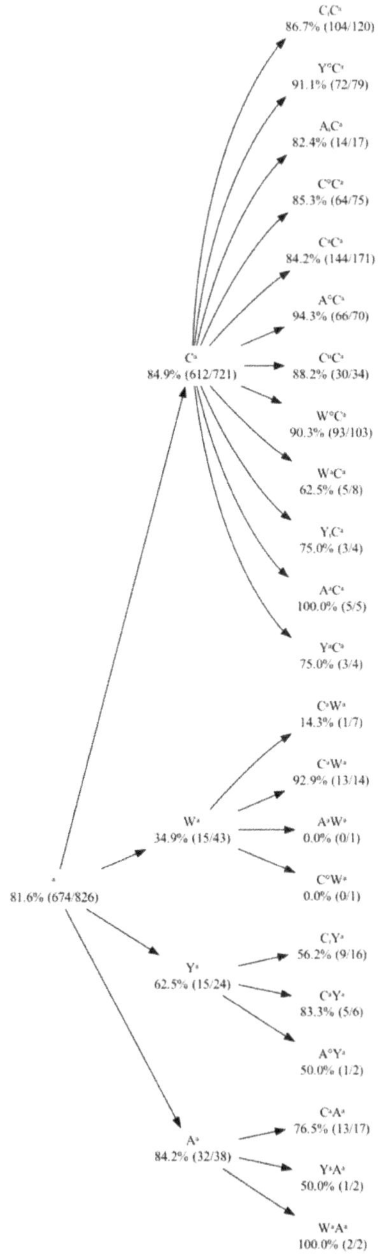

4.0. Conclusions

This paper describes the methodology developed for the encoding and understanding of partially dotted manuscripts. The dotting system is characterised by two main elements: not all vocalised syllables have been marked by a dot and the number of possible positions of dots in relation to their letter is massive. The development of an appropriate methodology has been an iterative process resulting from the interdisciplinary approach of traditional and digital philology, palaeography, and codicology, history of the text, computer science, and data analysis.

The computational pipeline has been created with the intention of having a "pipeline that both curates the text and provides a structure for text analysis" trying to solve the divide between encoding and analysis (Ohge and Tupman 2020).[16]

The development of the pointer for encoding the dots by means of vectors generated a novel visualisation of the dots position and the possibility of visualising the collation between two manuscripts. The pointer and visualisation are not only an instrument but produce meaning like the markup does in the digital editing as observed by Fiormonte, i.e., the markup language is not only an instrument to perform certain semiotic targets, but is in itself and produces a distinct semiotic dimension ("una dimensione segnica separata," 2003, 219). This tool and the approach

[16] An example of the possible results from the methodology of connecting encoding and analysis is given in the separate contribution on MS BnF ar.340c in this volume.

could be further developed and open new and cutting-edge directions of research.

A genuine collaboration between different disciplines offered also a possible solution in dealing with two contrasting principles at work when studying early dotted manuscripts characterised by a high degree of variation in placing the dots. The scholar aims at regularising the infinite variability of dot positions for their understanding but at the same time tries to capture this infinity variety. Variation is the essence not only of the text but also of the sign. According to Pallesen (2017, 8),

> [i]n classic methodological thinking, variation is a problem that is solved as a matter of statistical significance (in quantitative methodology) or saturation of categories (in qualitative methodology). However, in Bergson's (2010) terms, one might say that both of these ways of reasoning are extensive ways of thinking about variation, that is, variation between states and categories that are separable and exclude each other in space. However, thinking of multiplicity as qualitative (i.e., indivisible, multiple states interpenetrating each other) paves the way for another way of thinking of variation: a fundamentally qualitative way, namely, thinking of variation from within, as intensive. One way to do this in empirical work is by welcoming the notion that the same piece of empirical material comes into being in multiple ways depending on the context it resonates with and the experience of those involved.

The use of the pointer captures the editor's interpretation and preserves the variation of the dot sign without using the intermediation of the vowel symbol only. The dot's quantitative descriptors generated by the vectors can capture the infinite variability of the position against a letter while the qualitative analysis of the editor can capture the dynamics of the dot sign in the context of the whole manuscript page.

As the dotting system—which was not originally introduced in the first Arabic writing system—did not have *all* aspects governed by identical, fixed, and unique rules applied by all the dotters in every manuscript in exactly the same way, we developed and applied a new methodology in working with partially dotted manuscripts to measure and describe the variability of the dots' position. The methodology will show its potential when tested on larger amounts of data while in this project, it was tested on small sections of manuscript texts that scholars can manually scrutinise to detect patterns and behaviours.

The visualisation of a few samples of dotted letters in contrast with letters in another manuscript that has the same portion of text shows the degree of ambiguity of a dot when there are no clear clusters of positions/signifiers associated to their reading/signified, e.g., the continuum of single dots along the arm of isolated B in MS BnF ar.340c that signify /a/, /i/ and /u/ (Table 3). The disappearance of the dotting system was likely a consequence of this ambiguity and variation and the inappropriateness of a single sign (the dot) to represent the whole array of phenomena related to the reading and recitation of the Qurʾānic text.

References

Abbott, Nabia. 1939. *The Rise of the North Arabic Script and its Ḳurʾān Manuscripts in the Oriental Institute*. Chicago: The University of Chicago Press.

al-Dānī, Abū ʿAmr ʿUṯmān b. Saʿīd b. ʿUṯmān. 2004. *al-Muḥkam fī Naqṭ al-Maṣāḥif*, edited by Muḥammad Ḥasan Muḥammad Ḥasan Ismāʿīl. Beirut: Dār al-kutub al-ʿilmīyah.

Arberry, Arthur J. 1964 [1955]. *The Koran Interpreted.* London: Oxford University Press.

Aschenbrenner, Andreas, Tobias Blanke, Christiane Fritze, and Wolfgang Pempe. 2013. 'Data-Driven Research in the Humanities-the DARIAH Research Infrastructure'. In *The DATA Bonanza: Improving Knowledge Discovery in Science, Engineering, and Business*, edited by Malcolm Atkinson et al., 417–430. Minneapolis: John Wiley & Sons. https://doi.org/10.1002/9781118540343.ch20.

Baines, John, John Bennet and Stephen Houston. 2008. *The Disappearance of Writing Systems. Perspectives on Literacy and Communication*. London: Equinox Publishing.

Bechhofer, Sean, David De Roure, Matthew Gamble, Carole Goble, and Iain Buchan. 2010. 'Research Objects: Towards Exchange and Reuse of Digital Knowledge'. *Nature Precedings* 1–6. https://doi.org/10.1038/npre.2010.4626.1.

Buzzetti, Dino. 2002. 'Digital Representation and the Text Model'. *New Literary History* 33: 61–88.

Buzzetti, Dino, and Andrea Tabarroni. 1995. 'Database Edition of Non-collatable Textual Traditions'. Paper presented at The Electric Scriptorium: Electronic Approaches to the Imaging, Transcription, Editing, and Analysis of Medieval Manuscript Texts, A Physical and Virtual Conference, Calgary, 10–12 November 1995. http://web.dfc.unibo.it/buzzetti/

dbuzzetti/pubblicazioni/calgary.html, accessed 1 January 2024.

Cellard, Éléonore. 2021. 'The Written Transmission of the Qurʾan during Umayyad Times. Contextualising the Codex Amrensis I'. In *The Umayyad World*, edited by Andrew Marsham, 438–463. Abingdon: Routledge.

Déroche, François. 1983. *Les manuscrits du coran. Aux origines de la calligraphie coranique. Catalogue des manuscrits arabes. Deuxième partie: manuscrits musulmans, Tome I-1*. Paris: Bibliothèque Nationale.

Fedeli, Alba. 2013. 'The Kufic Collection of the Prussian Consul Wetzstein. The 1100 Leaves of the Universitätsbibliothek in Tübingen and Their Importance for Palaeography and Koranic Criticism'. In *Writings and Writing. Investigations in Islamic Text and Script in Honour of Dr Januarius Justus Witkam*, edited by Robert M. Kerr and Thomas Milo, 117–142. Cambridge: Archetype.

———. 2020. 'The Qurʾānic Text from Manuscript to Digital Form: Metalinguistic Markup of Scribes and Editors'. In *From Scrolls to Scrolling. Sacred Texts, Materiality, and Dynamic Media Cultures*, edited by Bradford A. Anderson, 213–245. Berlin: De Gruyter.

———. 2024. 'Early Qurʾānic Manuscripts: Re-mediating Their Manuscript Page in the Most Recent Digital Form as Part of the InterSaME Project'. In *The Qur'an and Its Handwritten Transmission*, edited by François Déroche, 53–104. Leiden: Brill.

Fiormonte, Domenico. 2003. *Scrittura e filologia nell'era digitale*. Torino: Bollati Boringhieri.

Gacek, Adam. 2009. *Arabic Manuscripts: A Vademecum for Readers*. Leiden: Brill.

Ibn-Ḵālawaih, Abū-ʿAbdallāh al-Ḥusain Ibn-Aḥmad. 1934. *Muḵtaṣar fī Šawāḏḏ al-Qurʾān*, edited by Gotthelf Bergsträsser. Leipzig: Brockhaus.

Ince, Barış. 2023. 'Arabe 330b. The Discovery of Two Canonical Readings'. *Journal of Islamic Manuscripts* 14 (2–4): 115–154.

Kabsch, Wolfgang. 1976. 'A Solution for the Best Rotation to Relate Two Sets of Vectors'. *Acta Crystallographica* A32 (5): 922–923.

Milo, Thomas. 2013. 'Toward Arabic Historical Script Grammar through contrastive analysis of Qur'ān manuscripts'. In *Writings and Writing: Investigations in Islamic Text and Script, in Honour of Dr Januarius Justus Witkam*, edited by Robert M. Kerr and Thomas Milo, 249–292. Cambridge: Archetype.

Nasser, Shady Hekmat. 2020. *The Second Canonization of the Qurʾān (324/936). Ibn Mujāhid and the Founding of the Seven Readings*. Leiden: Brill.

Ohge, Christopher, and Charlotte Tupman. 2021. 'Encoding and Analysis, and Encoding as Analysis, in Textual Editing'. In *Routledge International Handbook of Research Methods in Digital Humanities*, edited by Kristen Schuster and Stuart Dunn, 1–31. London: Routledge. https://doi.org/10.4324/9780429777028.

Pallesen, Eva. 2017. 'Documenting the Invisible—On the 'How' of Process Research: (Re)considering Method from Process Philosophy'. *Methodological Innovations* 10 (3): 1–10.

Posegay, Nick. 2021a. 'The Marking of Poetry: A Rare Vocalization System from an Early Qurʾān Manuscript in Chicago, Paris, and Doha'. *Journal of Near Eastern Studies* 80 (1): 73–89.

———. 2021b. *Points of Contact: The Shared Intellectual History of Vocalisation in Syriac, Arabic, and Hebrew.* Cambridge Semitic Languages and Cultures. Cambridge, UK: Open Book Publishers.

Robertson, Elizabeth, Áine O'Grady, John Barton, Stuart Galloway, Damiete Emmanuel-Yusuf, Matthew Leach, Geoff Hammond, Murray Thomson, and Tim Foxon 2017. 'Reconciling Qualitative Storylines and Quantitative Descriptions: An Iterative Approach'. *Technological Forecasting & Social Change* 118: 293–306.

Weisweiler, Max. 1930. *Universitätsbibliothek Tübingen. Verzeichnis der arabischen Handschriften.* Leipzig: Otto Harrassowitz.

Datasets

Dukes, Kais 2009–2017. *The Quranic Arabic Corpus.* Maintained by the quran.com team. School of Computing, University of Leeds. https://corpus.quran.com/, last accessed 1 January 2024.

Fedeli, Alba. 2023. *InterSaME Project Materials' (Version V1.0).* http://doi.org/10.25592/uhhfdm.13718, last accessed 1 January 2024.

King Fahd Quran Complex. *Tanzil Qur'an* [Unicode font text matching the Medina edition]. https://tanzil.net/docs/home, last accessed 13 February 2023.

Nasser, Shady H. *Encyclopedia of the [variant] readings of the Qur'an [EVQ]*. Harvard Digital Humanities. https://erquran.org/, last accessed 1 January 2024.

Noël, Geoffroy and King's Digital Lab. 2014–2024. *Archetype, Digital Resource for and Database of Paleography, Manuscripts and Diplomatic* (formerly known as 'The DigiPal Framework'). https://github.com/kcl-ddh/digipal and https://www.digipal.eu/, last accessed 17 October 2024.

A COMPUTATIONAL SYSTEM TO ANALYSE THE LAYER OF TAJWĪD NOTATION IN CONTEMPORARY QURʾĀNIC ORTHOGRAPHY[1]

Alicia González Martínez

The Quranic text relies on a precise system of phonetic notation that can be traced back to the early Islamic period, when the Qurʾān was mainly oral in nature and the first written renderings of it served as memory aids for this oral tradition. The early systems of diacritical marks created on top of the consonantal skeleton of the text motivated the creation and further development of a fine-grained system of phonetic notation that represented *tajwīd*: the rules of recitation. We explored the systematicity of the rules of *tajwīd* notation that is found in the Cairo Qurʾān, using a fully and accurately encoded digital edition of the Qurʾānic text. For this purpose, we implemented an algorithm that applies the *tajwīd* rules for removing or adding the layer of sign notation from the text of the Cairo Qurʾān. The value of these rules is that they apply to the complete Qurʾānic text, so they can be used as

[1] This research was part of the InterSaME project, which was funded by the DFG under a DFG-AHRC Cooperation.

 https://doi.org/10.11647/OBP.0498.10

precise witnesses to study its phonetic and prosodic processes. Additionally, from a computational point of view, the text of the Cairo Qurʾān can be used as a basis to compare Qurʾānic manuscripts, due to its richness and completeness. This allowed us to create a powerful digital tool to work with the Arabic script, not just within an isolated text, but automatically exploring a specific textual phenomenon in other manuscripts. The digital codification of the texts facilitates the study of the nature of the notation systems of diacritics added to the consonantal skeleton.

1.0. Introduction

The Cairo Qurʾān is currently the only complete Qurʾānic text fully and accurately encoded in digital form.[2] This makes it an excellent choice to use as a reference text for mapping other Qurʾānic texts, in order to study and compare them by means of computational methods. Hence the importance of having a complete understanding and precise analysis of its orthography and *tajwīd* notation in differentiated layers.

The phonetic component of the Cairo Qurʾān and its relationship with *tajwīd*—the rules governing correct recitation—has been subject to multiple analyses in order to create computational systems that aim to enhance pedagogical practices. However, to our knowledge no computational analysis has been conducted to investigate the interaction between *tajwīd* notation and

[2] We use the DIN 31635 standard to transcribe Arabic script throughout the article.

the orthography of the complete Qurʾānic text. This chapter reports the outcome of examining those interactions in the Cairo Qurʾān.

1.1. A Qurʾānic Text

Initially, the Qurʾānic text was recorded orally, but very early on it was accompanied with written artefacts that served as a memory aid to this oral tradition (Versteegh 2001, 55). Gradually, these written artefacts replaced the oral tradition as the main tool for preserving the Qurʾān. This led to the need for a phonetically accurate writing system that precisely encoded the oral language. For this purpose, Islamic scholars developed, over time, different systems of diacritical marks that served diverse functions and used different shapes. Some of them, having supposedly the same purpose, were even used concurrently. Broadly speaking, one type of diacritical mark was used to disambiguate consonants that were written with the same archigrapheme,[3] while the other type was used to indicate mainly vowels, both allowing the use of overlapping, contradictory diacritics. These two types of systems were not applied consistently to the base consonantal skeleton from the start but scattered through it. This complex and fluid notational landscape, in addition to the diver-

[3] An archigrapheme is the bundle of shared features between two or more graphemes, minus their distinctive features (Milo et al., 2019). For instance, ب and ت share the same archigrapheme ٮ when stripped out of their disambiguating consonantal marks.

gences that early Qurʾānic manuscripts exhibit, let us identify different readings of the text, i.e., different *qirāʾāt* قراءات,[4] which refer to the different methods of reciting the Qurʾān.[5] Closely related to *qirāʾāt* are the rules of *tajwīd*, which provide phonetic guidance on how the text should be recited. These rules, may or may not be indicated by specific diacritical marks in the text and, although the core system is shared among the different *qirāʾāt*, there are some variations.

The *qirāʾāt* constituted an essential tool used to standardise the Qurʾānic text (Nasser 2020, 2). The first standardisation of the Quranic text was said to have been undertaken by order of Caliph ʿUthmān and it is referred to as the ʿUthmānic text (UT).

Among the available canonical readings of the Qurʾān (*qirāʾāt*), the Ḥafṣ ʿan ʿĀṣim reading has become the most widespread contemporary reading tradition, as it was used as the model for the Cairo printed edition of the Qurʾān,[6] under the supervision of Al-Azhar in 1923–1924 (Puin 2009, 606; Nasser 2020, 8).[7] Other readings are still in used in some parts of the

[4] See Alba Fedeli's work on this same volume about *qirāʾāt*.

[5] The Prophet is said to have recited the same passage in various ways at various times (Graham 1987, 99).

[6] As Graham mentions, the text was not based on available manuscripts but upon the oral and written traditions recorded in the *qirāʾāt* literature, following the Ḥafṣ ʿan ʿĀṣim reading (1987, 55).

[7] Over the literature, there seems to be some confusion on the exact year of publication (Graham 1987, 211). Although the year indicated in the print of this first edition was 1919, the printing itself took several years to be finished (Puin 2009, 606).

world—for example Warš ʿan Nāfiʿ is still widely used in Morocco, Algeria and Tunisia (van Putten 2022, 5–6). [8]

Subsequently, the Cairo Edition was used as the most common model for the digital encoding of the Qurʾānic text. The Cairo Qurʾān reflects the Contemporary Qurʾānic Orthography (CQO), which diverges from Modern Standard Arabic (MSA) and the UT. For instance, CQO makes use of miniature letters inserted *amphibiously*—i.e., with a horizontal offset vis-à-vis the carrier grapheme—above the Qurʾānic Consonantal Text (QCT), whereas MSA and UT do not exhibit this trait (Milo 2009, 492).

1.2. Digital Qurʾāns

Having a complete and accurate encoding of the Qurʾānic text allows us to explore in a systematic way the rules governing *tajwīd* in CQO. To our knowledge, only two projects have created digital Qurʾānic texts that made use of CQO: the Tanzil Qurʾān and the DecoType Qurʾān.

Both Qurʾāns are actually based on the King Fahd Complex for the Printing of the Holy Qurʾān edition (1985), also known as the Medina Qurʾān. But this in turn is based on the second edition of the King Fuʾād Qurʾān, i.e., the Cairo Edition, published in 1952. According to Puin, the difference between the two is that the Medina Qurʾān is based on a handwritten copy made by the calligrapher ʿUṯmān Ṭaḥa, whereas the Cairo Qurʾān was printed

[8] Abuhamdia (2016) mentions that Nāfiʿ is in general followed in the Maghreb and in West African Muslim countries, Bin Al-ʿAlāʾ in Sudan and parts of Yemen, and ʿĀṣim in Afghanistan, India, Pakistan, Turkey and the rest of the Arab countries.

using movable type, hence the deviation of some calligraphic rules in this version (2009, 602).[9]

1.2.1. The Tanzil Qur'ān

The Tanzil project (https://tanzil.net) was created in 2007 with the aim to produce a digital Qur'ānic text that followed a reliable Unicode encoding and that was freely available for non-commercial purposes. The text is provided in different orthographic versions, including one in a complete *ʿuṯmānī* script. Although they provide a fairly accurate encoding of the *ʿuṯmānī* text, there are minor inconsistencies and, more importantly, do not use open *tanwīn* diacritics, i.e., U+08f0, U+08f1 and U+08f0, which are a type of *tajwīd* marking. [10] For instance, Q2:90:26 is encoded as عَذَابٌ instead of عَذَابࣰ. This sole omission makes the Tanzil Qur'ān unsuitable for the present study.

1.2.2. The DecoType Qur'ān

The DecoType Qur'ān was used to make the Muṣḥaf Muscat (https://mushafmuscat.om), a digital Qur'ān commissioned by

[9] From the point of view of the context, according to Philipp Bruckmayar, the Medina Edition is actually a complete plagiarism of the Cairo Edition, except for two letters (https://www.ideo-cairo.org/2021/12/the-cairo-edition-of-the-qur%CA%Bean-1924-texts-history-challenges, accessed 30 March 2023).

[10] These subtle encoding inconsistencies are normally handled properly by the rendering technologies, but the fact that they fail to provide a completely accurate encoding underneath poses a problematic challenge to studies aiming to explore, in fine detail, elements of the Arabic writing system, such as the present one.

the ministry of Endowments and Religious Affairs of the Sultanate of Oman and contracted out to the Dutch company DecoType. Its website was launched on 12 June 2017 (Milo 2022, 25). DecoType ignores conventional font technologies, which are based on legacy thinking and are constrained by the restricted technological capabilities of the printing press. Instead, they created a novel technology for digital typography—called the Advanced Composition Engine (ACE)—that makes use of the full potential of computers and that is capable of accurately displaying any Arabic script with absolute precision in an elegant and scalable way. By doing so, they created "arguably the most advanced typographical technology in the world" (Nemeth 2017, 410). As a result, the Muṣḥaf Muscat displays Arabic script as it was attested in actual manuscripts (van Lit 2020, 190–191), contrary to the ineffective movable types of the Cairo Edition, and in line with the *calligraphic* Medina Qurʾān.

An interesting and much desired side effect of using DecoType's rendering technology is that they do not need to resort to any *hacks* in the way they encode Arabic text, since they rely on a linguistically consistent separation of script encoding from script rendering. For example, Tanzil Qurʾān encodes Q56:36:1 as فَجَعَلْنَـٰهُنَّ, using Arabic *taṭwīl* (U + 0640) to *help* font technologies display the word correctly. On the contrary, DecoType encodes it as فَجَعَلْنَٰهُنَّ, without *taṭwīl*, leaving display decisions to ACE.

Though encoding practices as the one described above can easily be overcome by normalising the text, the lack of open *tanwīn* characters prevents us from studying *tajwīd* automatically.

Fortunately, DecoType includes them. This is another reason we chose this Qurʾānic text for our study.[11]

1.3. Previous Work

There have been several works on *tajwīd* that included a computational component. As we already pointed out, all of them aim at enhancing pedagogical needs. The most recent studies focus on speech recognition (Ahmad et al., 2018; Alagrami and Eljazzar, 2020), hence not relevant for the present work. Among the projects that involve text, we can mention two them: Alfaries et al. (2013) who developed a tool called *QurTaj* for automatically annotating *tajwīd*;[12] and Aqel and Zaitoun (2015), who described an expert system for helping non-Arabic Muslim speakers identify *tajwīd* rules.[13] However, neither of them offer a complete system of *tajwīd* rules addressing the whole Qurʾānic text.

---

[11] I would like to thank Thomas Milo for kindly giving me permission to use the DecoType Qurʾān for making the present study and for all his valuable insights on Unicode and CQO.

[12] *QurTaj* annotates *tajwīd* by describing contextual rules for each type of *tajwīd* phenomenon. The rules are defined on top of a tokeniser that splits the Qurʾānic text into words, letters and diacritics. Unfortunately, the system is only evaluated against the surah Al-Šuʿarāʾ الشعراء, which means that only 1.7% of the whole Qurʾānic text has been used to evaluate the rules.

[13] The system asks the user several questions about the orthographic context of the sequence and based on the results it identifies the rule. An evaluation to the system is mentioned by the authors, but no details about it are given.

2.0. *Tajwīd*

Tajwīd is the system of rules regulating the correct and clear oral rendering of the Qur'ān, in order to preserve the revelation, both in terms of its sounds, as well as its content (Nelson 2001, 14; 2006, IV:425). This consists of rules that govern how phonemes assimilate to their context, both within words and across word or morpheme boundaries.[14] Additionally, it includes rules for vowel lengthening and guidelines for pauses during speech, which mostly serve semantic purposes. In this sense, *tajwīd* rules play a central role in prosody and their study can be highly valuable for understanding how the latter works (Bohas et al. 1990, 96).

Below, we list the *tajwīd* rules in a non-comprehensive way, loosely following the description presented by Czerepinski (2003), but focusing on those rules that affect script and, sometimes, oversimplifying or excluding elements not directly relevant to the present study. We are not including Qur'ānic stops (ۖ، ۚ، ۙ، ۘ، ۗ) because we cannot make any contextual rules for them.

2.1. al-*Nūn* al-Sākinah النون الساكنة

Nūn not bearing any vowel-diacritic (*ḥarakāt*)—either with *sukūn* or without anything. This also includes the *tanwīn* mark of the indefinite article, which contains a *hidden nūn*. The *nūn* changes its pronunciation, or not, according to the following consonant:

---

[14] Assimilation is a phonological process where two sounds that are different become more alike (Fasold 2014, 44).

al-ʾiẓhār الإظهار – This consists of pronouncing every letter according to its articulation point. This happens when the *nūn* is followed by ء /ʾ/, ه /h/, ع /ʿ/, خ /ḵ/, ح /ḥ/ or غ /ġ/, which are conventionally called guttural letters (الحروف الحلقية), i.e., laryngeals, pharyngeals, and uvular fricatives (Watson 2002, 37). As there are no sound changes in this context, the notation is the default one. An example at a word boundary is مِنْ خَشْيَةِ Q2:74:30–31, and in internal position صَنْعَةَ Q21:80:2.

al-ʾidġām الإدغام – This refers to consonantal regressive assimilation (Abuhamdia 2016), and can be of various types:

- *ʾidġām bi-ġunna* إدغام بغُنّة: This happens when the *nūn* is assimilated by the following phoneme causing nasalisation (*ġunna* الغُنّة).
- *ʾidġām bi-ġunna kāmil* إدغام بغُنّة كامل: This is caused when the *nūn* is followed by م /m/ or ن /n/. As a result of the rule, the second phoneme of the cluster is geminated. This is marked in the *tajwīd* notation by not writing a *sukūn* on the first consonant and adding a *šadda* on the second consonant. In the case of *tanwīn*, for *fatḥa* and *kasra*, the two *ḥarakāt* are not placed exactly one above the other, but they are just partially overlapping, whereas in the case of *ḍamma*, instead of the conventional ligature, the *ḍamma* diacritics are written separately side-by-side. Examples of this rule are وَلْتَكُن مِّنكُمْ Q3:104:1–2 and لُوطٍ نَّجَّيْنَٰهُ Q54:34:7–8. There is no case of silent *nūn* followed by *mīm* in internal word

position. As for the *nūn* followed by *nūn*, it is marked with *šadda*, as to be expected.

- *ʾidġām bi-ġunna nāqiṣ* إدغام بغُنّة ناقص: This is caused when the *nūn* is followed by ي /y/ or و /w/. The first consonant of the cluster, i.e., the /n/, is assimilated into the glide, which retains a nasalisation. As the /n/ is not completely lost, the assimilation is not considered 'complete', so no *šadda* is added on the glide consonant. The only mark of this assimilation is the absence of the *sukūn* on the *nūn* or the displaced *tanwīn*. For example, فَلْيُؤْمِن وَمَن Q18:29:7–8 and حَسَنَةً يُضَٰعِفْهَا Q4:40:9–10. There is no *ʾidġām* within a word, only across word boundaries. We checked all the cases and found these 4 lemmas typically mentioned in the literature: بُنْيَٰنٌ، صِنْوَانٌ، قِنْوَانٌ، ٱلدُّنْيَا. They make 10 different word forms and a total of 125 occurrences.
- *ʾidġām bi-ġayr ġunna* إدغام بغير غُنّة: This occurs when the silent *nūn* is followed by ل /l/ or ر /r/. In this case, the nasalisation is completely lost in the assimilation and the liquid consonant geminated as a result. As in the case of the *ʾidġām bi-ġunna kāmil*, the first consonant of the cluster is stripped of the *sukūn*—or we find a displaced *tanwīn*—and the second letter is reinforced with a *šadda*. For example, يَكُن لَّهُۥ Q112:4:2–3 and رَّحِيمٌ رَّبَّنَآ Q14:36:15–37:1.

Czerepinski points to an exception, مَنْۜ رَاقٍ Q75:27:2–3, where a miniature *sīn* indicates that a pause (*sakt*) should be made between the two (2003). The function of this pause is probably to emphasize the personal pronoun, so it is done for the sake of semantics.

al-qalb القَلْب – This happens when the vowelless *nūn* is followed by ب /b/. In this case the /n/ changes its place of articulation to that of the /b/, turning into a /m/. In the *tajwīd* notation, the *nūn* carries a miniature *mīm* instead of a *sukūn*, and the *tanwīn* is done with a single ḥarakah plus a miniature *mīm* (below in the case of a *kasra*). Examples are مِنۢ بَعۡدِهِمۡ Q7:169:2–3, فَأَنۢبَتۡنَا Q.80,27,1 and غُرۡفَةَۢ بِيَدِهِۦۚ Q2:249:23–24.

al-ʾikḫfāʾ الإخفاء – A consonant that is not in any of the groups described above—i.e., not a guttural, liquid, glide, or nasal—when preceded by vowelless *nūn*, turns it into an approximant, i.e., the /n/ is assimilated to the following consonant leaving a nasalisation. The consonants are ت /t/, ث /ṯ/, ج /j/, د /d/, ذ /ḏ/, ز /z/, س /s/, ش /š/, ص /ṣ/, ض /ḍ/, ط /ṭ/, ظ /ẓ/, ف /f/, ق /q/, ك /k/. As the /n/ is not completely lost, in the *tajwīd* notation this rule is marked with the absence of *sukūn* above the *nūn* or with the displaced *tanwīn*. This rule works both in internal word position and at a word boundary. For example, مِن شَرِّ Q113:2:1–2, هَٰٓأَنتُمۡ Q4:109:1 and مُّسَمًّى ثُمَّ Q22:33:6–7.

2.2. *al-Mīm al-Sākina* الميم الساكنة

As happens with the *nūn*, the *mīm* may assimilate or not depending on the neighbouring consonants.

al-ʾikḫfāʾ al-šafawiy الإخ الشفوي – Non-vowelled /m/ followed by /b/. The *mīm* turns into an approximant and this is marked by the absence of *sukūn*. There are no cases inside a word. An example of the rule is هُم بِرَبِّهِمْ Q23:59:2–3.

al-ʾidġām al-miṯlayn الإدغام المثلين – Non-vowelled /m/ follows by /m/. There is complete assimilation, so the first *mīm* does not bear *sukūn* and the second *mīm* has a *šadda*. This context within a word is resolved with a single *mīm* with *šadda*. An example of this rule is لَهُم مِّن Q7:41:1–2.

al-ʾiẓhār al-šafawiy الإظهار الشفَوي – There is no assimilation and therefore no *tajwīd* notation. This happens with the rest of the consonants. For example, أَلَمْ تَعْلَمْ Q2:107:1–2.

2.3. *al-Lām al-Sākina* اللام الساكنة

This happens when the vowelless *lam* of the definite article precedes a coronal consonant.[15] In this context complete assimilation is supposed to occur, and the /l/ is totally lost, and the coronal consonant is geminated. In the *tajwīd* notation, as in previous cases, the *lām* does not bear *sukūn* and the following consonants has a *šadda*. This *silent* lām also occur when a vowelless *lām* is followed by ل /l/ or ر /r/, either between a word boundary or not. Examples ٱلتَّوْرَىٰةَ Q3:3:10 and بَل رَّفَعَهُ Q4:158:1–2.

There is an exception to this assimilation rule in بَلْ ۜ رَانَ Q83:14:2. As before, this context seems to be semantically motivated.

---

[15] The letter *jīm*, typically pronounced as a voiced palato-alveolar affricate, though part of this class, probably evolved from an original velar articulation *g, hence not assimilating in presence of the lām of the definite article (Watson 2002, 210).

2.4. *al-Madd* المدّ

From a very general perspective, the rules of *al-madd* refer to different types of lengthening of long vowels—in terms of duration—according to their context, so it is a sign indicating an overlong vowel (van Putten 2021).[16] We include here, not just the maddah sign per se, i.e., the diacritic ~, but also the miniature *waw* ۥ and the miniature *ya* ۦ.

al-madd al-wājib al-muttaṣil المدّ الواجب المتّصل – It occurs when a long vowel is followed by a hamza. In this case, a *madd* diacritic is added on top of the so called *madd* letter. For example, يَشَآءُ Q2:90:18.

al-madd al-jāʾiz al-munfaṣil المدّ الجائز المنفصل – This rule describes the same context of the previous letter, but when occurring at a word boundary. For example, بِهِۦٓ إِلَّا Q83:12:3–4.

al-madd al-lāzim اللازم المدّ – Simplifying, this context is basically met when a long vowel is followed by a geminated consonant. For example, ٱلْحَآقَّةُ Q69:1:5. There is also *al-madd al-lāzim* on top of some of the letters that appear at the beginning of some Qurʾānic surahs. For example, طسٓمٓ Q26:1:5.

al-madd al-ṣila المدّ الصلة – The enclitic pronoun of third person masculine singular -ه, or the *ha* of the feminine demonstrative singular هذه, when preceded by a vowel, is lengthened with a miniature *waw* or *ya*, for *ḍamma* and

[16] For a precise description of the use of *madda* in CQO see Milo (2009, 507)

kasra respectively, when it is not followed by *hamza* from the next word. For example, أَهْلَهُۥ Q2:126:10.

There are two exceptions to this rule: (1) يَرْضَهُ Q39:7:13 is not lengthened even though it meets the described context, and (2) فِيهِۦ Q.25:69:7 is lengthened though not adjusting to the context.

2.5. *al-ʾIdġām* for Consonants Other than *Nūn* and *Mīm*

When a vowelless consonant is followed by the same consonant—as it happened in the case of *al-ʾidġām al-miṯlayn* with the *mīm* letter—their assimilation is marked by the absence of *sukun* in the first one and a *šadda* in the second. For example, يُدْرِككُّمُ Q4:78:3. On the other hand, a consonant cluster of two letters that are not identical but similar in their place or manner of articulation can also cause assimilation and it's marked accordingly. For example, نَخْلُقكُّم Q77:20:2.

2.6. *al-Ṣifr al-Mustadīr* الصفر المُستَدير

A diacritic with the shape of a small high rounded zero—encoded in Unicode as U + 06df—that is placed on top of some letters *ʾalif*, *waw* and *ya*, indicate that these letters should not be pronounced neither in connection nor pause. For example, أَجْرَمُوا۟ Q6:124:21.

2.7. *al-Ṣifr al-Mustaṭīl al-Qāʾim* الصفر المستطيل القائم

A diacritic with the shape of a small high upright rectangular zero—encoded in Unicode as U + 06e0—on top of an *ʾalif* indicates that the *ʾalif* is additional in consecutive reading but should be pronounced in pause. For example, لَّٰكِنَّا۠ Q18:38:1.

2.8. *al-Sakt* السكت

The *al-sakt* is a gentle pause made without breathing while reciting. It is marked by a miniature *sīn*. We have few examples of this rule, and we need to consider them lexically; for example, the case seen below in مَنْۜ رَاقٍ Q75:27:2–3, that was blocking a rule of *ʾidġām*.

3.0. *Tajwīdiser*: A Computational System to Handle *Tajwīd* in CQO

The *Tajwīd*iser system consists of an algorithm that, given text digitally encoded in CQO, removes the layer of *tajwīd* notation using a set of cascade rewrite rules that reflect all the rules described in the previous section. Conversely, given some text in CQO without the *tajwīd* notation layer, a reversed set of rules are applied and the layer of *tajwīd* notation is restored. The rewrite rules are formulated as regular expressions and they are applied either within words, across word boundaries, or to both.[17] The system is implemented in the python programming language and the source code is publicly accessible on GitHub at https://github.com/kabikaj/tajweed. Additionally, a static HTML visualisation of the data can be viewed at https://kabikaj.github.io/tajweed/.

The primary outcome of this study consists of two key components: the implementation of the *tajwīd* rules, which can be

[17] There is not necessarily a one-to-one relationship with a regular expression rule and an orthographic rule.

found in the script tajweed.py, and the generated dataset, comprising an indexed Quranic text where each word is annotated with the relevant *tajwīd* rule or rules that apply to it by. This dataset can be further examined through the static website referenced in the preceding paragraph.

An example of a simple rule is the rule with id 't-assim': the sequence طت in internal word position is marking an *ʾidġām* process with the absence of the *sukūn*. This rule reinstates the *sukūn* by converting the sequence to طْت effectively removing the *tajwīd* marking. Conversely, the *sukūn* is added to a de*tajwīd*ised text to reinstitute *tajwīd*.

An example of a conditional rule is the rule with id 'HI': it stipulates that a miniature *yā'* above at the end of a word, preceded by the sequence of any short vowel and the genitive pronomical enclitic 'هِ', must be removed in order to erase *tajwīd*. Conversely, when adding *tajwīd*, the miniature *yā'* is restored after 'هِ', but only if the subsequent word does not start with a hamza.

To evaluate the correctness of the two sets of rules, we run a two-phase process on the Qurʾānic text. First, the *tajwīd*iser applies the set of cascade rewrite rules to remove the *tajwīd* and restore *sukūn* diacritics when required. Then, the set of reverse cascade rules are applied to the de*tajwīd*ised text to add back the *tajwīd* layer. At the end, two types of verifications are conducted: (1) that the original text and the restored *tajwīd*ised text match, and (2) that there are no missing marks of *tajwīd* in the de-*tajwīd*ised text. In this way, we can assure the effectiveness and accuracy of our rules.

From an overall perspective, we have three main types of rules: assimilation rules, elongation rules and pausal marks.

3.1. Assimilation Rules

This group includes *al-nūn al-sākina,*[18] *al-mīm al-sākina,*[19] *al-lām al-sākina* of the definite article,[20] as well as other assimilation processes (*ʾidġām*) affecting consonant clusters.[21] It is interesting to point out that, in order to describe the *lām sākina* rule affecting the definite article, we needed to count the part-of-speech of all the words of the Qurʾānic text, as the rule only affects nouns—or more properly speaking, اسم *ism* in the Arabic grammatical tradition, i.e., words that are not verbs فعل *fiʿl* or particles حرف *ḥarf*. Indeed, if we apply the rule for the assimilation of the article to all words, we over-generate and apply the rule to cases where the assimilation doesn't occur. To solve this problem, we used the morphosyntactic analyses provided by the corpus.quran.com project (Dukes and Habash 2010). We processed their data and mapped its linguistic information with our indexed Qurʾānic text.

---

[18] In the code, rules with ids 'N2.1.1.A', 'N2.1.1.B', 'N2.1.1.C', 'N2.1.1.D', 'N2.1.2.A', 'N2.1.2.B', 'N2.1.2.C', 'N2.1.2.D', 'N2.2.A', 'N2.2.B', 'N2.2.C', 'N2.2.D', 'N3.A', 'N3.B', 'N3.C', 'N3.D', 'N4.A', 'N4.B', 'N4.C', 'N4.D'.

[19] Rules with ids 'M1', 'M2'.

[20] Rule with id 'SHAMS'.

[21] Rules with ids with rules 'MITHL-bb', 'MITHL-dd', 'MITHL-kk', 'MITHL-ll', 'MITHL-yy', 'MITHL-hh', 'MITHL-ww', 'MITHL-tt', 'MITHL-rr', 'MITHL-ðð', 'MITHL-ff', 'MITHL-33', 'MTJNS-dt', 'MTJNS-td', 'MTJNS-tT', 'MTJNS-Tt', 'MTJNS-ṯð', 'MTJNS-lr', 'MTJNS-ðṮ', 'MTJNS-qk', 'MTJNS-bm', '*t-assim*'.

After that, we indicated in our assimilation rule for the definite article that it should only be applied to words tagged as nouns. The resulting reverse rule for removing and adding the notation layer of this rule is flawless, covering all cases.

Apart from the assimilation in the definite article, if we pay a closer look to the assimilations occurring on consonant clusters, regardless of whether they are at the word boundary or internally, all of them cause the first consonant to lose its *sukūn*. Then, if the assimilation is complete, i.e., the sound of the first consonant is totally lost, then the second consonant bears a *šadda*. On the other hand, if there are traces of the manner or place of articulation of the first consonant, no *šadda* is added into the second.

Obviously, the presence of otiose *ʾalifs* does not prevent the assimilations from taking place, for example عَصَواْ وَّكَانُواْ Q2:61:57–8. Apart from consonant clusters containing the same repeated phoneme, these are the contexts that cause complete or partial assimilation:

/n/ followed by any consonant that is not a guttural.

/m/ followed by a /b/ or /n/. The first, /mb/, only occurs at a word boundary. The sequence /b/ followed by /m/ only occur once, at the word boundary, and it also assimilates: مَّعَنَا ٱرْكَب Q11:42:14–15.

/d/ followed by /t/: both at a word boundary and in internal position. There are 45 cases. The reverse, /t/ followed by /d/, also occurs and assimilates, but there are only two cases, both at a word boundary: أَثْقَلَت دَّعَوَا Q7:189:21–22 and أُجِيبَت دَّعْوَتُكُمَا Q10:89:3–4.

/t/ followed by /ṭ/: at a word boundary, 14 cases. There are no cases in internal position. The reverse, /ṭ/ followed by /t/ only occurs in internal position four times (Q5:28:2, Q12:80:21, Q27:22:5 and Q39:56:7), and it also assimilates.

/ṯ/ followed by /ḏ/: at a word boundary, only one case: يَلْهَثۚ ذَّٰلِكَ Q7:176:20–21. There are no cases in internal position.

/l/ followed by /r/: operative at a word boundary; there are 12 cases in total, and no cases in internal position.

/ḏ/ followed by /ẓ/: only two cases and both at a word boundary: إِذ ظَّلَمُوٓاْ Q4:64:11–12.

/q/ followed by /k/: only one case, which is in internal position: نَخۡلُقكُّم Q77:20:2.

3.2. Elongation Rules

This group includes the *madd* rules containing the *madd* sign on top of *ʾalif*, *waw* or *ya*,[22] the miniature *waw*,[23] and the miniature *ya*.[24]

---

[22] Rules with rule ids 'MADD-hmz', 'MADD-hmz-A-sil', 'MADD-hmz-sp-1', 'MADD-hmz-sp-2', 'MADD-hmz-sp-3', 'MADD-hmz-sp-4', 'MADD-lzm', 'MADD-shdd-skn', 'MADD-sp-1', 'MADD-sp-2', 'MADD-sp-3', 'MADD-sp-4', 'MADD-sp-5', 'MADD-sp-6', 'MADD-sp-7', 'MADD-sp-8', 'MADD-sp-9', 'MADD-sp-A', 'MADD-sp-B', 'MADD-sp-C', and 'MADD-sp-D'.

[23] Rules with ids 'HU', 'min-u-1', 'min-u-2', 'min-u-3', 'min-u-4', 'min-u-5', 'min-u-6', 'min-u-7', 'min-u-8'.

[24] Rules with ids 'HI', 'min-y-1', 'min-y-2', 'min-y-3', 'min-y-4', 'min-y-5', 'min-y-6', 'min-y-7', 'min-y-8', 'min-y-9', 'min-y-A'.

The main rule for the elongation before a *hamza* is 'MADD-hmz', so it corresponds to *al-madd al-wājib al-muttaṣil* and *al-madd al-jāʾiz al-munfaṣil*. As for the *madd* before a geminated, i.e., the *al-madd al-lāzim*, the rules are 'MADD-lzm' and 'MADD-shdd-skn'.

The rules 'HU' and 'HI' define the elongation of the *ḍamma* and *kasra* of the enclitic pronoun, i.e., *al-madd al-ṣila*. As stated in the literature, there is only one exception to this rule, which we had to indicate: يَرْضَهُ Q39:7:13.

The rest of the rules indicated in this group are lexical, i.e., they correspond to specific word forms or lemmas, and thus would require a more detailed description that is outside of the scope of this analysis.

3.3. Pausal Rules

The pausal marks included in this study include three types: *al-ṣifr al-mustadīr*,[25] *al-ṣifr al-mustaṭīl al-qāʾim*,[26] and *al-sakt*.[27]

As already mentioned, it is important to note that some rules are applied only to specific word forms. This is especially true for the pausal rules. In some cases, this might mean that we didn't succeed completely in defining the context of a rule, so we needed to resort to combining the rule with a list of exceptions or restrictions. But in most of the cases, restricting a rule through a list of word forms indicates that the rule is related to semantics and not with the phonetic context. For example, the same word

---

[25] Rules with rule ids 'Sil-1', 'Sil-2', 'Sil-3', 'Sil-4', 'Sil-5', 'Sil-6', 'Sil-7', 'Sil-8', 'Sil-9', 'Sil-A', 'Sil-B', 'Sil-C', 'Sil-D', 'Sil-E', 'Sil-F', 'Sil-G'.

[26] Rules with ids 'P-sil-1', 'P-sil-2'.

[27] Rules with ids 'sakt-1', 'sakt-2', 'sakt-3'.

is repeated twice with different pausal marks at the end, first as قَوَارِيرَا۠ Q76:15:8 and then as قَوَارِيرَاْ Q76:16:1, meaning that in the first one, the ʾ*alif* should be read when making a pause; whereas in the second word, the ʾ*alif* should not be read when stopping. Obviously, we had to treat this case lexically.

As regards the *sakt* sign, we decided to include it because it affects few cases, although we could have left it aside as in the case of the Qurʾānic Stops, since we cannot define rules related to the context where it appears.

4.0. Discussion

A detailed study of the *tajwīd* notation layer based on the text of the Cairo Edition might not seem very interesting at first. The Fuʾād Muṣḥaf was not based on the study of the early Qurʾānic manuscripts, as it was thought that they reflected an imprecise script caused by the lack of competence of the scribes that crafted them (Puin 2011, 147). It might therefore seem that we should rather direct our efforts to produce critical editions of the earliest manuscripts. This is a valid point. But from the digital point of view, we can greatly benefit from having a complete and accurately encoded reference Qurʾānic text enriched with different layers of linguistic information that can be used as a linchpin for aligning the different Qurʾānic manuscripts and all phenomena described in the literature. Instead of producing disconnected and static digital editions, we should make use of the full potential of computational technology by building dynamic and robust systems based on a combination of accurately encoded texts and linguist rules. By doing so, we can generate alternative texts straight away.[28]

In the case of our study, we have implemented a set of rules that let us generate a Quranic text without *tajwīd*. In this scenario, adding a new rule to this system—for instance, a different set of assimilation rules for consonant clusters based on other readings than the one of Ḥafṣ' ʿan ʿĀṣim—is almost effortless. Furthermore, we can perform rigorous evaluations on this type of system, as in the case of this study, where we have proved that our two-phase conversion produces the same exact text as the original one.

The development of this type of system must satisfy the following desiderata:

- appropriate methodology directed to create dynamic systems of text encoding, instead of frozen and static representations of text
- accurate digital encoding making a clear distinction between a linguistically based script encoding versus a rendering mechanism for visualisation
- simple collation mechanisms
- linguistically based rules that can be applied to the base texts and to which we can potentially apply well-informed modifications in order to create alternative texts

A notable side effect of this work is that we have created an indexed catalog of Quranic words according to the specific rules

[28] This is inspired by the way the Advanced Composition Engine (ACE) deals with digital typography.

they are subject to, providing a valuable resource for future research and analysis, as well as for pedagogical purposes.

5.0. Conclusions

We have described and implemented a system for digitally handling the rules of *tajwīd* in CQO that addresses the full text of the Cairo Qur'ān. The rules of this system, which have been implemented using regular expressions, describe the contexts where each *tajwīd* phenomena must be applied, indicating possible exceptions and restrictions. All this information can be directly used to study more in depth the system of *tajwīd* rules governing the Ḥafṣ' ʿan ʿĀṣim reading according to the Cairo Qur'ān. More interestingly, this resulting Qur'ānic text enriched with an optional layer of *tajwīd* data could be used as a starting point to align and compare the different canonical readings of the Qur'ān, creating a mapping between the different manuscripts.

References

Abuhamdia, Zakaria Ahmad. 2016. 'Phonetically Motivated and Phonetically Unmotivated Assimilation in Tajweed'. *Journal of Philosophy, Culture and Religion* 17: 18–29.

Ahmad, Fadzil, Saiful Zaimy Yahya, Zuraidi Saad, and Abdul Rahim Ahmad. 2018. 'Tajweed Classification Using Artificial Neural Network'. Paper presented at the International Conference on Smart Communications and Networking (SmartNets), Yasmine Hammamemt, Tunisia, 16–17 November 2018.

Alagrami, Ali M. and Maged M. Eljazzar. 2020. 'Smartajweed Automatic Recognition of Arabic Quranic Recitation Rules'. Paper presented at the 6th International Conference on Computer Science, Engineering and Applications (CSEA 2020), Sydney, Australia, 18–19 December 2020.

Aqel, Musbah J., and Nida M. Zaitoun. 2015. 'Tajweed: An Expert System for Holy Qurʾan Recitation Proficiency'. *Procedia Computer Science* 65: 807–812.

Bohas, Georges, Jean-Patrick Guillaume, and Djamel Kouloughlu. 1990. *The Arabic Linguistic Tradition*. Washington, D.C: Georgetown University Press.

Czerepinski, Kareema C. 2003. *Tajweed Rules of the Qurʾan*, parts I-III. Jeddah: Dar al-Khair.

Dukes, Kais, and Nizar Habash. 2010. 'Morphological Annotation of Quranic Arabic'. In *Proceedings of the Seventh International Conference on Language Resources and Evaluation (LREC'10)*, edited by Nicoletta Calzolari, Khalid Choukri, Bente Maegaard, Joseph Mariani, Jan Odijk, Stelios Piperidis, Mike Rosner, and Daniel Tapias. Valletta: European Language Resources Association. https://aclanthology.org/L10-1190/.

Fasold, Ralph. W., and Jeff Connor-Linton (eds). 2014. *An Introduction to Language and Linguistics*. 2nd ed. Cambridge: Cambridge University Press.

Graham, William A. 1987. *Beyond the Written Word: Oral Aspects of Scripture in the History of Religion*. Cambridge: Cambridge University Press.

Milo, Thomas. 2009. ‘Arabic Amphibious Characters. Phonetics, Phonology, Orthography, Calligraphy and Typography’. In *Vom Koran zum Islam*, edited by Markus Groß and Karl-Heinz Ohlig, 493–520. Berlin, Tübingen: Verlag Hans Schiler.

———. 2022. *About Mushaf Muscat*. Hildesheim, Zürich, New York: Georg Olms Verlag.

Nasser, Shady. 2020. *The Second Canonisation of the Qurʾān (324/936)*. Leiden: Brill.

Nelson, Kritina. 2001. *The Art of Reciting the Qurʾān*. Cairo: The American University in Cairo Press.

———. 2006. ‘*Tajwīd*’. In *Encyclopedia of Arabic Language and Linguistics*, vol. 4, edited by Kees Versteegh, 425–428. Leiden: Brill.

Nemeth, Titus. 2017. *Arabic Type-Making in the Machine Age. The Influence of Technology on the Form of Arabic Type, 1908–1993*. Brill: Leiden.

Paret, Rudi. (2012). ‘Ḳirāʾa’. In *Encyclopaedia of Islam New Edition Online (EI-2 English)*, edited by Paul J. Bearman. Brill. https://doi.org/10.1163/1573-3912_islam_SIM_4383.

Puin, Gerd. 2009. ‘Quellen, Orthographie und Transkription moderner Drucke des Qurʾān’. In *Vom Koran zum Islam*, edited by Markus Groß and Karl-Heinz Ohlig, 606–641. Berlin, Tübingen: Verlag Hans Schiler

———. 2011. ‘Vowel Letters and Ortho-epic Writing in the Qurʾān’. In *New Perspectives on the Qurʾān*, edited by Gabriel Said Reynolds, 147–190. London: Routledge.

van Lit, Lambertus W.C. 2020. *Among Digitized Manuscripts. Philology, Codicology, Paleography in a Digital World*. Leiden: Brill

van Putten, Marijn. 2021. 'Madd as Orthoepy Rather than Orthography'. *Journal of Islamic Manuscripts* 12: 202–213.

———. 2022. *Quranic Arabic. From Its Hijazi Origins to Its Classical*. Studies in Semitic Languages and Linguistics. Leiden: Brill.

Versteegh, Kees. 2001. *The Arabic Language*. Edinburgh: Edinburgh University Press.

Watson, Janet. 2002. *The Phonology and Morphology of Arabic*. Oxford: Oxford University Press.

INDEX

accent dots, *see under* dots

accents, 5, 8–9, 14–16, 28, 30, 33, 35 n. 8, 39, 41, 98–99, 105–6, 177, 180–87, 195–96, 202, 205, 212–13, 215, 222, 233, 242–43, 259, 279 n. 7

Anaphora (book of), 135, 138, 141, 145

Arabic dialectology, 275, 291–92, 295, 298–300

Archetype for Qurʾānic Manuscripts (ArQuM), 390, 393, 396

archigrapheme, 319 n. 9, 391, 395, 439

assimilation (phonological), 3, 12, 230, 325 n. 16, 336, 346–47, 388, 420–21, 445 n. 14, 446–47, 449, 451, 454–55, 459–60

audibility, 131–32, 143–48

Bar ʿEbroyo, 30–33, 35, 39–40, 45, 54–55, 100–1

Beth Gazo (book of), 138

Bible, 10–11, 13, 29 n. 3, 34, 37–38, 41, 48–50, 52–54, 56, 98, 151–54, 203, 231, 234, 238, 242, 258, 260, 262–64, 266, 277, 301

Hebrew Bible, 5–17, **151–72**, **173–227**, 181–82, **229–74**

Syriac Bible, 1–2, 7–9, 13, 15, 28, 33, 38, 55, 96, 98, 100, 111, 126. *See also* Peshiṭta

Bible translation, 29 n. 3, 39, 48, 53

boundaries between words, 3, 322, 337, 445, 447, 452

Cairo Qurʾān, 437–41, 460

canonical hours, 132, 141–44

cliticization, 212, 214–15, 220–21

clitics, 178–80, 211–17, 220–22

codices, 7–12, 18, 29 n. 3, 33–34, 36–39, 41–44, 48, 51, 52 n. 18, 53, 55–57, 122, 151, 153–54, 156–57, 159–60, 162, 164–66, 234, 240–41, 245, 248, 263, 276, 319, 352. *See also* Masoretic codices

collation, 410, 412, 428, 459

Contemporary Qurʾānic Orthography (CQO), **437–63**

curriculum, 1, 33, 38–39, 41, 56

DecoType, 441–44

digital palaeography, 397
dots, 1–4, 6, 27–35, 37, 40–41, 42 n. 10, 43, 45, 51, **95–128**, 158, 160–63, 243–44, 249, 257, 276, 279–82, 291–94, **307–85**, **387–435**.
  accent dots, 28, 31, 34, 35 n. 8, 40–41, 45, **95–128**. *See also* accents
  non-pausal dots, 108, 113
  pausal dots, 108, 112–13, 122
  piercing dots, 331 n. 26, 341, 347, 349, 391–92, 394 n. 3, 397–98, 407
  placement of dots, 43, 162 n. 11, 361. *See also* dot position
  vowel dots, 249, **307–85**, 393, 401 n. 6. *See also* vowels
dot position, 307, 342–43, 346, 348–49, 351 n. 34, 368, 391–93, 394 n. 3, 402, 407–8, 410, 421, 426, 429
dotted words, 158, 356
dotter, pointer, 294 n. 15, 295, **307–85**, 391, 397, 406, 409, 412–13, 418, 420–22, 424, 430
eastern treatises, 97, 103, 111–14, 116, 118, 120, 123–25. *See also* western treatises
Egypt, 52 n. 18, 131, 232, 281, 292
encoding, 194, 387, 389, 391, 393, 397 n. 4, 409, 411, 428, 441–43, 459
Eucharist, 135–39, 141, 144–45
Fatimid, 249
Firkovitch collection, 230, 232–33, 276
Genesis, 96, 158, 193, 196–97, 199, 203, 205, 207 n. 14, 240, **275–305**
Genizah, 18, 230, 232, 264, 267, 276, 301
grammar, 8, 96 n. 2, 99, 102, 111, 113–15, 118–19, 122–24, 174, 263–65, 296
Ḥafṣ ʿan ʿĀṣim, 440
Hebrew Bible, *see under* Bible
Hebrew Masorah, *see under* Masorah
ʾidġām, 446–47, 449, 451–54
inaudibility, 132, 143–48
Indo-European, 180, 200, 213, 215
Jacob of Edessa, 32, 43–44, 97–103, 105, 108–12, 116, 119–23, 125, 130–31, 146
Jerusalem, 133 n. 5, 136, 232, 301
Judaeo-Arabic, 7, 9, 229, 267, 275–77, 278 n. 4, 279, 280 n. 8, 291–92, 294, 297–301

Karaite, 10–11, **229–74**, 276, 292
ketiv, 154, 157, 231, 237, 239–41, 261–62, 264–65. *See also* *qere*
Kūfa, 236
liturgy, 15, 57, 121 n. 6, **129–49**, 231, 263
liturgical services, 136–37
liturgical space, 132, 139–40
liturgical texts, 129–30, 132, 146–47
maqryānē, 96–97, 104
Masorah, 12–13, **151–72**, 241
  Hebrew Masorah, **151–72**
  Syriac Masorah, 33, 36, 55, 151–52, 154
Masoretic, 12–14, 16, 96–98, 103, 151 n. 2, 152, 155, 159–60, 163, 166, 234, 240, 247–48, 280–81. *See also* Tiberian
Masoretic annotations, 156, 247
Masoretic codices, 122, 157, 160, 162, 165–66, 248
mater lectionis, 27, 261–63, 282, 423
Mecca, 236
Medina, 236, 333, 352, 441, 442 n. 9, 443
midrash, 13, 155–56, 158–61, 240–41
multimodality, **129–49**
Muṣḥaf Muscat, 442–43
Muʿtazilī, 238
non-pausal dots, *see under* dots
On Persons and Tenses (by Jacob of Edessa), 97, 100, 102, 108, 111, 119, 125
orality, 1–3, 5, 7, 10, 14–17, 27, 37–38, 129, 131–32, 138–39, 143–48, **151–72**, 231, 260, 266, 309, 362–64, 437, 439, 440 n. 6, 445
orthography, 12–13, 38, 153, 156, 229, 232–33, 240–41, 259–63, 267, 275, 277–78, 297–98, 319, 423, 438–39, 441–42, 444 n. 13, 452 n. 17
otiose *ʾalif*, 455
palimpsests, 129, 132, 146–48, 249
paraša, 158, 161, 244–47, 258
partially dotted manuscripts, 307–9, 318–19, 321, 339, 351, 353, 389, 428, 430
Patriarch John of Sedre, 130–31, 146
patterns, 38, 104, 118, 125–26, 206, 249, 291, **307–85**, 389, 400–2, 406, 409, 411–12, 418–20, 423–24, 426, 430
pausal dots, *see under* dots
pausal marks, 51, 454, 457–58
Peshiṭta, **27–93**, 29, 32 n. 6, 38–39, 41, 48, 56, 137. *See also* Syriac Bible *under* Bible

piercing dots, *see under* dots
placement of dots, *see under* dots
pointer (vector-based tool), 393–94, 396–99, 401, 403, 406, 409–11, 413 n. 12, 421–22, 426, 428–29. *For* pointer *as in* one who adds vowel pointing, *see* dotter
prosodic phrase, 176–77, 181, 184, 197–98, 201–2, 206 n. 13, 207–8, 210–12, 215, 218–22
prosodic word, 176–80, 182, 184, 193, 210, 212–13, 215–16, 219–22
punctuation, 28, 30, 32–33, 35 n. 8, 39–41, 43, 45, 53, 56, 95, 97
Qenneshre monastery, 100–1, 103–4
qere, 154, 231, 237, 239, 241, 260–61, 264, 266. *See also* *ketiv*
qirāʾa, 234–35, 238
qirāʾāt, 4, 15, 234–35, 236 n. 7, 238, 309, 318, 323, 340, 351, 353, 355–58, 361–64, 440
Qurʾān, 2–4, 6–13, 15, 234–35, 238, 239 n. 12, 241 n. 13, 242, 249–58, 260, 264, 267, 312 n. 3, 367–68, 421 n. 13, 423, 424 n. 14, 437–43, 444 n. 11, 445, 460. *See also* Cairo Qurʾān, Muṣḥaf Muscat, Tanzil Qur'an
Qurʾānic Consonantal Text (QCT), 441
Qurʾānic manuscripts, 4–5, **307–85**, **387–435**, 440, 458
Rabban Rāmīšoʿ, 104
Rabbinic literature, 154–55, 157–58, 160–63, 165–66, 230–31, 237 n. 8, 239–40, 262
Rabbula gospels, 98
Ramle, 232
rasm, 233–34, 236, 241, 260, 262, 264, 266, 313–16, 321–22, 327, 329, 342 n. 30, 343, 350–51, 359–60, 363–68, 388, 410
Received Tradition, 32, 132, 142, 145, 147–48
relative chronology, 311–12, 315
Sanskrit, *see* Vedic Sanskrit
scribal habits, 12, 389, 401, 409
Sībawayh, 235, 339
šmāhe, 27 n. 1, 29 nn. 3–4, 33–57
sopherim, 154, 157–58
sunna, 235, 239 n. 12, 267
Syriac, 1–9, 14–15, 27–30, 33–34, 35 n. 8, 36–38, 40–41, 43–49, 52–57, **95–128**,

129–32, 134, 135 n. 10, 136–37, 139, 143, 145–48, 152, 166, 297, 339, 345
Syriac Bible, *see under* Bible
Syriac manuscripts, 33, 46, 122
Syriac Masorah, *see under* Masorah
Syriac Orthodox, **129–49**
tajwīd, 14, 337, **437–63**
Talmud, 166, 239–40, 265, 297
tanwīn fatḥa, 330 n. 24, 332, 340–41, 418, 421
Tanzil Qur'an, 423, 441–43
Targum, 301
terminology, 14, 45–46, 98, 120, 126, 165, 189 n. 5, 240, 339
Tetragrammaton, 258, 260, 266, 300
textuality, 12–13, 17, 129, 132, 138–39, 143–45, 147–48, 152, 155–58, 165–66, 194, 352, 390 n. 2, 410, 438
textual criticism, 154–55
Thomas the Deacon, 43–44, 97–103, 110–11, 120–21
Tiberian, 5–7, 11–13, 16, 159, 181–82, 184, 187, 198, 211–13, 233, 237, 240, 248, 264–65, 275, 278–79, 281, 291, 300. *See also* Masoretic
Tiberian cantillation, **173–227**
Tiberian vocalisation, 6–7, 11, 233, 301
transcriptions, 10, 229, 231–34, 241, 248–50, 258, 260, 262–66, 389, 391, 393–99, 401, 409, 423, 425 n. 15
ʿUthmānic Text (UT), 440–41
Vedic Sanskrit, 212–13
vocalisation, 1–9, 11, 14–15, 18, 33, 38, 41, 151 n. 2, 233, 241 n. 13, 242, 249, 259–60, 275, 278, 294–95, 297–98, 301, 308–9, 315 n. 7, 321, 326, 338–39, 359, **387–435**
vocalisation probability, 423–24, 427
vowels, 2–4, 6, 8–9, 27–28, 43, 261–62, 277, 291, 295, 297, 309, 313, 318, 321, 323, 326, 328–29, 331–33, 335–36, 339, 346, 354, 392, 401 n. 6, 423, 439, 450
vowel dots, *see under* dots
vowel grammatical import, 337, 339
vowel symbols, 333 n. 27, 425, 429
western treatises, 95 n. 1, 98, 101, 103, 116, 120, 124–26. *See also* eastern treatises
word class, 173–74, 179, 195–97, 219, 222
word order, 198 n. 10, 203, 205, 220, 222

About the Team

Alessandra Tosi and Geoffrey Khan were the managing editors for this book and provided quality control.

Tamar Karni performed the copyediting of the book in Word. The fonts used in this volume are Charis SIL, SBL Hebrew, SBL Greek, Scheherazade New, Estrangelo Edessa, Serto Jerusalem and Allan.

Annie Hine created all of the editions—paperback, hardback, and PDF.

Jeevanjot Kaur Nagpal designed the cover of this book. The cover was produced in InDesign using Fontin and Calibri fonts.

www.ingramcontent.com/pod-product-compliance
Lightning Source LLC
Chambersburg PA
CBHW062025290426
44108CB00025B/2776